COPYRIGHT AND CARTOGRAPHY

This open access book explores the intertwined histories of mapmaking and copyright law in Britain from the early modern period up to World War I, focusing chiefly on the 18th and 19th centuries. Taking a multidisciplinary approach and making extensive use of the archival record, this is the first detailed historical account of the relationship between maps and copyright. As such, it examines how the emergence and development of copyright law affected mapmakers and the map trade and how the application of copyright law to the field of mapmaking affected the development of copyright doctrine. Its explorations cast new light on the circulation of geographical knowledge, different cultures of authorship and creativity, and connections between copyright law, print culture, technology and society.

The book will be of interest to legal historians, intellectual property scholars and historians of the map and print culture, as well as those interested in the history of knowledge and how legal control over data has been exerted over time. It takes the reader back to the earliest attempts to establish who can own and control geographical information and its graphic representation in the form of a map. In so doing, it establishes a long history of tension between the interests of private enterprise, government and the public. The book's investigations end in the first decades of the 20th century, but the tensions it identifies persist in the 21st century, although today paper maps have been largely replaced by web-based mapping platforms and digital geospatial data.

Copyright and Cartography

History, Law, and the Circulation of Geographical Knowledge

Isabella Alexander

•HART•
OXFORD • LONDON • NEW YORK • NEW DELHI • SYDNEY

HART PUBLISHING
Bloomsbury Publishing Plc
Kemp House, Chawley Park, Cumnor Hill, Oxford, OX2 9PH, UK
1385 Broadway, New York, NY 10018, USA
29 Earlsfort Terrace, Dublin 2, Ireland

HART PUBLISHING, the Hart/Stag logo, BLOOMSBURY and the Diana logo are trademarks of Bloomsbury Publishing Plc

First published in Great Britain 2023

A catalogue record for this book is available from the British Library.

Library of Congress Cataloging-in-Publication data

Names: Alexander, Isabella, author.

Title: Copyright and cartography : history, law, and the circulation of geographical knowledge / Isabella Alexander.

Description: Oxford ; New York : Hart, 2023. | Includes bibliographical references and index. | Summary: "This open access book explores the intertwined histories of mapmaking and copyright law in Britain from the early modern period up to World War 1, focusing chiefly on the 18th and 19th centuries. Taking a multidisciplinary approach and making extensive use of the archival record, this is the first detailed, historical account of the relationship between maps and copyright. As such, it examines how the emergence and development of copyright law affected mapmakers and the map trade and how the application of copyright law to the field of mapmaking affected the development of copyright doctrine. Its explorations cast new light on the circulation of geographical knowledge, different cultures of authorship and creativity, and connections between copyright law, print culture, technology, and society. The book will be of interest to legal historians, intellectual property scholars, and historians of the map and print culture, as well as those interested in the history of knowledge and how legal control over data has been exerted over time. It takes the reader back to the earliest attempts to establish who can own and control geographical information and its graphic representation in the form of a map. In so doing, it establishes a long history of tension between the interests of private enterprise, government, and the public. The book's investigations end in the first decades of the 20th century, but the tensions it identifies persist in the 21st century, although today paper maps have been largely replaced by web-based mapping platforms and digital geospatial data. The eBook editions of this book are available open access under a CC BY-NC-ND 4.0 licence on bloomsburycollections.com. Open access was funded by the Australian Research Council"— Provided by publisher.

Identifiers: LCCN 2023008883 | ISBN 9781509958337 (hardback) | ISBN 9781509958375 (paperback) | ISBN 9781509958351 (pdf) | ISBN 9781509958344 (Epub)

Subjects: LCSH: Copyright—Maps—Great Britain—History. | Cartography—Great Britain—History.

Classification: LCC KD1330 .A44 2023 | DDC 346.4104/82—dc23/eng/20230410

LC record available at https://lccn.loc.gov/2023008883

ISBN: HB: 978-1-50995-833-7
ePDF: 978-1-50995-835-1
ePub: 978-1-50995-834-4

Typeset by Compuscript Ltd, Shannon

To find out more about our authors and books visit www.hartpublishing.co.uk. Here you will find extracts, author information, details of forthcoming events and the option to sign up for our newsletters.

For my mother,
who tells the best stories

ACKNOWLEDGEMENTS

A book project as long in the making as this one has accrued significant debts of gratitude along the way. The research was supported by Australian Research Council Discovery Project Award DP160100393. I also gratefully acknowledge the assistance of the State Library of NSW for awarding me the NSLA Honorary Research Fellowship in 2017, and Robinson College, Cambridge, which funded me to attend the London Rare Books School in 2012.

When thanking people, the first thanks must go to Lionel Bently, who suggested the topic back in 2010, never suspecting I would still be working on it over a decade later, and to Tomás Gómez-Arostegui, in particular for help in locating and interpreting primary material. Both of them have given support in the form of discussion and draft reading throughout. I am also enormously grateful to a large number of others who read drafts, commented on conference papers, assisted in locating material, engaged in discussion, and gave advice, feedback, and friendship. In particular, I thank Megan Barford, Ashley Baynton-Williams, Jose Bellido, Katherine Biber, Tracey Booth, Kathy Bowrey, Catherine Delano Smith, Joost Depuydt, Shaunnagh Dorsett, Douglas Duhaime, Matthew Edney, Louisiane Ferlier, Ruth Frendo, Michael Handler, Ian Killick, Sarah Kinkel Miller, Thomasin Litchfield, Nikki Lengkeek, Cristina Martinez, Jill McKeough, Nick Millea, Bénédicte Miyamoto, Alex Munt, William O'Reilly, Maggie Patton, Morgan Richards, Brad Sherman, Alecia Simmonds, Johanna Skurnick, Sarah Tyacke, Ana Vrdoljak, Adrian Webb, Genevieve Wilkinson, Greg Wood, Evana Wright, and Laurence Worms. Thank you to Ali Nasseri for the photography, and to the UTS DAB Production Support Unit for technical assistance with images. Many apologies to anyone I have forgotten here.

Invaluable research assistance was provided by Eloise Chandler, Nicole Davis, Astron Douglas, Kosta Hountalas, Divya Murthy, James Parish, Naomi Parkinson and Lucie-Lou Treguier.

In addition to those archivists and librarians mentioned by name above, I offer a huge thanks to the staff of the Beinecke Rare Book and Manuscript Library, British Library, Bodleian Library, Cambridge University Library, UKHO Archive, UK Post Office Archive, National Archives of the United Kingdom, National Archives of Australia, State Library of New South Wales, Stationers Company Archive, Imray Archive, National Library of Scotland, National Archives of Scotland, and Yale Center for British Art.

I have been privileged to have worked first at Robinson College, Cambridge, and then the UTS Faculty of Law, during the writing of this book and gratefully acknowledge both the institutional support and generous collegiality they have provided. Thank you also to Roberta Bassi and the team at Hart Publishing for their enthusiasm for the project, their support and their patience.

I have been working on this project for as long as my son has been alive, and so none of it would have been possible without the support and assistance of family and friends. Thank you from the bottom of my heart to my husband Matthew, my sisters Hattie and Chottie and their families, to Rachael, Bibi and Paddy, neighbours and friends *par excellence*, and to the fabulous footballing women of Dave's Dees, and Coach Dave, who are my village. I can never sufficiently thank my parents Hannah and Charles for their unwavering support in every way. And final thanks to Katharine and Robbie. This book would have been written much more quickly if it weren't for you, but life would not have been nearly as much fun.

TABLE OF CONTENTS

TABLE OF ABBREVIATIONS OF ARCHIVES AND LIBRARIES

BL	British Library
Bodleian	Bodleian Libraries, University of Oxford
CUL	Cambridge University Library
LMA	London Metropolitan Archives
NLA	National Library of Scotland
NRS	National Records of Scotland
PM	The Postal Museum, London
RA	Royal Academy of Arts Archive
SCA	Stationers' Company Archive
UKNA	National Archives, United Kingdom
UKHO	United Kingdom Hydrographic Office Archives

LIST OF ILLUSTRATIONS

Chapter 6

Chapter 7

Chapter 8

Chapter 9

Chapter 10

TABLE OF CASES

1

Introduction

In 1899 prominent Edinburgh mapmaker John G Bartholomew was holidaying in Jersey, hoping to improve his chronic asthma. But he was utterly unable to enjoy his break, and not just because he had brought the wet and foggy weather with him from Scotland. The affair that 'rendered rest quite impossible' was the lawsuit currently underway against him for copyright infringement. Writing to his cousin and business partner, Bartholomew lamented: 'It is a most sickening and worrying business and will be a lifelong warning to keep far from the tender mercies of such blackmailing sharks'.[1] Almost 100 years earlier, another defendant in copyright litigation involving a book containing maps, publisher Francis Newbery, spoke bitterly of his own reluctance to become involved in what he called 'the slow warfare of legal restraints and prosecutions'.[2]

Across the centuries, mapmakers and map publishers have found copyright law to be terrifying, tedious, or both. The same could perhaps be said of historians. For many, the law is something that happens to people, like rain or fog or asthma. This book hopes to persuade historians of the value in paying greater attention to copyright law. It seeks to expose the law as something that mapmakers influenced, as well as something to which they were subjected. At the same time, it hopes to convince legal scholars and lawyers of the value in digging deeper into the relationship between copyright, maps, and geographical knowledge. Lawyers tend to think of maps as telling us about the land they depict, generally in terms of property rights or territorial claims. But uncovering stories about how those maps were made gives us new stories about copyright law. In particular, it tells a story that complicates two of the central elements of copyright law: authorship and creativity.

Maps and copyright share some significant characteristics. Both stand at one remove from the tangible property they represent and facilitate dealings with that property without having to possess it physically.[3] Maps form a key element of the process by which land is described and registered, this abstraction moving land beyond its use value and allowing its exchange value to be realised. But maps are useful objects not just for their role in creating property rights. They are beneficial

[1] JG Bartholomew to Andrew Scott, 25 March 1899 (Bartholomew Archive, Business Records 952) (NLS).
[2] D Paterson, *Paterson's Roads*, 13th edn (London, Longman & Rees, 1803) viii–ix.
[3] See eg A Pottage, 'The Measure of Land' (1994) 57 *Modern Law Review* 361.

for wayfinding and navigation, education, imparting ideology, delineating territorial boundaries, and conveying social messages. Maps were already circulating in the commodity market as tangible artefacts *before* the coming of statutory copyright and mapmakers were using early legal forms such as privileges to try to regulate that market. Statutory copyright offered another way to regulate the market for maps as physical commodities, in the sense that it could be used to prevent anyone else from putting the same good on the market. Through its creation of intangible rights, which could themselves be transferred, it offered a way to commodify the information that the map contained, now that the information too could be exchanged on the market, including in different physical formats to that in which it was originally produced.

Yet, while copyright assisted in converting the use value of maps into exchange value by turning the labour expended on maps into property, the utility of maps for both private and public objectives meant that there was always a tension that copyright struggled to resolve. The very award of property rights over information so apparently in the public domain, through being observable by all, was contested. Over a period of 200 years, the case for asserting property rights in maps had to be repeatedly made and the extent of the rights negotiated to encompass competing ways to circulate the useful information they contained.

This book tells the story of how copyright came to be applied to maps and explores its role in the creation, publication, commercialisation, circulation, and use of maps as well as the geographical information they contain. It argues that the law assisted in stabilising 'the map' as a coherent category and concept.[4] At the same time, maps sit uncomfortably within the copyright regime that, in ideology if not in practice, centres the author as its organising principle and raison d'être. The logics underlying map production, use, and exchange are very different from those underlying the works from which copyright draws its justifications and upon whose idealised formats it structures its policy and regulatory format. Maps usually have multiple authors but mapmakers are less concerned with respecting the individual expression of their *authors* than they are with establishing *authority*. Maps are informational works, where that information is conveyed using both graphics and text, meaning that they straddle categories of copyright law which separate the literary and the visual. The book explores how these imperatives and factors have changed the work that copyright does in the market for maps and, in turn, impacted on the law itself.

This is a book written for two audiences: those interested in the history of the map and those interested in the history of copyright law. To bridge the disciplinary gap, this chapter starts by providing an overview of the field of map history, followed by an overview of that of copyright history. It also explains what the present study offers to each field and the value of combining them, before setting out how the book is structured and its contribution.

[4] MH Edney, *Cartography: The Ideal and Its History* (Chicago, University of Chicago Press, 2019).

I. History, Cartography, and Maps

Historiographical work on map history is of relatively recent origin and can be hard to summarise neatly. Those working in the field make distinctions between such terms as 'history of cartography', 'historical cartography', and 'history of mapping' but the categories do not exhibit hard boundaries and can flow into each other.[5] For most of the twentieth century, the 'history of cartography' was the province of geographers, historians, map librarians, and map collectors interested in the content of maps and tracking their 'improvement' in the display of geographical knowledge as a result of exploration, discovery, survey, and mathematical and technological advances. Matthew Edney refers to this as the empiricist approach and divides it into those carrying out 'traditional map history', which emphasises map content, and 'internal' map history, which emphasises map form and mapmaking.[6] What the two groups shared, according to Edney, was

> the modern, 'empiricist' conviction that maps are statements of geographical fact, that a map's significance is defined solely by the quality and quantity of its factual content, and that cartography is the singular enterprise of reconfiguring the world onto paper.[7]

From the 1980s, a new approach to the history of cartography began to emerge. Known as 'critical cartography', this approach was influenced by the work of theorists Jacques Derrida and Michel Foucault, as well as drawing more broadly on the work of anthropologists, sociologists, art historians, and literary and cultural scholars. Leading the way was British historical geographer JB Harley who, along with David Woodward, established the History of Cartography Project. Also called the New History of Cartography, or Socio-Cultural Map History, this broad approach sought to challenge the presumption that maps were simply statements of fact and could be judged upon that basis. It focused instead on seeing maps in terms of their sociocultural history.[8]

One of JB Harley's central contributions, following Foucault, has been to begin to construct a 'discourse of maps'. Thus, in one of his influential essays, he writes that he wishes to

> move the reading of maps away from the canons of traditional cartographic criticism with its string of binary oppositions between maps that are 'true and false,' 'accurate and inaccurate,' 'objective and subjective,' 'literal and symbolic,' or that are based on 'scientific integrity' as opposed to 'ideological distortion'.[9]

[5] C Delano-Smith, RJP Kain, and K Parker, 'Maps and Mapping, History Of' in A Kobayashi (ed), *International Encyclopedia of Human Geography*, 2nd edn, vol 8 (Amsterdam, Elsevier, 2020) 353.

[6] MH Edney, 'Academic Cartography, Internal Map History, and the Critical Study of Mapping Processes' (2014) 66 *Imago Mundi* 83, 84.

[7] Edney (n 6) 84–85.

[8] ibid 88.

[9] JB Harley in P Laxton (ed), *The New Nature of Maps: Essays in the History of Cartography* (Baltimore, The Johns Hopkins University Press, 2001) 53.

For Harley, maps should be read as a text or sign, rather than as a mirror of nature.[10] They are rhetorical images, which are 'never neutral, or value-free or ever completely scientific'.[11] Crucially, just as Foucault identified knowledge as a form of power, Harley emphasises that cartography is both 'a form of knowledge and a form of power'.[12] Influenced by the same thinkers and motivated by similar concerns is Denis Wood, whose work insists on the central role played by maps in the formation of the modern nation-state. For Wood, the power of maps is that they 'bring into being the territory *as we know it* to an extraordinary degree, for maps happen to be unrivalled as vehicles for the creation and conveyance of authority about and over territory'.[13]

Harley's ideas and interpretations have not been without their critics.[14] Yet, in stronger or weaker forms, they have proved influential in the work of scholars from a wide array of disciplines. The multi-volume *History of Cartography* has become a key vehicle for the transformation of the field, as Harley and Woodward increasingly encouraged their contributing authors to think differently about maps.[15] A body of work exploring the textual and discursive aspects of maps has emerged,[16] as well as studies examining the role of maps in the construction of empire[17] and the production of geopolitical territories.[18] Philosophers, sociologists, and political scientists also drew attention to the relationships between maps, the construction of sociospatial identity,[19] and sovereignty.[20]

The present work has drawn on insights from these bodies of work. It sees maps as material products of cultural practices and projects (nation building, imperial expansion, cultural hegemony, economic and trading ambitions) and seeks to be attentive to the relationship between maps and power. However, at the same time it is concerned not to reduce its examinations into a single ideology or search

[10] JB Harley, 'Texts and Contexts' in ibid 35–36.
[11] ibid 37.
[12] JB Harley, 'Maps, Knowledge and Power' in Harley (n 9) 55.
[13] D Wood, *Rethinking the Power of Maps* (New York, The Guilford Press, 2010) 52 (original emphasis).
[14] JH Andrews, 'Meaning, Knowledge, and Power in the Map Philosophy of J.B. Harley' in Harley (n 9).
[15] Delano-Smith, Kain, and Parker (n 5) 360.
[16] D Turnbull, *Maps Are Territories; Science Is an Atlas: A Portfolio of Exhibits* (Geelong, Deakin University, 1989).
[17] MH Edney, *Mapping an Empire: The Geographical Construction of British India, 1765–1843* (Chicago, Chicago University Press, 1997); S Ryan, *The Cartographic Eye: How Explorers Saw Australia* (Cambridge, Cambridge University Press, 1996).
[18] D Foliard, *Dislocating the Orient: British Maps and the Making of the Middle East, 1854–1921* (Chicago, University of Chicago Press, 2017).
[19] H Lefebvre, *The Production of Space*, D Nicholson-Smith (trans) (Oxford, Blackwell, 1991); B Latour, *Science in Action: How to Follow Scientists and Engineers through Society* (Cambridge, MA, Harvard University Press, 1987); B Anderson, *Imagined Communities: Reflections on the Origin and Spread of Nationalism* (London, Verso, 1983).
[20] J Branch, *The Cartographic State: Maps, Territory, and the Origins of Sovereignty* (Cambridge, Cambridge University Press, 2013).

for discursive power functions. More specifically, it responds to Matthew Edney's recent call for a processual history of mapmaking. Arguing that sociocultural critiques place too much emphasis on ideology and, in their tendency to engage in synchronic analysis of single maps or genres, are overly reliant on outdated work by empiricist, internal map historians, Edney urges the adoption of an alternative approach. This approach would apply critical perspectives to the topics of internal map history and would extend 'the study of map form and map-making practices to encompass the ways in which maps are circulated and consumed'.[21]

This book draws on studies of material culture through its focus on maps as artefacts, physical objects that are constructed, moved through space, exchanged for value, and used in differing ways.[22] It also draws on the history of the book in its concern with the communications circuits in which texts are produced, circulated, and consumed.[23] This approach might seem to have little interest in the territories, spaces, and places being mapped; yet, the content of the maps themselves is also of significance. A further concern of the book is with the circulation of knowledge itself. Therefore, the knowledge that each map contains and the way it is presented, constructed, and disputed is also important. For each inquiry the question being asked is: how did the law of copyright impact on this aspect of the map?

II. What is a Map?

The shift noted in the above discussion from traditional and empiricist, internal, histories of cartography to sociocultural histories of cartography also involved a shift in thinking about what constituted a 'map'. The traditional and empiricist historians (where they thought it necessary to do so) adopted definitions that saw a map as a representation in a plane of all or part of the earth's surface.[24] Likewise, the definition one finds in the Oxford English Dictionary focuses on the scientific and mathematical attributes as the relevant qualifying features when it defines a map:

> A drawing or other representation of the earth's surface or a part of it made on a flat surface, showing the distribution of physical or geographical features (and often also including socio-economic, political, agricultural, meteorological, etc., information), with each point in the representation corresponding to an actual geographical position according to a fixed scale or projection.[25]

In 1987 Harley and Woodward offered a new definition of the map that moved away from seeing it solely as a technical construct. For them, '[m]aps are graphic

[21] Edney (n 6) 94.
[22] M Brückner, *The Social Life of Maps in America, 1750–1860* (Chapel Hill, University of North Carolina Press, 2017).
[23] R Darnton, '"What Is the History of Books?" Revisited' (2007) 4 *Modern Intellectual History* 495.
[24] Edney (n 6) 22.
[25] 'map, n.1', OED Online, September 2022 (Oxford University Press).

representations that facilitate a spatial understanding of things, concepts, conditions, processes, or events in the human world'.[26] In adopting this definition, Harley and Woodward deliberately sought to expand the field to encompass celestial maps, maps of imagined cosmographies, and maps made by cultures other than the European. Under this new definition, the history of cartography can encompass prehistoric rock art, works by Indigenous peoples, propaganda maps, and stylised maps such as Henry Beck's famous map of the London Underground.[27]

Recently, Edney has thrown down the gauntlet with the sweeping proposition that all attempts to define the 'map', by whomever they are made, are both misguided and fundamentally flawed. This is because scholars insist on seeing 'the map' as a generic category, whereas in fact it is an historically created one.[28] One symptom of this misunderstanding is the assumption that an essential commonality can be identified between such terms as 'map', 'chart', and 'plan'. Yet, each of these entail different types of imagery that reflect different ways of seeing the world. Maps 'delineate regions of the world or the whole world beyond the ability of one individual to observe and survey directly'; plans 'delineate parts of the world observed and measured by one surveyor or organised teams of surveyors'; and charts 'delineate the hydrosphere'.[29]

Edney argues that the insistence on treating such images as forming part of a coherent category called 'the map' derives from a deeply held, culturally constructed, and previously unexamined belief in 'the ideal of cartography'. He describes the ideal of cartography as

> an interlocking and resilient web of mutually reinforcing preconceptions, each of which sustains basic convictions that seem to be common-sense propositions about the nature of maps. These preconceptions and convictions together construe cartography to be the apparently transcultural endeavour of translating the world to a paper or screen, with the shared goal of advancing civilization by perfecting a singular archive of spatial knowledge through the use of universal techniques of observation and communication.[30]

In his ground-breaking book, Edney goes on to deconstruct the ideal by exposing its underlying assumptions and their limitations and flaws, before examining how the ideal emerged in the nineteenth and twentieth centuries. In order to avoid being trapped within the ideal's misconceptions, he again advocates the processual approach to map studies and to avoid the use of the word 'cartography' altogether, except insofar as it refers, knowingly, to the ideal. Thus, rather than referring to 'the

[26] JB Harley and D Woodward (eds), *The History of Cartography, Vol 1. Cartography in Prehistoric, Ancient and Medieval Europe and the Mediterranean* (Chicago, University of Chicago Press, 1987) xvi.

[27] For a history of this map, see JH Long, 'London Underground Map' in M Monmonier (ed), *The History of Cartography, Vol 6. Cartography in the Twentieth Century* (Chicago, University of Chicago Press, 2015) 788–92.

[28] Edney (n 4) 2.

[29] ibid 3.

[30] ibid 4.

history of cartography', scholars should rather describe their efforts as 'mapping history' or 'map history/studies/scholarship'.[31]

The use of the word 'cartography' in the title of this book means to adopt this understanding of cartography as an idealised category and its findings in fact endorse and extend Edney's argument. Edney submits that the foundation of the ideal was laid by European states at the very end of the eighteenth century, when they began to undertake systematic territorial surveys, using the new mathematical and scientific practice of triangulation.[32] Adopting as its key periods of examination the eighteenth and nineteenth centuries, this study reveals copyright law to have been another agent that helped to inform and consolidate the ideal of cartography as it arose and ensured its survival into the present day.

III. History, Intellectual Property, and Copyright

Copyright law is one branch of the broader legal category of intellectual property (IP) law. Today, the broader category also covers trademark law, patent law, design rights, plant breeders' rights, trade secrets, and other regimes such as geographical indications and database rights. This book is concerned with the law of copyright, which emerged in England as a statutory right in authors in 1710, despite having older origins in both the Crown's power to grant patents and royal privileges, as well as trade regulation and the guild system.

The first historical narratives of copyright law emerged in the eighteenth century in the course of the various legal skirmishes that came to be known as 'the battle of the booksellers'. The matter at stake was the legal question of whether copyright existed as a common-law right prior to the passing in 1710 of An Act for the Encouragement of Learning by vesting the Copies of printed Books in the Author or Purchasers of such Copies during the Times therein mentioned (popularly known as the Statute of Anne).[33] The significance of the question for contemporaries was whether, having established an historical pedigree for the right, they could further argue that the common-law right continued to exist *after* the passing of the Statute, such that the rights the booksellers held in the books they printed and published were perpetual. The statutory rights under the Act expired after a maximum period of 28 years.[34] History was therefore critical to the parties on both sides of the argument. In one 1761 case, counsel for the plaintiff

> presented the courts with the first extended pre-history of copyright, taking the judges back through the bye-laws of the Company of Stationers, the printing patent cases of the

[31] ibid 6–8.

[32] ibid 103–11.

[33] 8 Anne c19.

[34] For details on this period, see R Deazley, *On the Origin of the Right to Copy: Charting the Movement of Copyright Law in Eighteenth Century Britain (1675–1775)* (Portland, OR, Hart, 2004); M Rose, *Authors and Owners: The Invention of Copyright* (Cambridge, MA, Harvard University Press, 1993). For more information on the debates over common-law copyright, see also M Rose, 'The Author as

> late seventeenth century, and the *Licensing Act* 1662; back through the various decrees of the Star Chamber, the incorporation of the Stationers, and the origins of the prerogative right to grant printing privileges; back to the very introduction of printing itself by Caxton in 1471.[35]

This was history pressed into service as legal precedent. The next attempts at historical exegesis came in the legal treatises of the nineteenth century, again with underlying agendas. Robert Maugham's 1828 copyright treatise was written to support the campaign for the reform of the library deposit provisions, while later legal scholars used their treatises as platforms to further the rights of authors.[36] Into the twentieth century, however, copyright history continued to be an 'internal' history, carried out by legal scholars, and focusing on legal doctrine, as found in the statutes and cases. However, increasingly it began to attract the attention of librarians, book historians, literary historians, and others more interested in the mechanisms of the book trade, and publishing history.[37]

Having moved out of barristers' chambers and law faculties, copyright history (like map history) was soon influenced by poststructuralist thinkers. Particularly influential in the 1980s was the work of Roland Barthes and Michel Foucault on the concept of authorship. Important work by Martha Woodmansee, Peter Jaszi, and Mark Rose has explored the relationship between copyright law and the birth of the author in the eighteenth century. For these writers, copyright law worked to consolidate the 'Romantic' view of the author as the genius creator of original and unique works.[38] Since the 1980s, interest in copyright's history has continued to grow and expand in directions too numerous to list here. Some histories are theoretically inflected, others explore authorship, book trade history, national and international legal developments, specific subject matters, and industries.[39]

This book joins this flourishing field and, in its exploration of maps, turns its attention to a subject matter that has received little direct attention from copyright historians or copyright scholars more generally. The handful of works that

Proprietor: *Donaldson v. Becket* and the Genealogy of Modern Authorship' (1988) 23 *Representations* 51; HT Gómez-Arostegui, 'Copyright at Common Law in 1774' (2014) 47 *Connecticut Law Review* 1.

[35] R Deazley (2008) 'Commentary on *Tonson v Collins* (1762)' in L Bently and M Kretschmer (eds), *Primary Sources on Copyright (1450–1900)*, www.copyrighthistory.org/cam/tools/request/showRecord.php?id=commentary_uk_1762.

[36] RA Maugham, *A Treatise on the Laws of Literary Property* (London, Longman, 1828). See also JJ Lowndes, *An Historical Sketch of the Law of Copyright*, 2nd edn (London, Saunders & Benning, 1842); GT Curtis, *A Treatise on the Law of Copyright* (London & Boston, Maxwell & Son and Little & Brown, 1847); WA Copinger, *The Law of Copyright in Works of Literature and Art* (London, Stevens and Haynes, 1870).

[37] For example, J Feather, *Publishing, Piracy, and Politics: An Historical Study of Copyright in Britain* (New York, Mansell, 1994); C Blagden, *The Stationers' Company: A History 1403–1959* (London, Allen & Unwin, 1960).

[38] M Woodmansee and P Jaszi (eds), *The Construction of Authorship: Textual Appropriation in Law and Literature* (Durham, NC, Duke University Press, 1994); Rose, *Authors and Owners* (n 34); D Saunders, *Authorship and Copyright* (London, Routledge, 1992).

[39] For an overview and bibliography, see I Alexander and HT Gómez-Arostegui, *Research Handbook on the History of Copyright Law* (Cheltenham, Edward Elgar, 2016).

consider the relationship between copyright and maps do so largely in relation to the question of the difficulties to be found in applying copyright to factual works.[40] To focus on this particular issue is to find oneself locked into the ideal of cartography. Once the ideal is recognised as just that, a myriad of new perspectives opens up. In addition, we can further identify the role played by law and lawyers in constructing and maintaining this ideal.

IV. Copyright, Creativity, Authorship, and Culture

Viewing maps as cultural, creative, and commercial material artefacts means that examining their production, circulation, and use can also inform our understanding of the relationship between copyright, creativity, and cultural production. Copyright law is generally understood in both the legal and general community to be a law aimed at encouraging and protecting creativity. For governments, it is increasingly important in international trade and is seen as a policy lever for economic growth. Yet these understandings are based on the general assumption that copyright provides incentives for authors to produce creative work, which in turn promotes the widespread dissemination of knowledge and learning, and thus the 'continual forward march of creative and intellectual progress'.[41] However, as Julie Cohen has argued, this account is seriously incomplete because creativity is always invoked but never explored and we know very little about 'how cultural progress actually proceeds or about how copyright law affects its direction and content'.[42] The failure to interrogate creativity and its fruits in any real sense means there is also no true understanding of authorship and how it operates in practice, despite the fact that all of copyright is premised on the existence of an author.[43] A second assumption, flowing from the first, is that identified by Laura J Murray et al; namely, that IP laws have effects on behaviour that can be predicted and achieved. Yet, as they point out, 'effects attributed to IP statute and case law are often, in fact, results of cultural, professional, economic, and ideological circumstances in which IP law is invoked or imagined, occasionally, opportunistically, or instrumentally'.[44]

There is, however, a growing body of scholarly work investigating the interactions between copyright law, creativity, and culture. Since the 1998 publication

[40] See eg JF Whicher, 'Originality, Cartography, and Copyright' (1963) 38 *New York University Law Review* 280; DB Wolf, 'Is There Any Copyright Protection for Maps after Feist?' (1991–92) 39 *Journal of the Copyright Society of the U.S.A.* 224; H Klepper, 'Originality in Cartography: The Standard for Copyright Protection Ninth Circuit Survey: Patent & Copyright Law: II' (1980) 10 *Golden Gate University Law Review* 469.

[41] JE Cohen, *Configuring the Networked Self: Law, Code and the Play of Everyday Practice* (New Haven, Yale University Press, 2012) 62.

[42] ibid.

[43] ibid 64.

[44] LJ Murray, ST Piper, and K Robertson, *Putting Intellectual Property in Its Place: Rights Discourses, Creative Labor, and the Everyday* (New York, Oxford University Press, 2014) 1.

of Rosemary Coombe's seminal work, *The Cultural Life of Intellectual Properties*, the field has expanded in many directions to include ethnographic and historical studies,[45] work by cultural studies scholars,[46] and studies investigating creative practices in fields that do not fit neatly into copyright categories – such as fashion designers, comedians, tattoo artists, chefs, or graffiti and street artists.[47] Kathy Bowrey has recently highlighted the need to pay closer attention to the relationship between the author and copyright by recognising how the idea of authorship shifts over time, and is embedded in and affected by contractual relationships, business affairs, media formats, entertainment technologies, marketing, and advertising.[48]

This book adds to this body of scholarship through its detailed examination of how mapmakers and map users interacted with copyright law over two centuries. Significantly, the field of mapmaking is not a field we conceive of today as 'creative', yet maps have been subject of copyright law as 'prints' at least since the Engravings Act of 1767, if not that of 1735. Observing copyright's longstanding application to maps and exploring how mapmakers responded to it already starts to put pressure on the assumptions about the role of copyright law and the place of creative authorship. This is even more true as maps are almost never the product of a single maker. Geographers, surveyors, navigators, draughtsmen, engravers, printers, colourists, and publishers – often more than one in each category and perhaps with different specialisations – may all be involved in the production of any one map. Yet, since the very beginning of copyright protection for maps, it tended to be the publisher who was treated as the author for the purposes of the relevant statutes.

Paying attention to how maps are made draws attention to the point made by Denis Wood that most mapmaking

> is a convoluted social process in which dozens of hands participate in the construction of a map – so that authorship is typically impossible to assign – and these maps are the most authoritative and at the same time the center around which *all* other maps circulate at greater or lesser remove.[49]

[45] Such as those found in M Biagioli, P Jaszi, and M Woodmansee (eds), *Making and Unmaking Intellectual Property: Creative Production in Legal and Cultural Perspective* (Chicago, Chicago University Press, 2011); also, W Slauter, *Who Owns the News? A History of Copyright* (Stanford, Stanford University Press, 2019).

[46] For example, J Meese, *Authors, Users, and Pirates: Copyright Law and Subjectivity* (Cambridge, MA, MIT Press, 2018).

[47] For example, M Iljadica, *Copyright Beyond Law: Regulating Creativity in the Graffiti Subculture* (Portland, OR, Hart, 2016); Murray, Piper, and Robertson (n 44); E Fauchart and EA von Hippel, 'Norms-Based Intellectual Property Systems: The Case of French Chefs' (2008) 19 *Organisation Science* 187; D Oliar and Cr John Sprigman, 'There's No Free Laugh (Anymore): The Emergence of Intellectual Property Law and the Transformation of Stand-Up Comedy' (2008) 94 *Virginia Law Review* 1787; A Perzanowski, 'Tattoos and IP Norms' (2013) 98 *Minnesota Law Review* 511.

[48] K Bowrey, *Copyright, Creativity, Big Media and Cultural Value: Incorporating the Author* (London, Routledge, 2021).

[49] Wood (n 13) 52.

For mapmakers and map users, the authority of a map did (and does) not lie in the names of the owners of the many hands that brought it to fruition but, rather, to the authority under which it was produced and, as the eighteenth century gave way to the nineteenth, the extent to which the map could be said to embody the ideal of cartography.

The present study is largely organised around instances of copyright litigation. While Rosemary Coombe rightly observes that an examination of the social life of the law must go beyond reported cases or litigated disputes, for this historical study the cases are often the best, if not the only, source of evidence remaining.[50] They expose moments of tension which suggest what was unusual and what was not tolerated, thus giving indirect evidence of the everyday.[51] The legal documents produced as part of the legal process are invaluable sources for non-legal relations, providing crucial evidence of how people worked inside, outside, and around the law. The study allows us to set the law alongside other everyday practices, using evidence gleaned from the legal process, to generate greater knowledge about maps as a significant form of cultural production.

V. Copyright and the Circulation of Geographical Knowledge

Study of the production, circulation, and appropriation of knowledge has, in the twenty-first century, become the focus of a new field of scholarship known as the history of knowledge. Indebted to the work of Foucault, Thomas S Kuhn, Donna Haraway, Adrian Johns, and many other cultural historians and historians of science, it is still a relatively young and evolving field.[52] While clearly closely related to the history of science and the history of technology, practitioners of the history of knowledge urge a move away from a focus on the making of scientific knowledge to look at how knowledge moves and how that movement is continuously shaping knowledge.[53] Although a focus on the 'material and social dimensions'[54] of knowledge, including institutions, are important features of work in the field, law has rarely been a topic of exploration. As copyright is an area of law designed specifically to regulate the production of knowledge-bearing texts

[50] RJ Coombe, *The Cultural Life of Intellectual Properties* (Durham, Duke University Press, 1998) 9.

[51] A similar point is made by Adrian Johns in *The Nature of the Book: Print and Knowledge in the Making* (Chicago, University of Chicago Press, 1998) citing Marc Bloch's observation that 'a good cataclysm suits our business' in *The Historians' Craft* (New York, Knopf, 1953) 75.

[52] See J Östling, D Larsson Heidenblad, E Sandmo, A Nilsson Hammar, and K Nordberg, 'The History of Knowledge and the Circulation of Knowledge: An Introduction' in J Östling, E Sandmo, D Larsson Heidenblad, A Nilsson Hammar, and K Nordberg (eds), *Circulation of Knowledge: Explorations in the History of Knowledge* (Lund, Nordic Academic Press, 2018).

[53] JA Secord, 'Knowledge in Transit' (2004) 4 *Isis* 95, 654–72. See also, ibid.

[54] J Renn, 'From the History of Science to the History of Knowledge – and Back' (2015) 57 *Centaurus* 37, 41.

and other artefacts, it is perhaps surprising it has received so little attention from those working in the field.

In terms of copyright doctrine and policy, knowledge is sometimes equated with 'information' or 'facts', which have long been said to fall outside the scope of copyright's protection. This was stated by Justice Willes in 1769 in the famous case of *Millar v Taylor*:

> [S]o all the knowledge which can be acquired from the contents of a book, is free for every man's use: if it teaches mathematics, physic, husbandry; if it teaches to write in verse or pose; if by reading an epic poem, a man learns to make an epic poem of his own; he is at liberty.
>
> But printing is a trade or manufacture. The types and press are mechanical instruments: the literary composition is as the material; which always is property. The book conveys knowledge, instruction, or entertainment: but multiplying copies in print is quite a distinct thing from all the book communicates. And there is no incongruity, to reserve that right; and yet convey the free use of all the book teaches.[55]

The point has been repeated ever since in different ways but with the same message: copyright does not protect facts, data, ideas, information, concepts, or knowledge.[56] The terms are not, however, interchangeable. In the field of data science, it is said that 'data precedes information, which precedes knowledge, which precedes understanding or wisdom'.[57] Here, 'data' represents raw elements ('facts') that, when accumulated and given meaning, become 'information', while 'knowledge' can be seen as the processing of both data and information by humans. Renn defines knowledge as 'encoded experience'. He continues: 'Based on experience, it is, at the same time, the capacity of an individual, a group or a society to solve problems and to anticipate appropriate actions'.[58]

To insist that copyright cannot prevent someone from taking the information or knowledge from a text or image and using it in a different way is perhaps to underestimate the ways that copyright law (indeed intellectual property law) is shaping that knowledge and determining the conditions of its transmission. This relationship has not gone unobserved. For example, it has been emphasised by Peter Drahos and John Braithwaite in *Information Feudalism: Who Owns the Knowledge Economy?*[59] Indeed, the term 'knowledge economy' has recently been adopted by the European Union when considering its copyright policy, although the implication is that living in a 'Knowledge Economy' is something new and unique to this point in history.[60]

[55] *Millar v Taylor* (1769) 4 Burr. 2303 at 2331.

[56] See also Trade Related Aspects of Intellectual Property Agreement, Article 9(2): Copyright protection shall extend to expressions and not to ideas, procedures, methods of operation or mathematical concepts as such.

[57] R Kitchin, *The Data Revolution: Big Data, Open Data, Data Infrastructures & Their Consequences* (London, SAGE, 2014) 9.

[58] Renn (n 54) 40.

[59] P Drahos with J Braithwaite, *Information Feudalism: Who Owns the Knowledge Economy?* (New York, New Press, 2002).

[60] European Commission, *Green Paper: Copyright in the Knowledge Economy* (16 July 2008) COM (2008) 466 Final.

This book seeks to explore the role of copyright law in the 'knowledge economy of society'; that is, the institutions governing the production, dissemination, and appropriation of knowledge.[61] Its focus is on geographical knowledge and the material artefacts in which knowledge travels: maps and books. The location explored is largely Great Britain. The timeframe is expansive, but the main focus begins at the start of the eighteenth century and continues to the outbreak of World War I. This is the period during which London became the global leader in mapmaking, as well as the Imperial centre, and the law which developed in Britain was exported to its colonies with ongoing influence into the present day. During this period there was a growing interest across society in scientific knowledge of all kinds. This interest had its roots in the ideas of the Western Enlightenment, including a commitment to bettering the human condition, humanity, and cosmopolitan sensitivity, which flowed into opposition to inhumane practices such as torture and slavery. It professed toleration of different beliefs; adherence to basic liberties of worship, speech and communication; intellectualism; and commitment to cultivating the powers of the mind for understanding the world around them.[62] Most importantly, Enlightenment thinkers shared a belief in 'the power of learning as a means of bringing about improvement',[63] which flowed into a growing interest in 'information management, data collection and knowledge production'.[64] This occurred in a flourishing print culture, embodied not only in the profusion of encyclopaedias and dictionaries of arts and sciences[65] but also in the rapidly growing and transforming field of geography and mapmaking.

A further aspect of the Enlightenment project was a drive to make the economy produce more wealth, and to increase economic welfare, using newly acquired practical knowledge.[66] One important way this was achieved in Britain was through the global trade made possible by the strength of its navy and merchant shipping fleet, as well as its imperial holdings. As the eighteenth century gave way to the nineteenth, state intervention in a number of fields (taxation, welfare, labour, commerce) increased, as did its interest and investment in the gathering of information. Britain's empire continued to expand, as did her dominance over global trade. Maps and geographical information played a vital role in the accumulation of British power and wealth, even if direct causality cannot be ascribed to them,[67] and the expansion of imperial sovereignty was complex, uneven, and

[61] Renn (n 54) 41.

[62] RB Sher, *The Enlightenment and the Book: Scottish Authors and Their Publishers in Eighteenth Century Britain, Ireland, and America* (Chicago, University of Chicago Press, 2007) 16–17.

[63] ibid 17.

[64] J Rudolph, *Common Law and Enlightenment* (Woodbridge UK, The Boydell Press, 2013) 24.

[65] See R Yeo, *Encyclopaedic Visions: Scientific Dictionaries and Enlightenment Culture* (Cambridge, Cambridge University Press, 2001).

[66] See J Mokyr, *The Enlightenment Economy: An Economic History of Britain 1700–1850* (New Haven, Yale University Press, 2009) 30.

[67] J Black, *The Power of Knowledge: How Information and Technology Made the Modern World* (New Haven, Yale University Press, 2014) 252.

far from uniform.[68] Beyond Britain, the period also saw the rise of the modern, territorial state.

Although mapping played a critical part in all of these developments, their exegesis is not the central concern of this book. As Branch has argued, the mapmakers of the eighteenth century were not consciously setting out to foster an understanding of space as being geometric nor creating an image of a world as made of 'homogenously territorial states'.[69] They were not deliberately promoting an ideology of empire nor setting out to effect the dispossession of Indigenous peoples. Rather, the effect of maps on changing understandings about political authority was 'in part a by-product of market demand for maps in the early modern period'.[70] Commercial factors first dictated the widespread adoption of geometric mapping practices, as well as aesthetic choices and subject matters. By the time that government-sponsored mapmaking projects emerged in Britain at the very end of the eighteenth century, the ground had been laid by the privately produced, geometric, graticulated maps of the previous century. Pedley also emphasises the need to pay more attention to the many factors involved in the creation and circulation of maps. Her important work on commercial mapping in the eighteenth century demonstrates that

> [t]he process of compilation, publication, and distribution was subject to the availability of resources – money, labour, and materials. These market conditions could affect the content and form of the final printed map as much as the availability of the raw survey data that comprised the map's content.[71]

The structures, practices and customs of the map trade are thus crucial to the work that maps do in the world. Their interaction with one of the main legal fields to regulate them is the subject of this book. Before the examination commences in chapter two, the final section of this Introduction provides some background on the process of mapmaking in the period covered by the book, for an audience unfamiliar with the technology under review. Chapter two then provides an overview of mapmaking in premodern Europe, looking at how early English mapmakers sought to make use of the legal instruments of patent and privilege that pre-dated the modern copyright regime. It uses three case studies – the *Britannias* of Richard Blome and John Ogilby and a new edition of William Camden's *Britannia* – to explore the role played by these early forms of protection on these mapmakers' businesses. Chapter three is the first of three chapters focusing on the eighteenth

[68] See L Benton, *A Search for Sovereignty: Law and Geography in European Empires 1400–1900* (Cambridge, Cambridge University Press, 2009).
J Black, *The Power of Knowledge: How Information and Technology Made the Modern World* (New Haven, Yale University Press, 2014) 252; S Dorsett, 'Mapping Territories' in S McVeigh (ed), *Jurisprudence of Jurisdiction* (Abingdon, Routledge, 2007) 137–58.

[69] J Branch, 'Mapping the Sovereign State: Technology, Authority, and Systemic Change' (2001) 65 *International Organization* 1, 21.

[70] ibid.

[71] M Sponberg Pedley, *The Commerce of Cartography: Making and Marketing Maps in Eighteenth-Century France and England* (Chicago, University of Chicago Press, 2005) 11.

century. It describes the passing of three Engravings Acts in 1735, 1767, and 1777, and how 'maps, charts and plans' became the subject of statutory copyright protection. Chapter four then traces the impact of this legislation through detailed examination of six legal disputes involving maps that had been copied without authorisation. It explores the interaction between Enlightenment ideology, mapmaking, and legal regulation, looking not only at how the law affected the business practices and relationships of London mapmakers, but also at the significance of the maps which were the subject of the litigation. Because these cases also offered courts the opportunity to interpret and develop the nascent law of copyright, the chapter also examines how the application of the new law to a new subject matter in turn affected the development and interpretation of copyright law. Chapter five examines a series of legal battles that arose concerning an increasingly popular geographical text of the late eighteenth century: the road book. It explores how these disputes negotiated the boundary between image and text in the context of copyright litigation.

The next three chapters move into the nineteenth century. The most significant development in this period was the emergence of state mapmaking through two official state bodies, the Ordnance Survey and the Hydrographic Office. The rise of state-sanctioned mapmaking brought to the fore themes that had been simmering in the background in earlier periods, in particular, tensions between claims of private mapmakers, state mapmakers, and the public in general in relation to the commercialisation of geographic knowledge or information. Chapter six focuses on the Ordnance Survey and reveals how the transition of mapmaking from a trade that was largely funded and organised privately to one directed by the state placed new pressure on the relationship between the geographic data and its processing into the commodity form of the map. Drawing on existing studies of the Ordnance Survey, as well as the extensive archival record, it focuses on the Ordnance Survey's shifting attitudes towards copyright law and its efforts to balance its aim of ensuring the greatest circulation of its publicly funded survey data with the need to recoup its investment and manage its budget. In particular, it explores the Survey's relationship with private mapmakers and mapsellers, and the difficulties involved in creating geographical data, transforming it into geographical information, and circulating that information in the marketplace in a commercially viable manner.

Chapter seven looks at the establishment of the UK Hydrographic Office and, like the chapter before, explores its attitudes towards copyright law and the circulation of its naval charts. It identifies the same conflict as discussed in the previous chapter between the desire to make publicly funded information as widely available as possible and the need to commercialise it to cover costs, but examines its different inflection in the maritime context. It details the cooperation and conflict between the UKHO and private chartmakers and chartsellers, and the particular tensions arising from the economic significance of maritime trade and the devastating impact of inaccurate charts on the lives of sailors.

The rise of state mapmaking dramatically changed the conditions in which the private trade operated but did not lead to its demise. Chapter eight explores how the private trade responded to changing economic and social conditions, and the rise of new map uses and, thus, new markets to reach. It explores the continuing challenge of articulating claims to property rights, as well as evidence of infringement, while subscribing to the cartographic ideal of maps as objective factual representations of the earth and how this sat uncomfortably with the rise of the Romantic authorship ideal in copyright law. In addition, it shows how changes in the statutory framework of copyright led to the inclusion of maps within the regime for literary property while continuing to be covered by the regime for engravings and prints, and the uncertainty this caused for litigants and judges.

The final substantive chapter, chapter nine, brings us into the early twentieth century. It shows how the Hydrographic Office continued to take little interest in copyright law, while the Ordnance Survey looked increasingly to legislation to resolve disputes with the private trade over the use of its data and name. It traces the legislative enactment of Crown copyright law in the Imperial Copyright Act 1911, and the role played by the Ordnance Survey in this endeavour. It then goes on to examine the Ordnance Survey's first foray into copyright litigation and application of the new statutory provision.

This book is full of people. It adheres to the not always fashionable view that history, and laws, are made not by forces, or movements, or ideas, but by the people who adopt, embody, and enact them. In this book, most of the people are not legislators, judges or legal reformers, but everyday people – mapmakers, engravers, publishers, geographers – seeking to use the law to achieve commercial or cultural objectives, or caught up in law's processes and powers against their will. While the legal documents relied upon can be used to expose aspects of everyday practices, the book also demonstrates how the interactions of people with the law, through the bringing of litigation, work to create legal doctrine through the generation of precedent. The stories told in this book are also stories of the development of key copyright doctrines such as the idea-expression dichotomy; of the constant tension between private rights and public interest; and of the commodification of information. They can be seen as offering empirical evidence that could be used to assess the popular utilitarian theory that copyright law offers incentives to creativity. In addition, they highlight the poor fit of the authorship paradigm of copyright law for many forms of cultural production, which, like maps and geographic texts, are the work of many different hands.

This book is also full of maps. In almost every case, the maps at issue in the various disputes are not 'important' maps, in the sense that scholars have written about them as 'making history' or 'changing the world'.[72] They are often not the first of anything – not the products of new technologies nor the introduction of new techniques of representation nor the first image of a newly explored or charter territory. But they gave rise to disputes, sometimes incurring significant legal costs, and giving rise to substantial monetary claims, meaning they were important to those making and selling them for commercial reasons. And the reasons

[72] See eg S Winchester, *The Map That Changed the World: The Tale of William Smith and the Birth of a Science* (London, Penguin, 2002).

each of the maps was commercially important leads to questions as to each map's significance in terms of the knowledge embedded in it – the ideology it embodied or reinforced, the social and political values it espoused, or the data it contained. In some cases, the maps were so 'insignificant' in terms of their lasting value as material objects that no copies of them can be located today; yet even, or perhaps especially, these maps can be seen to reflect and respond to the social, political, cultural, and economic conditions of their creation. Uncovering the legal lives of these maps thus uncovers the social, political, cultural, and economic lives of the maps and texts in question, as well as those of their creators and users.

VI. The Making of Maps

Before turning to the first substantive chapter of this work, this introduction provides some brief context on mapmaking. The process of mapmaking has been well documented elsewhere but will be summarised here for those unfamiliar with its intricacies.[73] A basic understanding of the methods, actors, technologies, and costs involved in bringing a map into physical form is integral to appreciating its significance as a material object, and phenomenological experience, to its makers, distributors, and purchasers. Such an understanding is also essential to appreciating some of the tensions produced by the disconnect between the map as material object and the map as legal object, in particular when it comes to questions of authorship and the allocation of rights.

A. Acquiring the Information

As Mary Pedley has observed: 'There are, in the end, only two ways to make a map: by going outside, and by staying inside; that is, either by one's own direct observation or by the completion of the work of others'.[74] Thus, while mapping begins with observation of the world outside, not all maps commence with a direct process of survey, measurement, or description. Many maps, especially early maps, were made by compiling and combining the work of others. While a surveyor would travel the country taking measurements and making sketches, the map compiler would avail himself of existing maps, surveys in manuscript, textual descriptions, and reports of travellers.

Direct surveying was the costliest form of information acquisition. The expenses involved not only paying the surveyors themselves but the provision of horses or mules, people to tend them, and tents for land surveys; sea vessels and crews for maritime surveys; and, in both cases, expensive instruments such as compasses

[73] See D Woodward (ed), *Five Centuries of Map Printing* (Chicago, University of Chicago Press, 1975).

[74] Pedley (n 71) 19.

and theodolites.[75] Compilation was also expensive. A compiler needed mathematical knowledge to create projection and scale, ability with foreign languages, and time.[76] After the survey, if carried out, and the compilation were complete, a draughtsman was needed to prepare a manuscript copy of the map.

B. Printing the Map

If the decision was taken to print a map, a new set of costs would arise and a new set of actors would be required. Three broad categories of printing method were used to produce graphic images in our period: relief, intaglio, and planar printing. Relief printing is the oldest, developed in the fifteenth century by Gutenberg and others for movable type. It is often called letterpress but to produce images wood blocks were used. The wood blocks would have a two-level surface, the upper level carrying the image and receiving the ink. Once inked, the blocks would stamp the image onto paper.[77] The earliest maps were made using wood blocks. However, by the end of the sixteenth century, intaglio printing had taken over as the method of choice for most mapmakers. Intaglio printing involved starting with a smooth metal plate and cutting lines into it using line engraving, drypoint, etching, mezzotinto, or some other method. For maps, the preferred metal was copper and the preferred incisive method was line engraving.[78] First the copper had to be prepared to make it smooth and shiny. It was then rubbed with wax, spread evenly over the plate using a feather. The design was then transferred to the wax in reverse. Next the lines were incised onto the plate. Line engraving involved running the point of a graver, or burin, along the line, removing some of the metal. Etching involved scratching through the wax coating and applying acid to eat away at the metal. As this process did not result in such fine lines, it was mostly used for decorative features.[79]

It seems that the same sequence tended to be followed in relation to the order in which features were engraved. First came the outline, then the writing, and then the specific features such as rocks, hills, woods. In larger print establishments, different elements would be completed by different individuals (see Figure 1).[80] A final stage, also a specialist task, might be the addition of a decorative cartouche containing the map's title and details of those involved in its production (such as the surveyor, compiler, printer, and publisher), but also often conveying messages about the region being mapped and expressing relationships of power.[81]

[75] ibid 36.
[76] ibid 26.
[77] AH Robinson, 'Mapmaking and Map Printing: The Evolution of a Working Relationship', in Woodward (ed) (n 73) 1, 5.
[78] C Verner, 'Copperplate Printing' in Woodward (ed) (n 73) 51, 52.
[79] ibid 53.
[80] ibid 64.
[81] Pedley (n 71) 57–63; GNG Clarke, 'Taking Possession: The Cartouche as Cultural Text in Eighteenth-Century American Maps' (April 1988) 4 *Word & Image* 455, doi.org/10.1080/02666286.1988.10436193.

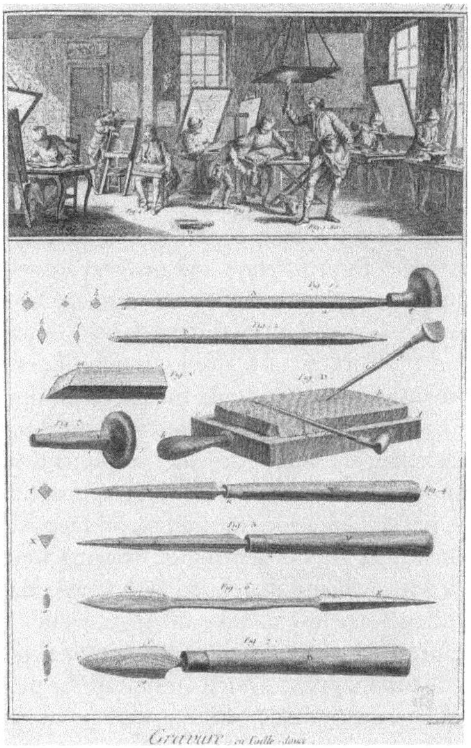

Figure 1 A copperplate engraver's workshop and tools, from *Recueil de Planches, sur les Sciences, les Arts Libéraux, et les Arts Méchaniques, avec leur explication, vol V* (Paris, Briasson, 1762) (Supplement to D Diderot and J R d'Alembert, *Encycloépdie; ou Dictionnaire raisonné des science, des arts et des métiers* (Paris, Briasson, 1751–1780)
Image courtesy of the State Library, NSW, RB/F034/22.

At several points during the engraving process, proof copies would be printed to check for accuracy and corrected where necessary.[82] Once the engraving was complete and checked, the plate was ready for the press. Unlike letterpress, which was printed on a flatbed press, copperplates were printed on a roller press. This involved using dynamic pressure to squeeze the ink from the incised lines onto the paper.[83] Ensuring the valuable copperplate could produce large numbers of impressions before it required retouching was also the job of a skilled specialist.[84] Both ink and paper needed to be of good quality and represented a significant cost. In the eighteenth century, France was the centre of paper manufacture for the

[82] Verner (n 78) 66–67.
[83] ibid 67.
[84] T Clayton, 'Engraving and Printing' in MH Edney and M Sponberg Pedley (eds), *The History of Cartography. Vol 4. Cartography in the European Enlightenment* (Chicago, University of Chicago Press, 2020) 1254.

whole of Europe.[85] Ink was applied to dampened paper using an inking ball and the plate itself was heated while it was being inked.[86] The printed paper was hung to dry, a process that could take up to six weeks.[87] A final stage was the application of colour and this was generally done by hand. Not all maps were coloured but colour was more than decorative because it could be used to indicate important information such as contours, water depth, and so on. Colouring could increase the final price of a map by between 50 and 200 per cent.[88]

Lithography was invented by Alois Senefelder in Bavaria around 1796 as he searched for a cheaper way to print plays and musical scores.[89] Lithography is a planar method, meaning it involves transferring an image from a smooth surface to paper, rather than from a raised or incised surface.[90] To produce a lithograph, the artist draws upon the surface of a stone, usually limestone, with a greasy crayon. A chemical solution is applied to fix the grease to the stone and then the surface is washed with water and the stone rolled with printing ink. Because water and grease repel each other, the ink sticks only to the crayon drawing. Paper is then laid over the stone and both are pulled through a press, transferring the image from the stone to the paper. Senefelder himself recommended a slightly different approach for maps, in which lines of writing or drawing were engraved into the stone or etched into it with acid and then filled with grease for greater precision.[91]

Lithographic printing was slow to take off in England. It did not overtake copperplate printing until the second half of the century, with the exception of the specific field of railroad mapping, which embraced the process in the 1830s.[92] Lithographic printing became popular with mapmakers because it allowed them to avoid the time-consuming, labour-intensive, and expensive step of copperplate invention. It also offered a new solution to the ever-present problem of keeping maps up to date. Inserting new information on copper plates was costly and time-consuming, as it necessitated new rounds of drafting and engraving. With lithography, it became often cheaper to issue an entirely new map than to update an existing one.[93] A variation on lithography, anastatic printing, attracted some attention in the late 1840s but never really took off.[94] By the final decade of the century photolithography had become the main way of reproducing maps. Here the maps were drafted in black ink on photographic paper which was then exposed on a zinc or aluminium plate. Photography was also being used by this time to reproduce images, including three-dimensional terrain models.[95]

[85] Pedley (n 71) 66, and see Appendices 1 and 2 for the range of prices in the eighteenth century.
[86] Verner (n 78) 68.
[87] Pedley (n 71) 65.
[88] ibid 67–69.
[89] D Bryans, 'The Double Invention of Printing', (2000) 13 *Journal of Design History* 287, 288.
[90] WW Ristow, 'Lithography and Maps 1796–1850' in Woodward (ed) (n 73) 77.
[91] ibid 80.
[92] ibid 100–101.
[93] Brückner (n 22) 92.
[94] Ristow (n 90) 101–2.
[95] KS Cook, 'Reproduction of maps by printing' in M Monmonier (ed), *The History of Cartography, Vol 6. Cartography in the Twentieth Century* (Chicago, University of Chicago Press, 2015) 1308–9.

Over the course of the nineteenth century, almost every aspect of the printing process became mechanised. The first major innovation was the Fourdrinier paper-making machine which allowed paper to be made in continuous rolls, cutting manufacturing time and increasing availability from the 1820s.[96] Other technological improvements included the steam-powered case-iron press with rotary cylinders, paper-folding and book-binding machines, hot-metal typesetting machines, the rotary four-colour printing press, and in 1904 the offset printing press.[97] All of these innovations impacted on the nature of the labour required to make maps, but they remained a specialist, collaboratively-produced item.

[96] M Monmonier and JH Cameron, 'Paper' in M Monmonier (ed), *The History of Cartography, Vol 6. Cartography in the Twentieth Century* (Chicago, University of Chicago Press, 2015) 1048.
[97] ibid 1308.

2

Early Encounters: Protecting Maps and Atlases 1400–1700

I. Introduction

In 1500 few Europeans used or understood maps. By 1600 they had become familiar quotidian objects collected and used by rulers, nobles, and merchants. They had also become legal objects. By this I mean not that they were used for legal purposes (although of course they were) but that they had acquired legal status through legal instruments of protection. In Europe (including Britain) this instrument was the 'privilege', granted by royalty or a government and, in Britain, a second instrument was guild-based registration. This chapter explains and explores these forms of protection in the sixteenth and seventeenth centuries in order to lay the foundations for the book's central focus on statutory copyright law, which emerged in the eighteenth century. It covers a period that has been the subject of considerable scrutiny by map historians. The surge of interest in maps that occurred over the course of the sixteenth century, or the growth of 'map consciousness',[1] has led to the period being labelled a 'cartographic revolution'.[2] However, there has been very little recognition of the legal context in which this occurred or its significance in relation to the ways maps were created, circulated, and consumed. Misunderstandings are also common, with historians sometimes making broad statements or assumptions about the existence and treatment of 'intellectual property' or 'copyright' without attending to their legal underpinnings.[3]

This chapter seeks to remedy this gap by setting out the ways maps could be protected against copying in the sixteenth to early eighteenth centuries. It will also draw out some aspects of the relationship between legal protection and the different roles and purposes of maps in early modern Europe, as well as the impact of legal

[1] See D Buisseret, 'Introduction' in D Buisseret (ed), *Monarchs, Ministers and Maps: The Emergence of Cartography as a Tool of Government in Early Modern Europe* (Chicago, University of Chicago Press, 1987) 2, and other chapters in the collection.

[2] See eg PDA Harvey, *Maps in Tudor England* (Chicago, Chicago University Press, 1993) ch 1.

[3] For the history of the term 'intellectual property' see J Hughes, 'Copyright and Incomplete Historiographies: Of Piracy, Propertization, and Thomas Jefferson' (2005–6) 79 *Southern California Law Review* 993–1084 and J Hughes, 'A Short History of "Intellectual Property"' (2012) 33 *Cardozo Law Review* 1293. The term 'copyright' or 'copy right' began to be used around 1678. See DW Nichol, 'On the Use of "Copy" and "Copyright": A Scriblerian Coinage?' (1990) 12 *The Library, 6th series*, 110–120.

protection on mapmakers and the map trade, focusing in particular on Britain. The chapter covers two centuries, a period of remarkable political, social, and economic change; thus, many themes can be only touched upon. I am indebted to many excellent existing studies of the period, which have explored in detail the use of maps for administrative purposes including: tax collection; settling boundaries and improving infrastructure;[4] land management;[5] and as tools of government[6] such as waging war,[7] nation building,[8] exploration,[9] and imperial expansion.[10] Other important works have examined the role of early modern maps in exerting and maintaining power[11] and in transforming Europeans' understanding of spatial awareness.[12]

It was not just government that was interested in maps in this period. Indeed, as Peter Barber notes:

> [A]fter 1550 most maps, charts and plans were produced not for the Crown but for those groups in society that were better able to pay for them and now grasped their importance: predominantly merchants and members of the landed gentry.[13]

Merchants commissioned charts to guide their commercial voyages, while the gentry began to employ estate surveyors to protect and manage their lands.[14] During this period, maps also became objects of consumption. In a much-quoted extract of his 1570 preface to Euclid's *Elements of Geography* (c 300BC), Elizabethan scholar John Dee observed a new fashion of map collecting in England:

> Some to beautify their halls, parlours, chambers, galleries or studies or libraries with … some other[s] to view the large dimension of the Turk, the wide empire of the Muscovite, and the little morsel of ground where Christendom … is certainly known … some other[s] for their own journeys … into far lands, or to understand other men's travels.[15]

[4] See, in particular, RJP Kain and E Baigent, *The Cadastral Map in the Service of the State: A History of Property Mapping* (Chicago, Chicago University Press, 1992).

[5] RJP Kain, 'Maps and Rural Land Management in Early Modern Europe' in D Woodward (ed), *History of Cartography: Vol 3, Cartography in the European Renaissance Part I* (Chicago, Chicago University Press, 1998) 705.

[6] See Buisseret (ed) (n 1); RL Kagan and B Schmidt, 'Maps and the Early Modern State: Official Cartography' in Woodward (ed) (n 5) 661–79.

[7] J Hale, 'Warfare and Cartography, ca.1450 to ca.1640' in Woodward (ed) (n 5) 719–37.

[8] R Helgerson, *Forms of Nationhood: The Elizabethan Writing of England* (Chicago, University of Chicago Press, 1992).

[9] F Fernández-Armesto, 'Maps and Exploration in the Sixteenth and Early Seventeenth Centuries' in Woodward (ed) (n 5) 738–59; S Tyacke, 'Chartmaking in England and its Context, 1500–1660' in Woodward (ed) (n 5) 1722–53.

[10] Kagan and Schmidt (n 6).

[11] JB Harley, 'Silences and Secrecy: The Hidden Agenda of Cartography in Early Modern Europe' (1988) 40 *Imago Mundi* 57.

[12] B Klein, *Maps and the Writing of Space in Early Modern England and Ireland* (Basingstoke, Palgrave Macmillan, 2001).

[13] P Barber, 'England II, Monarchs, Ministers and Maps, 1550–1625' in Buisseret (ed) (n 1) 57, 58.

[14] ibid 58–59.

[15] Quoted in J Black, *Mapping Shakespeare: An Exploration of Shakespeare's World Through Maps* (London, Bloomsbury, 2018) 58.

The quote captures an emergent market for maps and suggests their varied purposes and broad interest for Elizabethan readers and viewers outside government circles. This interest was only to intensify over the next century and a half.

Maps in the early modern period were thus the result of a complex and varying interplay between state and private interests. They were increasingly used for national, imperial, and commercial ends or valued as commodities in their own right; yet, at the same time, they were the product of humanist approaches to learning and the value of knowledge. These intertwining purposes – sometimes complementary, sometimes contradictory – are reflected in their legal status. To draw out these themes, this chapter begins by describing the use of privileges and registration for maps, as well as books of geography, tracing their use through continental Europe before focusing on Britain. It then narrows its gaze to pay particular attention to three case studies, each involving a different geographical book called *Britannia*. The first case study is that of Richard Blome (1636–1705), perhaps the most active of the seventeenth-century mapmakers in seeking legal protection for his ventures, whose *Britannia* was published in 1673. The second looks at John Ogilby (1600–76) and his *Britannia*, published in 1675. The third example involves a *Britannia* that was originally published much earlier, a book written by William Camden and first published in 1586, without maps, called *Britannia*. Popularly known as Camden's *Britannia*, a new translation, with maps, was published in 1693 and was the cause of litigation in 1701.

While all of these were books of maps, they were not all the same type of book. Scholars have identified three emerging geographic subdisciplines in the seventeenth century. The first type was mathematical geography, which was closely related to practical mapmaking, influenced by the Egyptian mathematician and astronomer Ptolemy (c 100–170AD), and concerned with plotting coordinates and making measurements. The second, descriptive geography, was influenced by Greek geographer Strabo (c 64BC–c 24AD) and portrayed physical, political, and cultural features of foreign lands. The third type was chorography, which encompassed interests in genealogy, antiquities, local history and topography.[16] Publishing ventures in each genre might incorporate maps as well as text. Blome's books, including his *Britannia*, fell largely into the second category of descriptive geography. Ogilby's *Britannia* contained 200 pages of text and 100 pages of maps which, although not plotted on a Cartesian plane or graticule, had been measured and, so, shared characteristics with mathematical geography. Camden's *Britannia* was a foundational work of chorography. While these were not the only maps of England produced during the period whose makers made use of the strategies under discussion, they provide illuminating case studies, particularly when juxtaposed with each other. Their shared subject matter, Britain, also offers an opportunity to explore the relationship between

[16] LB Cormack, *Charting an Empire: Geography at the English Universities, 1580–1620* (Chicago, University of Chicago Press, 1997) 37–38.

legal protection and visual conceptualisations of an 'imagined community' of the nation.[17]

The case studies allow an exploration of how mapmakers engaged in creating such images of the nation-state and, in the absence of direct state support, used a range of legal tools and commercial strategies in their attempts to bring the works to market and make them a success. Looking at the publishing operations of Richard Blome and John Ogilby, alongside the story of Camden's *Britannia*, highlights the role of law in the creation and circulation of geographical knowledge at the end of the seventeenth century. An ingenious array of strategies, from lotteries to subscriptions and royal favours such as tax relief and paid offices, were developed to underwrite a series of ambitious ventures in the latter half of the seventeenth century, alongside the legal tool of royal privileges. When these legal tools are considered as a commercial strategy, we can see that the costs involved in producing such expensive works meant that even being protected against competition was not sufficient to make many maps or geographical books financially viable, let alone successful, for their creators.

II. Privileges in Continental Europe

The desire of those involved in the book and print trade to exercise monopolies over their output can be traced back to the decades following the invention of the printing press by Johannes Gutenberg in Mainz around 1440. The tool employed to create such monopolies was one that already existed – the patent or privilege. The terms patent and privilege were often used interchangeably alongside other terms such as licence or warrant but, as is explained below, their meanings were not identical. While this is sometimes referred to as copyright protection, patents and privileges differ from modern copyright in important ways. Whereas modern copyright law establishes a statutory property right open to all, a privilege was a personal favour granted to one or more specified individuals, often in return for some service or benefit. In this way, privileges formed part of the complex web of patronage transactions that constituted the basis of much social and political interaction in early modern Europe.[18]

Since the thirteenth century, the Venetian Republic had been granting monopoly rights to foreigners bringing new skills, techniques, and inventions to the city, making it a flourishing centre of trade and technology.[19] The first known patent

[17] See B Anderson, *Imagined Communities: Reflections on the Origin and Spread of Nationalism* (London, Verso, 1983).

[18] See GF Lytle and S Orgel (eds), *Patronage in the Renaissance* (Princeton, Princeton University Press, 1981).

[19] J Kostylo, 'From Gunpowder to Print: The Common Origins of Copyright and Patent' in R Deazley, M Kretschmer, and L Bently (eds), *Privilege and Property: Essays on the History of Copyright* (Cambridge, Open Book Publishers, 2010) 21, 23.

was granted by the Venetian Republic in 1469 to German printer Johannes of Speyer (Johann de Spira), granting the exclusive right to operate a printing press in the city for five years.[20] The patent specified that anyone else who tried to set up a press would be subject to fines and the confiscation of their tools and books.[21] The Venetian authorities clearly saw this patent as being no different to the many thousands of others they granted to makers of products as divergent as gunpowder and dumplings.[22]

Soon, however, a different type of privilege was being granted; not over the technology of printing but over specific printed works. From 1489 such privileges began to be granted in the German and Italian states with increasing frequency. The grantors of the privileges included: ecclesiastical authorities conferring exclusive rights to print breviaries within their dioceses; governments such as the Venetian Republican; and royalty, including the King of Naples and the Duke of Milan.[23] Other parts of Europe soon followed, with sovereigns and church authorities, including the Papacy, granting privileges within their controlled territories. While the specifics of the privileges could and did vary, in general they would bestow upon the holder rights to print the work in question to the exclusion of all others and, on occasion, rights to prevent the importation of copies and/or the printing and importation of translations and abridgements. Privileges would be specified to last for a number of years and could be granted to printers, authors, or court favourites, who might in turn assign the right on to another. They frequently included details of the penalties that would flow in case of breach, usually being fines and confiscation of copies.

Privileges represented a permission to print and, in general, this meant permission to be the *only* person to print. Each jurisdiction developed its own system of censorship and different methods for that system to interact with the grant of the exclusive right.[24] In France, for example, Francis I ordered in March 1521 that new works should be examined and approved by the University of Paris and the Faculty of Theology if they related to the Christian faith or Holy Scripture, before being placed on the market. In 1566 Charles IX went further and merged the privilege and licence to print into one act of royal permission, a system that lasted until the end of the Ancien Régime in 1789.[25] Papal privileges were popular as they could offer exclusive rights not only in the Papal States where the Pope wielded secular power but across all lands under the Pope's spiritual control. In such privileges the penalties for breach could include automatic

[20] J Kostylo, 'Commentary on Johannes of Speyer's Venetian Monopoly (1469)' in L Bently and M Kretschmer (eds), *Primary Sources on Copyright (1450–1900)*, www.copyrighthistory.org.

[21] E Armstrong, *Before Copyright: The French Book-Privilege System 1498–1526* (Cambridge, Cambridge University Press, 1990) 2.

[22] Kostylo (n 19) 24.

[23] Armstrong (n 21) 2–7.

[24] See A Griffiths, *The Print Before Photography: An Introduction to European Printmaking 1550–1820* (London, The British Museum Press, 2016) 97–99.

[25] Armstrong (n 21) 100.

excommunication.[26] To obtain a Papal privilege, it was necessary to apply first to Papal censorship authorities, initially the Master of the Sacred Palace and later the Congregations of the Inquisition and of the Index, for permission to publish the book. Once this *licenza dei superiori* or *superiorum permissu* was obtained, the privilege could be sought.[27]

From the early sixteenth century, mapmakers across Europe were seeking privileges and sometimes licences, from their rulers to print their maps in much the same way as printers and authors of books. In 1511 Konrad Peutinger of Augsburg received an Imperial privilege from Emperor Maximilian to print the Itinerary of Emperor Augustinus which specifically referred to 'libros et chartas' (books and maps).[28] In the Low Countries, Gemma Frisius and Gaspar Van der Heyden received imperial charters from Holy Roman Emperor Charles V in the 1530s for terrestrial and celestial globes.[29] From the 1550s, Gerardus Mercator also sought imperial licences and privileges for his own globes and maps, as well as from the Senate of Venice and the Court of Philip II of Spain at Brussels.[30] In France a map of Italy that formed an illustration in a book was singled out as expressly included in the book privilege of 1515, while the *Vraye Description de la Ville et Chasteau de Guines* included a statement that it was published 'avec privilege de sa majesté' ('with the privilege of his majesty') in 1558.[31] Another early privilege was granted in 1608 to François Quesnel for his *Map of Paris*.[32] Several mapmakers sought and received Papal privileges, such as the Florentine painter and engraver Antonio Tempesta for his map of Rome in 1593.[33]

The mapmakers seeking these privileges were participating as members of the same system to which the book trade belonged and presumably for similar reasons – protecting the exclusivity of their market. While there is little evidence of positive enforcement of such privileges, that they could be effective may be seen in the apparent rivalry between the creators of the first two modern atlases, Abraham Ortelius and Gerard de Jode. Jason Harris's research suggests that Ortelius was able to use the 10-year printing privileges he had acquired for his *Theatrum Orbis Terrarum* in 1569 to prevent de Jode from receiving a privilege from the Council of Brabant for his competing work, *Speculum Orbis Terrarum*, until 1579. However,

[26] JC Ginsburg, 'Proto-Property in Literary and Artistic Works: Sixteenth-Century Papal Printing Privileges' in I Alexander and HT Gómez-Arostegui, *Research Handbook on the History of Copyright Law* (Cheltenham, Edward Elgar, 2016) 237.

[27] ibid.

[28] See 'Imperial Privilege for Konrad Peutinger, Augsburg (1515)' in Bently and Kretschmer (eds) (n 20).

[29] N Crane, *Mercator: The Man Who Mapped the Planet* (London, Phoenix, 2003) 75.

[30] ibid 171, 182, 262–66.

[31] Armstrong (n 21) 205.

[32] K Scott, 'Maps, Views and Ornament: Visualising Property in Art and Law. The Case of Pre-Modern France' in Deazley, Kretschmer, and Bently (eds) (n 19) 255, 259.

[33] See JC Ginsburg, 'The 1593 Antonio Tempesta Map of Rome' in C op den Kamp and D Hunter (eds), *A History of Intellectual Property in 50 Objects* (Cambridge, Cambridge University Press, 2019) 40; 'Petition from and Privilege granted to Antonio Tempest for a map of Rome (1593)' in Bently and Kretschmer (n 20).

Harris concedes that de Jode's delay in publishing might also have been due to other factors, such as difficulty in obtaining support from his peers and funding.[34] And the ability to enforce privileges against potential copyists might not have been their only function. As Katie Scott has observed,

> the credit of royal attention converted the time and money invested in producing a book and acquiring a privilege into symbolic capital that could later be reconverted into material capital accumulated from higher sales. This in turn eased access to finance for the next publishing enterprise.[35]

Privileges granted in Europe in the sixteenth and seventeenth centuries can thus be seen to have played a number of possible roles in supporting the production and commercialisation of printed maps.

III. Patents, Licences, and Registration in Britain

In Scotland and England, consecutive sovereigns also granted printing privileges from the time of James IV (1488–1513) and Henry VIII (1491–1547) respectively.[36] However, seeking a privilege for individual works was not the only method of exercising monopolistic control over books in England, where the key to controlling the book trade was the Stationers' Company. This London guild received its charter from Mary I in 1557 and, over time, assumed practical control over the printing, buying, and selling of books.[37] Concerned about the threats of heresy and treason, successive monarchs issued decrees requiring books to have a licence before they could be printed and the Stationers' Company was expected to exercise its monopoly in such a way that this could be enforced. The Company devised a registration system according to which only licensed books could be registered.[38] The power of the Company was enforced in part through the Star Chamber (court set up under the king's prerogative) and its ecclesiastical equivalent the High Commission, but this was far from being a harsh and oppressive censorship regime in practice. Indeed, by the 1640s, according to John Feather, 'censorship of content had been intermittent almost to the point of being random'.[39] For the Company, however, the central concern was controlling the trade in its own interest and ensuring its members maintained their monopolies over the book market.

[34] J Harris, 'Reading the First Atlases: Ortelius, De Jode and TCD volume M.aa.9' (2004) 49 *The Long Room* 28.

[35] K Scott, *Becoming Property: Art, Theory and Law in Early Modern France* (New Haven, Yale University Press, 2018) 41–42.

[36] Armstrong (n 21) 9–11.

[37] See C Blagden, *The Stationers' Company: A History 1403–1959* (London, Allen & Unwin, 1960).

[38] HT Gómez-Arostegui, 'What History Teaches Us about Copyright Injunctions and the Inadequate-Remedy-at-Law Requirement' (2008) 81 *Southern California Law Review* 1197, 1216; L Kirschbaum, *Shakespeare and the Stationers* (Columbus, Ohio State University Press, 1955) 31–32.

[39] J Feather, 'Controlling the Press in Restoration England' (2013) 74 *Publishing History* 7.

With the abolition of the Star Chamber in 1641, the power of the Stationers' Company began to wane. During the Civil War (1642–51) and Interregnum (1649–60), similar mechanisms for regulation were developed through legislation.[40] After the Restoration in 1660, press regulation continued and was carried out through a series of Licensing Acts enforced by a Surveyor of the Press. Increasingly this was in cooperation with the Stationers' Company, whose members' interest in enforcing their own valuable privileges could only be enhanced by working together with those seeking to stamp out unlicensed printing.[41] During this entire period, therefore, the Company controlled most of the book trade by requiring books to be entered in the Register held at Stationers' Hall, either before or at the time of publication. Only members of the Company could register books and disputes over title or cases where one member printed a book registered by another member were frequently dealt with, at least in the first instance, by the Company through its Court of Assistants and, as time went on, by the superior courts of England.[42]

While most of the registrations at Stationers' Hall were for books, there were also a number of individual prints (prints not forming part of a book) registered.[43] A survey of the Register from 1562 to 1698 reveals over 40 registrations of books that either contained maps or were books of maps, such as atlases, and over 20 registrations of maps as individual prints.[44] Often the entry was quite specific that the map in question was on a single sheet of paper. For example, in 1657 John Owsley registered *A New Mapp of the Whole World in Many Places Amended by the Author N. J. Piscator, and Augmented and Enlarged by Jo: Bleau Ano Dni 1657, in One Sheet of Paper, Printed on One Side*.[45] The following year John Macocke registered *A new and exact map of the World, &c, together with a descripcon of the principles of geography &c, cutt in copper in one sheet of paper*.[46] Some of these maps and books were clearly imports, so that what was being sought was the exclusive right to sell copies in England. Others were newly created, such as John Overton's *A New and Plaine Mapp of the Citty of London, Shewing the Streets, Lanes, Allies, Courts, Churches, Halls & Other Remarkable Places, as They are Now Rebuilt 1676*, which he registered on 17 January 1675.[47] Overton was a map and printseller and

[40] ibid 9; Gómez-Arostegui (n 38) 1217.

[41] Feather (n 39) 10–21.

[42] Blagden (n 37); Gómez-Arostegui (n 38) 1217–18.

[43] Malcolm Jones has recorded well over 300 prints in his study of the Register between 1562 and 1656: M Jones, 'Engraved Works Recorded in the Stationers Registers, 1562–1656: A Listing and Commentary' (2002) 64 *The Volume of the Walpole Society* 1.

[44] This review was carried out initially using E Arber (ed), *A Transcript of the Registers of the Company of Stationers 1554–1640AD*, 5 volumes and GE Briscoe Eyre (ed), *A Transcript of the Registers of the Worshipful Company of Stationers 1640–1708 AD*, 3 volumes, then supplemented with a search of the Stationers' Register Online, stationersregister.online/.

[45] GE Briscoe Eyre (ed), *A Transcript of the Registers of the Worshipful Company of Stationers 1640–1708 AD*, vol 2 (London, Privately Printed, 1913) 163 (27 January 1657).

[46] ibid 2, 170 (25 March 1658).

[47] ibid 3, 14 (17 January 1675).

a member of the Stationers' Company, and he also registered his map of Bristol at Stationers' Hall. Yet he was an exception rather than the rule. As Sarah Tyacke has pointed out, very few map and printsellers of the sixteenth and seventeenth centuries were members of the Company. She has identified 35 mapsellers in London in the period from 1650 to 1710, of whom only nine were Stationers.[48] Furthermore, of them, it seems only William Fisher, William Garrett, Richard Blome, and Overton made use of the Register.

Notwithstanding the influential role of the Stationers' Company on the book and print trade, seeking a royal privilege remained an important path to exclusive protection. Indeed, some of the most lucrative printing privileges – those covering such things as statutes, law books, Bibles, primers, psalters, and almanacs – were owned by members of the Company.[49] As noted earlier in this chapter, the terms privilege, licence, patent, and warrant, have often been used interchangeably, but their meanings are not identical. Before 1695, a licence referred to an official imprimatur as to the work's political or religious suitability, but by the middle of the eighteenth century was synonymous with privilege as meaning permission to print.[50] Warrant tended to mean a privilege providing exclusive rights to a class of works, as noted above.[51] The most authoritative form of privilege was one enrolled as letters patent. The labyrinthine process for acquiring a patent in the seventeenth century has been described by both Arnold Hunt and Sean Bottomley[52] and it changed little over the centuries, being famously satirised by Charles Dickens in 1850.[53] The patentee-to-be would commence by addressing a petition either in person to the King, to the Privy Council, or one of the secretaries of state. This petition would then be referred for legal advice to the Attorney General or Solicitor General. If approved, a bill was prepared for the King to sign. As Hunt explains: 'This formed the authority for a Bill of Privy Signet, which in turn formed the authority for a Writ of Privy Seal, which in its turn formed the authority for Letters Patent under the Great Seal'.[54] A copy of the patent was enrolled in Chancery and the original, with Great Seal attached, became the possession of the patentee.

The process was both onerous and expensive and, perhaps unsurprisingly, not all those seeking protection proceeded all the way to enrolment. I use the term

[48] S Tyacke, 'Map-Sellers and the London Map Trade c1650–1710' in H Wallis and S Tyacke (eds), *My Head Is a Map: Essays and Memoirs in Honour of R.V. Tooley* (London, Francis Edwards and Carta Press, 1973) 63, 67.

[49] Gómez-Arostegui (n 38) 1197, 1213–15.

[50] S Rogers, 'The Use of Royal Licences for Printing in England, 1695–1760: A Bibliography' (2000) 1 *The Library* 133, 136–37.

[51] ibid.

[52] The following description is based on A Hunt, 'Book Trade Patents, 1603–1640' in A Hunt, G Mandelbrote, and A Shell (eds), *The Book Trade and Its Customers 1450–1900* (Winchester, St Paul's Bibliographies, 1997) 27, 37; S Bottomley, *The British Patent System during the Industrial Revolution 1700–1852: From Privilege to Property* (Cambridge, Cambridge University Press, 2014) 36–39.

[53] C Dickens, 'A Poor Man's Tale of a Patent', *Household Words*, 19 October 1850. See also, Bottomley (n 52) 33.

[54] Hunt (n 52) 37.

'patent' to refer only to those privileges that received the Great Seal and were enrolled in Chancery, and the terms 'licence' or 'warrant' to refer to privileges which did not reach that stage. The reasons for pursuing a licence all the way to enrolment as a patent, and incurring the significant costs and effort that would entail, remain unclear. Not getting a licence enrolled might seem to present a risk to the privilege-holder needing to enforce it against another party. Certainly, holding a patent would make some aspects of enforcement simpler; for example, a patent's authenticity would be treated as incontrovertible in a court of record (a court whose proceedings are recorded in writing, allowing for the possibility of appeal).[55] Yet it seems in many cases, for both books and maps, simply receiving the royal warrant was sufficient. In the case discussed at the end of this chapter, *Swall v Wild*, the parties were able to obtain an interlocutory injunction (an injunction which lasts until a full hearing of the case is conducted and a final judgment given) on the strength of a mere licence. Once received, the text of the warrant in question would frequently be reproduced in the front matter of a book, the words *cum privilegio regis* (with the king's privilege) included upon the map itself (often within the cartouche), or the privilege referred to in advertising material. As noted above, this suggests that while the licence may have served some role in deterring potential copiers, its chief importance may have in fact lain in the royal stamp of authority it proclaimed and the prestige it conferred upon the work.

The earliest privilege for maps may have been that granted to Christopher Saxton by Elizabeth I in 1577.[56] Saxton had been employed by Thomas Seckford, Master of Requests, to survey the counties of England and Wales, a task that was probably begun in 1574 and completed in 1579. This enormous undertaking produced the first national survey of the kingdom and the publication of the first national *Atlas of England and Wales*. Saxton carried out his own surveys as well as making use of contemporary geographical information. The work was funded by Seckford but the Crown was heavily involved in its production; much interest was taken in it by William Cecil, Lord Burghley, who received proof copies of each map as they were produced.[57] Royal patronage of the project is indicated by the presence of the Royal Arms engraved upon each map and the Queen's approval of the project is further indicated by several marks of appreciation towards Saxton, including several grants of land and office.[58]

Crown sponsorship of the project is revealed by the Privy Council pass granted on 11 March 1576 to Saxton 'to be assisted in all places where he shall come for the view of meet places to describe certain counties in cartes'.[59] A second order of assistance for his survey of Wales was made on 10 July 1576.[60]

[55] I am grateful to HT Gómez-Arostegui for this point.

[56] C66/1159 f21 (UKNA).

[57] IM Evans and H Lawrence, *Christopher Saxton: Elizabethan Map-Maker* (West Yorkshire & London, Wakefield Historical Publications & The Holland Press Ltd, 1979) 9.

[58] ibid 66–73.

[59] ibid Appendix 15, 163.

[60] ibid Appendix 8, 147.

On 22 July 1577, Saxton received letters patent from Elizabeth. This patent, granted two years before the completed *Atlas* was published, set out that Saxton had already travelled through 'the greatest parte of this oure Realme' and had drawn diverse 'trewe and pleasaunte mappes chartes or plates' of the counties, and the cities, towns, villages, and rivers therein. It granted Saxton (and his assignees) the sole privilege and licence to print and sell maps, charts, and plats (another term for map) of the realm of England and Wales or of any county or other part thereof for a period of 10 years. It further forbade any other person from printing and selling such maps, as well as from importing any made in foreign countries. Anyone in breach of the grant would forfeit £10 and any copies already printed to Saxton.[61]

One interesting (although not unique) feature of the patent was that it directly charged the Master and Wardens of the Stationers' Company to aid and assist Saxton in his exercise of the privilege. A second feature of interest was that it did not apply to a specific work but to any maps depicting England and Wales or any part thereof. A third element that stands out is the explicit statement of public benefit and encouragement to be found, the patent stating its object is 'for the better incouraginge of the saide Christofer to procede in this his so profitable and beneficiall an enterprise to all manner of persons'.[62] A fourth point worth noting is that the patent was granted to Saxton himself, while at the same time explicitly recognising that the 'greate coste expenses and charges' had been borne by his employer Seckford.[63] The patent's language thus recognised the usefulness of the maps to sovereign and realm, as well as the labour and cost required to achieve it. The patent can be seen as a mechanism to protect the conversion of this utility into an exchangeable commodity.

Saxton's maps were hugely popular and commercially successful, and their production was a significant event in map history. For the first time, they allowed Englishmen to take 'effective visual and conceptual possession of the physical kingdom in which they lived'.[64] Both Richard Helgerson and Bernard Klein explain that the maps were created at either the behest of Elizabeth or her privy council and represent, at least in part, Tudor propaganda. Klein points out that

> Elizabeth's image graces the frontispiece of the collection and the patronage system that led to its production can be traced in the hierarchical line that leads, on nearly every page of the atlas, from the cartographer's compass though the heraldic motto of his patron Thomas Seckford to the omnipresent arms of the Tudors.[65]

This view of the maps as proclaiming Elizabeth I's mastery of her realm and emphasising its internal coherence is the one on display in the famous 'Ditchley portrait'

[61] C66/1159/21 (UKNA).
[62] ibid.
[63] ibid.
[64] Helgerson (n 8) 107.
[65] Klein (n 12) 101.

Figure 2 Known as 'the Ditchley Portrait', this painting of Elizabeth 1 by Marcus Gheeraerts the Younger shows the Queen standing on Saxton's map of Britain, with her feet on Oxfordshire

of Elizabeth standing on Saxton's map of England (see Figure 2).[66] However, Helgerson points out an ideological effect of the maps that was perhaps, ironically, the opposite of what the Queen and her advisers intended, in that they allowed Englishmen and women to see the land as separate to the monarch, enabling the development of a national and local identity that was distinct from loyalty owed to the king or queen.[67]

Saxton's atlas 'determined the visual image of England and of its constituent parts for over a century to come'.[68] The image he created appeared not only in derivative maps but was absorbed into designs for frontispieces, cartouches, portraits, tapestries, and playing cards.[69] This may in part be due to the fact that this was to represent the high-water mark of royal support for mapmaking ventures for many years. While the government continued to use maps, by the end of Elizabeth's reign it had become a 'mere consumer' of them.[70] John Speed, Saxton's successor and most famous of all the seventeenth century English cartographers, did not receive a similar level of direct royal patronage but was supported by Sir Fulke Greville, favourite of Elizabeth I and supporter of James I, which allowed him to produce his two atlases, *The Theatre of the Empire of Great Britaine* (1611) and *Prospect of the Most Famous Parts of the World* (1627).[71] Speed dedicated his *Theatre* to James, the 'Inlarger and Uniter

[66] Marcus Gheeraerts the Younger, *Elizabeth I (the 'Ditchley portrait')*, c1592. National Portrait Gallery, London, NPG 2561, www.npg.org.uk/collections/search/portrait/mw02079/Queen-Elizabeth-I-The-Ditchley-portrait.

[67] Helgerson (n 8) 114ff. See also Klein (n 12) 102–104.

[68] V Morgan, 'The Cartographic Image of 'The Country' in Early Modern England' (1979) 129 *Transactions of the Royal Historical Society* 129, 133.

[69] Morgan (n 68) 148–53.

[70] Barber (n 13) 84.

[71] A Baynton-Williams, 'John Speed', mapforum.com/2022/01/14/biography-john-speed/.

of the British Empire',[72] and his first map reflects James's unifying agenda by covering the entire British Isles.[73] Speed was self-deprecating of his own efforts, admitting in the *Theatre's* introduction that: 'I have put my sickle into other mens corne, and have laid my building upon other mens foundations'[74] but he did make considerable improvements to the maps of Saxton and other predecessors such as William Norden and William Smith.[75] In addition, as Klein and Helgerson have argued, Speed continued the transformation begun by Saxton of separating land and monarch. Speed's maps are distinguished by the presence of elaborate heraldry of the gentry, which marginalises the royal insignia also present on the maps and, thus, 'contributed to the emergence of a conception of England defined not exclusively in relation to its monarch, but to all the leading families of the gentry'.[76]

The gentry was the chief market for Speed's atlases and it was not he who sought a privilege for *The Theatre* but George Humble who, with his uncle John Sudbury, operated the most successful publishing and printselling business in London.[77] On 7 April 1608, Humble received a royal patent to print 'a book compiled by John Speed called "The Theatre of the Empire of Great Britayne" with cartes and maps' for a period of 21 years.[78] It does not appear that a similar privilege was sought for the *Prospect* and, in 1658, George Humble's son William appears to have assigned his rights in both works to William Garrett, a Stationer, who entered them in the Register at Stationers' Hall on 24 March 1658, as well as epitomes or abridgements in octavo.[79] A modern lawyer would be tempted to interject here to ask what 'right' Humble could be assigning? The patent had long expired, Humble was not a Stationer, and no other positive law could establish the 'estate, right & title in the book or copie'[80] referred to in the Register's entry. The answer must be that possession of the plates, combined with custom of the trade, operated to create a transaction that could be treated as property and was accepted as such by those in the map and book trade.

Saxton and Speed's patents were granted for projects that were already underway. However, in some cases, patents were granted for more speculative projects. On 11 March 1618, Aaron Rathborne and Roger Burges were granted a patent lasting 21 years to engrave and print maps and descriptions of London,

[72] 'Dedication' in J Speed, *The theatre of the empire of Great Britaine presenting an exact geography of the kingdomes of England, Scotland, Ireland and the iles adjoining: with the shires, hundreds, cities and shire-townes, within the kingdome of England, divided and described by Iohn Speed* (London, 1611).

[73] Klein (n 12) 105.

[74] 'To the Well-affected and Favourable Reader' in Speed (n 72).

[75] C Delano-Smith and RJP Kain, *English Maps: A History* (London, The British Library, 1999) 74–75. See also Baynton-Williams (n 71).

[76] Klein (n 12) 108.

[77] Baynton-Williams (n 71).

[78] C66/1770/23 (UKNA); ibid.

[79] Briscoe Eyre et al (n 44) 2, 219–220 (24 March 1658).

[80] ibid.

Westminster, York, Bristol, Norwich, Canterbury, Bath, Oxford, Cambridge, and Windsor.[81] However, Rathborne and Burges failed to produce any town plans, which, as Lawrence Worms points out, demonstrates the drawbacks of the system. If operating as intended, the existence of such a broad patent would prevent anyone else from producing any town plans either and, indeed, no town plans were produced during the life of the patent.[82] Other patents were even broader. In 1547 a patent known as 'the grammar patent' was granted to Reyner Wolfe. Directed mainly at schoolbooks, the patent also referred to maps, charts, and 'other things of that kind'.[83] The patent eventually ended up in the hands of John Norton, Printer to the King in Latin, Greek and Hebrew, in 1603. Although the extent of the protection is questionable, the only maps made during the period that Norton held the patent were made with his involvement, with the signal exception of Speed's maps, which had their own patent, as noted above.[84]

Broader yet, and with even greater potential chilling effect was the infamous and much-contested patent granted to Thomas Symcock and Roger Wood in 1619 for everything printed on one side of paper only.[85] In 1623 the patent was reissued, now explicitly naming maps among the included items.[86] Yet even before that, Humble and Speed had been among those petitioning the House of Commons against the patent.[87] After a long campaign by the Stationers' Company and others, the Court of Chancery eventually found against Symcock (now sole patentee) in 1631.[88] It does not appear that Wood or Symcock produced any maps during the previous 12 years nor did anyone else, suggesting again that map production had been suppressed by the existence of the monopoly.[89]

Following the Restoration, the practice of granting royal licences to both maps and geographical works continued, although none of the Stuarts before Charles II showed much interest in mapping projects. Very few of the licences granted were ever enrolled as patents. One project in which Charles II clearly took some interest was William Petty's survey and maps of Ireland. These flowed from the Down Survey, which Petty had been appointed to undertake in 1654 under Cromwell during the Protectorate. The object of the survey was to enable a valuing of the land, which could then be transferred to the soldiers who had defeated the Irish in the

[81] C66/2152/12 (UKNA).

[82] L Worms, 'The London Map Trade to 1640' in D Woodward (ed), *History of Cartography: Volume 3, Cartography in the European Renaissance Part II* (Chicago, Chicago University Press, 2007) 1693, 1715.

[83] ibid.

[84] ibid.

[85] WW Greg, *A Companion to Arber, Being a Calendar of Documents in Edward Arber's Transcript of the Registers of the Company of Stationers of London 1554–1640* (Oxford, Clarendon Press, 1967) 59.

[86] ibid 65–66.

[87] ibid 168.

[88] For a detailed discussion of the controversy, see W Alexander Jackson, *Records of the Court of the Stationers' Company, 1602 to 1640* (London, Bibliographical Society, 1957) xvi–xxii; Hunt (n 52) 34–35.

[89] Worms (n 82) 1716–17. Alastair Mann details a similar case in Scotland, where the Privy Council granted rights to printer Thomas Finlayson in 1606 for works including maps: Mann, 'Mapping North Sea Print Networks'.

war of 1648 and to whom Cromwell was now indebted.[90] The Down Survey thus facilitated a 'ruthless transfer of the land of Ireland to an immigrant landlord class'.[91] Petty, however, had his own personal ambitions and early on had conceived the plan of using the information gathered to produce an atlas of Ireland.[92] As Brenna Bhandar has recently shown, Petty was deeply influenced by Baconian empiricism and his survey aimed to reduce both land and people to economic units of value. In this way, land use was tied to notions of racial difference and both were woven into an ideology of improvement and the creation of wealth. Petty's survey and the maps that followed, argues Bhandar, represent the beginnings of using racial taxonomy and classification to reconceptualise human life 'within emergent political economies of land, labor and commerce' and that this was 'inextricably tied up with colonial spaces'.[93] Although the survey was begun under Cromwell, Charles II was sufficiently interested in the project that he granted a licence in 1660 to Petty for his maps of Ireland. In 1664 Petty petitioned the King again, explaining he had 'Beene at many hundred pounds' charge, and severall yeares' labour in composing a most exact map of that kingdome' and seeking payment.[94] In 1665 the Act of Explanation, passed as an element of Charles II's partial reversal of Commonwealth policies, also granted Petty's claim.[95] The maps were eventually engraved in Amsterdam and published in atlas form as *Hiberniae Delineatio* in 1685.[96]

Unsurprisingly, given England's growing imperial and commercial ambitions, an area of particular interest to the Crown was maritime charts and navigation aids. Charles II continued Cromwell's development of maritime power, by building more ships, as well as his bid to take control of trade networks through the Navigation Acts (1660, 1663 and 1673) and strengthening naval discipline through the Articles of War Act (1652), Press Act (1659), and Naval Discipline Act (1661). Success in the three wars against the Dutch between 1651 and 1675 followed, establishing England's maritime supremacy, whereupon the focus moved to the riches of the Atlantic.[97] Charles II granted a licence to John Seller in 1670–71 for two treatises on navigation, the *English Pilot* and the *Sea Atlas*, for a period of 30 years.[98] Seller, an instrument maker, was the first Englishman to attempt

[90] B Bhandar, *Colonial Lives of Property: Law, Land and Racial Regimes of Ownership* (Durham, NC, Duke University Press, 2018) 40.

[91] P Linebaugh and M Rediker, *The Many-Headed Hydra: Sailors, Slaves, Commoners, and the Hidden History of the Revolutionary Atlantic* (Boston, Beacon Press, 2000) 122.

[92] RA Skelton, *County Atlases of the British Isles 1579–1850: A Bibliography, Part 4 (1671–1703)* (London, Map Collectors' Circle, 1968) 162.

[93] Bhandar (n 90) 46–47.

[94] Skelton (n 92) 163.

[95] An Act for the Explaining of some Doubts Arising upon An Act intituled An Act for the better execution of His Majesties gracious Declaration for the Settlement of His Kingdom of Ireland, and satisfactions of the several interests of Adventurers Souldiers, and other his Subjects there (1665) 17 Charles II c.2.

[96] Skelton (n 92) 164, 169.

[97] Linebaugh and Rediker (n 91) 145–48.

[98] SP44/34, 76–7 (UKNA).

to compete with the Dutch charts upon which all European navigators relied.[99] He appears to have sought this privilege in response to a specific commercial threat, for the text of the licence noted that the King had been informed of attempts to copy and reprint the works, 'but under another Title, to the great prejudice and discouragement of the said John Seller'. It continued:

> We taking the same into our Princely consideration and minding the great usefullnesse of this Work, have thought fit to the future encouragement hereby to declare our Pleasure, and accordingly we do by these presents strictly prohibit and forbid all our Subjects within our Kingdoms of Great Britain and Ireland to copy, epitomise, or reprint the said Treatises of Navigacon intitled the English Pilot and the Sea Atlas in whole or in part, or under any other Name or Title whatsoever, or to Copy or Counterfeit any of the Maps, Platts, or Charts that shall be in the said Treatises.[100]

Other examples of Crown sponsorship of maritime works include James II's 14-year licence to Daniel Newhouse in 1685 for *The Whole Art of Navigation* and William and Mary's licences granted to Greenvile Collins in 1691/2 for his *Coasting Pilot*.[101]

Once 'map consciousness' had taken hold of the upper echelons of society, it is not difficult to deduce the Crown's motivation in granting privileges for maps and charts. The instrument allowed them to provide encouragement for ventures considered valuable without having to take a directory role and with little financial outlay or obligation (although this could be provided separately if requested). Clearly, these licences were seen as worth acquiring by mapmakers, but what exactly was their value in commercial terms and how did this relate to the Crown's objectives? In addition, how did the privilege system interact with the Stationers' Company's registration system in the context of mapmaking? To address these questions, we turn now to explore the commercial practices of two important mapmakers and rivals of the late seventeenth century: Richard Blome and John Ogilby. Blome and Ogilby came to mapmaking from different backgrounds but used a similar range of commercial strategies to support their cartographic ventures, including the use of subscription publishing, traditional advertising, and a variety of forms of royal patronage. Blome, as a member of the Stationers' Company, also had recourse to protection through the Register. Both of them entered into expensive undertakings, with varying degrees of success, to produce large-scale, multi-volume geographical works. We will then turn to consider a third major geographical publication, a seventeenth-century edition of Camden's *Britannia*, and the legal action brought by three booksellers against an alleged copier on the strength of their royal privilege.

[99] C Verner, 'John Seller and the Chart Trade in Seventeenth-Century England' in NJ Thrower (ed), *The Compleat Plattmaker: Essays on Chart, Map and Globemaking in England in the Seventeenth and Eighteenth Centuries* (University of California Press, 1978) 127, 127–28.

[100] SP44/34, 76 (UKNA).

[101] SP44/336, 249–50, SP44/343, 240–1 (UKNA) (see also ch 4).

IV. The Legal and Commercial Strategies of Richard Blome

Richard Blome (1635–1705) was perhaps the most active of seventeenth-century mapmakers in seeking legal protection for his ventures. Made free of the Stationers' Company by patrimony in August 1660, the year Charles II was restored to the throne, Blome began his career as a ruler of paper and a heraldic printer.[102] However, he soon turned to the publication of geographical works. Blome had an ambitious publishing agenda, envisaging multiple volumes containing both maps and political, historical, and cultural description. In so doing, he was seeking to participate in the Renaissance humanist revival of interest in classical traditions, including the geographical works of Strabo, combined with a growing interest in empirical observation.[103] Foreign travel and the observation of foreign parts was considered to be an essential part of the education of a gentleman, particularly one destined for public service.[104] But not everyone could travel and atlases and other works of chorography allowed those who stayed at home to also be abreast of national and global geographies. As Blome noted in the preface of his *Geographical Description* in 1670, 'we cannot travel so well with the Body, yet at least-wise we would visit, behold, and contemplate [the Earth] with our minds'.[105] Publishing such works, however, required significant investment and a range of strategies for dissemination.

Eight years after Blome was made free of the Stationers' Company he embarked upon his grand geographical plans. At this stage, he appears to have envisaged a major project of three volumes of geographical works. According to his prospectus, Volume I would be a translation of German geographer Varenius's *Geographica Generalis*; Volume II would be a world atlas taken from French geographer Nicholas Sanson entitled *A Geographical, Hydrographical and Chorographical Description of the Four Parts of the World*; and Volume III would be a description of Britain.[106] These three volumes were all entered in the Stationers' Register on 31 May 1668.[107] Interestingly, all three had first been registered by Blome (or possibly his father Jacob) on 28 May 1663.[108] Blome entered one more book of geography in the Register in the 1660s: *A Generall Discripcon of the Kingdomes, Countreys, Isles &c in Affrica* on 10 April 1669.[109] This work does not seem to have

[102] Skelton (n 92) 140.
[103] B Shapiro, *Political Communication and Political Culture in England, 1558–1688* (Stanford, Stanford University Press, 2012).
[104] ibid 56–59.
[105] Quoted in GA Sullivan, 'The Atlas as Literary Genre: Reading the Inutility of John Ogilby's Britannia', Thirteenth Kenneth Nebenzahl Jr Lectures in the History of Cartography, Newberry Library, 1999.
[106] Skelton (n 92) 140.
[107] Briscoe Eyre et al (n 45) 389–90 (31 July 1668).
[108] ibid 2, 323 (28 May 1663).
[109] ibid 2, 399 (10 April 1669).

proceeded to publication, although an English edition appears under the imprint of Blome's rival John Ogilby.[110] In 1671 Blome again returned to the Register for protection for *A Discripcon of the Island of Jamaica* on 9 November.[111] This work, which included a map of Jamaica, was published in 1672.

At the same time, Blome also sought royal privileges and patronage for his works. On 14 March 1669, as the second volume of his grand project neared completion, Charles II granted him 21 years of protection for 'a book of Geography, in three Volumes, in folio, illustrated with great variety of delightful & usefull maps'.[112] It seems likely that Blome was seeking protection for the same three companion volumes he had already entered in the Stationers' Register.[113] But first he had to raise the funds for publication and sought to do so by attracting subscribers. On 28 October 1669, Blome announced the imminent publication of the *Geographical Description* in the *London Gazette* and invited those concerned in the subscription to come to his house in the Savoy.[114] However, Blome was not simply relying on press advertisement but also on royal influence. On 10 July 1669, Charles II had issued a further order, recommending that the nobles and learned society subscribe to one or more of Blome's books in order to 'encourage him to finish this his commendable design'.[115] This letter was prefixed to the *Geographical Description* itself. Moreover, in either 1669 or 1670, an advertisement was issued by the King's Command recommending the purchase of 'an exact Book of Geography taken from the notes and travels of the famous Monsieur Sanson'.[116]

A Geographical Description of the Four Parts of the World was published in 1670 and Blome dedicated it to Charles II for his 'undeserved encouragement'.[117] It contained 24 maps copied from Nicholas Sanson's maps issued in his *Cartes Generales de toutes les Parties du Monde* (1658) and was the first world atlas published in England since Speed's *Prospect* in 1627.[118] Blome also included a 'Testimony and Approbation' signed by several members of the Royal Society, stating they had supervised and approved the work. Blome used the publication of this volume to push his upcoming books. In the preface to the *Geographical*

[110] A Baynton-Williams, 'Richard Blome', www.mapforum.com/2022/07/13/biography-richard-blome/.
[111] Briscoe Eyre (n 44) 2, 436 (9 November 1671).
[112] SP44/30,156 (UKNA).
[113] Although note that Baynton-Williams believes that the third book entered, *A Survey or Descripcon of the British Isles*, was a smaller project that was abandoned, with some of the plates to appear later in his *Speed's Maps Epitomiz'd*: Baynton-Williams (n 110). Skelton believes that Blome had two sets of county maps engraved for him concurrently – larger maps, which appeared in *Britannica*, and smaller maps, which appeared much later in *Speed's Maps Epitomiz'd*. Skelton, *County Atlases, Part 4* 104.
[114] Sarah LC Clapp, 'The Subscription Enterprises of John Ogilby and Richard Blome' (May 1933) 30 *Modern* 371.
[115] SP44/30, 158 (UKNA).
[116] SP29/441 f151 (c1669–1670) (UKNA).
[117] Richard Blome, *A Geographical Description of the Four Parts of the World taken from the Notes and Workes of the Famous Monsieur Sanson, geographer to the French King, and other eminent travellers and authors* (London, printed by TN for R Blome, 1670).
[118] Baynton-Williams (n 110).

Description, he indicated future offerings, namely the two volumes referred to above and a fourth volume, which would be a hydrographical description of the world.[119] Charles II's letter of recommendation of 10 July 1669, inserted in the text after the dedication, also promoted the future volumes. The King noted that Blome 'hath in obedience to our particular Command prepared one of the Volumes of the said Work to be a large description of Our kingdoms of England, Scotland and Ireland, and the Islands thereto belonging'.[120] In order to assist Blome in his stated desire to 'rectify those great & many errours committed in all books & Maps yet extant', the King requested all the Justices of the Peace, sheriffs, mayors, high constables, and others to give him aid and assistance.[121] The advertisement of either 1669 or 1670, recommending the purchase of the *Geographical Description*, also noted that Blome was currently preparing a larger description of the British Isles, including a map of every county of England, and, if the nobility or gentry wished their names, titles, and coats of arms to be included within, they should make the request of Blome before the next Hilary Term (January).[122] This was the work that came to be titled *Britannia*.[123]

In 1670 Blome issued a prospectus, or proposal, for his *Britannia*, which referred to the King's request for assistance, specifying the kind of information he would require: the names of market towns and their location, such as proximity to rivers or the sea; size of towns; number of churches; market days and what is sold there; existence of fairs; places of antiquity; castles and forts; and so on. The proposal seemed in some respects intended also to ward off complaints about omissions, with Blome writing he issued the proposal 'that none may take exceptions if omitted in the said Work as having no notice thereof'. Subscribers were invited to pay 20s in return for one book, in which they would have their coat of arms affixed to the map of the county to which they are related, and could pay an additional 5s for every additional county in which they wished to be mentioned.[124] By 1673 the price had increased for new subscribers and an additional offer was made for a larger size colour edition for: 'Those that are curious in their books'.[125] There were 812 subscribers, including Charles II (whose name leads the list), and the Duke of York (later James I) (see Figure 3).[126]

However, even subscriptions were not enough to cover the costs and Blome sought additional royal favour. On 18 July 1672, he was granted a royal warrant

[119] This work was never registered and Skelton claims it had to be abandoned after John Seller obtained the licence referred to earlier from Charles II in March 1671: Skelton (n 113) 90. I am not aware of the evidence Skelton relied upon to make this assertion.

[120] SP44/30, 158–59 (UKNA).

[121] ibid.

[122] SP29/441 f151 (c1669–1670) (UKNA).

[123] R Blome, *Britannia: or, A Geographical Description of the Kingdoms of England, Scotland, and Ireland, with the Isles and Territories thereto belonging* (London, R Blome, 1673).

[124] Maps 187.1.1(16) (BL). Reproduced in Skelton (n 113) 141.

[125] Term Catalogue, Vol 1, 149 (24 Nov 1763).

[126] Clapp (n 114) 372.

Figure 3 The first page of list of supporters and subscribers for Richard Blome's *Britannia*, headed by the King

Image courtesy of the State Library, NSW, RBDQ924A/49.

allowing him to import 4,000 reams of royal paper free of the customs duty of 12d a ream. The licence explained it was granted because Blome had

> undertaken a very laudable and useful work of geography in the setting forth our kingdoms and dominions with maps and tables, wherein he has proceeded so far at his own charge as to finish one volume, and has presented the same to us.[127]

In 1673 Blome sought a further royal licence for a volume he referred to as a 'Description of your Majesty's Dominions with Maps now ready for the Press'. The licence he sought would include a 21-year

> prohibition for any others to reprint the same in whole, or in part, or to observe the method, or print any the like Alphabetical Tables, or to Coppy any of the said Mapps or Sculptures which shall be in the said Book or by any other means prejudice him in the sale thereof.[128]

This work was published in 1673 under the title of *Britannia* with 49 maps, based mainly on those of Speed (see Figure 4).[129] On 29 September 1675, Blome petitioned the King again, stating he had completed 'his 2d Volume (called Britannia)' and now had two remaining volumes ready for the press, the first being *Arts of Cosmography and Geography*, which is a translation of Varenius, and the second, 'Geographicall & Hydrographicall Tables of the Known Countrys & Kingdoms in the World'.[130] In order to help him to finish these works, he asked for a Royal Licence to import 8,000 reams of royal paper free from customs duties.[131]

[127] Calendar of Treasury Books, Vol 3, 1668–1672.

[128] SP29/337 f235 (UKNA). Note that this use of the word 'sculpture' refers to the process of engraving to produce designs or figures in relief or intaglio (from the Latin, sculpere, to carve or engrave) rather than the modern meaning of a three-dimensional artwork.

[129] R Blome, *Britannia, or, A Geographical Description of the Kingdoms of England, Scotland, and Ireland, with the Isles and Territories Thereto Belonging* (London, Printed by Tho. Roycroft for the undertaker, Richard Blome, 1673); Delano-Smith and Kain (n 75) 105.

[130] SP29/373 f264 (UKNA).

[131] ibid.

Figure 4 The map of the county of Devonshire from Richard Blome, *Britannia, or, a geographical description of the kingdoms of England, Scotland, and Ireland, with the isles and territories thereto belonging* (London, printed for Thomas Roycroft for the undertaker, Richard Blome, 1673)

Image courtesy of the State Library, NSW, RBDQ924A/49.

In 1681 Blome published *Speed's Maps Epitomiz'd*, which consisted of crudely reduced copies of Speed's maps.[132]

The translation of Varenius eventually appeared in 1682 under the title *Cosmography and Geography* and was again financed through subscriptions.[133] For the next 13 years, Blome turned his attention away from cartographical works. However, on 7 November 1695, he was granted a licence by William III for 14 years for the sole printing and selling of a book titled 'A Survey or Description of our

[132] The history of the plates is uncertain and Blome's object in producing such a work is unclear. Skelton suggests it may have been an attempt to exploit the ongoing popularity of Speed's maps in a more accessible format than *Britannia* 'without infringing the copyright still owned by Bassett and Chiswell': Skelton (n 92) 158–159. In referring to 'copyright', Skelton seems to be mistaking the reference to the work having been 'licensed to be reprinted' in the front matter of Bassett and Chiswell's 1676 edition of *The Theatre of the Empire of Great Britain*. However, as the statement is attributed to Roger L'Estrange, the Press Licensor, it seems more likely that this refers to the publishers having received permission to publish, rather than a royal privilege protecting them against rival copies. I have been unable to locate any such royal privilege.

[133] Clapp (n 114) 373.

Cities of London & Westminster with the Liberties and Parts adjacent and also of the Several American Plantations which will be illustrated with a great many useful ichnographical maps'.[134] In addition to granting the licence, the king expressed his 'Royall approbation' of the project and recommended his loyal servants assist Blome 'in such particulars as shall be desired', as well as to subscribe to the work.[135] The licence also directed the Master, Warden, and Company of Stationers to take notice that the work would be entered in the register, as indeed it was on 30 November 1695.[136]

This project also seems to have been abandoned, although Ashley Baynton-Williams notes there is evidence that at least some of the maps were completed. He suggests that the reason the project foundered may have lain in the difficulty of compiling accurate and up-to-date maps of London and the costs involved in such a project.[137] Evidence of Blome's need to raise more finance can be found in a petition of 29 April 1696, in which he requested that his Majesty grant him 'to farm for a term of years the fines as shall arise from the place of the Clerk of the Market within the Verge of his Majesty's Court', paying the usual fee of 20 per cent into the Exchequer.[138] This office conferred upon its holder the right to collect the fines raised by this court for market-based misdemeanours. It is not clear from the petition whether Blome was seeking the position or already held it and wished to 'farm' (or sublet) it to someone else, presumably for payment.

Blome's final cartographic project also remained incomplete. On 21 September 1705, he was granted a licence by Queen Anne, along with recommendatory letters, to publish a book entitled *The Britannick Empire*, which was to be printed in folio with 'a great Variety of Mapps & Sculptures'.[139] The licence was to last for 14 years and prohibited anyone else from reprinting the said book in whole or in part, epitomising the book, printing it 'in any Language or Speech whatsoever', copying or counterfeiting any of the maps or engravings, or selling any such books, without the consent of Blome.[140] Blome died shortly after the licence was granted and the book was never published.[141]

Neither the licences, registrations, and subscriptions, nor the intellectual support of the Royal Society, were enough to allow Blome to produce original work or carry out new surveys, despite the requests made by Charles II to furnish him with information. He was condemned by contemporaries for his lack of originality, with antiquary Anthony à Wood writing that Blome 'scribbled and transcribed from Camden's Britannia and Speed's Maps' and that he got his livelihood by

[134] SP44/346 f167–68 (UKNA).
[135] SP44/436 f167 (UKNA).
[136] Rogers (n 50) 148.
[137] Baynton-Williams (n 110).
[138] SP44/238, 75 (UKNA).
[139] SP44/353, 98–9 (UKNA).
[140] ibid.
[141] Blome's will was proved on 22 October 1705, PROB11/484/405 (UKNA).

'progging tricks'.[142] Others accused *Britannia* of being 'a most entire piece of theft out of Camden and Speed' and 'a most notorious piece of plagiarism'.[143] However, originality had never been Blome's object and he made no claim to it. In the preface to *Britannia*, he explained: 'I do not own my self the Author, but the Undertaker of this Work, it receiving Birth from divers Manuscripts'. He openly acknowledged the maps were taken from Speed and the information from Camden and that, while his maps were not 'without fault', his view was that 'there are none (nor ever will be any) made without fault'.[144] Yet, with generosity (perhaps to his rival Ogilby), he went on:

> yet there may be some that by new Surveys may pretend to do much in the rectifying all such errors, and to make them faultless, which I should be heartily glad to see, as being a Work of such general good.[145]

Tracing Blome's efforts to both protect and promote his works, especially *Britannia*, demonstrates the very real commercial difficulties facing mapmakers in Restoration England.

V. John Ogilby: Science, Commerce, and Royal Patronage

John Ogilby (1600–76) was one of the more colourful mapmakers of the seventeenth century. Like Blome, Ogilby conceived a multi-volume cartographical project on a grand scale and, like Blome, pursued a number of different avenues of fundraising and advertisement to try to make the project commercially viable. Ogilby, however, turned to mapmaking late in life. His first career as a dancer ended following an injury, following which he became in turn a dancing-master, soldier, poet, theatre manager and owner, and translator and bookseller of the classics.[146] His interest in cartography followed from a second life-changing catastrophe, when his entire stock of books was destroyed in the Great Fire of London in 1666. Thereafter he and his step-grandson William Morgan were appointed 'sworn viewers', helping to arbitrate property boundary disputes in London's devastated areas.[147]

[142] Skelton (n 92) 140. 'Progging' is British slang meaning to forage or prowl about for food or timber.
[143] Bishop William Nicolson in 1696 and Richard Gough in 1780 respectively. Quoted in ibid 142.
[144] Richard Blome, 'Preface to the Reader,' (n 123).
[145] ibid.
[146] Ogilby's fascinating and somewhat mysterious career has inspired recent claims he was a royalist agent and his *Britannia* hid a secret invasion plan: A Ereira, *The Nine Lives of John Ogilby: Britain's Master Map Maker and His Secrets* (London, Duckworth Overlook, 2016).
[147] J Ogilby and JB Harley, *Britannia: John Ogilby, London 1675. With an Introduction by Dr. J.B. Harley* (Amsterdam, Theatrum Orbis Terrarum, 1970) vii; L Worms, 'Maps and Atlases,' in J Barnard, DF McKenzie, and M Bell (eds), *The Cambridge History of the Book in Britain. Volume IV: 1557–1695* (Cambridge, Cambridge University Press, 2002) 241.

Ogilby announced his grand project, *The English Atlas*, in a proposal dated 10 May 1669. There he set out his ambition of 'Conquest of the whole World' through a 'New and Accurate Description' of its four quarters, Africa, America, Asia, and Europe, illustrated with large maps and embellished with 'sculptures', or engravings. Europe would consist of two volumes, with the second consisting only of Britain.[148] Ogilby's title draws a direct link between the expansionist colonial ambitions of England and many Englishmen, and the humanist intellectual tradition with its new empiricist leanings discussed above.[149] He hoped to appeal to a broad base of potential subscribers, who were encouraged to put down a first payment of 20s for each volume, with a further 20s being paid for the first two volumes, and two payments of 10s for each of the final three volumes. Anyone who subscribed to all five volumes would receive an additional copy.[150]

Ogilby was not a member of the Stationers' Company, so the option of entering his books on the Register in his own name was not open to him.[151] From the time of the Restoration, however, he had begun seeking privileges for works he had published during the Commonwealth as well as his new ventures.[152] On 20 April 1668, he was granted a licence for 'an Exact Description of Africa'.[153] The following year, on 1 November 1669, he received a 15-year licence for his much more ambitious project: 'a Description of the world, viz. Africa, America, Asia and Europe, in several Volumes, adorn'd with Sculptures'. This licence also reaffirmed earlier licences for his earlier works including *Aesop's Fables* and translations of Virgil and Homer. It forbade anyone from printing or reprinting the volumes, or from copying or counterfeiting the 'sculptures or ingravements' therein. Anyone offending would 'answer the contrary at their utmost perill'. The licence also directed the Stationers' Company to take particular notice 'that due obedience been given to this Our Royal Command'.[154] Unlike the licence granted to Blome, it did not include a prohibition against epitomes.

The first volume, the description of Africa, was published in 1670 and included the text of the licence in its introductory material.[155] Volumes on China, Japan,

[148] 'A Proposal Concerning an English Atlas' 10 May 1669, Wood 658 f.792 (Bodleian).

[149] See A Fitzmaurice, *Humanism and America: An Intellectual History of English Colonisation, 1500–1625* (Cambridge, Cambridge University Press, 2003) and Shapiro (n 103) especially ch 3.

[150] 'A Proposal Concerning an English Atlas' 10 May 1669 Wood 658 f.792 (Bodleian).

[151] On at least two occasions Ogilby's works were registered as having been assigned to stationers. On 18 April 1661 Ogilby's book *His Majesty's Entertainments Passing through the City of London to his Coronation* was registered by Thomas Roycroft and, on 2 May 1675, Ogilby's translation of Virgil was registered by Master Guy: Briscoe Eyre et al (n 45) 291, 510 (9 November 1671).

[152] KS Van Eerde, *John Ogilby and the Taste of the Times* (Folkestone, Dawson & Sons, 1976) 82–84.

[153] SP44/30, 127 (UKNA).

[154] SP44/25, 131v–132r (UKNA).

[155] J Ogilby, *Africa Being an Accurate Description of the Regions of Ægypt, Barbary, Lybia, and Billedulgerid, the Land of Negroes, Guinee, Æthiopia and the Abyssines : With All the Adjacent Islands, Either in the Mediterranean, Atlantick, Southern or Oriental Sea, Belonging Thereunto : With the Several Denominations Fo Their Coasts, Harbors, Creeks, Rivers, Lakes, Cities, Towns, Castles, and Villages, Their Customs, Modes and Manners, Languages, Religions and Inexhaustible Treasure : With Their Governments and Policy, Variety of Trade and Barter : And Also of Their Wonderful Plants, Beasts,*

America, and Asia quickly followed. Although the works were entitled 'atlases', they were not simply collections of maps. The works did contain maps but they were included alongside substantial written information about the history, geography, and culture of the parts of the world described therein. None of this information was particularly original or new and comprised mostly translations of travellers' accounts.[156]

However, even in 1671, planning was underway for something far more ambitious and original still – a new survey of the entire country, to be called *Britannia*. On 14 August 1671, Charles II, 'out of Our Inclination to Promote so Great and Useful a Work', issued an instruction to 'all Persons whom it may concern in the several and respective Counties' to give assistance to Ogilby or his appointee for the production of the volume on Great Britain.[157] Ogilby issued a prospectus, probably around February 1672, advertising for further subscribers and claiming that the King and Queen had offered to contribute £500 each to the project. In this same prospectus Ogilby laid out the intention of his *Britannia*, which would set it above the earlier works of Camden, Speed, and even the very recent offering of Blome:

> The Author seriously considering that whatever of this nature has been hitherto attempted, comes infinitely short of the Perfection the Importance of the Subject requires: whether Respect be given to the Historick Part, in which not a Tenth, and sometimes a Twentyeth Part of the Towns have been so much as mention'd: nay, oftentimes the very Hundreds wholly omitted; or the Geographick Part, wherein, as Mr Norden complains, *No Actual Dimensuration was every perform'd but a Computation of Distances, by a Cursory Perambulation, made up the Original Work*, from Whence, whatever Mr *Cambden*, *Speed* or of late one *Blome* have since done, are but onely Copy'd, with this ill Fate, That as the Original Errors were not onely transferr'd to, but augmented by the additional ones of the later Mapps; so now, lastly, the very Performance it self rendred so much worse than the meanest of what was before Extant.[158]

Ogilby promised six volumes to remedy these ills, the first four being a historical and geographical description of England, with county maps produced using new surveys. The fifth volume would be an 'Ichnographical and Historical Description' of the principal roads in England and Wales, and the sixth would be a 'New and Accurate Description' of London. Ogilby estimated the cost of the entire project to be £20,000, £14,000 of which would be devoted to the road survey.[159]

Birds and Serpents : Collected and Translated from Most Authentick Authors and Augmented with Later Observations: Illustrated with Notes and Adorn'd with Peculiar Maps and Proper Sculptures (London, John Ogilby, 1670).

[156] D Hodson, 'The Making of John Ogilby's *Britannia*' (unpublished paper), cited in C Delano-Smith, 'Milieus of Mobility: Itineraries, Route Maps and Road Maps' in JR Akerman (ed), *Cartographies of Travel and Navigation* (Chicago, University of Chicago Press, 2006) 305.

[157] MS Aubrey 4 f244 (Bodleian). Writ of Assistance to John Ogilby, the King's Cosmographer, SP44/36, 31 (24 August 1671) (UKNA).

[158] J Ogilby, 'Mr Ogilby's Design for Carrying on his Britannia' (167–?) BrSides Edea 167 (Yale University Library).

[159] ibid.

In 1672 Ogilby met with several members of the Royal Society – Robert Hooke, John Aubrey, and Christopher Wren – to draw up a list of queries to be sent around pursuant to the King's order of 14 August 1671. The queries ranged from the broad ('Of the County in general', 'Cities, Towns Corporate, Market Towns and Fair Towns') to the specific ('What Part of the Countrey is Arrable, Pasture, Meadow', 'Peculiar Customs or Manners of the Countrey').[160] Although there is little evidence that the list of queries was widely circulated, Ogilby did at least embark upon something nobody had attempted since Saxton – an actual attempt at measuring the roads. With surveyors Gregory King and Richard Shortgrave, assisted by unnamed others, 7,519 miles of road were measured using only a perambulator (measuring wheel) and a theodolite (surveyor's compass).[161] Robert Hooke was deeply involved in helping Ogilby design the sheets and maps, as well as in raising capital.[162]

However, there were still insufficient funds. On 11 July 1672, Charles II recommended Ogilby's work to the nobility, universities, churchmen, sheriffs, and justices on the basis he intended 'to illustrate England and Wales more fully by an actual survey, a work never before performed by any' and which would 'be a charge much exceeding his private fortune'.[163] Again the King noted he and the Queen would be subscribing £1,000.[164] In the end only £1,900 could be raised by subscription.[165] On 18 December 1672, Charles II provided further indirect assistance by granting Ogilby a licence to erect a standing lottery selling off existing copies of his works.[166] Ogilby had used this method with some success in the past but, although it was reported that the King himself had attended, not enough was raised to carry the project through to its originally envisioned scale. The King and Queen withdrew their subscription of £1,000, instead granting a further licence in 1673 permitting Ogilby to import custom-free paper for two years, which was claimed to represent an equal amount.[167] A final source of funding was Ogilby's appointment as His Majesty's Cosmographer and Geographic Printer, offices that commanded an annual payment of £13 6s 8d.[168]

Another financial challenge facing Ogilby was a falling out with his principal surveyor, Richard Shortgrave, in late 1673.[169] The dispute related to an

[160] Wood 658 f793 (Bodleian).

[161] Ogilby and Harley (n 147) xiii, xv.

[162] EGR Taylor, 'Robert Hooke and the Cartographical Projects of the Late Seventeenth Century (1666–1696)' (1937) 90 *The Geographical Journal* 529; Ogilby and Harley (n 147) xv.

[163] SP44/36, 93 (UKNA).

[164] ibid.

[165] 'Proposals by William Morgan His Majesty's Cosmographer, for Vending Mr Ogilby's Works in a Standing Lottery, to enable him to finish Britannia, with the Second Part of Asia, and Europe' (1676/7) (Wing (2nd edn) M2755 Bodleian).

[166] SP44/36, 147–48. Index of Patent Rolls, Charles II, 17–31, 237 (UKNA).

[167] SP44/26, 156–57; SO3/16, 689 (October 1873) (UKNA).

[168] Ogilby referred to himself thus on the title page of his volume entitled *America; being the latest and most accurate description of the new world ...* (London, printed by the Author, 1671). However, the first record of his being formally appointed comes in 1675: SP44/40A, 77 (UKNA).

[169] Hooke's diary of 12 December 1673 notes: 'To Ogilby, Shortgrave and he squabbled': Van Eerde (n 152) 126.

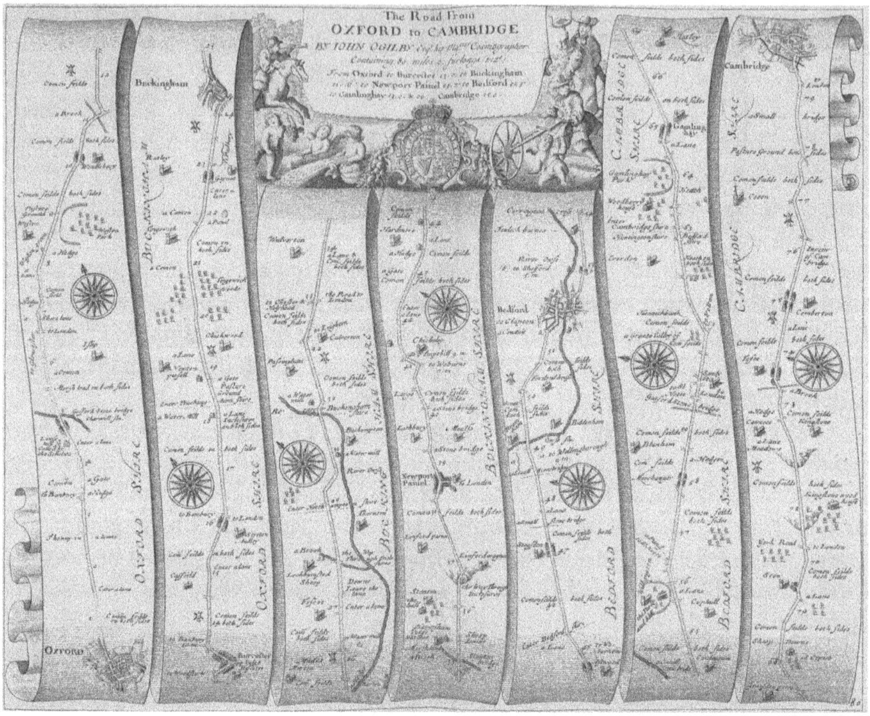

Figure 5 Map of the Road from Oxford to Cambridge from Ogilby's *Britannia* (London, 1675)

© The British Library Board 457.f.1 f081.

alleged miscalculation of the total amount Ogilby had agreed to pay Shortgrave, and Ogilby commenced proceedings in Chancery. There, he not only accused Shortgrave of accepting more money than had been agreed but of poor-quality work; namely, errors and omissions in calculating distances and setting down and naming landmarks.[170]

Ultimately, only one volume of Ogilby's grand plan for *Britannia* was completed during his lifetime. This was the projected fifth volume, the *Book of Roads*, published in 1675. Still envisaging the project would continue, Ogilby published it under the title *Britannia, volume the first, or, An illustration of the Kingdom of England and dominion of Wales by a geographical and historical description of the roads thereof.* The book contained 200 pages of written description and 100 pages of maps, presented in the 'strip map' format (see Figure 5), invented 400 years earlier by Matthew Paris.[171] Although the final book contained only half the

[170] Complaint of John Ogilby, 1 February 1674, C9/409/96 (UKNA).

[171] Delano-Smith (n 156) 46–54; C Delano-Smith, 'Matthew Paris Itinerary Map (c.1250)' in *The Times History of the World in Maps* (London, Harper Collins, 2014) 36–39.

number of maps promised in 1672 and a third of the measured miles promised in an advertisement of 1675, it was a historic achievement. Depicting 73 of the main roads of England and Wales, the volume provided the most current and accurate highway information available and was the first to make consistent use of the measurement that came to be known as the statute mile (1,760 yards to the mile). It also popularised the scale of one inch to one mile.[172] Ogilby's *Britannia* was significantly more successful than Blome's volume of the same name. Several months after it appeared, Ogilby and his step-grandson William Morgan produced another edition of the road maps but without the descriptive text, entitled *Itinerarium Angliae, or, A Book of Roads*.[173] By April 1676, the maps were also being advertised as available for individual sale at 6d a sheet and two further impressions of *Britannia* were published before Ogilby's death on 4 September 1676.[174]

Even as his health failed, Ogilby was apparently seeking to complete the original sixth volume of his projected *Britannia*, the map of London. Again with the assistance of Robert Hooke, Ogilby sought, and received, financial support for this project but this time from the Court of Aldermen of the City of London.[175] With London's reconstruction following the Great Fire underway, it is perhaps not surprising that this body should have had a particular interest in documenting their city's rise from the ashes.[176] The surveying was carried out by William Leybourne, who had been one of six professional surveyors chosen by the Corporation of London to re-survey the City after the Great Fire.[177] The Court of Aldermen not only gave financial support, it also 'was pleas'd … to grant him a Licence for proceeding in the said Work'.[178] They also appointed a Committee to oversee its progress.[179] *A large and accurate map of the City of London*, which consisted of 20 sheets measuring four feet seven inches high and eight feet four inches wide, was eventually published by Morgan in 1677, after Ogilby's death.[180] It was dedicated to the Lord Mayor, Aldermen and Sheriffs of London.

[172] Ogilby and Harley (n 147) v.

[173] *Itinerarium Angliae: Or, A Book of Roads, Werein are Contain'd The Principal Road-Ways of His Majesty's Kingdom of England and Dominion of Wales* (London, Printed by the Author at his House in White-Fryers, 1675).

[174] Ogilby and Harley (n 147) xviii.

[175] ibid 533–34. Records detailing the assistance given to Ogilby for the London survey can be found at Rep 78 f207b and Rep 79 f105 (LMA).

[176] R Hyde, 'The Ogilby and Morgan Survey of the City of London – 1676' in *A large and accurate map of the City of London: ichnographically Describing all the Streets, Lanes, Alleys, Courtyards, Churches, Halls and Houses &c. Actually Surveyed and Delineated, By John Ogilby; introductory notes by Ralph Hyde* (Lympne Castle, Kent, Harry Margary [for] Guildhall Library, London, 1976).

[177] Taylor (n 162) 529, 533.

[178] Court of Aldermen Order, 19 June 1673, Bagford Colln. Harl. 5946 (BL), reproduced in Hyde (n 176).

[179] ibid.

[180] J Ogilby, W Morgan, and W Hollar, *A large and accurate map of the City of London: ichnographically Describing all the Streets, Lanes, Alleys, Courtyards, Churches, Halls and Houses &c. Actually Surveyed and Delineated, By John Ogilby, Esq; His Majesties Cosmographer* (London, J Ogilby, 1677).

What motivated Ogilby to undertake such an ambitious, even impossible, project? And what was the purpose of *Britannia* itself? For the monarchs who supported him, the works represented an opportunity to foster an image of their kingdom as both unified and flourishing. This was particularly important for Charles II following the Restoration, and for William and Mary following the Glorious Revolution of 1688. Ogilby spelled this out explicitly for Charles II in his preface to *Britannia*, claiming it would play a role in:

> Reviving and Propagating the great Soul of the World, Commerce and Correspondency, in maintaining Privileges, encouraging Industry, and inciting the whole Kingdom to a Noble Emulation of recovering a Pristine Splendor, establishing a Present Greatness, or laying the Foundations of a Future Glory.[181]

In his dedication to Charles II, he described the volume as

> an Important Novelty, the Scale of Peace and War, whereby … a True Prospect of This Your Flourishing Kingdom may be Taken, Pregnant Hints of Security and Interest Gather'd, and the Considerable Augmentation of its Extent, beyond Vulgar Estimation, more Certainly Collected.[182]

Laying on the flattery, he pointed to earlier rulers whose territories had been accurately surveyed, from 'the Persian Princes' and 'the Macedonian Conqueror' (Alexander the Great) to Julius Caesar.[183]

Sullivan considers that the reference to 'augmentation' refers literally to a more precise measurement, which resulted in an increase in the count of miles in the kingdom, and metaphorically as expressing the text's impact in increasing the glory of Britain.[184] Alan Ereira, more speculatively, asserts a still more literal meaning for the preface, arguing it proclaims the true purpose of *Britannia*, which was to provide information for a military invasion of Britain aimed at securing absolute power for Charles II.[185]

In terms of Ogilby's own motivation or purpose, his biography reveals him to be a highly versatile and energetic entrepreneur, willing to take financial risk and able to recover from adversity. *Britannia* was certainly high-risk but Ogilby may well have seen it as high-reward. Sullivan notes that Ogilby's *Britannia*, as well as his other books, were 'designed to gain him the approbation and support of monarchs, aristocrats and wealthy merchants, and its lavish form is absolutely central to that task.'[186] The dizzying ambition of Ogilby's scheme leads Donald Hodson to discern a more prominent role of the Royal Society than is often credited. Nothing in Ogilby's background suggested a particular skill or interest in surveying or geography. What he brought to the venture was his business acumen and enthusiasm; the Royal Society brought the scientific skills and ambition to

[181] Ogilby, *Britannia, volume the first*, Preface.
[182] Ogilby, *Britannia, volume the first*, Dedication.
[183] ibid.
[184] Sullivan (n 105).
[185] Ereira (n 146).
[186] Sullivan (n 105).

replace the maps of Saxton with something reflecting their vision of Britain as a leader in the advancement of scientific knowledge.[187]

Whatever Ogilby's objective, he and Blome were far from alone in seeking to undertake ambitious geographical projects in the second half of the century. John Seller received royal patronage to undertake 'a great and elaborate work of an actual survey of England and Wales, comprising complete maps of every county in a large book in folio entitled "Atlas Anglicanus"'.[188] Only a handful of new maps were produced.[189] John Adams proposed a survey of England and Wales on an astronomical basis. He also had the support of Robert Hooke and other members of the Royal Society and had travelled 25,000 miles by 1684. Although he was promised some support by the Treasury Lords and received some subscriptions, no maps were produced.[190] The well-respected London publisher Moses Pitt was another who formulated a grand scheme for an *English Atlas* in 12 volumes. He too compiled a list of queries with the assistance of the Royal Society and sought to raise money by subscription. Subscribers included Charles II and Queen Catherine, the Duke of York, and a very large number of noblemen, merchants, scholars, and colleges of the university.[191] Charles II gave encouragement and a gift of £300 pounds but, by 1691, only four volumes had appeared.[192] Yet again, the venture foundered on the huge costs involved.[193]

Although Ogilby failed to achieve his complete vision for his *English Atlas*, he achieved more than any of his colleagues and rivals. Having produced such an expensive volume as *Britannia*, he clearly saw that copying was a threat to his perceived market and another measure of the book's popularity was the speed with which it was copied. Already in January 1676 Ogilby was complaining to the Secretary of State about 'Mr Basset and Mr Chiswel, who have robbed my book and falsely printed certain tables'.[194] Bassett and Chiswell had converted Ogilby's graphic presentation into typographical word maps. Copies of these maps were inserted into Speed's *Theatre of the Empire of Great Britain* and bound in a pocket volume called *The English Travellers Companion*. In response, Ogilby and Morgan produced their own typographic road maps as well as a letterpress reduction in a narrow format suitable for being carried in a pocket, clearly aimed at travellers.[195] By the fourth impression in 1689, this was being called *Mr Ogilby's*

[187] D Hodson, 'The Early Printed Road Books and Itineraries of England and Wales' (PhD Thesis, University of Exeter, 2000) 407–408 (available in the Forum Library, Exeter, and British Library microfilm no. DX215546. I am grateful to Dr Hodson for providing me with a copy).

[188] Taylor (n 162) 536.

[189] ibid.

[190] ibid 536–38.

[191] Wood 658 (Bodleian).

[192] EGR Taylor, '"The English Atlas" of Moses Pitt, 1680–83' (1940) 95 *The Geographical Journal* 292; Taylor (n 162) 538–40.

[193] Moses Pitt was imprisoned for debt before completing the project but this arose not from his losses from the *Atlas* but from unfortunate property investments: Taylor (n 192) 298.

[194] SP29/378 f.40 (UKNA).

[195] J Ogilby, *Mr Ogilby's Tables of His Measured Roads. So Digested, that any great Road or Branch may readily be found; with the General and the Particular, Computed & Measur'd Distance, and the Distinction of Market and Post-Towns* (London, printed by the Author, 1676). See Hodson (n 187)

and William Morgan's Pocket Book of Roads.[196] However, and notwithstanding the legal protections he had obtained, Ogilby did not take direct legal action, limiting his complaints to advertisements in the *London Gazette* and influential members of the government.[197] Legal action was, however, taken in relation to yet another *Britannia*, produced in the very last years of the century and it is that publication to which we now turn.

VI. Camden's *Britannia* and the First Law Suit

The first book of maps to be the subject of a law suit over unauthorised copying was a far less ambitious undertaking than that of Ogilby. The work known as Camden's *Britannia* was not an original or new publication in 1701 when the suit was commenced. William Camden, a respected Elizabethan antiquary, first published his *Britannia* in May 1586. This first edition combined history and topographic description, falling into (and largely helping to create) the genre known as chorography. Camden appears to have received a privilege from Elizabeth for the work, which proclaims on its title page *Cum gratia & priuilegio Regiae Maiestatis* (with the grace and privilege of her Majesty the Queen).[198] Written in Latin, the common language of the Renaissance elite, the work was immediately popular. By 1590 it had been reprinted three more times in England and twice in Germany.[199] A fourth, larger, edition was published in London in 1594. The work began its life as a small quarto with no maps and a single woodcut of a medieval inscription as its only illustration. The sixth edition, the last to be published during Camden's lifetime, was published in 1607 in folio. It was also the first to contain maps, most of which were taken from the well-known English county maps of William Saxton and John Norden.[200] Despite its title, the main focus of the work was on England and Wales, with shorter sections devoted to Scotland and Ireland.

493–506. The advertisement of the work also refers to the piracy: 'Mr Ogilby to prevent the Injury design'd Him and the Kingdom, by the Publishers of certain Tables stolen out of his Book (so ignorantly and carelessly Collected and Printed, that they are fill'd with false Computations and Directions …) did Print his own Tables in 4 Broad-sides': Skelton (n 113) 148.

[196] J Ogilby and W Morgan, *Mr Ogilby's and William Morgan's Pocket Book of the Roads, with their Computed and Measured Distances … the Fourth Impression. To which is added several Roads … With a Table for the ready finding any Road, City, or Market-Town, and their Distance from London. And a Sheet Map of England … By William Morgan, Cosmographer to their Majesties* (London, printed for the Author, and Christopher Wilkinson, 1689). For details of this and subsequent editions, see HG Fordham, *John Ogilby (1600–1676), His Britannia, and the British Itineraries of the Eighteenth Century* (London, Oxford University Press, 1925) 168–74.

[197] Tyacke (n 48) 68.

[198] G Camdeno [William Camden], *Britannia sive Florentissimorum Regnorum, Angliae, Scotiae, Hiberniae, et Insularum Adiacentium ex intima antiquitate Chorographica descripto* (London, Per Radulphum Newbery, 1586).

[199] RC Richardson, 'William Camden and the Re-discovery of England' (2004) 78 *Transactions of the Leicestershire Archaeological and Historical Society* 108, 113.

[200] S Piggott, 'William Camden and the Britannia' in RC Richardson (ed), *The Changing Face of English Local History* (Oxford, Routledge, 2018) 20–21.

However, like Saxton's atlas, Camden's *Britannia* is seen as having played a significant role in creating a unified national space, first through words and then with Saxton's maps.[201] According to Denys Hay, 'Camden did more to unite Britain in the long run than did King James', a statement Richardson interprets as referring to *Britannia's* formulation of a concept of 'Englishness' grounded in local history.[202] The combination of maps and text also made the work attractive to a wider audience and therefore enhanced its commercial appeal.[203]

The work was translated into English by Philemon Holland in 1610 and registered at Stationers' Hall in both English and Latin on 4 June 1610 for a group of six Stationers.[204] The shares passed through several different sets of hands as the original owners died or sold up, with changes in their ownership being recorded on the Stationers' Register. The book's popularity also led to the production of abridgements. The first of these was another Latin edition, known as Vitellius's *Camden's Britannia Contracta.* Originally printed in Amsterdam with maps by Peter van den Keere, an English version was being sold by George Humble in 1617.[205] An English language abridgement appeared in 1626, printed by John Bill.[206] This is probably the same version for which Gilbert Diglan applied for a 21-year privilege in 1624.[207]

On 10 April 1693, a proposal for printing a new translation of Camden's *Britannia* by subscription was issued. This was the work undertaken by Edmund Gibson, later bishop of Lincoln and then London, but at this stage an undergraduate at Oxford. Gibson brought together a team of contributors with the aim of improving upon Philemon Holland's translation, including such notables as Samuel Pepys and John Evelyn.[208] The proposal alleged that copies of Camden's *Britannia* in English were 'very Scarce and Dear', at no less than three pounds, despite the translation being 'very ill'.[209] It therefore promised a new translation, with new maps including new county maps by Robert Morden. It claimed that the maps would be so costly to revise and print that the price of the book would be 32s in sheets for subscribers, or 27s 6d to anyone who subscribed to all six, with a seventh volume supplied gratis.[210]

London booksellers Abel Swall and Awnsham Churchill were granted a licence by William and Mary for Gibson's translation of Camden's *Britannia* on 6 July 1693. Swall and Churchill had promised their Majesties they had been at 'Considerable Charge … in obtaining many new Discourses and Observations,

[201] See Klein (n 12) 143–45.
[202] D Hay, *Annalists and Historians* (London, Methuen, 1977) 151, quoted in Richardson (n 199) 112.
[203] Morgan (n 68) 145.
[204] E Arber (ed), *A Transcript of the Registers of the Company of Stationers 1554–1640AD*, Vol 3 (London, 1875–77) 196.
[205] RA Skelton, *County Atlases of the British Isles 1579–1850: A Bibliography, Part 2 (1612–1646)* (London, Map Collectors' Circle, 1964) 12.
[206] ibid 55–56.
[207] Petition of Gilbert Diglan for Camden's Britannia Epitome, Add MS 69912 ff88-9 (BL); Hunt (n 52) 33.
[208] Piggott (n 200) 12, 23.
[209] Wood 658 (806) (Bodleian).
[210] ibid.

relating thereunto, and in Graving new Mapps'.[211] The licence prohibited reprints and abridgements, and the importation of copies printed overseas, for the term of 14 years and asked both the Stationers' Company and the Customs Officers to take note of the privilege.[212] The book itself was published in 1695.[213]

Six years later, on 30 May 1701, Swall and Churchill commenced a suit in Chancery against the bookseller Joseph Wild and the printers John Brudenall, Sarah Parker, John Gardiner, and John Cholmly, alleging that they had either printed or imported 'great quantities or numbers' of the book or a book purporting to be an abridgement thereof, in contravention of the licence.[214] The court granted their request for an injunction on 31 May, pending an answer by the defendants.[215] On 5 June, the defendants put in an answer.[216] The lead defendant was Joseph Wild, who stated that the other defendants were simply acting as his servants, agents, and porters. Wild claimed it was not Swall and Churchill's new translation of Camden's *Britannia* that he had printed but a translation of Vitellius's *Camden's Britannia*, which had been printed in Amsterdam in 1639. Joseph Wild claimed that 'being advised the same was a very usefull Booke and would sell well if translated into English did sometime about Christmas last at his great Expense and Charge cause the said Book to be translated'.[217] This book was entitled *Camden's Britannia Abridged*. Wild claimed it was lawful for him to sell this book, despite the claimants' licence, because it was not the same book nor an abridgement of it nor did it use the same maps.[218] On 19 June 1701, the defendants filed an affidavit and asked for the injunction to be dissolved.[219] No further records have been found so it is likely that the dispute settled. As we saw in relation to Blome and Ogilby, the litigation demonstrates the difficulties faced by those undertaking such ambitious projects when so many different versions and editions circulated so freely.

VII. Conclusion

This chapter has explored the long history of using legal instruments, royal favour, and guild protection to support the investment of labour and capital in the making of maps. Since the sixteenth century, mapmakers have sought to protect the exclusivity of their product in the marketplace using a range of tactics. Tracing this long

[211] SP44/343, 306–307 (UKNA).
[212] ibid.
[213] E Gibson (ed), *Camden's Britannia, Newly Translated into English: with large Additions and Improvements* (London, Swalle and Churchill, 1695).
[214] Complaint of Abel Swall, Awnsham Churchill and John Churchill, 30 May 1701, C6/324/8 m1 (UKNA).
[215] C33/296 f340 (UKNA).
[216] Answer of Joseph Wild, John Brudenall, Sarah Parker, John Gardiner and John Cholmly, 5 June 1701, C6/324/8 m2 (UKNA).
[217] ibid.
[218] ibid.
[219] C41/34 East no 863.

history of attempts to prohibit copying has shed new light on the different roles played by maps and their various uses for assorted people and purposes. Maps were valued for their aesthetic appeal because their display could demonstrate the erudition and status of their owner, or the scientific prowess of the nation that produced them. For rulers, maps could foster a shared vision of national unity and an illusion of territorial control they hoped to wield in order to transform the illusion into a reality. The rise of the printing press meant that a map could become a reproducible commodity. However, as we have seen, the labour and expense required to make maps, and the comparatively small size of the market for them, meant that the exchange value very rarely exceeded the use value. As the state, in the form of the sovereign ruler, had little appetite for directly producing these useful objects, it needed to continue to encourage the market to do so, thus intervening indirectly in the form of privileges, patents, licences, and trade protectionism.

Royal privileges might have provided encouragement to produce such works, but they could also be a discouragement to others due to their monopoly effects. Looking in detail at the publishing operations of Richard Blome and John Ogilby alongside the story of Camden's *Britannia* highlights the role of law in the creation and circulation of geographical knowledge as well as in the visual articulation of royal authority, national identity, and imperial ideology that maps enabled and fostered. However, the costs involved in producing such works were so high that that even using the legal tools of the privilege or guild registration to protect against competition was not sufficient to make many maps or geographical books financially viable, let alone successful, for their creators. An ingenious array of strategies, from lotteries to subscription to royal favours such as tax relief and paid offices, were developed to underwrite a series of ambitious ventures in the latter half of the seventeenth century. Yet the enormous costs continued to militate against carrying out original surveys and even projects based largely on copying existing materials were prohibitively expensive to compile, engrave, and print.

That such ventures were attempted at all invites consideration of their significance. The *Brittaniae* of Blome and Ogilby, and Gibson's new translation of Camden's *Britannia* sought to convey a wide array of different kinds of knowledge about the world – historical, geographical, and cultural – to their readers. The audience for such works was not yet the general public and the subscription lists reveal the customers were almost entirely members of the nobility, gentlemen, scholars, and clergy. These readers were not seeking travel guides but, rather, knowledge of the world.[220] The involvement of the Royal Society in the ventures of Blome and Ogilby emphasises that these works were also coming to be embedded in humanist learning and scientific circles.

[220] Catherine Delano-Smith and Garret Sullivan have argued that even Ogilby's *Britannia*, with its groundbreaking, newly measured roads, should not be seen as a tool for wayfinding but, rather, as an indoor entertainment: Delano-Smith (n 156) 53–54; Sullivan (n 105).

Royal privileges were not simply legal tools with commercial implications but an integral element of a social order that retained feudal overtones, even as England was transforming into a parliamentary monarchy. The relationship between the monarch and the petitioner for a privilege was expressed, rhetorically in many cases, as personal. Patents and privileges were granted to a 'trusty and well-beloved servant' and framed in terms of loyalty and protection as a personal favour, while their advantages would accrue to the realm. Included in the preface to a book or referred to on the face of a map or on a title page as being printed *cum privilegio regis*, privileges conferred an authority and prestige that registration with the Stationers' Company could not. Yet both systems were coming under increased pressure by the end of the seventeenth century. Mounting hostility to the monopolistic control of the book trade by the Stationers' Company and the censorial power of the state combined to form a new legal order in the passing of the Statute of Anne in 1710. The old regime based upon royal favour, loyalty, and guild-based protection would fall away, replaced by a new order to which we now turn.

3

Enlightenment Mapmaking and Lawmaking Part One: The Legislation

I. Introduction

By the end of the seventeenth century, the system of regulating the book trade through the Stationers' Company, alongside the system of royal privileges, was coming under increasing strain. Opposition to royal grants of monopolies and parliamentary patronage, censorship, and the power of the Stationers' Company all began to come together to force changes to the way that the book trade was regulated. This chapter explores the impact of these changes on the map trade as the statute passed to enact changes for the book trade (the Statute of Anne) came to be used as a model for new legislation aimed at the trade in engravings and prints and, by extension, maps. After briefly describing the Statute of Anne, the chapter describes three subsequent Acts, each developing with greater specificity its object of protection and the scope that protection would take. It was the second of these Acts that specified that maps, charts, and plans formed a class of print to be protected against copying and, thus, for the first time grouped these three distinct types of image into one legal category. Both Christian Jacob and Matthew Edney have pointed out the etymological instability of the three words, and their gradual closure as categories under the single term of 'map'.[1] Edney points out that: 'Each set of imagery entails a particular conception of the world, which it depicts with different strategies and techniques, in order to support specific functions; each set is produced and consumed within certain social institutions and contexts'.[2] He asks why they must be thought of as things that possess a common character and finds the answer in the existence of the cultural hegemony of the ideal of cartography. In this chapter, we see the institution of law playing its own role in creating and sustaining this cultural hegemony though the creation of a legal category. Chapter four explores how the content of that category was fleshed out by the courts.

[1] C Jacob in EH Dahl (ed), *The Sovereign Map: Theoretical Approaches in Cartography throughout History*, T Conley (trans) (Chicago, University of Chicago Press, 2006) 18–21; MH Edney, *Cartography: The Ideal and its History* (Chicago, University of Chicago Press, 2019) 3–4.

[2] Edney (n 1) 3.

II. The Statute of Anne 1710

Two years after Charles II came to the throne of England in 1660, a Printing Act was passed, conferring the power to control seditious and treasonable works upon Parliament.[3] The Act was initially expressed to last for two years but was repeatedly extended until it lapsed for the last time in 1695.[4] The Stationers' Company lobbied for legislation that would protect their interest by preventing books printed by their members from being pirated but were unsuccessful. Opposition to the royal use of monopolies, through the granting of patents and privileges as discussed in the previous chapter, had been growing for some time, as had opposition to the power of the Stationers. By the start of the eighteenth century, the London booksellers had abandoned attempts to shore up their control through linking regulation of the trade with censorship, and began to focus solely on their business interests and orderly trade.[5] Their petitions to Parliament invoked the plight of authors, who would no longer be able to support their wives and children if they could not sell copies of their works to booksellers. They combined these arguments with appeals to the interest of the public in the spread of learning.[6]

These appeals culminated in 1710 in the passing of An Act for the Encouragement of Learning, by Vesting the Copies of Printed Books in the Authors or Purchasers of such Copies, during the Times therein mentioned, popularly known ever since as the Statute of Anne.[7] It created an exclusive right to print books that was held by the author of the book in question and which, if infringed, would give rise to liability for penalties and forfeitures. While the statute continued to provide that books be registered at Stationers' Hall, it severed the link between censorship and trade regulation by addressing only the latter issue. Furthermore, it broke the hold of the Stationers' Company over the book trade by providing that one did not need to be a member of the Company to register a book.[8] The right lasted for a period of

[3] An Act for Preventing the Frequent Abuses in Printing Seditious, Treasonable and Unlicensed Books and Pamphlets, and for Regulating of Printing and Printing Presses 1662 (13 & 14 Car II c. 33).

[4] (1664) 16 Car II c 8; (1664/5) 16 & 17 Car II c7; (1665) 17 Car II c4; (1685) 1 Jac II c 17; (1692) 4 & 5 Wm & M c 24.

[5] For a detailed examination of this period and its relationship to copyright legislation, see R Deazley, *On the Origin of the Right to Copy: Charting the Movement of Copyright Law in Eighteenth Century Britain (1675–1775)* (Portland, OR, Hart, 2004) 1–50.

[6] For a summary, see I Alexander, *Copyright Law and the Public Interest in the Nineteenth Century* (Oxford, Hart Publishing, 2010) 21–23. This was not a new strategy; a petition of 1641 urging the adoption of a new printing statute blended the need to control seditious printing with appeals to protect the labour of authors and the investment of printers: 'Reasons to induce the passinge of the Bill touching printing', SP16/484 f121 (UKNA).

[7] An Act for the Encouragement of Learning, by Vesting the Copies of Printed Books in the Authors or Purchasers of such Copies, during the Times therein mentioned (1710) 8 Anne c. 19 (Statute of Anne).

[8] Statute of Anne, s 2. See also HT Gómez-Arostegui, 'The Untold Story of the First Copyright Suit Under the Statute of Anne' (2010) 25 *Berkeley Technology Law Journal* 1247.

14 years and, if the author were living at the end of that time, the right would last for a second period of 14 years.[9]

Historians have debated the purpose and aim of Parliament in passing the Statute of Anne. John Feather interprets it as allowing a small and wealthy group of booksellers to retain control of the London book trade,[10] while Lyman Ray Patterson sees the Statute as an attack on the Stationers' monopoly.[11] Ronan Deazley argues that Parliament's central concern was the continued production of useful books.[12] Tomàs Gómez-Arostegui uncovers the role played by a dispute over Samuel Butler's *Hudibras* which may have been a key impetus for the bookseller's 1709 petition to Parliament.[13] It is also, perhaps, important to view it as part of a shift in ideas about property, as identified in particular by JGA Pocock, who sees the period after 1690 and the Financial Revolution as one of conflict between old 'landed interests' and new 'monied interests'.[14] As society was increasingly perceived as being based upon commerce, in the sense of 'the exchange of forms of mobile property',[15] copyright legislation can be seen as also reflecting this shift through its transformation of the property right from one bestowed by the crown (and thus a product of corruption – in theory if not reality in the case of the book trade) to one created by statute and now a mobile object embedded in the market. This new approach clearly had a broader appeal, in particular for the other main cultural form of the period whose commercial value lay in its ability to be reproduced and multiplied: prints and engravings.

III. The Engravings Act 1735

The Statute of Anne applied only to books and, therefore, books containing maps would have fallen within its scope. But what of maps published only as single or multiple sheets? This question engaged an uncertainty about the protection of engravings more broadly. On the face of the Statute, it would seem that engravings published as separate prints would not fall within its scope, yet it was not unheard of for individual prints to be registered at Stationers' Hall.[16] Either way, engravers clearly perceived there was a gap in protection. In 1735 seven prominent

[9] Statute of Anne, s11.

[10] J Feather, 'The Book Trade in Politics: The Making of the Copyright Act of 1710' (1980) 8 *Publishing History* 19, 37.

[11] L Ray Patterson, *Copyright in Historical Perspective* (Nashville, Vanderbilt University Press, 1968) 147.

[12] Deazley (n 5) 46.

[13] Gómez-Arostegui (n 8) 1299–1306.

[14] JGA Pocock, *Virtue, Commerce and History: Essays on Political Thought and History, Chiefly in the Eighteenth Century* (Cambridge, Cambridge University Press, 1985) 109.

[15] ibid.

[16] For example, the Reverend John Watson registered two copperplates in 1761: *The South East View of the Town of Halifax* and *A South East Prospect of Halifax Church*. He later published a book, also registered at Stationers' Hall, which incorporated both prints.

engravers presented a petition to Parliament seeking protection against 'divers Printsellers, Printers and other persons' who had 'of late, too frequently, taken the Liberty of copying, printing, and publishing great Quantities of base, imperfect, and mean, Copies and Imitations thereof'.[17] This activity, complained the petitioners, was 'to the great Detriment of the Petitioners, and other Artists, and to the Discouragement of Arts and Sciences in this Kingdom'.[18] The ringleader of the petitioners was the most famous engraver of the day, William Hogarth, alongside his co-petitioners, George Lambert, Isaac Ware, John Pine, Joseph Goupy, and Gerard Vandergucht, also well-known engravers.

A bill was introduced and passed through both Houses of Parliament, receiving Royal Assent on 15 May 1735.[19] The new Engravings Act gave exclusive printing rights to any person who 'shall invent and design, engrave, etch or work in *Mezzotinto* or *Chiaro Oscuro* … any historical or other print' for a term of 14 years from first publication. It also protected anyone who 'from his own Works and Invention shall cause to be designed and engraved, etched or worked in *Mezzotinto* or *Chiaro Oscuro*, any historical or other Print or Prints'. Anyone who copied and engraved, etched, or printed any such print without the consent of the owner, or who knowingly sold or imported such a print would be liable to forfeit the plates and printed sheets, and pay the sum of 5s for every print found in their custody. The plates and prints would be destroyed, while the money would be shared between the King and the person bringing the action.[20]

The Act gave rise to several further uncertainties. Most relevant for present purposes is the question of whether it applied to maps. They were, after all, prints and were produced using the techniques of engraving and etching that were specifically referred to in the Act. But the wording of the Act created potential limits on its scope as it referred only to persons who did 'invent **and** design, engrave, etch or work in *Mezzotinto* or *Chiaro Oscuro*' (emphasis added). As Cristina Martinez and I have observed elsewhere, this phrasing sets up 'invent' as a cumulative condition to be satisfied alongside one of the listed techniques.[21] So, in order to receive protection, the person must have invented the print. What did this mean in 1735? Both design and invention were 'slippery concepts'[22] in the eighteenth

[17] *Journal of the House of Commons (JHC): Vol 22*, 7 February 1734/5, 364.

[18] *JHC: Vol 22*, 7 February 1734/5, 364. See also, R Deazley, 'Commentary on the Engravers' Act (1735)' in Bently and Kretschmer (eds), *Primary Sources on Copyright*, www.copyrighthistory.org/cam/tools/request/showRecord.php?id=commentary_uk_1735.

[19] An Act for the encouragement of the Arts of Designing, Engraving and Etching Historical and other Prints, by vesting the Properties thereof in the Inventors and Engravers, during the Time therein mentioned (1735) 8 Geo II c. 13 (Engravings Act 1735).

[20] Engravings Act 1735, s 1.

[21] I Alexander and CS Martinez, 'The First Copyright Case under the 1735 Engravings Act: The Germination of Visual Copyright?' in W Slauter and S Delamire (eds), *Circulation and Control: Artistic Culture and Intellectual Property in the Nineteenth Century* (Cambridge, Open Book Publishers, 2021) 39–76.

[22] K Scott, *Becoming Property: Art, Theory and Law in Early Modern France* (New Haven, Yale University Press, 2018) 247.

century but 'invention' here seems to be seeking to capture the person who came up with the idea for the engraving, which they then executed, and distinguishing them from the person who simply made engravings of works already in existence, such as paintings. This reading of the Engravings Act is confirmed by the fifth section, which provided specific protection for the engraver (and co-petitioner) John Pine for his prints of the Spanish Armada tapestries hanging in the House of Commons 'in the same Manner as if [he] had been Inventor and Designer of the said Prints'.[23] The result of this interpretation, as has been often observed, was that (aside from Pine) the main beneficiary of the Engravings Act 1735 was Hogarth himself. He was unusual among his fellow engravers in that his prints were original designs, frequently satirical works, rather than engravings of paintings by the Old Masters.[24]

Could maps, charts and plans be said to arise from 'invention' or not? Did it matter that they were a representation of the physical world and not a work of imagination? Here it is worth considering that there had, in fact, been a suggestion in the House of Lords for a broader approach, with one lord proposing 'to Amend the Bill & make it more general by extending it to prints Ingrav'd from old paintings, provided the same be Ingrav'd by the Consent of the Proprietors of such Paintings'.[25] Pine, who was present, commented that 'the Engravers would have been glad to have had the Bill more general, but that the House of Commons were not inclined to make it so extensive'. That, he explained, was the reason he had sought a clause relating to the Lords' tapestries.[26] George Vertue, another of the petitioners, was also unhappy with the restriction, complaining in 1751 that if the Act 'had been plain full and strong as I did propose it at the Committee of the parliament – it might have been of true benefit to those artists that became superior in skill, and practice'.[27] He went on to explain that by this he meant:

> That the license should be all those who Engravd works from paintings of any kind. if they did actually do them originally from paintings – or statues or buildings – or any other artfull works. such only to have the licence – and not to be coppyd in Engravings by any others from there prints, in any part, or the whole – under such penalties as the Act directs for 14 years to come – although the person that Engraves does not design or drawn or paint or Invent the originals. from whence such Engravings are done. this would truely & certainly be the true encouragement – without hazard & law suits.[28]

Vertue was right about the lawsuits. In 1738 Elizabeth Blackwell brought a suit in the Court of Chancery against a number of London printsellers who had been engraving and selling unauthorised copies of botanical prints she had drawn and

[23] Engravings Act 1735, s 5.
[24] D Hunter, 'Copyright Protection for Engravings and Maps in Eighteenth-Century Britain' (1987) 6 *The Library* 128, 140.
[25] ibid 135.
[26] ibid.
[27] G Vertue, *Note books*, Vol III, 22 Walpole Society (1933–34) (Oxford, Walpole Society 1934) 156.
[28] ibid.

engraved.[29] In this first case to be brought under the new Act, the defendants argued that the prints did not fall within the scope of the statute because they 'are only Copies from Nature & no Inventions & the Statute designed this Benefit only to persons who formed Designs out of their own fancy as Historical Allegorical Prints &c'.[30] The Lord Chancellor, Lord Hardwicke, did not accept the argument. He found it was clear that the prints fell within the Act's protection, explaining that, to make his case, the defendant 'must shew me that these prints of medicinal plants are in any other book or herbal whatsoever, in the same manner and form as they are represented here'.[31] Of particular relevance to the question of maps, the Lord Chancellor is also reported to have remarked:

> I am of the opinion that if there should be a print published of any building, or house and gardens, or that great design Mr Pine's of the city of London, they will all come properly within this act of parliament; or else it would be narrowing it greatly and making it of little use.[32]

The case of *Blackwell v Harper* would therefore suggest that an engraving of a map or chart would fall under the Engravings Act 1735, so long, perhaps, as it was not copied from another map. However, a second question remained as to the Act's scope, which was also pertinent for mapmakers and sellers. This issue arose in another suit brought in the Court of Chancery on 27 November 1752 by Thomas Jefferys, one of the leading mapmakers of the day, against the proprietors of *The London Magazine*.[33] The engraving that was the subject of the litigation was not a map but a print depicting the vessels of the Society of the Free British Herring Fishery, which the defendants had reproduced in the pages of the *Magazine*. The defendants demurred to Jefferys's bill of complaint, arguing that the print did not come within the scope of the statute because Jefferys had procured another person to invent, draw, and design the print, rather than doing it himself. Lord Hardwicke accepted this argument, stating: 'It is not within the statute, which was made for encouragement of genius or art; if it was, any person who employs a printer or engraver would be so too'.[34]

This decision dealt a blow to any claim that the Engravings Act 1735 would apply to maps where the initial drawings had been done by someone other than the person bringing the legal action. This was a problem. As explained in chapter one, maps were the work of many hands. The person known as the 'mapmaker' performed a role we might today think of as the publisher – he (and it was almost always he) would arrange for the map to be drawn (or copied), engraved, and printed, putting up the capital and arranging for sale and distribution. Some

[29] For a more detailed discussion of this case see Alexander and Martinez (n 21).

[30] Add. MS 36,015 (II. Ff. 207) Mar 1738/Oct 1741, 248–49.

[31] *Blackwell v Harper* (1740) 2 Atk 93, 94–95.

[32] 2 Atk 93, 94. Words to a similar effect were also reported in *Blackwell v Harper* (1740) Barn C. 210, 212 and Add. MS 36,015 (II. Ff. 207) Mar 1738/Oct 1741, 249.

[33] *Jefferys v Baldwin* (1752) Amb 164.

[34] ibid 164.

mapmakers, such as Thomas Jefferys, did draw and engrave their own maps but even those multi-skilled individuals could not do so in every case and still run a viable business.

A second question is: did mapmakers themselves think that they were protected by the 1735 Act? Without any contemporary statements, the only evidence of such a belief can be found on the maps themselves. As was discussed in the previous chapter and above, registration at Stationers' Hall had been necessary to obtain full protection against copying in the years before the passing of the Statute of Anne. The statute had continued the requirement of registration for books for those seeking the penalties provided for under the Act. The Engravings Act 1735 did not require that prints be registered. Instead, it drew on the more common practice in the print trade of inserting the name of the engraver on each print. The Act thus set out that the term of protection would 'commence from the Day of first publishing thereof, which shall be Truly engraved, with the name of the Proprietor on each Plate, and printed on every such Print or Prints'.[35] The precise meaning of this requirement had also been an issue in *Blackwell v Harper* because Elizabeth had included the words 'Eliz. Blackwell delin sculp et Pinx [designed, engraved, and painted]' on each plate but she had not named herself specifically as proprietor nor had she included a date of publication. Lord Hardwicke considered this not to be an impediment to receiving protection under the Act and that the statement adequately met the Act's requirement as to ownership.[36] However, because she had not included the date of publication, she was not entitled to the penalties under the Act and could only be awarded an injunction.[37]

Over time, print publishers would come to develop these criteria into a formula, generally placing at the foot of a print the line 'Published according to the Act of Parliament' (or a similar phrase), accompanied by the name of the publisher and a date. A survey of maps from the period between 1735 and 1767 (when the next statute was passed) reveals that it was not uncommon for mapmakers to include this publication line on their maps, as well as on topographical plans and charts, although it was not the invariable practice. Even after 1767, when protection of maps became clearer, not all mapmakers included a date upon their maps. Indeed, dating a map is likely to have placed a mapmaker on the horns of a dilemma, requiring them to balance the advantages of statutory protection against the revelation that a map was out of date or superseded.

Neither the Statute of Anne nor the Engravings Act 1735 supplanted the system of royal licences. Shef Rogers has observed that there was an initial rush to register in 1710 but thereafter the number of books registered at Stationers' Hall dramatically declined.[38] Licences were sought for both maps and geographical

[35] Engravings Act 1735, s 1.
[36] For more detail, see Alexander and Martinez (n 21).
[37] (1740) 2 Atk 93, 95.
[38] S Rogers, 'The Use of Royal Licences for Printing in England, 1695–1760: A Bibliography' (2000) 1 *The Library* 133.

books. For example, in 1721 William Mayo was granted a licence for a map of Barbados and a plan of Bridgetown but he also entered the work in the Stationers' Register.[39] In 1723 Aubrye de la Motraye was also granted a licence for a book of travels 'with proper Cutts and Maps',[40] while in 1743 Stationer Thomas Astley received a licence for *A New General Collection of Voyages and Travels*, including the charts and maps contained therein, and directly forbade the copying or counterfeiting 'the maps and Sculptures thereof, either in great or in small'.[41] That same year a group of 18 prominent booksellers received a licence for an updated edition of Herman Moll's *The Compleat Geographer*, which they explained included 70 maps 'all new drawn and engraved by Emanuel Bowen, according to the latest Discoveries and Surveys; printed in distinct half Sheets, the full Size of the Book, making of themselves a compleat Atlas'.[42] The latter two licences mentioned that the works in question would be of great service to those concerned in trade and navigation. Other licences were granted in 1757 to Samuel Dunn, a mathematics teacher, and William Owen, a bookseller, for a pair of globes,[43] and to Elizabeth Pattilo for geographical, chronological, historical, geometrical, astronomical, and philosophical cards designed for the amusement and instruction of young people.[44] In 1759 bookseller John Coote received a licence for *A New Geographical Dictionary*, illustrated with new maps,[45] and for *A New and Complete Collection of Voyages & Travels*: 'Illustrated with near Three hundred elegant Copper Plates, consisting of Perspective Views, Maps, Sea Charts, Draughts of Harbours, Heads of the Principal Navigators and Travellers and drawings of the most curious animals, Vegetables and Minerals'.[46]

The licences reflected the continued interest of both monarch and populace in tales of travel and other opportunities for geographical education but also the ongoing perception that such licences had a value. The standard fee for a licence was £8 1s, a cost that remained fixed over the early part of the century.[47] As seen above in the case of Mayo, a licence holder might also seek registration with the

[39] William Mayo, Licence to publish a Map of Barbados (11 November 1721), SP44/361, 88–89. See ibid 159 (UKNA).

[40] Aubrye de la Motraye, Licence to print his Book of Travels (27 April 1723), SP44/361A, 32–33 (UKNA).

[41] Thomas Astley, Licence to print a new general collection of voyages and travels (18 October 1743), SP44/309, 195–97 (UKNA).

[42] William Innys, Richard Ware, Aaron Ward, John and Paul Knapton, John Clarke, Thomas Longman, John Osborn, Henry Whitridge, Richard Hett, Charles Hitch, Stephen Austen, Edmund Comyns, James Hodges, Andrew Millar, John and Henry Pemberton, and John Rivington, Licence to print *A Compleat System of Geography* SP44/367, 338–41 (UKNA).

[43] Samuel Dunn and William Owen, Licence to Print *The Universal Planispheres or Terrestrial & Celestial Globes in Plano* (7 November 1757), SP44/371, 364–66 (UKNA).

[44] Elizabeth Pattilo, Licence to Print a work calculated both for the amusement and instruction of youth (14 December 1757), SP44/371, 369–70 (UKNA).

[45] Coote, Licence to Print *A new Geographical Dictionary* (23 May 1759), SP44/371, 458–59 (UKNA).

[46] Coote, Licence to print *A new and Compleat Collection of Voyages and Travels* (21 December 1759), SP44/371, 493–94 (UKNA).

[47] Rogers (n 38) 143.

Stationers' Company which, since the passing of the Statute of Anne, was open to non-Stationers. The cost of registration was 6d but also required nine copies of the book or work in question to be deposited, representing a significant additional cost.[48] Mayo can be seen to be covering all the bases for his map of Barbados – not only did he acquire a licence and registration, he specifically included a statement within his cartouche that the map was 'Authorized by His Majesty's Royal Licence' and below the cartouche was printed 'Engrav'd by John Senex 1722'. Also within the cartouche, Mayo noted the map was the produce of 'an Actual & Accurate Survey' approved by the Royal Society, suggesting that both the approval and the licence operated together to bestow authority upon his claims about his survey and his resultant map.[49]

IV. The Engravings Act 1767

The question of whether maps were protected by the 1735 Engravings Act was clarified in a statute passed in 1767. The initiative for amending the 1735 Act came from the Society of Artists of Great Britain (SAGB). This society was made up of a group of painters, sculptors, architects, engravers, and others (such as medallists and seal cutters), who came together to work for the promotion of the arts in Britain. They determined that a first step would be to hold a public exhibition of their work, which took place in 1760 with the backing of the Society for the Encouragement of Arts, Manufactures and Commerce (SEAMC). By 1761 rivalries and differing views over whether to charge the public for such exhibitions had split the SAGB into two. The majority of the SAGB distanced itself from the SEAMC and began to hold exhibitions with an entry fee. A second group, the Society of Free Artists, sought to distance itself from any imputation of commercial self-interest and set up on their own, still backed by the SEAMC. William Hogarth became a member of the SAGB, notwithstanding his earlier opposition towards the formation of a public academy of arts like the Paris Académie Royale de Peinture et de Sculpture.[50]

The inadequacies of the 1735 Act appear to have first been drawn to the attention of the SAGB's committee in 1761. At its meeting on 28 November of that year, the committee resolved to direct a sum of money towards obtaining an amendment to the Act. At that time seven of the directors were painters, two were sculptors, two were engravers, and the final three were a seal cutter, a chaser, and a medallist. In January 1762, a strategy was decided upon: the Society would fund a

[48] ibid. Statute of Anne, s 5.

[49] William Mayo, *A New & Exact Map of the Island of Barbadoes in America: According to an Actual & Accurate Survey Made in the Years 1717 to 1721 Approved by the Royal Society & Authorized by His Majesty's Royal Licence* (London, 1722), Maps K.Top.123.117.2 TAB (BL).

[50] M Hargraves, *'Candidates for Fame': The Society of Artists of Great Britain 1760–1791* (New Haven, Yale University Press, 2005) chs 1 and 2.

test case under the Act. James McArdell, one of the directors and a leading mezzotint engraver, would be given a sum of 30 guineas in order to bring a case that would 'try the force' of the 1735 Act.[51] On 6 April, the resolution was changed to apply to McArdell or any other person who wished to prosecute any person who copied his works. The singling out of McArdell at first instance makes it clear that the particular aim of the Society was to test the extent to which the Act might protect engravings that copied paintings, as McArdell's main business was making engravings of the works of leading painters such as Joshua Reynolds. However, the committee also had a broader purpose in mind. On 5 January 1762, the committee again discussed reform of the 1735 Act and noted it 'was of Opinion that Sculptors should be included so as to secure their Casts – Portraits – that the Penalty should be enlarged & that those who may be cast shall pay Costs'.[52]

In 1764 the Act was tested in the manner envisaged, although not by McArdell. Instead, an action was brought in the Court of Common Pleas by Robert Edge Pine, a politically radical artist and son of the engraver John Pine, discussed above. The action was brought against London printseller Robert Withy and related to a print of Pine's painting of radical politician John Wilkes. The verdict was given for Pine but a newspaper report observed it was 'subject to the opinion of the Court, whether pirating of portraits is equally included, as well as historical pieces, in the act against pirating of prints'.[53]

The committee of the SAGB continued to work towards reform of the Act and a number of suggestions were made for its improvement. Some related to increasing the penalties, while others pertained to the types of engraving that could be protected. In relation to the latter, there were suggestions that architectural and landscape prints should also be included.[54] Finally a draft bill was drawn up and sent to Serjeant William Whitaker, the Society's General Counsel, for his opinion. Whitaker was not impressed with some aspects of the bill, making a number of amendments and comments in a rather crabbed hand. In particular, he was opposed to the Society's desire to extend the Act to include protection of sculptors, which he considered 'altogether improper' and likely to give rise to opposition.[55] As drafted, the bill covered any person who should

> invent or design, engrave, etch or work in Mezzotinto or Chiaro Oscuro or from his own Work design or Invention shall cause or procure to be designed engraved etched or Worked in Mezzotint or Chiaro Oscuro any Historical print or prints or any print or prints of any portrait Conversation Landscape or Architecture or any other print or prints whatsoever.[56]

[51] Minutes of Committee Meeting, 19 January 1762, Royal Academy of Arts/Society of Artists Papers ('SA/'), SA/1 (RA).

[52] Hargraves (n 50) 50.

[53] *Lloyd's Evening Post*, 23–25 July 1764.

[54] Minutes of the Meetings of the Directors of the Society of Artists of Great Britain, 14 March 1767, SA/10 (RA).

[55] SA/23/1 (RA).

[56] SA/23/1 ff.1, 2 (RA).

In a different hand, written in pencil rather than the ink used by Whitaker and inserted after the word 'Architecture', were added the words 'Map Chart or Plan'.[57]

The directors asked Sir George Hay, the member for Sandwich, a lawyer and prominent government speaker, to introduce the bill to Parliament. Hay had been a friend of the now-deceased William Hogarth, which seems likely to be the reason he was chosen.[58] The bill was referred to a committee headed by Hay and, on 14 May 1767, Jane Hogarth petitioned Parliament for personal protection in respect of her husband's prints, the copyright in some of which had now expired.[59] The committee made some amendments and the Act was passed in the Commons and the Lords, receiving Royal Assent on 28 June 1767.[60]

Frustratingly, the record is silent on the question of why the words 'map, chart or plan' were added to the bill or at whose instigation. They were added in the House of Commons after the bill had returned from the committee and been engrossed; just before this the bill had been sent to the House of Lords[61] and could thus have been added at the suggestion of a Member of Parliament. They could also have come from the SAGB, as we know from a letter sent from its solicitor Nathaniel Barwell to Francis Milner Newton on 18 May 1767 that changes were still possible.[62] Could the change have come from Paul Sandby, one of the SAGB's directors? An established painter and engraver, Sandby had begun his career as a draughtsman to the military survey in Scotland. A second candidate might be architect John Gwynn, another director. His *Essay on Design* had included complaints about the lack of skill shown by travellers in general principles of surveying. He argued that if more travellers 'had been initiated in these Acquirements … we should, by this Time, have seen the Geography of the Globe much corrected than we now find it'.[63] Gwynn had been active in pressing for legislative reform, including an extension of term but, although his collection of essays, *London and Westminster Improved*, contained a number of engraved maps and plans of the city of London, he did not specifically refer to extending legislative protection to them.[64] Or perhaps Thomas Jefferys was behind the addition.

[57] SA/23/1, ff.2 (RA).

[58] Hargraves (n 50) 60.

[59] See CS Martinez, 'Hogarth [née Thornhill], Jane (d. 1789), printseller and businesswoman' *Oxford Dictionary of National Biography* (9 July 2020) www-oxforddnb-com.rp.nla.gov.au/view/10.1093/ref:odnb/9780198614128.001.0001/odnb-9780198614128-e-310187 and CS Martinez, 'Jane Hogarth: A Printseller's Imprint on Copyright Law' in CS Martinez and CS Roman (eds), *Female Printmakers, Printsellers and Print Publishers in the Eighteenth Century: The Imprint of Women ca. 1700–1830* (Cambridge, Cambridge University Press, forthcoming).

[60] *Journal of the House of Lords (JHL): Vol 31*, 29 June 1767, 660. An act to amend and render more effectual an act made in the eighth year of the reign of King George the Second for encouragement of the arts of designing, engraving, and etching, historical and other prints; and for vesting in, and securing to, Jane Hogarth widow, the property certain prints (1767) 7 Geo II c38 (Engravings Act 1767).

[61] *JHC: Vol 31*, 25 May 1767, 383.

[62] SA/32/1 (18 May 1767) (RA).

[63] J Gwynn, *An Essay on Design including Proposals for erecting a Public Academy* (London, Ino. Brindley, 1749) 59.

[64] J Gwynn, *London and Westminster Improved* (London, printed for the Author, 1765).

He was certainly on intimate terms with the engravers of the day and had worked directly with many of them. He had already tried the force of the 1735 Act and, as we will see, would be the first to try the 1767 Act. Until further information comes to hand, the mystery will remain.

The SAGB had achieved a considerable success in their reforming efforts. Although the attempt to extend the Act to cover sculptures was not successful nor was their hope of increasing the penalties, the scope of the Act was certainly broadened and made more certain. It now covered not only 'historical' prints but specifically referred to the other different types of print, including the catch-all phrase 'any other print or prints whatsoever'.[65] Furthermore, the print in question no longer had to be invented and designed, engraved, or etched by the person seeking protection, or even caused or procured to be engraved from his own work, invention, or design. Those activities were still protected, but Section 2 now held that the protection extended to those who caused engravings to be made that were 'taken from any picture, drawing, model or sculpture, either ancient or modern'.[66] The Act now clearly applied to engravings of other artworks already in existence. In addition to extending the Act's scope, the time period within which an action could be brought was extended to be within six months of the offence being committed[67] and, although the committee had rejected the increased penalties, a successful plaintiff could recover 'full costs of suit' in an action at law.[68] A final significant change to the 1735 Act was the extension of the term of protection from 14 years to 28 years.[69] This meant that engravings were now protected for longer than books, as the Statute of Anne still provided for a split term of 14 years in the first instance, with a possible second term of 14 years if the author were still alive at its expiry.[70] Jane Hogarth's petition was also successful and she was awarded a further term of 20 years of protection for William Hogarth's engravings.[71]

V. The Engravings Act 1777

Despite the success of the SAGB, the 1767 Act had two key flaws. First, engravers considered its enforcement provisions still too weak. Second, in providing protection for those who made engravings of existing works, be they paintings, sculptures, or other engravings, the statute failed to specify how to accommodate

[65] Engravings Act 1767, s 1.
[66] ibid s 2.
[67] ibid s 5.
[68] ibid s 6.
[69] ibid s 7.
[70] Statute of Anne, ss 1, 11.
[71] See Martinez, 'Jane Hogarth' (n 59).

the rights of the owner of the original work. The SAGB's draft had engaged with this issue by including a section that provided:

> No person shall be entitled to the Benefit or protection of this Act who shall engrave, etch, or Work any print taken from any picture drawing model or sculpture during the life of the painter drawer modeller or sculptor thereof respectively without Authority in Writing under their respective Hands for that purpose first had and obtained.[72]

The clause was struck out, probably by Whitaker, but no reason is given as to why.

On 5 February 1777, a group of engravers and artists presented a petition to the House of Commons. This group, which included two SAGB directors, William Byrne and William Woollett, the court engraver, Francesco Bartolozzi, and painter and engraver Paul Sandby, complained that since the passing of the last Act:

> Several base, imperfect, and mean Prints have been fraudulently engraved and vended, with the Names of some of the Petitioners attached thereto, with a View to deceive the Public, and make the same pass for the Works of the Petitioners whose Names were made use of, to their very great Detriment and Discredit, and to the Discouragement of the Arts aforesaid.[73]

The member who introduced the petition (whose name is unfortunately not recorded) was reported as arguing that 'the people whose petition he had in his hand deserved their attention; for in every branch of commerce, property ought to be secured, which it will be found upon enquiry is not the case among these gentlemen'.[74] Sir Edward Ashley, who seconded the motion, observed that

> the article of engraving was at present in the way of becoming a branch of commerce, in which we might rival the French, who had made it a most lucrative one; that the only means of doing it was to grant the prayer of the petition.[75]

A bill was brought into the House of Commons but rejected in the Lords.[76] A second bill was brought in that was successful in the Lords and, accordingly, received Royal Assent on 6 June 1777.[77] This Act made only minor changes to the previous two Acts. It provided that any person who engraved or caused or procured to be engraved any print covered by the Act without the express consent of the proprietor of that print in writing and attested by two witnesses would be liable to legal action in which the proprietor could recover damages assessed by the jury, together with double costs of suit.[78] In this way, the need for consent

[72] SA/23/1 f.3 (RA).

[73] *JHC: Volume 36*, 1777, 116–17.

[74] *London Chronicle*, 4–6 February 1777, 8.

[75] ibid.

[76] *JHC: Vol 36*, 116, 117, 191, 264, 403; *JHL, Vol 35*, 149, 197, 202, 207, 208.

[77] *JHC: Vol 36*, 511, 517, 539; *JHL: Vol 35*, 223, 229, 235, 240. *An Act for more effectually securing the Property of Prints to Inventors and Engravers, by enabling them to sue for and recover Penalties in certain Cases* (1777) 17 Geo. III c.57 ('Engravings Act 1777).

[78] Engravings Act 1777. Note that 'double costs' of suit actually mean 1½ times the cost of suit: W Tidd, *The Law of Costs in Civil Actions* (London, Wheldon and Butterworth, 1793) 56.

was made explicit and the shift of the penalty to damages opened up the potential for much higher awards than would be allowed under the 1735 Act's provision of recovering five shillings for every sheet found in the offender's custody, half of which would go to the King and half to the person bringing the action.

VI. Conclusion

The three Engravings Acts of the eighteenth century would remain the basis for protecting all types and genres of engraving against unauthorised copying until they were repealed in 1911 and replaced with a statute that brought all the different kinds of copyright subject matter into a single statute.[79] The impetus for their passing had largely come from engravers, who argued that protection against copying was needed if the art of engraving were to be encouraged and improved within the realm. The inclusion of maps, charts, and plans within this regime seems largely to have occurred because they were specific types of print engraved, sold, and dealt with by the same people who engraved, sold, and dealt with other types of print. It does not seem to have flowed from any policy or objective to encourage mapmaking specifically.

There were, however, other venues in which mapmaking was being encouraged in eighteenth-century England. The SAGB's former ally and latter-day rival, the Society for the Encouragement of Arts, Manufacture and Commerce, set up its own initiative of offering monetary awards and, later, medals for the production of new county surveys between 1759 and 1809.[80] Another initiative to encourage the production of geographical knowledge was the establishment of the Board of Longitude in 1714, which offered a reward of £20,000 for a method that would find longitude at sea. After its main purpose was achieved (famously with John Harrison's chronometers and lunar tables), the Board turned its attention to fostering improvements in navigational instruments and naval charts.[81] This broader discourse, emphasising the need for cartographic improvement, would come to influence the statutes' interpretation in both legal argument and judicial decision-making. It is the statutes' impact on the map trade and their consideration in the courts to which we now turn.

[79] Copyright Act 1911 c46. See ch 9.

[80] JB Harley, 'The Society of the Arts and the Surveys of English Counties 1759–1809' Part (i) (1963) 112 *Journal of the Society of the Arts* 43; JB Harley, 'The Society of the Arts and the Surveys of English Counties 1759–1809', Part (ii) (1964) 112 *Journal of the Society of the Arts* 119; JB Harley, 'The Society of the Arts and the Surveys of English Counties 1759–1809', Part (iii) (1964) 112 *Journal of the Society of the Arts* 269; JB Harley, 'The Society of the Arts and the Surveys of English Counties 1759–1809', Part (iv) (1964) 112 *Journal of the Society of the Arts* 538.

[81] P Johnson, 'The Board of Longitude 1714–1828' (1989) 99 *Journal of the British Astronomical Association* 63.

4

Enlightenment Mapmaking and Lawmaking Part Two: The Litigation

I. Introduction

It was the penultimate year of the eighteenth century and barrister Thomas Erskine was at the top of his game. Famed for his legal oratory, Erskine had been retained by naval chartmaker William Heather in a copyright suit against his former employer John Hamilton Moore. In a speech filled with rhetorical flourish, Erskine argued that if the court did not find in Heather's favour,

> the wisdom of the legislature would be defeated, a stop would be put to the enlargement of human knowledge, and to the future discoveries of men of science, to all works of invention and improvement whatever; and it would be totally impossible hereafter, ever to place any dependence on a Sea Chart, a thing of the utmost importance in carrying on the vast trade of this commercial country.[1]

The 'enlargement of human knowledge' was of course a central concern of Enlightenment ideology, which placed reason, experience, and experiment at the core of its desire to understand and improve society. While the precise contours and nature of 'the Enlightenment' have long been the subject of debate,[2] it can broadly be said that Enlightenment thinkers shared a belief in 'the power of learning as a means of bringing about improvement'.[3] The philosophers of the Enlightenment turned their rational gaze to debate questions of religion, politics, identity, and the human condition. The study of natural philosophy and natural history – later known simply as 'science' – formed an essential element of Enlightenment discourse, centred around Newtonian mathematics but spreading into fields we know today as botany, chemistry, physics, and medicine. Emerging theories and new discoveries were also enthusiastically promoted to the (literate) public

[1] *Trial of John Hamilton Moore for Pirating a Chart: Sittings after Term, March 1798, before Lord Kenyon and a Special Jury of Merchants* (London, Plummer, 1798) 3.

[2] See eg works such as P Gay, *The Enlightenment: An Interpretation, Volume 2: The Science of Freedom* (London, Wildwood House, 1970); R Porter, *Enlightenment: Britain and the Creation of the Modern World* (Harmondsworth, Penguin Books, 2000).

[3] RB Sher, *The Enlightenment and the Book: Scottish Authors and Their Publishers in Eighteenth Century Britain, Ireland, and America* (Chicago, University of Chicago Press, 2007) 17.

through lectures and demonstrations.[4] 'Practical geographical investigation'[5] was also an important feature of Enlightenment Britain, with the Pacific sea voyagers and the terrestrial explorers of Europe, Africa, and South America changing the way people understood the shapes of continents, as well as the plants and animals of the world.[6] Having studied the world by observing and reasoning about it, another preoccupation of Enlightenment thinkers was to measure and classify it. This impulse can be seen both in the botanical work of Swedish naturalist Carl von Linné (Linnaeus), as well as the growing numbers and popularity of encyclopaedias and scientific dictionaries.[7]

The ideal behind encyclopaedias, 'that rational enquiry can reduce all ideas and data to a common and understandable basis', also lay at the heart of eighteenth-century mapmaking. Matthew Edney explains that Enlightenment scholars placed the map at the centre of 'mathematical cosmography', a complex interweaving of astronomy and geography.[8] Mapmaking was both a metaphor for and epitome of Enlightenment ideology because one of the Enlightenment's most basic ideas was that: 'Critical and logical thought based on experience and observation – reason in the period's understanding – would lead to greater and more perfect knowledge of the physical world and the human condition, and so allow improvements in both'.[9] Ideas such as this would come to play a role in copyright litigation, which in turn helped establish an enduring definition of cartography as 'a factual science'.[10]

Trade and commerce were the other key concerns of eighteenth-century Britons to which Erskine alluded. By the start of the century, international trade had been rapidly expanding for many decades. Britain was uniquely placed to take advantage of this by reason of its colonies, control over trade routes, involvement in the slave trade, and commercial monopolies such as that of the East India Company. In England there was a 'consumer revolution', which saw men and women from all social classes buying and consuming unprecedented amounts of goods.[11] Items that were previously luxuries became 'decencies' or even 'necessities', while new luxury products emerged and leisure itself was commercialised.[12] Intimately connected with the rise of commerce were war and empire. Between 1689 and 1783

[4] Porter (n 2) 130–44.

[5] CWJ Withers, *Placing the Enlightenment: Thinking Geographically in the Age of Reason* (Chicago, University of Chicago Press, 2007) 5.

[6] ibid.

[7] See R Yeo, *Encyclopaedic Visions: Scientific Dictionaries and Enlightenment Culture* (Cambridge, Cambridge University Press, 2001).

[8] MH Edney, 'Mathematical Cosmography and the Social Ideology of British Cartography, 1780–1820' (1994) 46 *Imago Mundi* 101.

[9] ibid 104.

[10] JB Harley, 'Texts and Contexts in the Interpretation of Early Maps' in JB Harley (ed), *The New Nature of Maps: Essays in the History of Cartography* (Baltimore, The Johns Hopkins University Press, 2001) 33, 35.

[11] N McKendrick, J Brewer, and JH Plumb, *The Birth of a Consumer Society: The Commercialization of Eighteenth-Century England* (London, Hutchinson & Co, 1983).

[12] N McKendrick, 'Introduction' in ibid 1; JH Plumb, 'The Commercialization of Leisure in Eighteenth-Century England' in ibid 265–85.

Britain fought five major wars over a total of 53 years.[13] Pursuing these conflicts entailed an extraordinary level of expenditure on both the navy and military. This was achieved through increases in taxation, the use of public deficit finance, and the growth of administrative government.[14] The relationship between all these factors was codependent. Military, particularly naval, dominance secured colonies and trade routes, which in turn financed their own maintenance. As Pocock has observed, 'commerce was an aggressive action' and trade was 'intimately connected with the concepts of external relations and national power'.[15]

Erskine thus skilfully wove together several key ideals of eighteenth-century society in his address to the court – Enlightenment ideals surrounding scientific progress, the importance of scientific discoveries, and the centrality of commerce and trade to Britain's economy, social interactions, and imperial ambitions – all of which coalesced when it came to the question of copying charts and maps. This chapter examines the interplay of these factors over a period in which both copyright law and mapmaking were transformed, and explores the extent to which each impacted upon the transformation of the other. It does so by examining in detail six court cases that involved the application of the statutes discussed in the previous chapter to disputes over the copying of maps and charts.

These disputes and their participants played an important role in stabilising the category of 'maps, charts, and plans' as set out in the legislation and in embedding in that category Enlightenment-inflected concepts of accuracy and utility. At the same time, this research uncovers a rich vein of information about the trade practices of eighteenth-century London mapmakers and their legal and extra-legal interactions with each other. It reveals the deployment of copyright law by mapmakers to protect their investment against free-riders and copiers, which in turn allowed the trade itself to consolidate and transform. Finally, it demonstrates how the application of copyright law to maps and charts affected the development of copyright legal doctrine and the emergence of legal principles that were designed to complement and support Enlightenment ideals.

Additionally, each litigated case offers opportunities for examining the links between the different roles played by maps in eighteenth-century society, politics, and economics, and the different ways in which they were significant and valuable both as objects and in terms of knowledge that they contained. The relationship between all of these developments is critical but not straightforward. While it is common for claims to be made that maps and charts facilitated imperial acquisition and administration, and facilitated trade by expanding global knowledge and networks, the line of cause and effect cannot be simply drawn. Maps were not just used for commerce; they were commodities themselves. While the activities

[13] J Brewer, *The Sinews of Power: War, Money, and the English State, 1688–1783* (Harvard University Press, 1990) 29.

[14] ibid xvii.

[15] JGA Pocock, *The Machiavellian Moment: Florentine Political Thought and the Atlantic Republican Tradition* (Princeton, Princeton University Press, 1975) 425.

that fostered a growing interest in maps and charts – scientific exploration, war, and trade – were state sponsored, mapmaking was not. The making and circulation (selling) of maps remained almost entirely in the hands of a small number of private traders throughout most of the century. For these traders, maps were commercial objects, their forms and formats dictated by the market. Increasingly found on the walls and in the libraries of the literate classes, maps could be played as games, featured on screens or playing cards, or kept in pockets as handkerchiefs. They illustrated books, appeared in magazines, and adorned the walls of schoolrooms.[16]

But the growing popularity of maps as both tools of empire and desirable possessions did not mean that the trade of mapmaking was itself booming. By 1760 Britain may have achieved maritime dominance[17] but the cartographic community was, in the words of Yolande Hodson, 'characterised … by indigence'.[18] This was because mapmaking was a high-risk business, involving significant levels of expenditure on engraving, copperplates, and paper.[19] These costs were too high for any but the most successful firms to generate a profit. Mapsellers entered into labyrinthine arrangements for the raising of finance and the sharing of profits. And, in an environment where production costs were so great, the cost of carrying out new surveys was prohibitive to most members of the trade. Creating a new map generally involved compiling the necessary information from a variety of existing materials. Even the growing amount of data and knowledge of foreign parts was gathered by explorers in a piecemeal way and it was often many years before it was incorporated into the maps and charts made and sold in London.[20] Whether compiled from existing sources or created from a new survey, acquiring and processing the necessary information represented perhaps the most significant cost in mapmaking, as it required the longest amount of time, the greatest intellectual skill, and the most expensive instruments. These were, therefore, costs that many mapmakers sought to eliminate. As Mary Pedley states: 'Copying, reengraving and selling someone else's labor were lifeblood to the map trade throughout the entire eighteenth century'.[21]

While most mapmakers either copied existing maps or purchased engraved plates and made minor updates or changes before reissuing them with a new title, this practice of copying sat uneasily alongside the rhetoric of the maps themselves. These new titles proclaimed the maps as 'new and accurate', 'new and complete',

[16] MS Pedley, *The Commerce of Cartography: Making and Marketing Maps in Eighteenth-Century France and England* (Chicago, University of Chicago Press, 2005) 6.

[17] Brewer (n 13) xiv.

[18] Y Hodson, 'Maps, Charts and Atlases in Britain, 1690–1830' in MF Suarez, SJ and ML Turner (eds), *The Cambridge History of the Book in Britain: Volume V, 1695–1830* (Cambridge, Cambridge University Press, 2009) 762.

[19] For detail on the costs involved, see Pedley (n 16) 35–70.

[20] For more on exploration and mapmaking, see Withers (n 5) ch 5.

[21] Pedley (n 16) 96. Yolande Hodson has also noted that 'the practice of plagiarism … was, for many a map and chart publisher, an economic necessity': Hodson (n 18) 763.

'new and improved'.[22] In this way, mapmakers sought to align their products with the scientific revolution underway and demonstrated their awareness that the market too was interested in the quest for scientific advances. Although these claims were often no doubt misleading or false, there was a transformation occurring. Laurence Worms has argued that the latter half of the century saw a maturing of commercial cartography and a growing cadre of mapmakers who prized accuracy over outdated reprints and aspired to a greater range of coverage than was offered by piecemeal county surveys.[23] Worms characterises this as a 'battle between ancients and moderns' and suggests that, following the ultimate victory of the moderns, private, individual mapmakers handed cartography over to publicly-funded bodies such as the Ordnance Survey and the Hydrographic Office, which took mapmaking forward into the next century.[24]

To examine the extent to which copyright law played a role in this transformation, we turn to consider the cases that were brought under the Engravings Acts. Before considering the cases in detail, however, it is necessary to outline briefly the state of copyright law more generally in the period. As noted in the previous chapter, the Statute of Anne had applied to books since 1710 but its focus was largely upon the problem posed by multiple people wishing to publish the same book, and many aspects of its scope remained unclear. Perhaps the most pressing question left unanswered by the statutory text was whether there was a common-law copyright that existed alongside the Statute of Anne, with the result that booksellers could be said to hold copyright in their more valuable properties in perpetuity. A considerable body of scholarship has considered the series of cases that culminated in the landmark decisions of *Millar v Taylor* (1769) and *Donaldson v Becket* (1774).[25] But, beginning in the 1720s and continuing throughout the century, booksellers began to bring cases before the courts that raised other questions about the statute's scope, such as: Did the Act extend to things other than books? Did it apply to unpublished writings, such as letters? Did it affect grants of privileges? And did it only apply when *identical* books were published or could it also be used to prevent the publication of partial copying or copying by abridgement or summary?

Under the Statute of Anne, as well as the Engravings Acts, disputes over copyright could be litigated in any 'Court of Record at Westminster'; namely, the King's Bench, Court of Common Pleas, and Court of Exchequer.[26] However, for most of the century the only remedies available in those courts were the penalties provided in these Statutes (one penny per sheet under the Statute of Anne or 5 shillings per

[22] Pedley (n 16) 188.

[23] L Worms, 'The Maturing of British Commercial Cartography: William Faden (1749–1836) and the Map Trade', (2004) 41 *The Cartographic Journal* 5.

[24] ibid 11.

[25] See eg HT Gómez-Arostegui, 'Copyright at Common Law in 1774' (2014) 47 *Connecticut Law Review* 1; R Deazley, *On the Origin of the Right to Copy: Charting the Movement of Copyright Law in Eighteenth Century Britain (1675–1775)* (Portland, OR, Hart, 2004); M Rose, 'The Author as Proprietor: *Donaldson v. Becket* and the Genealogy of Modern Authorship' (1988) 23 *Representations* 51.

[26] Statute of Anne, s 1, Engravings Act 1735, s 1.

print under the Engravings Act 1735) and forfeiture of infringing copies, although the Engravings Act 1777 did introduce the possibility of damages.[27] In addition, the book had to have been registered at Stationers' Hall and the action brought within three months of the offence.[28] For various reasons (explained by Tomàs Gómez-Arostegui[29]), litigants preferred the Court of Chancery, where they were able to obtain relief through interlocutory and final injunctions preventing future infringements, and an account of profits made by the defendant through their past infringing activities.[30] However, very few of these cases progressed as far as a hearing. As Justice Willes explained in *Millar v Taylor*: 'Few Bills against Pirates of Books are ever brough to a Hearing. If the Defendant acquiesces under Injunction, it is seldom worth the Plaintiff's while to proceed for an Account; the Sale of the Edition being Stopped'.[31] Because so few cases reached a hearing, let alone a formal judgment, in any of the courts, the law developed slowly and tentatively. The few decisions that were handed down were often considered relevant to cases brought under any of the statutes. Yet, with few judicial pronouncements to lay down clear principles and binding precedents, litigants and lawyers were left feeling their way to a great extent, both in relation to cases brought under the Statute of Anne as well as the Engravings Acts. How the various parties sought to make sense of the new statutory regime and apply it to their business activities is what we turn to consider now.

II. Testing the Statute with a Map Game: The Case of *Jefferys v Bowles* (1770)

Three years after the Engravings Act 1767 received Royal Assent, the first case involving a single sheet map was brought before the Court of Chancery.[32] The plaintiff was Thomas Jefferys who, as we have seen, had already tested the 1735 Act in relation to a print of shipping vessels – hardly the kind of artistic print produced by the likes of William Hogarth. Jefferys was one of the leading mapmakers of his day and was appointed as official geographer to Frederick, Prince of Wales, and his son Prince George, becoming Geographer to the King upon George's ascension to the

[27] See ch 3.

[28] Statute of Anne, ss 2, 10.

[29] HT Gómez-Arostegui, 'What History Teaches Us about Copyright Injunctions and the Inadequate-Remedy-at-Law Requirement' (September 2008) 81 *Southern California Law Review* 1269–73.

[30] For the procedure followed in Chancery and detail on the different types of injunctions as well as disgorgement of profits, see HT Gómez-Arostegui, 'Equitable Infringement Remedies before 1800' in I Alexander and HT Gómez-Arostegui (eds), *Research Handbook on the History of Copyright Law* (Cheltenham, Edward Elgar, 2016) 195.

[31] *Millar v Taylor* (1769) 4 Burr. 2303, 2324.

[32] For a more detailed study of this case, see I Alexander and CS Martinez, 'A Game Map: Object of Copyright and Form of Authority in Eighteenth-Century Britain' (2020) 72 *Imago Mundi* 163.

throne as George III in 1738.[33] Although little is known of his early life, by the 1760s he was employing around a dozen staff – engravers, cartographical draughtsmen, and compilers – with an especially flourishing line in North American maps. However, in 1766 he was declared bankrupt. JB Harley speculates that Jefferys' financial difficulties might have flowed from his over-investment in the English county surveys. Where Jefferys had been able to obtain data for his foreign maps at very little expense from his wide-ranging network of sources including naval captains and colonial surveyors, the county surveys necessitated much greater levels of investment, including costs such as surveyors, labourers, instruments, and horses.[34] Harley uses the story of Jefferys' bankruptcy to emphasise the small profit margins of mapmaking, the chronic lack of capital in the business, and to suggest that 'the eighteenth-century mapseller could not afford to be other than a plagiarist'.[35]

By 1767, however, Jefferys was back in business, having been assisted by 'some Friends who were compassionate enough to re-instate me in my shop'.[36] And in 1770, he was bringing a case to the Court of Chancery against an alleged plagiarist. The map in question was not one of the county maps in which he had so perilously invested nor was it one of the North American maps for which he was well-known. Rather, it was a novel kind of map product – a map that was also a game. This was *The Royal Geographical Pastime or the Complete Tour of Europe*, (see Figure 6) published in 1768 and followed by two more map games, *A Complete Tour Round the World*, and *A Complete Tour Thro' England and Wales*, both published in 1770. These were games of chance, rather than skill, played by two to six players taking turns to spin a totum to move around the board.[37] The map itself was a copperplate engraving, hand-coloured, cut into squares then mounted on linen and folded into squares so it could fit into a slip-case. The rules were printed in letterpress and affixed to both sides of the map. All three games were dedicated to the Prince of Wales (later George IV).

At the same time that Jefferys published his second and third maps, rival publisher and printseller Carington Bowles issued his own map game of Europe under the title *The Royal Geographical Amusement or the European Traveller Designed from the Grand Tour by Dr Nugent* (see Figure 7). Like Jefferys' map, Bowles's version was coloured, framed by letterpress texts on each side, and sold with a totum. On 15 February 1770, Jefferys sought an order in Chancery to halt its sale.[38] Why did Jefferys choose this map game as the vehicle for testing the

[33] JB Harley, 'The Bankruptcy of Thomas Jefferys: An Episode in the Economic History of Eighteenth-Century Map-Making' (1966) 20 *Imago Mundi* 27, 31, 35.

[34] ibid.

[35] ibid 48.

[36] ibid 46.

[37] A totum (or teetotum) was a spinning top with eight flat sides marked with numbers. It performed the same function as a die but was considered more appropriate for children as it did not carry the same associations with gaming: J Shefrin, '"Make It a Pleasure and Not a Task": Educational Games for Children in Georgian England' (1999) 60 *The Princeton University Library Chronicle* 251.

[38] Complaint of Thomas Jefferys, 15 February 1770, C12/1318/18 m1 (UKNA).

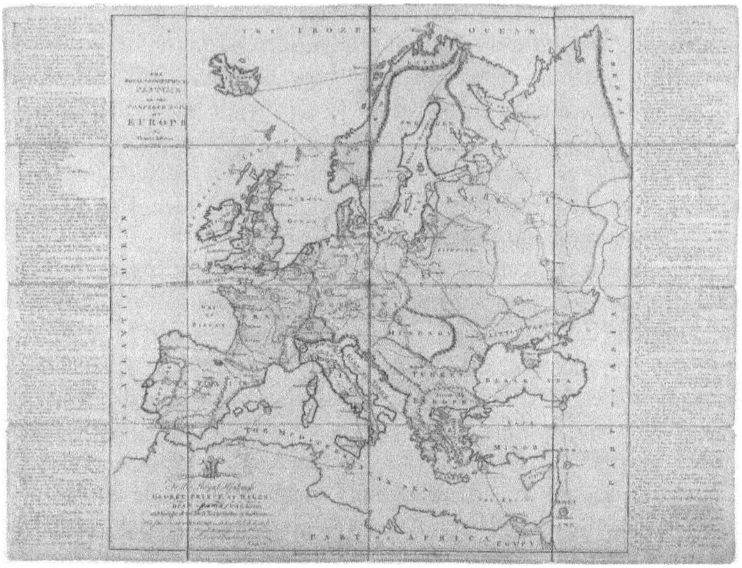

Figure 6 Thomas Jefferys' map game, *The Royal Geographical Pastime or the Complete Tour of Europe*, (London, Thomas Jefferys, 1768)

Image courtesy of the National Library of Wales NLW South MAP (Antiquarian Map 3545).

Figure 7 Carington Bowles' map game, *The Royal Geographical Amusement or the European Traveller Designed from the Grand Tour by Dr Nugent*, (London, Carington Bowles, 1770)

Image courtesy of Yale Center for British Art GV1199.R69 1770.

Acts? The answer is likely related to the rising popularity of this emergent market. As noted above, the eighteenth century saw maps involved in a wide array of consumer products, and it is not surprising the trade also began to respond to the growing Enlightenment emphasis on geography and mapping in children's education by creating a new market with map games. John Spilsbury, a former apprentice to Thomas Jefferys, was the first to produce dissected maps but the first educational map game for children in which the map itself was the playing board was published and designed in 1759 by John Jefferys (no relation to Thomas).[39] Thomas Jefferys seems to have indeed copied this idea nine years later.[40]

The games, however, were more than a simple pastime. They operated as a vehicle not just for imparting Enlightenment ideologies surrounding the acquisition of knowledge to the next generation, but also as a vehicle for the ideology of English power, both domestic and abroad. This can be seen in the rules of the game, printed in letterpress, and arranged down each side of the map, which proclaim that the winner is 'he who is fortunate enough to gain' London. Other stops and moves also reflect ideas of nationalism and a celebration of English military might. In Bowles's game, for example, the player who lands on Minorca is told the town was 'taken by the English in 1708, and famous for its excellent harbor. This being a lucky number, the traveller is to be carried forward to Turin.' In Jefferys' game, city stops include Cherburg, 'taken by the English in 1758', and Vigo, where the traveller stays one turn 'to see this town which was burnt by the English, 1702.'

Religious messages are also encoded. In both games Rome is a penalty stop. In Bowles's game, the player who reaches Rome must 'stay two turns to view the ancient and modern curiosities, and to reflect on the abuses of the papal government', while in that of Jefferys, 'the Traveller, who is supposed to have indiscreetly kissed the pope's toe, must be banished to Bergen, in Norway (No.11) and miss four turns'. Jefferys' game further identifies cities home to religious reformers John Huss (Jan Hus) and John Calvin. The games also celebrated the British Crown and the Hanoverians. In Bowles's map, Hanover is singled out for favour: 'the capital of our king's German dominions; this being a fortunate number, the traveller will be removed to Brussels'. In Jefferys' map, it is Strelitz, 'where the Traveller will be shewn the splendid court of our Queen's brother; this being a fortunate number, he is to be removed to Vienna'.

Jefferys' games were carefully calculated to please his royal patrons but he must also have hoped to reach a wider audience and the new copyright law offered an opportunity to protect his market exclusivity. To take on Bowles, Jefferys engaged two legal counsel with considerable experience in copyright litigation: Robert

[39] Shefrin (n 37) 259. See eg Spilsbury's advertisement in the *St James Chronicle or the British Evening Post*, 19 June 1762, 4 which mentions that maps were made 'for the Purposes of introducing young Ladies and Gentlemen insensibly to the Knowledge of Geography' and 'are contained in neat Boxes, which preserve them from being lost'.

[40] The Jefferys map, which is currently held in the National Library of Wales (and shown at Figure 6 above), was actually sold in a slip-case, stating it was printed and sold for Spilsbury: See catalogue entry for *The Royal Geographical Pastime, or the Complete Tour of Europe* (Thomas Jefferys, London, 1768) Antiquarian Map 3545 (Llyfrgell Genedlaethol Cymru/National Library of Wales).

Bicknell and Alexander Wedderburn. Wedderburn would go on to argue in favour of common-law copyright four years later in the famous case of *Donaldson v Becket*;[41] he subsequently became Chief Justice of the Court of Common Pleas as Baron Loughborough and later still rose to the position of Lord Chancellor. In his bill of complaint Jefferys relied on both the 1735 Engravings Act and the 1767 Engravings Act. He stated that he did 'with great Labour and Assiduity & at a considerable Expence Contrive and Invent a Method of Teaching Young Persons the Use of the Maps and Charts' and that he had 'well hoped that he should have fully Enjoyed and Reaped the Sole Benefit of the Labour and Industry as aforesaid Pursuant to and Compliant with' the two Acts of Parliament.[42] However, he was not seeking the remedies provided for in those statutes but had brought the case in Chancery seeking equitable remedies, chiefly an injunction, but also delivery up of unsold prints and an account and payment of the defendant's profits. The court granted his injunction on 19 February 1770, stating it would last until the defendant put in his answer.[43]

Bowles engaged the Attorney-General William de Grey, along with a Mr Kett, as his counsel. Four years later de Grey too would play a significant role in *Donaldson v Becket* when, as Lord Chief Justice of the Common Pleas, he expressly rejected the existence of common-law copyright.[44] In his answer to the bill of complaint, Bowles admitted that he had indeed published a game entitled *The Royal Geographical Amusement, or the European Traveller Designed from the Grand Tour by Dr Nugent*.[45] He also admitted that he had approached Jefferys twice in 1768, proposing to take up a half share of the right to print, publish, and sell the game but that Jefferys' price of 100 guineas was too high, so he refused to deal any further with him. However, Bowles denied being liable under the statutes on several bases. First, he claimed that, far from having copied Jefferys' map, Jefferys had copied from him. According to Bowles, the map used by Jefferys was copied, with some 'trifling variations',[46] from a map of Europe designed and engraved by Monsieur Palairet and owned by Bowles himself. Second, Bowles argued, it was not correct that Thomas Jefferys had invented and designed the game himself. Instead, Bowles claimed, he himself had purchased the copperplate, 'invention', and 'all his right and interest therein' from the game's true inventor, John Jefferys, who had engraved and published a game entitled *Journey Through Europe or the Play of Geography* on 14 September 1759.[47]

[41] (1774) 7 Bro PC 88; 4 Burr 2303.
[42] C12/1318/18 m1 (UKNA).
[43] C33/433 f 161v (19 February 1770) (UKNA).
[44] *Donaldson v Becket* (1774) 7 Bro PC 88; 4 Burr 2408. See also R Deazley, 'The Myth of Copyright at Common Law' (2003) 62 *Cambridge Law Journal* 106, 121.
[45] Answer of Carington Bowles, 7 March 1770, C12/1318/18 m2 (UKNA).
[46] ibid.
[47] A copy of this map game is reproduced in FR Beaman Whitehouse, *Table Games of Georgian and Victorian Days* (Royston, Herts and Harborne, Birmingham, Priory Press Ltd, 1951) 6. There is no indication given of where this copy is held.

The wording here is of interest, in particular his claim that he had acquired title to the game through his purchase of not only the copperplates but also the 'invention' and 'right and interest'. It is not stated when this purchase occurred but, as Bowles explains that John Jefferys engraved his name on each print according to the Act of Parliament, it suggests the former at least believed that the 1735 Act created a property right that could be enforced and possibly traded. It is interesting that his answer suggests that he also acquired John Jefferys' 'invention' via this sale. What he meant by this is unclear and perhaps he and his lawyers were themselves not sure, but simply picking up on the words in the statute.[48] More concretely, Bowles accused Jefferys of employing the engraver Louis Delarochette to copy John Jefferys' game, changing some of the rules and historical and geographical anecdotes, and publishing it under a different name to elude the Acts of Parliament.

Bowles continued by denying that Jefferys:

> is or ever was in fact the proprietor thereof in such sense as to be entitled to the benefit of the Acts of Parliament in the bill mentioned or either of them he not being as this defendant believes the original inventor or claiming under the original inventor but being only the engraver thereof.[49]

Moreover, he argued, the rules and historical and geographical anecdotes did not fall under the Act as they were on letterpress rather than copperplate. In addition, Bowles contended that he had not used the same map as Thomas Jefferys but that his map was copied or traced from a plate engraved for him by a Mr Lodge and finished by a Mr Ellis. Bowles pointed to many differences between his game and that of Jefferys. He claimed that: his map included latitude and longitude; the numbers on his map were different; it included different places; and, while the rules and directions were identical, the historical and geographical anecdotes were different. He explained these distinctions did not result from his desire to avoid the Engravings Acts but to ensure that his map closely followed a book called *The Grand Tour* by Dr Nugent. Finally, Bowles denied he had printed and published 1,000 copies of the game, as Jefferys had alleged, stating he had printed only 50 copies, published only 29, and disposed of only nine copies at a price of 8s each or thereabouts. He admitted that he did intend to publish two more games – like Jefferys, one of England and Wales and one of the World – and asked that he not be enjoined against doing so.[50]

When Bowles made his answer on 7 March 1770, the court ordered that the injunction be dissolved unless the Plaintiff showed good cause to the contrary on 17 March.[51] Jefferys' counsel argued that the injunction be continued but

[48] See ch 3.
[49] C12/1318/18 m2 (UKNA).
[50] ibid.
[51] C33/433 f421v (7 March 1770) (UKNA).

the Lords Commissioners of the Great Seal[52] referred the matter to a Master in Chancery[53] by consent of counsel on both sides. The Master in Chancery, Mr Pechell, was ordered to examine whether the defendant's copperplate 'is of the same size and scale and has the same marginal notes and directions or Instructions and is in all respects the same as the first Plate published by the [Plaintiff]'.[54] Unfortunately, there is no record of the Master's decision and the final resolution of the case is not known.

The case is, however, instructive in several respects. As the first person to bring litigation under the 1767 Act, we can see Jefferys feeling his way, not entirely sure how this new protection will play out. His uncertainty can perhaps be reflected in his approach to the publication line on each of his map games. For the first game, Jefferys complied with the requirement of the Engravings Act 1735 that the date of first publishing and publisher's name be engraved on each plate. The publication line centred in the lower margin reads: 'Published according to the Statute of the 7th. of George IIId Jan 1st 1768 by T. Jefferys the Corner of St. Martins Lane'. The next two map games included a similar publication line on the left-hand side of the lower margin, giving the date of publication as 1 January 1770. On the right-hand side, a second publication line warns: 'Entered in the Hall Book of the Stationers Company, and whoever presumes to Copy it will be prosecuted by The Proprietor, who will reward any Person that shall give Information of it'.[55] However, it appears from the Stationers' records that neither map was actually registered until 30 December 1770.[56] Was this a response to Bowles's suggestion that the letterpress could not be covered under the Engravings Act? Bowles and his legal team also seemed unsure how to proceed, putting forward a wide range of arguments, perhaps hoping at least one of them would gain traction with the judge.

Despite not proceeding to a decree, this dispute did assist in clarifying the scope of the new Engravings Act 1767. Because Jefferys brought the case, despite not having done the engraving himself, and his complaint was neither objected to by the defendant nor thrown out by the court on this basis, it became clear that it was possible for a publisher to bring an action in respect of a work engraved for them by another. As a result, the statute was of use to mapmakers who engaged printers to engrave maps under their instruction. The instruction to the Master also revealed some of the things that the court ought to consider in such cases.

[52] This is the term used when the office of Lord Chancellor fell vacant and was held in the interim by more than one person. In 1770 the Lords Commissioners were Sir Sidney Stafford Smythe, Henry Bathurst, and Sir Richard Aston.

[53] A master in chancery was one of the court officers who assisted the Lord Chancellor.

[54] C33/433 f267v (17 March 1770) (UKNA).

[55] T Jefferys, *The Royal Geographical Pastime Exhibiting a Complete Tour Round the World in with are delineated the North East and North West Passages into the South Sea and other modern Discoveries* (London, 1770); T Jefferys, *The Royal Geographical Pastime Exhibiting a Complete Tour Thro' England and Wales* (London, 1770).

[56] *Register of Entries of Copies, 29 Sep. 1746–30 Dec. 1773* (TSC/1/E/06/09) (SCA).

As there was no Chancery-ordered resolution in the case, we can surmise that the case settled. It seems that Bowles continued to sell versions of *The European Traveller* until the 1780s as further prints were advertised. He did, however, remove the word 'Royal' from the title, substituting his own name, and made changes to the colouring.[57] These alterations increased the differences between his game and that of Jefferys. In addition, when Bowles published a *Geographical Game of the World* in 1790, he used a map very different to that of Jefferys (although the letterpress rules remained fairly similar).[58]

III. Breaching a Publishing Agreement: The Case of *Bowles v Sayer* (1780)

It was to be 10 years before another dispute over maps was brought before the Court of Chancery. This case was not brought under the Engravings Act 1767, although it did invoke its provisions. While it did not progress far beyond the initial stages of complaint and answer, it reveals the parties exploring the impact of this new statutory regime on existing ways of doing business. Once again Carington Bowles was involved but this time he was the plaintiff. The defendant was Robert Sayer, a prominent London printseller, who had taken over Philip Overton's business by 1748 and was one of those who had assisted Jefferys back into business after his bankruptcy. Sayer acquired some of Jefferys' stock of plates and manuscript material at that time, later purchasing more from his estate.[59]

The map in question depicted Scotland and can, like the game map in the previous case, be seen to lie at a moment of mapmaking transition. Carington Bowles's father and uncle had published a single sheet map of 'Scotland or North Britain with considerable improvements according to the newest observations' in 1730.[60] The map that gave rise to the dispute, however, was in four sheets and likely based on James Dorrett's map of Scotland of 1750, which included new information from surveys undertaken at the expense of the Duke of Argyll, Dorrett's employer.[61] This four-sheet map was used as the basis of a number of later maps, both English and Scottish.[62]

[57] Alexander and Martinez (n 32) 167.

[58] C Bowles, 'Bowles's Geographical Game of the World, in a New Complete and Elegant Tour through the Known Parts thereof, Laid down on Mercator's Projection' (London, 1790). Reproduced in A Baynton-Williams, *The Curious Map* 102.

[59] L Worms and A Baynton-Williams, *British Map Engravers: A Dictionary of Engravers, Lithographers and Their Principal Employers to 1850* (London, Rare Book Society, 2011) 587.

[60] *A New Mapp of Scotland or North Britain with Considerable Improvements According to the Newest Observations* (London, Printed and sold by Tho Bowles print and map seller next the Chapter House in St Pauls Church yard and John Bowles print and map seller at the Black Horse in Cornhill, 1731).

[61] DG Moir, *The Early Maps of Scotland to 1850* (Edinburgh, Royal Scottish Geographical Society, 1973) 92.

[62] ibid 92.

It is also likely to have used information acquired from the Board of Ordnance's Military Survey.[63] This survey began after the Jacobite rebellion of 1745 demonstrated the severe deficiencies in England's geographical knowledge of the Highlands and its significant military implications. The Military Survey heralded a surge of military mapping undertaken by the Board, with the explicit aim of quelling Jacobite unrest and defending against future attack.[64] As Carolyn Anderson explains, these military mapmakers 'were charged with planning, constructing, and recording landscapes of and for military action – a conjunction of forts, barracks, batteries, roads and battlefields'.[65] For most European states at the time, the main areas of military activity were fortification, movement, and battle.[66] These interests can be seen reflected on Bowles's and Sayer's map, beginning with its extended title: *A New and Complete Map of Scotland, and Islands thereto belonging, From Actual Surveys, the Shires properly Divided and Subdivided, the Forts lately Erected, & Roads of Communication or, Military Ways; Carried on by His Majesty's Command: the Times wherein and Places whereof the most remarkable Battles have been fought. Likewise the Roman Camps, Forts, Walls & Military Ways: the Danish Camps & Forts. Also the Seats of Nobility in each Shire distinguished with several other remarkable Places that occur in the History of Scotland.* Military interests can be observed in the cannon and weaponry decorating the cartouche, as well as the ship of the line sitting offshore. The English crown sits atop the Lion of Scotland, which could represent Scotland's military subjugation, although the message (if such it is) might be undermined by the fact that the cannon appears directed at the Naval vessel (see Figure 8).

Perhaps more significant in the cartouche are the mapping and surveying implements sitting atop. The military mapping of Scotland was the British state's first concentrated foray into state-directed cartography with the aim of asserting territorial control and also involved an early deployment of a new technology of mapping, the trigonometrical survey. Matthew Edney has argued that triangulation represented a shift away from the Enlightenment's encyclopaedic approach to mapping, in which reason offered the foundation for a scientific approach to mapmaking. He explains that, because triangulation was so much more precise over different scales and landscapes, 'it represented a dramatic extension of state power'.[67] By incorporating some of this new, scientifically generated data in their map of Scotland, Bowles, and Sayer offered customers a taste of what was to come, presaging the Scottish

[63] ibid.

[64] For a fascinating and detailed examination of Scottish military mapping in this period, see C Anderson, 'Constructing the Military Landscape: The Board of Ordnance Maps and Plans of Scotland, 1689–1815' (PhD Thesis, University of Edinburgh, 2010).

[65] ibid 1.

[66] ibid 86, 115.

[67] MH Edney, 'Reconsidering Enlightenment Geography: and Map-Making: Reconnaissance, Mapping, Archive' in DN Livingstone and CWJ Withers, *Geography and Enlightenment* (Chicago, University of Chicago Press, 1999) 165, 191.

Figure 8 Cartouche from Carington Bowles, Robert Sayer & J Bennett, *A New and Complete Map of Scotland*. The map is undated but includes Bennett's name, indicating it is one of the maps produced under the arrangement that led to the litigation

Enlightenment and rise of Scotland as an intellectual leader of British (private) mapmaking in the nineteenth century.[68]

Capitalising on this interest, Carington Bowles entered into a joint venture with Robert Sayer and Sayer's business partner, John Bennett,[69] in 1766 to publish a map of Scotland in four large copperplates. According to Bowles, it had been agreed between them that if either party sold off all their prints, they would purchase prints from the other before printing any new copies. However,

[68] I am grateful to Laurence Worms for discussions on this point (personal correspondence). For the rise to prominence of Scottish mapmaking firms Bartholomew and W & AK Johnston, see chs 7 and 9.

[69] *Bowles v Sayer* (1780) C12/1656/12. Bennett's active involvement in the litigation is questionable. He had been diagnosed as insane in 1781 and committed to an asylum in 1783. In 1784 Sayer took steps to dissolve the partnership: *Sayer v Bennett* (1784) 1 Cox 107. Bennett's name disappears from the partnership in 1785: S Fisher, *The Makers of the Blueback Charts: a history of Imray, Laurie, Norie & Wilson Ltd*, (St Ives UK, Imary Laurie Norie & Wilson, 2001) 47.

according to Bowles, Sayer sold all his copies and then arranged for new sheets to be printed with some small variations, without informing Bowles, and then sold the new impressions at a price below that which Bowles and Sayer had originally agreed upon.[70] Clearly infuriated at this double-crossing behaviour (or 'unfair and fraudulent Dealing'), Bowles brought a suit in Chancery complaining of the breach of this agreement, suggesting that Sayer and Bennett be ordered to account to him his share of the profits and that they be ordered to fulfil the agreement. He sought an injunction that would prevent Sayer and Bennett from continuing to print and sell copies of this map and a writ of subpoena requiring them to appear and answer his complaint.[71]

Interestingly, Bowles did not directly refer to the Engravings Acts in his bill of complaint. According to his complaint, he had relied on an older way of enforcing compliance with agreements to take shares in copperplates – possession of the plates. As he explained,

> for the mutual security of your Orator and the said Robert Sayer against any fraudulent or sinister attempt of either of them against the other and to prevent the taking off or printing of any Copies of the said Map without the mutual consent of both.[72]

Sayer would keep two plates in his possession, while Bowles would keep the other two in his. Although Bowles did not refer to the Engravings Acts, Sayer did so in his answer. Sayer, like Bowles, was well aware of the Engravings Acts. In 1770 he had brought an unsuccessful action in the Court of Common Pleas against Cluer Dicey for copying and selling a print of the King of Denmark.[73] In that case, Sayer was nonsuited because he had not engraved his name and date of first publication on the print in question, as required by the 1735 Act.[74] Six years later he and Bennett were defendants in an action brought in the Court of the King's Bench by Thomas Watson relating to unauthorised copying of a print. The verdict went against him and he had to pay £200 in damages.[75]

Responding to Bowles, Sayer conceded that he had printed additional copies but claimed this was because Bowles had, in the past, pirated Sayer's map of Ireland.[76] Seeking to escape the impact of the 1767 Act, Sayer also contended that

[70] C12/1656/12, m1, 2, 12 January 1780 (UKNA).

[71] C12/1656/12 m1, 12 January 1780 (UKNA).

[72] C12/1656/12 m1, 12 January 1780 (UKNA).

[73] *Sayer qui tam &c v Dicey et al.* (1770) 3 Wilson KB 60; 95 ER 933. See D Stokes, 'Another Look at the Dicey-Marshall Publications, 1736–1806' (2014) 15 *The Library* 111. Thanks to Cristina Martinez for pointing me to this source and helping me identify Dicey.

[74] Engravings Act 1735, s 1.

[75] *Watson v Sayer and Bennett* (1776) printed in JC Oldham, *The Mansfield Manuscripts and the Growth of English Law in the Eighteenth Century*, Vol 1 (Chapel Hill, University of North Carolina Press, 1992) 744.

[76] This is probably John Rocque, *A Map of the Kingdom of Ireland: Divided into Provinces Counties and Baronies*, which also appeared in the Kitchin's *General Atlas* published by Sayer.

the map in question could not be protected by that Act, as it had been published before it came into force.[77] He explained that

> the said Map of Scotland not being protected by the said Act of parliament as hereinbefore is mentioned the said Complainant may from a printed Copy of the two plates in the possession of these Defendants engrave or cause to be engraved onto new Copper plates such part of the said Map of Scotland as is contained in the said plates in the possession of these Defendants and may from such new engraved plates print or cause to be printed as many Copies thereof as he shall think proper without the consent or knowledge of these Defendants or either of them and may also sell and dispose of all such Copies to this own separate emolument and thereby take the same benefit from such now engraved plates as these Defendants have done from their aforesaid new engraved plates.[78]

It is interesting to observe Bowles here suggesting that the map could not be protected, when in the earlier litigation he had emphasised John Jefferys' use of the publication line required by the Engravings Act 1735. Perhaps he thought the failure to add such a line to the Scotland map disqualified it from protection under the Engravings Act 1735, or perhaps the lack of clarity surrounding both statutes and the extent of their application meant he could make the most expedient argument in each case.

The dispute between Bowles and Sayer and Bennett arose from a fairly typical commercial arrangement made between members of the print and map trades, in which the ownership of copperplates was shared, as was the outlay for printing, composition and engraving. As Mary Pedley's analysis of the letters between Thomas Jefferys and William Faden demonstrates, relationships between traders were crucial to the success of the trade as a whole, and the trade's high-risk nature and its small profit margins made joint ownership of maps essential.[79] Trust was crucial, particularly in light of long and complex lines of credit between those involved in making and selling the maps but inevitably it would, from time to time, break down. Towards the end of their answer, Sayer and Bennet reveal their own complaints of the relationship, noting that they and Bowles 'have several plates in partnership together' and that Bowles 'hath from time to time been very troublesome to these Defendants before they could get his consent to print editions or impressions of such last mentioned plates'. They observed that they had a joint interest in a 24-sheet Map of London, which 'wants to have the new buildings added there to [*sic*] but the said Complainant hath always refused and declined to join the Defendants in the expense of adding such new buildings thereto', causing them 'loss of the

[77] C12/1656/12, m3, 4, 29 June 1780 (UKNA).
[78] C12/1656/12, m3, 29 June 1780 (UKNA).
[79] M Pedley (ed), *The Map Trade in the Late Eighteenth Century: Letters to the London Map Sellers Jefferys & Faden* (Oxford, Voltaire Foundation, 2000) 3.

profit which might have arisen and been made in case such plates had been improved and used in the common and usual line of business as they ought to have been'.[80]

The Engravings Act 1767 offered a new strategy for mapmakers to negotiate such breakdowns and perhaps gain an advantage. However, the market was so small and the market players so close-knit and reliant upon each other that collaboration may have been more important than competition. The initial bill was lodged in June 1780 but by the following May it was recorded that the parties had 'accommodated' their differences and the plaintiff's bill was dismissed without costs.[81] The detail of the relationship that is provided in the fulsome pleadings reveals the parties articulating existing trade practices and attempting to map them onto the new statutory regime. For example, Bowles explains how his agreement with Sayer encompassed what would appear in the cartouche, and Sayer's betrayal is evidenced by his erasure of the 'Advertizement … added to show the property of the said Map to be in your Orator jointly with the said Robert Sayer'.[82] Likewise, we learn that the pre-copyright strategy of managing compliance with such agreements was through physical possession of the copperplates. However, as can be seen, this would not be effective in the case of a partner who could afford to have new plates engraved. Sayer's explanation that his actions responded to Bowles's unauthorised copying indicates that, in the days before copyright legislation, behaviour was also regulated by the perceived ability of a competitor to retaliate. The Engravings Acts began to change the stakes by introducing a new tool to regulate trade behaviour. However, by 1780 there were still very few cases interpreting it. Unsurprisingly, therefore, parties were still unsure of the extent to which they could rely upon their provisions to enforce publishing agreements.

IV. Improvement and Progress: The Moore Cases (1785–97)

The next three cases to be brought under the Engravings Acts were connected in several ways. Each of them involved a sea-chart, each involved the same defendant, all ended up before the Court of the King's Bench, and all proceeded to a judgment.[83] While fewer of the legal records can be located for these cases,

[80] C12/1656/12 m4, 29 June 1780 (UKNA).

[81] C33/455 f497, 26 May 1781 (UKNA).

[82] C12/1656/12 m1, 12 June 1780 (UKNA). I am grateful to Ashley Baynton-Williams for help in analysing the different cartouches and their possible dating. The reversal of the names of Sayer and Bowles, the addition of Bennett, and the removal of all names in the cartouches of different versions of the maps can be compared at www.copyrightcartography.org/cases/bowles-v-sayer/.

[83] For a more detailed discussion of these cases and their impact on copyright law, see I Alexander, 'Sayer v. Moore (1785)' in J Bellido (ed), *Landmark Cases in Intellectual Property Law* (Oxford, Hart Publishing, 2017) 59.

some of the legal argument has been preserved by the parties publishing their own accounts and the first of the cases was reported by Sir Edward Hyde East in his King's Bench case reports (now part of the English Reports).[84] In these cases we see for the first time judges applying the new statutes and developing principles which would cast a long shadow over copyright law.

The defendant in each case was John Hamilton Moore, a colourful character who attracted loyal friends as well as legal foes. Born in a village near Edinburgh in 1738 and educated in Ireland by a celebrated mathematics teacher, Mr Ballendine, Moore entered the Royal Navy but left to become a schoolteacher. While working in this profession, Moore wrote *The Practical Navigator and Seaman's New Daily Assistant*. Published in 1772, this was to become the most popular navigational text of the day. Moore wrote and published more books – *The Practical Observer* (1775), *A New and Complete Collection of Voyages and Travels* (1778), and *The Young Gentleman's and Lady's Monitors* (1780). In 1781 he moved to London, setting up business first in the Minories and then at Tower Hill.[85] Close to the river Thames and Trinity House,[86] Moore had moved to the heart of nautical London, alongside the premises of instrument makers and chandlers, its streets bustling with seamen. Moore advertised courses in navigation at a cost of five guineas with boarding accommodation provided if necessary. He also offered for sale books, charts, and nautical instruments such as compasses, quadrants and sextants, drawing and calculating instruments, and telescopes.[87]

By establishing this business, Moore was joining a small and interdependent community of nautical publishers. In the earlier part of the century, the trade had been dominated by a single firm, the partnership of Richard Mount and Thomas Page. Their business consisted largely of acquiring old copperplates from publications such as Seller's 1693 *English Atlas* and refurbishing them. But by the end of the century, the firm's business declined.[88] New players began to enter the market – not just Moore but also Robert Sayer, David Steel, William Heather, William Faden, and Aaron Arrowsmith. The business interests of these players were interlinked in many ways. William Faden had inherited Thomas Jefferys' business, including his position as geographer to the King. He had not, however, acquired Jefferys' stock of sea-charts and plates, which had been purchased from the estate by Robert Sayer.[89] Heather had worked for Moore, David Steel had been an apprentice with Mount

[84] East included his report of *Sayer v Moore* as a footnote to his report of *Cary v Longman*, which is discussed in ch 5.

[85] Worms and Baynton-Williams (n 59) 460–61; Fisher (n 69) 19; 'Obituary', (1807) 77 *Gentleman's Magazine* 1174.

[86] Trinity House had been given a charter by King Henry VIII in 1514 to regulate pilotage of ships in the 'King's streams'. In the seventeenth century it was given further powers over licensing pilots in the Thames, seamarks and ballast age, and lighthouses. See www.trinityhouse.co.uk/about-us and S Tyacke, 'Chartmaking in England and its Context, 1500–1660' in D Woodward (ed), *History of Cartography: Volume 3, Cartography in the European Renaissance Part 2* (Chicago University Press, 2009) 1725.

[87] Fisher (n 69) 19–20.

[88] ibid.

[89] Harley (n 33) 46.

and Page, and Aaron Arrowsmith may have worked for Faden.[90] Their places of business were all located along the Thames, they used the same draughtsmen and engravers, and they sometimes published in partnership.[91] They sold and copied each other's charts and sometimes, as we shall see, they fell out and ended up in court. The first case against Moore was brought by Robert Sayer, the second by Steel, and the third by Heather.

Critical to both the application and interpretation of the law in each of these cases, as well as to their outcomes, was the question of what made a good sea-chart and a growing understanding of the importance of that question for Britain's commercial and imperial ambitions. Britain might rule the waves but this was not due to the accuracy of her sea-charts. Up until the seventeenth century, English mariners, insofar as they used charts at all, relied on hand-drawn maps compiled using French, Portuguese, Dutch, and Spanish materials. The market for printed sea-atlases was dominated by the Dutch, with English translations produced for the English market.[92] Recognising that his lack of knowledge of the English coastline left him vulnerable to attack, Charles II appointed Captain Greenvile Collins to survey the coasts in 1681. Collins noted that he had been commissioned because 'there were no Sea Charts or Maps of these Kingdoms but were Dutch, and Copies from them and those very erroneous'.[93] Samuel Pepys, who was Clerk of the Acts to the Navy, and later held positions in Trinity House and the Admiralty, also complained about the lack of good maps in this period.[94] In 1770 Captain James Cook continued the complaints, writing in his journal that

> it is not [previous navigators] that are wholy to blame for the faultiness of the Charts, but the Compilers and Publishers, who publish to the world the rude Sketches of the Navigator as Accurate surveys, without telling what authority they have for so doing; for were they to do this we should then be as good or better judge than they, and know where to depend upon the Charts, and where not. Neither can I clear Seamen of this fault; among the few I have known who are Capable of drawing a Chart or Sketch of a Sea Coast I have generally, nay, almost always, observed them run into this error. I have known them lay down the line of a Coast they have never seen, and put down Soundings

[90] Fisher ((n 69) 5) describes Arrowsmith as Faden's assistant but Worms and Baynton-Williams are more circumspect: see Worms and Baynton-Williams (n 59) 26.

[91] Fisher (n 69) 5.

[92] Tyacke (n 86) 1722–53; S Fisher, 'The Organisation of Hydrographic Information for English Navigators – Five Hundred Years of Sailing Directions and Charts' (2001) 54 *Journal of Navigation* 157–59; C Verner, 'John Seller and the Chart Trade in Seventeenth-Century England' in NJ Thrower (ed), *The Compleat Plattmaker: Essays on Chart, Map and Globemaking in England in the Seventeenth and Eighteenth Centuries* (University of California Press, 1978).

[93] 'Preface' in G Collins, *Great Britain's Coasting Pilot: The First Part being a New and Exact Survey of the Sea-coast of England from the River of Thames to the Westward with the Islands of Scilly and from thence to Carlile … with Directions for Coming into the Channel between England and France* (London, Freeman Collins, 1693).

[94] JR Tanner (ed), *Samuel Pepys's Naval Minutes*, Publications of the Navy Records Society 60 (London, 1926) 135 as cited in HM Wallis, 'Geography is Better than Divinitie. Maps, Globes and Geography in the Days of Samuel Pepys', in Thrower (ed) (n 92) 1, 18.

where they never have sounded; and, after all, are so fond of their performances as to pass the whole off as Sterling under the Title of a Survey Plan, etc.[95]

Over the course of the seventeenth century, English shipping began to expand rapidly, with the number of ocean-going ships doubling by 1700 and doubling again by 1800 as trade with the East Indies became increasingly important.[96] Parliament attempted to address the situation by establishing the Board of Longitude in 1714, as noted in the previous chapter. However, the Admiralty had no regular surveying service analogous to that provided by the military engineers of the Corps of Ordinance for the Army. Surveys were thus left largely to personal initiatives of pilots, masters, and Trinity House officers, while publication was left to the commercial firms or the authors themselves.[97] The private chartmakers relied on receiving information by returning Navy captains. In numerous editions of his *Practical Navigator*, Moore lamented that it was 'a general Complaint among Seamen, that few Sea Charts are found correct'.[98] He advised them to follow his instructions, which would allow them to make their own corrections to existing charts or even to make new ones. For his own publications, he appears to have been reliant on information garnered from his seagoing contacts to update publications he had copied from elsewhere.

In 1783 Moore published his first map, *A New and Correct Chart of North America from the Island of Belleisle to Cape Cod*[99] (see Figure 9). This was the map that Robert Sayer accused him of copying. At this time, Sayer was considerably more established than Moore in the publishing and printselling business. Of the mid-eighteenth-century chartmakers, only Sayer and Bennett had a sufficiently strong financial position to commission surveys, such as one in 1777 of the Irish Sea from Joseph Huddart, an East India Company captain.[100] They also had the advantage of having purchased the major share of Cook's charts of Newfoundland from Jefferys. Sayer, as we have seen, had already been involved in one copyright dispute involving a map and in two other copyright cases involving engravings, one in the King's Bench and one in the Court of Common Pleas.[101] For this case, Sayer elected to bring his action before the Court of the King's Bench. While Chancery tended to be the forum of choice in copyright-infringement cases, we can only

[95] J Cook, Captain WJL Wharton (ed), *Captain Cook's Journal During his Voyage Round the World made in H M Bark Endeavour 1768–71* (London, Elliott Stock, 1893).

[96] Fisher (n 69) 3; see also DW Waters, 'The English Pilot: English Sailing Directions and Charts and the Rise of English Shipping, 16th to 18th Centuries' (1989) 42 *Journal of Navigation* 317.

[97] An example is the charts of Murdoch Mackenzie, who was ordered by the Admiralty to survey Ireland and the west coast of Britain. His charts were engraved by the commercial mapmaker Emmanuel Bowen and he published them himself in 1776. Hodson (n 18) 777.

[98] J Hamilton Moore, *The Practical Navigator, and Seaman's New Daily Assistant*, 6th edn (London, JH Moore, 1781) 243.

[99] Fisher (n 69) 141.

[100] ibid 56.

[101] See above nn 72, 75.

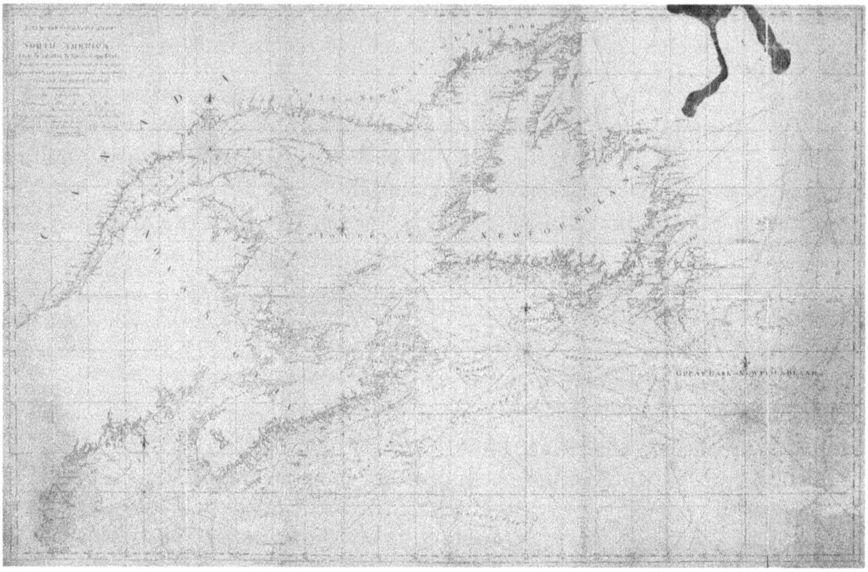

Figure 9 *A new and correct chart of North America from the Island of Belleisle to Cape Cod* (London, JH Moore, 1783) was John Hamilton Moore's first chart and the one that landed him in trouble with Robert Sayer

speculate as to why Sayer chose the King's Bench. It may have been due to the recent passing of the Engravings Act 1777, which meant he could seek damages and double costs of suit (he had had damages awarded against him in the earlier case brought by Watson), or he may have wanted a favourable ruling on a matter of law. He sought the enormous amount of £10,000 in damages.[102]

The case was heard before Lord Mansfield on 28 February 1785 before a 'special jury'; that is, a jury comprised of merchants who would be aware of the commercial aspects of the case.[103] William Mansfield, who sat as Chief Justice of the King's Bench from 1756 to 1788, has been called 'the founder of modern

[102] Estimates of what this sum would be worth today vary depending on the calculation method employed. According to the website www.measuringworth.com, measured as a commodity or real wage, it would amount to £1,276,000 in 2019.

[103] The foreman of the Special Jury, to whom the letter detailing much of our information on the case was written, was James Bogle French. French, a merchant of St Swithin's Lane and slave-owner on Grenada, was involved in the sale of rum to America. See 'Legacies of British Slave-ownership' www.ucl.ac.uk/lbs. For an examination of the different types and development of special juries, see JC Oldham, 'The Origins of the Special Jury' (1983) 50 *The University of Chicago Law Review* 137; JC Oldham, *Trial by Jury: the 7th Amendment and Anglo-American Special Juries* (New York, New York University Press, 2006). For Lord Mansfield's use of special juries comprised of merchants, see JC Oldham, *English Common Law in the Age of Mansfield* (Chapel Hill, University of North Carolina Press, 2004) 20–27.

commercial law'.[104] He too had a history in copyright litigation, having acted as counsel in the most important copyright cases before Chancery, and was well-known for his support of natural law-based arguments in favour of common-law copyright. Sitting on the bench in the famous 1769 case of *Millar v Taylor*, he had sought to cement this doctrine in law, along with the notion that the finite terms in the Statute of Anne did not terminate this common-law right.[105] However, this was ultimately unsuccessful and his ruling was overturned in *Donaldson v Becket*, when the House of Lords voted against its continued existence.[106]

Several witnesses appeared for Sayer, including William Faden, who confirmed that Sayer had purchased Thomas Jefferys' charts of North America at an auction of Jefferys' estate. Two engravers, Delarochette and Winterfelt (or Winterfield), also appeared for Sayer. Delarochette was a well-respected map engraver who often worked with Faden and testified that he had engraved the North American charts for Sayer using the charts from Jefferys but with improvements, and that the whole exercise would have cost Sayer between £3,000 and £4,000. He further expressed his belief that Moore's chart was a copy of Sayer's. Winterfelt gave evidence that he had been employed by Moore to make the copies and stated he had copied the Gulf Passage from Sayer's chart.[107]

Moore, however, produced his own witnesses, drawing on his contacts from the nautical world. Captain John Stephenson[108] appeared and testified that Moore's charts were not the same as Sayer's but were 'essentially different'.[109] Admiral Campbell FRS, the Governor of Newfoundland, and William Wales FRS, an astronomer who had sailed with Cook, also appeared to swear that Sayer's maps were erroneous and dangerous, and that Moore's offered significant improvements over them. Where Sayer's witnesses had focused on the physical act of copying, Moore's concentrated on map content and claimed that his maps were the more accurate. It was this strategy that led to Moore's success. As the judge hearing the case, Lord Mansfield's role was to sum up the evidence to guide the jury and set out the relevant legal principles. Although this was the first case in which the King's Bench had been called upon to apply the Engravings Acts to charts or maps, he

[104] NS Poser, *Lord Mansfield: Justice in the Age of Reason* (Montreal, McGill-Queen's University Press, 2013) 4.

[105] *Millar v Taylor* (1769) 4 Burr 2303, 2398.

[106] *Donaldson v Becket* (1774) 7 Bro PC88; 4 Burr 2408.

[107] *Sayer v Moore* (1785) 1 East 361n, 362n. See also Oldham (n 75) 770–71.

[108] Susanna Fisher states that Captain John Stephenson was a coal trade master and close friend of Moore's who provided him with information on the North Sea and Thames estuary, Fisher (n 69) 21, 24, while *Skelton suggests he was a Royal Navy Master, who had produced a number of charts for both Sayer and Moore; RA Skelton, 'Copyright and Piracy in Eighteenth-Century Chart Publication' (1960) 46 *The Mariner's Mirror* 207, 209. These could be two different career stages for the same man. Some case reports use 'Stephenson', while others use 'Stevenson'. For consistency, this chapter uses only the former, except in references where the original spelling is observed.

[109] 'Extracts from a Letter written to James Bogle French, Esq, Foreman of the Special Jury who tried the Cause in the King's Bench, at Guildhall, between Messrs Sayer and Bennet, Plaintiffs, and Mr John Hamilton Moore' in J Hamilton Moore, *The New Practical Navigator* (London, JH Moore, 1793).

drew on the more extensive law relating to copyright in books and the interpretation of the Statute of Anne. He stated:

> The Act that secures copy-right to authors guards against the piracy of the words and sentiments; but it does not prohibit writing on the same subject … So, in the case of prints, no doubt different men may take engravings from the same picture. The same principle holds with regard to charts; whoever has it in his intention to publish a chart may take advantage of all prior publications.[110]

Summing up the evidence, he observed:

> In deciding we must take care to guard against two extremes equally prejudicial; the one, that men of ability, who have employed their time for the service of the community, may not be deprived of their just merits, and the reward of their ingenuity and labour; the other, that the world may not be deprived of improvements, nor the progress of the arts be retarded … If an erroneous chart be made, God forbid it should not be corrected even in a small degree, if it thereby become more serviceable and useful for the purposes to which it is applied.[111]

Following this instruction, the jury found in favour of Moore and awarded him £37 10s in costs.[112]

However, it was not long before Moore was again a defendant in an infringement case, this time brought by his close neighbour David Steel. Steel operated a book and chart shop, also selling mathematical and navigational instruments, in Little Tower Hill.[113] Steel alleged that Moore had copied *A Chart of the East Coast of England, including the Navigation from the South Foreland to Flamborough Head from the Latest Observations and Survey*, which had been drawn by John Chandler and published by Steel in 1782. He was claiming £3,000 in damages.

Moore employed the same approach to his defence as he had in the case against Sayer. Captain Stephenson again appeared as a witness, alongside James Porteous, master of the royal yacht *Augusta*. Both witnesses pointed out the numerous errors in Steel's charts and attested to the superiority of Moore's. Stephenson claimed he had found 106 differences between Moore's and Steel's charts. He also claimed that the Elder Brethren of Trinity House, to whom Chandler had dedicated his charts, were arguably more culpable than Chandler for the errors as they had not properly examined them before giving their approval. According to the report, the jury would have found in Moore's favour but Steel consented to a nonsuit (which required him to pay Moore's costs). Lord Kenyon declared 'he heartily concurred with the Jury, and expressed his indignation that such erroneous Charts as Mr Steel's should be published'.[114]

[110] *Sayer v Moore*, 361n.
[111] ibid.
[112] KB139/101 f138v.
[113] MM Witt, *A Bibliography of the Works Written and Published by David Steel and His Successors, with Notes on the Lives of David Steel and His Heirs* (London, Anthony & Setitia Simmonds, 1991) 3, 4.
[114] *Steel v Moore* (1789), reported in *The Sunday Gazette* and republished by Moore: 'Extract from the Sunday Gazette of the 8th March 1789', in Moore, *The New Practical Navigator.*

Moore continued to publish his charts as well as other travel texts and, by 1791, was styling himself 'Hydrographer and Chartseller to the Duke of Clarence'.[115] However, it seems he had a knack for upsetting his colleagues. In 1793 an action was brought against him by well-respected London bookseller George Robinson for breaching an agreement Moore and Robinson had made in respect of *The New Practical Navigator*.[116] In 1794 an anonymous broadsheet was circulated that accused him of 'debauching his servant', 'offering to bribe a villain to swear a false debt against her', 'robbing and hiring others to rob the late Mr Robert Sayer', and 'plundering the property of his neighbour Mr Steel'.[117] In that year Moore also fell out with his former assistant William Heather. Having learnt the trade with Moore, Heather had left in 1792 to start his own business. Initially relations between the two were good and Heather printed and sold Moore's charts as well as copies of *The New Practical Navigator*.[118] But things soon soured and, in 1794, Moore brought an action against Heather in the King's Bench seeking recovery of £1,270, which Moore alleged was owed from the time of his employment.

Heather brought a suit in the Court of Chancery, seeking an order to stop the trial pending discovery. In his bill of complaint Heather accused Moore of neglecting his business and being given to intoxication and irregularity. He alleged that Moore had asked him to go into partnership with him but, when he refused, Moore had become angry and threatened to ruin him.[119] Moore eventually responded, explaining he had employed Heather to assist him so that he could continue his work in planning, constructing and laying down charts, writing books on navigation, instructing seamen in navigation, and in making his charts 'more correct and useful than any other charts'.[120] When his wife became ill he had visited her in the country and thus had been forced to leave more of the business in Heather's hands.[121] He insisted that Heather owed him money and, when Heather did not respond, the injunction suspending the action at law was dissolved.[122] No further records relating to the recovery action in the King's Bench have been located.

Two years later, in 1797, Heather brought a second suit in Chancery against Moore, this time for copyright infringement. Heather and his partner William Williams alleged that Moore had pirated *A New and Correct Chart of the Coasts of France Spain & Portugal drawn from the Latest Observations & Surveys by William Heather*, which they had published in 1793 (see Figure 10).[123] The case then moved

[115] See J Hamilton Moore, *The Practical Navigator and Seaman's New Daily Assistant*, 9th edition (London, B Law and Son, GGJ and J Robinson, JH Moore, 1791) title page.

[116] *George Robinson v John Hamilton Moore*, 31 July 1793, *Morning Herald*, 4.

[117] A copy of the broadsheet may be found in the archives of Imray Laurie Norie & Wilson Ltd. Also reproduced in Fisher (n 69) 2.

[118] See entries in the English Short Title Catalogue, estc.bl.uk, and the title page of Moore, *The New Practical Navigator*.

[119] C12/206/24 mm1-2, 26 February 1795. I have not located any documents relating to the King's Bench action.

[120] C12/206/24 mm3-6, 26 February 1795 (UKNA).

[121] ibid.

[122] C33/489 f500v, 20 July 1795 (UKNA).

[123] C12/225/16, C33/496 ff 161, 372, C33/497 f439.

to the King's Bench where it was heard in March 1798 before Lord Kenyon and a special jury of merchants.[124] Now it appeared that Heather had learnt more than chart publishing from Moore and was able to turn his tactics against him. Heather and Williams engaged two leading King's Counsel, Thomas Erskine and William Garrow, as well as a third barrister, George Holroyd. Like Erskine, Garrow was famous for his oratory skills and defence of civil liberties in high-profile cases. John Stephenson appeared again as a witness but this time for Heather. Now Stephenson testified that it was Moore's charts that contained 'several dangerous omissions', which had been remedied in Heather's chart. John Norie, another of Moore's former employees, also gave evidence that Moore's chart was a copy.

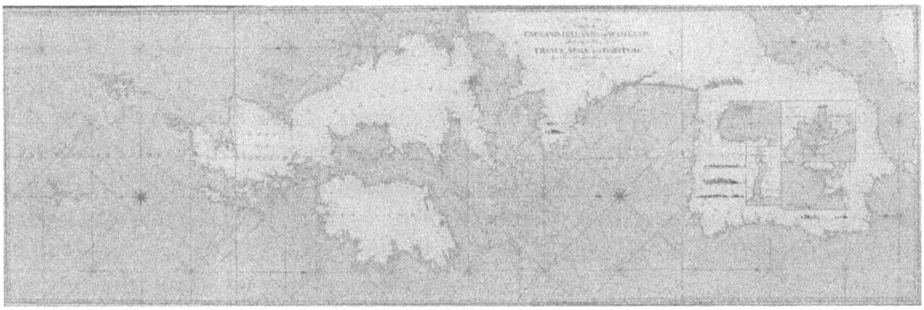

Figure 10 John Heather's *A New and Correct Chart of the Coasts of France Spain & Portugal* (London, J Heather, 1793) was the subject of the third of the copyright infringement cases against John Hamilton Moore in 1797
Image courtesy of the Biblioteca Digital Hispanica, (MR/5/I SERIE 39/15).

Thomas Erskine had served as a midshipman in the navy before turning to the law, an experience which might have sharpened his rhetoric in this particular case. He began by explaining that the policy of the legislation was 'to secure to these different descriptions of persons who had been at great labour and expence, the fruits of their labours, by preventing others for a certain period from copying their works'.[125] He then claimed that the defendant had not even taken the trouble of drawing his own map, let alone collecting any useful information, but had made merely colourable alterations. However, despite having 'minutely copied the Plaintiff's Chart … Mr Moore had, through his negligence, omitted islands, rocks and shoals by wholesale, which omissions rendered his Chart very dangerous, and would often prove fatal to the lives of Mariners'.[126]

[124] *Express and Evening Chronicle*, 1–3 March 1798, 1; *Trial of John Hamilton Moore*.
[125] *Trial of John Hamilton Moore*, 1.
[126] ibid 2.

In his defence, Moore acknowledged that the chart was a copy but denied it belonged to Heather and Williams, claiming he had copied it from his own publications. His witnesses were two engravers, Warner and Chapman, as well as two other witnesses whose occupations are not identified. However, as the *Express and Evening Chronicle* noted, 'their evidence fell far short of proving the alleged fact'.[127] Lord Kenyon was clearly persuaded by Erskine's arguments and the witnesses for the plaintiffs. Observing that 'the face of nature is open to everybody, but no person is permitted to copy another person's property',[128] he instructed the jury that the defendant had clearly copied the plaintiffs' chart. The jury found for the plaintiffs. Although the reports do not record whether any damages were awarded, one claims that the Chancery injunction was lifted and Moore's copperplates were destroyed, as were all the impressions taken from them. Moore also 'refunded' the money for those charts he had sold and paid all the Costs of Suit in Chancery.[129]

The cases against John Hamilton Moore convey the strong impression Moore may have been something of a disruptive influence in a close-knit circle of traders. After losing the case to Heather, his business went downhill. At least twice his maps were blamed for the loss of ships at sea in court martial proceedings. In each case the captain blamed Moore's chart for the wreck of their ships and was consequently exonerated.[130] He seems to have also spent some time in the Marshalsea for a debt owed to his shopman George Woulfe.[131] Then he lost his sight following an illness and became embroiled in a dispute with his son-in-law, Robert Blachford.[132] Moore was declared bankrupt on 1 August 1806 and died in Essex on 30 October 1807.[133] Yet, despite all this conflict, we can still discern traces of cooperation and interdependence between these chartmaking neighbours. Notwithstanding their legal disputes, William Heather left legacies to Moore's two 'natural or reputed daughters' (one of whom had married Blachford) upon his death in 1812.[134] Heather's business was purchased by John Norie (who had also worked for Moore and appeared as Heather's witness in the copyright suit) with George Wilson. Norie also purchased Steel's business in 1819. Robert Sayer's business continued to flourish. He served on the court of the Stationers' Company but declined the position of Master and he was able to purchase a large country house in Richmond in 1776.[135] He died a very wealthy man in 1794 at the age of 65. On his death he was succeeded in business by his assistants Robert Laurie

[127] ibid 1.
[128] ibid 4.
[129] ibid 5.
[130] ADM1/5355 (27 December 1800), ADM1/5369 (17 April 1805) (UKNA).
[131] IND1/6289 (UKNA).
[132] Blachford claimed the two went into a partnership which was later dissolved; Moore maintained he was taken advantage of and tricked: C13/51/11, C13/487/49 (UKNA).
[133] Worms & Baynton-Williams (n 59) 461.
[134] Fisher (n 69) 82.
[135] ibid 58.

and James Whittle.[136] Eventually, in 1904, the four firms founded by Moore, Sayer, Steel, and Heather merged to form Imray Laurie Norie & Wilson Ltd.[137]

Alongside their revelations of intricate personal relationships, the cases also reveal a complex interplay between copyright law and Enlightenment ideals surrounding scientific mapmaking and the expansion of knowledge, as well as the need for more accurate charts to carry on commerce, war and empire, and trade competition. As noted at the start of this chapter, map titles of the eighteenth century almost always carried claims of being 'new and accurate', 'new and exact', and so on. As Pedley has explained, this rhetoric was an important advertising tool.[138] Moreover, by including such statements, mapmakers were also participating in the broader Enlightenment discourse of knowledge production and validation. Ascertaining the authority under which a map was made was increasingly important but all the more so in the case of shipping, where chart accuracy was a matter of life or death. As Murdoch Mackenzie wrote in his 1774 *Treatise of Maritime Surveying*:

> Wherever the Safety of Shipping is concerned, the Public has a Right to some Satisfaction with respect to the Nature and Grounds of the Publication. It is not sufficient to say in the Title, that it is an actual Survey; or a new and accurate Survey: it ought to be accompanied with, at least, a short Account of the fundamental Operations, and Manner in which the Survey was conducted.[139]

One way of establishing this authority was to provide a geographical memoir to accompany a map.[140] Another was to incorporate statements on the map itself, as David Steel did on his *Chart of the East Coast of England*. That chart contained a statement that it had been 'honoured with the Approbation of the Right Honourable Master, Wardens and Elder Brethren of the Trinity House'.[141] A third, which emerges in the three cases against Moore, was the courtroom.

In these cases, we can discern two practices in relation to claims of accuracy and authority: first is the use of such claims being deployed to escape a charge of infringement; second is the courtroom itself becoming another venue in which the map's authority is established. Relevant to the first of these were questions of projection, scale, and conformity with Enlightenment mathematical principles, as well as the authority of the witnesses. In *Sayer v Moore* Captain John Stephenson explained that the errors arose in Sayer's map because of a failure of projection: while the latitudes and longitudes had been taken from the same authorities as Moore had used, the erroneous principles upon which Sayer's map was based meant that the course and distance between places was incorrect on his charts.

[136] PROB 11/1242/92 (UKNA).

[137] The firm is now based in St Ives, Cambridgeshire, where it continues to produce sailing charts in paper and digital form: See www.imray.com. See ch 7 for the histories of the various mergers.

[138] Pedley (n 16) 188.

[139] ibid 188–89.

[140] Edney (n 67) 186–90.

[141] Chandler, *Chart of the East Coast of England.*

Stephenson explained that Moore's maps 'were constructed upon the true principles of Mercator's sailing; but Mr Sayer's were neither Plane nor Mercator's Charts: they were contrary to every received principle of geography and navigation, and consequently erroneous'.[142]

A second authoritative witness was William Wales, a Fellow of the Royal Society and Master of the Royal Mathematical School in Christ's Hospital, who had sailed on the *Resolution* with Cook.[143] Wales agreed with Stephenson, adding that the latitudes and longitudes of the two maps differed, particularly in the West Indies. The third witness, Admiral Campbell, went further still, explicitly linking the production of accurate maps to national pride in an imperial context. Campbell, who had introduced Cook to the Royal Society, stated that when he had examined Sayer's charts

> at his station in Newfoundland, he was grieved for the honour of his country, that such a publication should originate in England, and often wished to have had the power of suppressing it entirely, by burning all the Charts, and destroying the plates'.[144]

In *Steel v Moore* Stephenson appeared again, offering to point out 106 places where errors in Steel's chart were corrected in Moore's. James Porteous, Moore's second witness, gave evidence so compelling that Steel's counsel agreed to be nonsuited and Lord Kenyon was moved to express his own indignation at Steel's temerity in publishing such poor-quality charts.[145]

By making a finding of non-infringement on the basis that one map did not simply copy but also improved another, the court gave the imprimatur of scientific and navigational superiority to one of the publications in dispute. The participants then ensured that this message was amplified beyond the legal sphere. Moore began by inserting short descriptions of the *Sayer v Moore* and *Steel v Moore* cases in the ninth edition of *The Practical Navigator*.[146] Two years later in *The New Practical Navigator*, he published much more detailed descriptions of both cases. In the case of the former, he included a letter which Mr Stephenson was said to have written to the foreman of the jury, itself in response to a paragraph in the *Public Ledger* (which I have been unable to locate).[147] In the same volume, Moore also published a report of *Steel v Moore*, which was extracted from the *Sunday Gazette*.[148] Unsurprisingly, Moore did not publish a report of *Heather v Moore* but a pamphlet containing a report of the case was published, with only the printer identified.[149] It is probably not too fanciful to suppose that Heather was involved.

[142] Moore (n 109).
[143] EI Carlyle, 'Wales, William' (*bap.* 1734, *d.* 1798) in *Oxford Dictionary of National Biography*, Rev D Howse, (Oxford, Oxford University Press, 2004). www.oxforddnb.com.rp.nla.gov.au/view/article/28457.
[144] ibid.
[145] 'Extract from the Sunday Gazette of the 8th of March, 1789'.
[146] Moore (n 115).
[147] ibid.
[148] ibid.
[149] *Trial of John Hamilton Moore.*

These reports were far from neutral; each emphasised the qualifications of the witnesses in favour of their own arguments and each minimised or ignored the credentials of those on the other side. For example, in *Steel v Moore* Captain Stephenson was prevented from giving all his evidence (the court apparently satisfied with not hearing details of each of the 106 errors he had located), yet the extract makes some amends for the lack by enumerating several of them. The pamphlet published following Heather's victory also follows its report of the case with five additional pages of evidence of the errors in Moore's map and finishes with a final rhetorical flourish:

> In short, the omissions and errors in Mr. Moore's Chart are so numerous, and several of them so exceedingly dangerous, that the negligence of the Engraver, and the inattention of the Publisher, must excite the indignation of every one, who properly regards the safety of our valuable Shipping, our extensive Commerce, and our inestimable Seamen![150]

These publications therefore performed a similar role to geographical memoirs by providing an account of the charts' production, as well as a validation of other textual claims made upon the chart as to their authority, accuracy, and superiority. In this way the court and the law of copyright were pressed into service as a badge of legitimacy attached to the geographic outputs of the mapmaker himself.

V. Thresholds of Protection and Infringement: The Case of *Faden v Stockdale* (1797)

The final case this chapter considers involved a dispute between William Faden and the publisher and bookseller John Stockdale. Faden had been a witness for leading print and mapseller Robert Sayer in his action against Moore; now he appeared as plaintiff in his own right. Born in London in 1749, Faden had been apprenticed to a decorative and jobbing engraver before setting up in partnership with Thomas Jefferys' son, Thomas Jefferys the younger, in the St Martin's Lane premises of Jefferys the elder in 1773.[151] The partnership was dissolved in 1776 but, in 1783, Faden received the title of Geographer in Ordinary to the King, Thomas Jefferys the younger having surrendered it in his favour. Soon Faden was one of the most commercially successful mapmakers in London, competing with Robert Sayer (although also, as the litigation just mentioned demonstrates, collaborating at times).[152] For Laurence Worms, Faden was in the vanguard of a new, modern breed of mapmakers, committed to importing the best maps from abroad and investing in engraving and publishing new surveys of the British Isles.

[150] ibid, 8.
[151] Worms (n 23) 5, 8.
[152] ibid 8, 10.

An active member of the Smeatonian Society of Civil Engineers, he was also the engraver and printer for the plans of their schemes involving canals, harbour improvements, dock improvements, and the like.[153]

The map that led to the legal action, however, was a map of the island of Saint Domingo. Faden accused the bookseller John Stockdale of publishing a copy of the former's map in Bryan Edwards's book *An Historical Survey of the French Colony in the Island of Saint Domingo*. This was a map capturing a topic of considerable contemporary interest and one in which Faden had made significant investment according to his legal complaint. Saint Domingo (now Haiti) was one of the most prosperous of the West Indies colonies. It had been colonised by both the Spanish and the French, who had introduced slavery to increase agricultural production, and was Europe's main source of both coffee and sugar. In 1791 reports began to arrive in Britain that the slaves were rebelling against their conditions and seeking an end to slavery on the island.[154] The price of sugar skyrocketed, leading to public indignation, and the debate over abolition intensified. William Wilberforce wrote: 'People here are all panic-struck with the transactions in St. Domingo' and feared that the insurrection would spread to British colonies.[155] A pamphlet war broke out in 1792 in which Saint Domingo featured prominently and in 1793 the British sent troops to conquer the colony and restore slavery. Mortality was astronomically high and in May 1797 a debate was forced in Parliament over withdrawing troops.[156] One prominent speaker was Bryan Edwards, a Jamaican slave owner, member of parliament, and anti-abolitionist.[157] Edwards had already made his views known through the *Historical Survey*, which Stockdale had published months before. While some attacked the *Historical Survey*, in other quarters it was welcomed; Edwards became a respected authority on the topic and the book was frequently reprinted.[158]

Faden had published his map of Saint Domingo in 1796, (see Figure 11) and he complained that the map Stockdale had included in Edwards's book to provide the by-now expected geographical context for his polemic was a brazen copy (see Figure 12). Faden was not going to let this pass uncontested. In his bill of complaint to the Court of Chancery, Faden claimed that in 1794 he had employed 'several persons to assist him in compiling and drawing the same from the best authorities engraving the same at a considerable Expense'. He explained he later procured better materials on the Spanish part of the island and so made corrections and improvements to the earlier map. Stockdale then approached

[153] ibid 9, 10.
[154] D Geggus, 'British Opinion and the Emergence of Haiti, 1791–1805' in J Walvin (ed), *Slavery and British Society 1776–1846* (London: Macmillan Education UK, 1982) 123.
[155] ibid 124–25.
[156] ibid 128.
[157] RB Sheridan, 'Edwards, Bryan (1743–1800), Planter and Politician', *Oxford Dictionary of National Biography* (online) 23 September 2004, www-oxforddnb-com.rp.nla.gov.au/view/10.1093/ref:odnb/9780198614128.001.0001/odnb-9780198614128-e-8531.
[158] Geggus (n 154) 129.

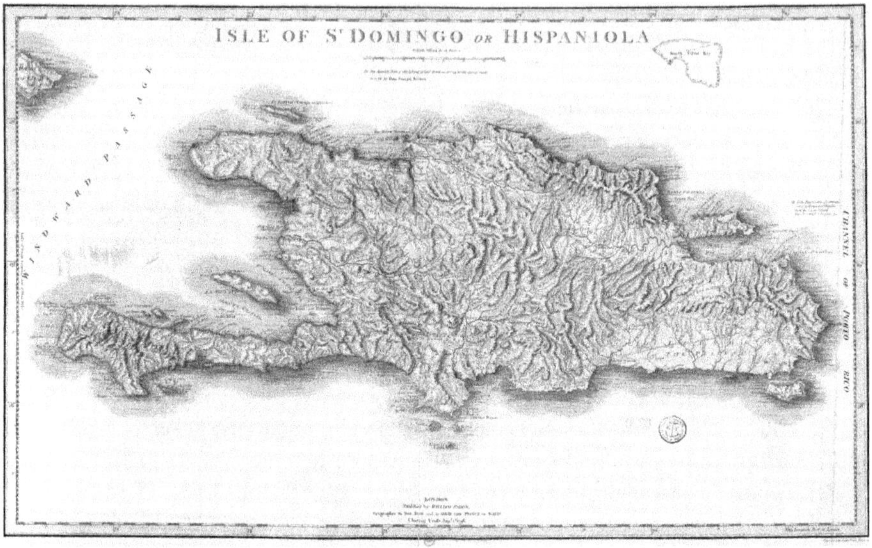

Figure 11 William Faden's *Isle of St Domingo or Hispaniola* (London, Faden, engraved by John Cooke, 1796) measured 760 × 480mm, too large to be easily tipped into a book
Image courtesy of the Bibliotèque National de France (ark:/12148/cb406333836).

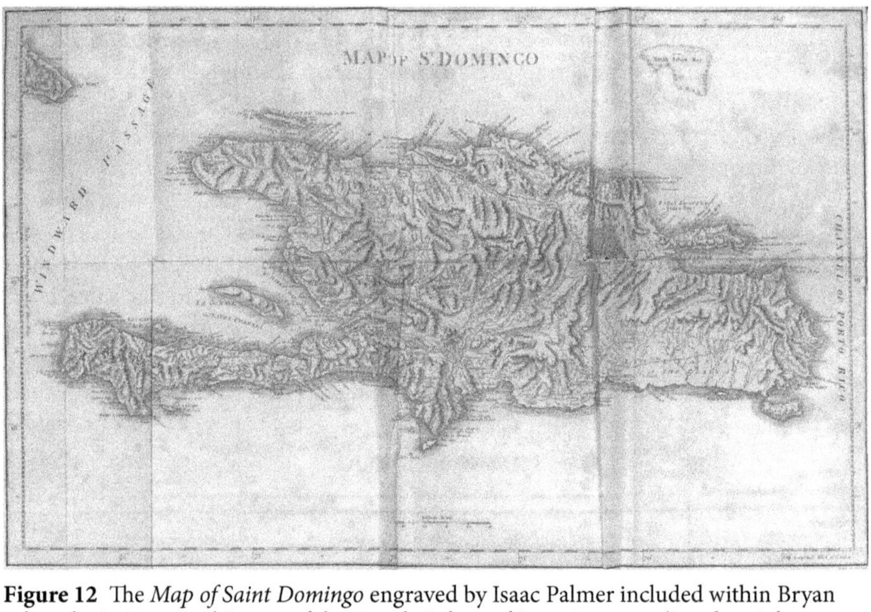

Figure 12 The *Map of Saint Domingo* engraved by Isaac Palmer included within Bryan Edwards *An Historical Survey of the French Colony of Saint Domingo* (London, John Stockdale, 1797)
Image courtesy of General Collection, Beinecke Rare Book and Manuscript Library (CF 1921 E38).

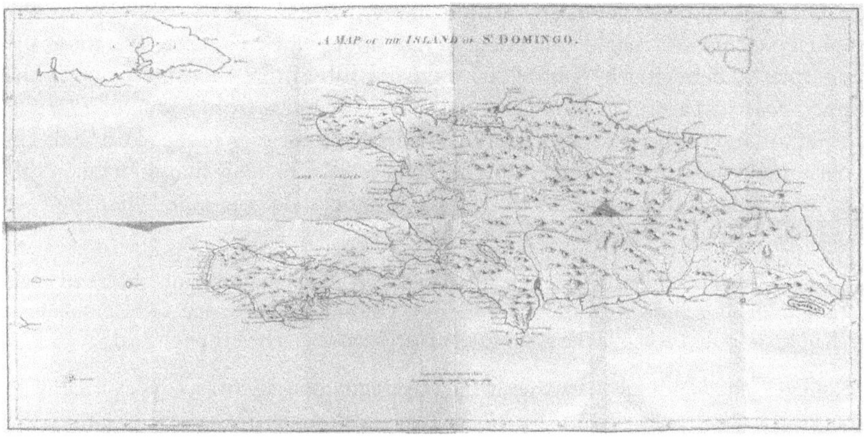

Figure 13 In the 1801 edition of Bryan Edwards, *An Historical Survey of the French Colony of Saint Domingo* (London, John Stockdale, 1801), Stockdale replaced the copy of Faden's detailed map with a much simpler version that could not be mistaken for a copy
Image courtesy of General Collection, Beinecke Rare Book and Manuscript Library (CF 1921 E38 1801).

him, asking to purchase the copperplates but he had declined, only later to find Stockdale had inserted a copy of the map into his book and refused to remove it.[159] Faden asked the court to order Stockdale to deliver up to Faden the copperplate to be destroyed, together with all remaining copies or impressions of the map and an injunction restraining Stockdale from selling any further copies of the map 'or any thing of the like Nature or kind of upon any such or the like plan'.[160] Faden also produced an affidavit to the same effect and was joined in the affidavit by the engraver Isaac Palmer. Palmer deposed that in December 1795 he had been approached by Stockdale to engrave a map of Saint Domingo Island which would be bound up and published in the *Historical Survey*. Stockdale had then delivered to him a drawing 'which was an Outline upon a reduced Scale and from a printed Impression of the Map of the said Island of Saint Domingo published by the said other Deponent William Faden' which Stockdale gave to him 'with Directions to copy the Names and finish the Plan Work from it'.[161]

The injunction was granted to last until Stockdale made his answer,[162] which he did on 16 May 1797.[163] Stockdale responded by claiming Faden was not the original inventor of the map, as the latter claimed, but that he had copied it at small expense from another map called the *Saint Domingo Pilot*, as well as other

[159] Complaint of Faden, C12/672/12 m1, 3 May 1797 (UKNA).
[160] ibid.
[161] C31/283 f2, 3 May 1797 (UKNA).
[162] C33/496 f321v, 3 May 1797 (UKNA).
[163] C12/672/12 m2, 16 May 1797 (UKNA).

foreign maps, and not from any actual survey made by the complainant or any employee of his. Stockdale conceded he had approached Faden to purchase the copperplates, believing he would sell them for little more than the price of the copper, based on a similar purchase he had recently made from Faden of a map of the Netherlands. Stockdale also admitted he had taken Faden's map to an 'eminent geographer', who drew up a copy on a reduced scale. Stockdale had then taken this copy to Palmer and asked him to engrave it. Stockdale contended that the case should be dismissed because

> he had an equal Right to have the said Map drawn and engraved upon a reduced Scale and to publish and sell the same for his own Use and benefit as the said Complainant had to draw and compile the same from other Maps then already published.[164]

He alleged that Faden's map was 'very erroneous and incorrect', presumably in an appeal to the reasoning in the *Moore* cases, although, in the case of a map not intended for navigation or any kind of wayfinding, it is hard to see the argument having any force.[165]

On 25 July 1798, the Master of the Rolls heard oral argument and ordered Faden to bring an action at law against Stockdale for what he claimed was due to him within three months and stated the injunction would stand while he did so.[166] On 23 February 1799, Faden brought his case before the King's Bench. According to the *London Chronicle*, after examining his first witness, Faden proposed the case be halted and that he would accept one shilling in damages, 'which, after some conversation, took place'.[167] Having succeeded at law, Faden was entitled to a permanent injunction and, when Stockdale published a second edition of the book in 1801, he used a different, much less detailed map of the island (see Figure 13).

The facts as claimed by the parties do not entirely explain their behaviour. While it is easy to see why Stockdale would have wanted to publish Edwards's book and to include a map, it is less clear why he wanted to purchase the copperplates from Faden. Stockdale explained he did so to save himself the expense of having new plates engraved but Faden's map was too large to be easily tipped into a book. Even the reduced map had to be folded several times to fit. Perhaps Stockdale underestimated the ongoing market Faden envisaged for the map, making him reluctant to offload the copperplates on the cheap. Stockdale's decision to get new plates engraved at a reduced scale posed a new problem for the nascent law of copyright. Faden was clearly concerned by this, as he emphasised in his complaint that 'the circumstances of its being reduced to a smaller scale makes no difference to the Identity of the said Map'.[168] Stockdale's response to this was to argue that his

[164] ibid.
[165] C12/672/12 m 1, 16 May 1797 (UKNA).
[166] C33/504/107v-108r, 25 July 1797 (UKNA).
[167] *London Chronicle*, 26–28 February 1799, 202; *Morning Herald*, 25 February 1799, 3.
[168] C12/672/12 m1 (UKNA).

use of Faden's map was no different from what Faden had done when he compiled his map from a variety of existing published sources. Stockdale argued that Faden could not claim ownership as 'inventor' of the map unless he himself had made a survey or commissioned one. Faden, however, had made no such claim, merely saying that he had 'formed a resolution to compile and publish' the map and that he 'employed several persons to assist him in compiling and drawing the same from the best authorities'.[169]

The dispute, therefore, again raised the question of how different a second map had to be from its source in order to escape a finding of infringement, as well as the threshold question of what one had to do in order to create a map that would be protected by copyright. It seems the Master of the Rolls did not accept Stockdale's claim that a new survey was required, as he continued the injunction and seemed to believe Faden would succeed in his case at law. Before the King's Bench, the signs of success must have been sufficiently in Faden's favour for Stockdale to settle the case. Thus, despite not giving rise to a reasoned, reported judgment, this dispute did result in development of the law through the court's tacit acceptance that a map drawn on a different scale could amount to an infringement (in a case where there was no claim of improvement) and confirmed again that a mapmaker did not have to create the map from an entirely new survey in order to be considered its owner under the Engravings Acts.

VI. Conclusion

The enactment of the Engravings Acts had a significant impact upon the eighteenth-century London map trade. The legal records created by disputes between mapmakers reveal them grappling to understand how this new legal regime would impact their trade and looking for ways to shape that law to achieve a competitive edge and good commercial outcome. This was a period of transformation for the trade, as mapmakers sought to rely less on outdated reprints and to invest in new surveys and the new, 'scientific', approach to knowledge generation and circulation, which formed such an essential element of Enlightenment thought. Copyright played its own role in this transformation. Maps were still expensive, labour-intensive commodities to produce. Following from the decision in *Jefferys v Baldwin*, discussed in the previous chapter, and consolidated in *Jefferys v Bowles*, the property right that the Engravings Acts created could be held by the mapmaker who brought together the labour and provided the materials and technologies necessary for their production. As the eighteenth century gave way to the nineteenth, publishing partnerships of the kind we saw in the case of

[169] C12/672/12 m1 (UKNA).

Bowles v Sayer began to decline and print and plate stocks began to be consolidated into fewer hands.[170] It seems likely that copyright law played a role in this shift by offering security external to trade custom and partnerships. It might also have encouraged investment in the acquisition of new data through surveys by its explicit recognition that property rights would result in the output. While the longer-term effects of the law may be more speculative, it is clear from the disputes examined that copyright law was quickly seen by mapmakers as a useful new tool to help regulate the circulation of these commodities within the market.

Copyright law was also useful in helping to establish the authority of the map. One way it achieved this was through the publication line. As discussed in chapter two mapmakers had long used the granting of a royal privilege to lend authority to their maps. Following the passing of the Engravings Acts, maps increasingly featured a publication line such as 'Published as the Act directs' or words to that effect, with the name of the mapmaker and the date. While this was a statutory requirement, it also operated as a form of authority, proclaiming the map's protected status under the law. Following his dispute with Bowles over the map games, we saw Jefferys use the publication line to offer a warning to would-be copiers. Another way of using copyright to establish the authority of the map was on display in the sea-chart cases. By including their own reports of the legal proceedings within their publications, in particular the testimony of the authoritative, 'scientific' witnesses, Moore and Heather were able to deploy the law of copyright as a badge of authority attached to the product itself. To borrow the phrase of David Livingstone, the courtroom came to be another 'venue of science'; that is, a site in which scientific meaning is made and interpreted.[171] And the effects went beyond the specific maps in issue, with the cases helping to consolidate 'the map' as a category of material object with specific characteristics, chief amongst which being its claim to authority through its scientific features and mathematical accuracy. Although each map was different, with a different purpose and audience, the law considered them all to fall within the same legal regime and the same category within that regime.

This is not to say that the application of copyright law to maps was in any way settled or clear during this period. Indeed, the characterisation of maps as objective, scientific representations of the world sat in some tension with the idea that they could be the object of a proprietary right. Much ink had been spilled on the question of quite how property could arise in ideas, words, and letters during the literary property debates of the mid-eighteenth century.[172] The map cases resolved this tension by emphasising the labour and expense of producing useful maps and, in particular, charts and characterising those who copied them as unfairly

[170] Pedley (n 16) 196.

[171] DN Livingstone, *Putting Science in its Place: Geographies of Scientific Knowledge* (Chicago, University of Chicago Press, 2003).

[172] For a detailed discussion of the cases and argument which comprised the 'literary property debates' see the works cited in n 25. For an analysis of how the law and legal thinkers grappled with the concept

free-riding on that labour. As Thomas Erskine explained to the jury in *Heather v Moore*, the law's policy was to secure to 'persons who had been at great labour and expence, the fruits of their labour, by preventing others for a certain period from copying their works'.[173]

The perhaps more difficult tension was how to reconcile protecting the exchange value of one map over the use value of its competitor. This was captured in Lord Mansfield's famous warning in *Sayer v Moore* that it was necessary to 'guard against two extremes equally prejudicial', namely, failing to reward 'ingenuity and labour' or depriving the world of 'improvements' and 'the progress of the arts'.[174]

In the case of *Heather v Moore*, Thomas Erskine fleshed this out more fully in argument. The reason that a monopoly could subsist in such a thing as a chart, despite it not being entirely original or new, was, according to Erskine, because charts had at last reached 'that state of perfection which enables the Navigator to go with safety from one part of the world to another'.[175] This had been achieved because 'various persons have contributed to fill up the measure of human knowledge, for the benefit of mankind, by inserting their discoveries, and adding something to that which was known before'.[176] Indeed, it was this very perfection which led to charts being copied. As Erskine explained:

> It was impossible for a man to make a Chart of the British Channel, and not to place the Capes and Promontories as they had been before; Ireland lay West of England, and Scotland North of England; but the great perfection and utility of Charts consisted in their accuracy, in having every place which appeared on them placed in its exact latitude and longitude, and in pointing out to the Navigator every danger which ought to be avoided. A Chart was not the work of fancy, and if a man, by way of being ingenious, should take it into his head to make a Chart, placing Ireland East of England, and Land's-end where Berwick now stands, he would be in no great danger of having his right to such a Chart invaded.[177]

Here Erskine achieved two rhetorical ploys that would continue to impact on copyright law both as applied to maps and more generally. First, he deployed Enlightenment reasoning to depict a 'good' map as being objective and neutral, fashioned by science rather than fallible humans. Second, he sought to align copyright law with Enlightenment values in relation to the progress of knowledge, as well as serving the demands of empire and mercantilism. It is also apparent that the judges involved in the three cases, Lord Kenyon and Lord Mansfield, seem to have conceived of their roles as interpreting the law in a way which would

of intangible property in these debates, see B Sherman and L Bently, *The Making of Modern Intellectual Property Law* (Cambridge, Cambridge University Press, 1999).

[173] ibid.

[174] *Sayer v Moore*, 361n.

[175] *Trial of John Hamilton Moore*, 2.

[176] ibid.

[177] ibid.

further Enlightenment ideology, in particular scientific accuracy, as well as British commercial and imperial interests. Lord Mansfield began his directions to the jury with the portentous announcement that: 'The rule of decision in this case is a matter of great consequence to the country'.[178] He clearly envisaged his task as one of finding a solution that would foster 'improvements', 'progress of the arts', and the usefulness of knowledge. Lord Kenyon likewise saw clear links between these ideals and outcome of the cases before him, and he sought to influence the jury to reach a verdict that favoured accuracy by focusing on the evidence relating to navigational science. Thus, in each case, the legal decision as to whether copyright was infringed was informed by an assessment of who had produced the 'better' map – and better meant more accurate, more scientific in appearance, more in tune with Enlightenment ideology, and more useful to the commercial and military needs of the expanding empire.

[178] *Sayer v Moore*, 361n.

5

Legal Highways and Byways: Road Books in Court

I. Introduction

This chapter focuses on a specific geographical genre – the road book – and a series of cases that arose over unauthorised copying in the last decades of the eighteenth century in Scotland and England.[1] The road book was the predecessor of the road atlas. The earliest versions consisted only of written itineraries rather than maps but, by the eighteenth century they were coming to include both. In fact, it is the relationship between written description of a route and its graphic representation that make the disputes over these publications of particular interest. Eighteenth-century traders, litigants, and members of the public were divided as to whether this was the same information being presented in different ways and, if so, what that meant when it was copied. Some claimed that the use of copyright to restrict the flow of lists of places and distances was absurd, even dangerous. But the information was expensive to acquire and maintain. With growing numbers of business and leisure travellers upon the road, this information was more in demand than ever and road books were valuable and useful commodities. Legal disputes were inevitable.

This chapter starts by setting out a brief history of the road book genre before turning to the first dispute, which arose in Scotland over Taylor and Skinner's *Maps of the Roads of North Britain* published in 1775. It then looks at a series of cases that occurred in England several years later and involved, directly or indirectly, the market-leading publications, *Paterson's Roads* and *Cary's British Itinerary*. It explores the difficulties experienced by contemporaries in explaining how copyright could arise in geographical facts and identifies the reliance on the concept of labour – both physical and mental – that we witnessed in earlier chapters, as well as its limits. It also notes that, in seeking to disseminate the same information in different formats (visual and textual) and market offerings (different sizes and prices), book and mapsellers were starting to identify the value of the information itself as opposed to simply the material form in which it was offered on the market.

[1] Material in this chapter was included in I Alexander, '"Manacles Upon Science": Re-evaluating Copyright in Informational Works in Light of 18th Century Case Law' (2014) 38 *Melbourne University Law Review* 317 and I Alexander, 'The Legal Journey of Paterson's Roads' (2015) 67 *Imago Mundi* 12.

This required them to insist upon an identity between graphic depictions of those facts (maps) and textual ones (lists of distances and roads), which was not always readily accepted. Finally, it observes the moulding of copyright law to achieve a balance between protecting the investment of those who first placed the information on the market, and the need to keep that information flowing to generate more economic value.

The eighteenth century witnessed a 'transport revolution', in which passenger travel speed increased, freight charges dropped, and road traffic grew.[2] Where the maps and charts discussed in previous chapters engaged matters of national identity and Enlightenment concerns with knowledge, learning, and progress, the road books discussed in this chapter were seen as still more directly instrumental in their usefulness to road users by those who wrote and published them. Improved roads and transport meant more goods could be exchanged using them, with positive effects on the domestic economy, and fostered a market for information about those roads. And it was not just goods or people that were transported by road, but also the post, which included newspapers, orders, invoices, banknotes, and market information.[3] Just as the roads were conduits of information circulation, so too were the road books that informed the public about them. At the same time, as we shall see, the discourse surrounding road books and their claims to mathematical, measured accuracy continued to draw on Enlightenment ideals.

II. Starting the Journey: The History of Road Books

In medieval and early modern times, those who wished to travel to an unfamiliar location by land relied on written itineraries rather than maps. At first produced in manuscript form, from the sixteenth century printed itineraries began to appear, although the earliest of these were not free-standing publications but generally attached to books on other subjects such as chronicles and almanacs.[4] As discussed in chapter two, in the 1670s, with the support of members of the Royal Society, John Ogilby sent out surveyors to map the roads of Britain, armed only with a perambulator (or waywiser) to measure distances and a surveyor's compass or theodolite to measure changes in direction. In 1675, Ogilby published his groundbreaking *Britannia*, which provided the most up to date and accurate highway information yet available. Significantly, it also made consistent use of measurement

[2] See E Pawson, *Transport and Economy: The Turnpike Roads of Eighteenth-Century Britain* (London, Academic Press, 1977).

[3] T Barker and D Gerhold, *The rise and rise of road transport, 1700–1990* (Cambridge, Cambridge University Press, 1993) 42.

[4] See D Hodson, 'The Early Printed Road Books and Itineraries of England and Wales' (PhD Thesis, University of Exeter, 2000) 20–1.

of 1,760 feet to the mile (later, the statute mile). Although the volume represented only a small part of a much larger global cartographical project (which Ogilby had had to abandon due to lack of funds and perhaps energy), it was the first road atlas in Great Britain and, therefore, the foundation publication of an enduring cartographic genre.[5]

It is highly unlikely that the book in its entirety was ever taken on the road, given that it weighed nearly seven kilograms.[6] The evocative strip maps were not, however, the only way that Ogilby presented his newly acquired data. Each plate was followed by a leaf of text containing additional information of use to the traveller, including a table of measured and computed distances between principal towns along the road, and a wealth of data such as road quality, rivers crossed, turnings, signposts, coach stages, market and fair days, inns and accommodations, and short topographical and historical observations of major towns and cities.[7] He also produced a *New Map of the Kingdom of England and Dominion of Wales. Wherreon are Projected all ye Principal Roads Actually Measured and Delineated* which was published with the *Britannia* in 1675.[8] In 1676 Ogilby published a slightly abridged version of the work, *Itinerarium Angliae*, which removed most of the letterpress. This was presumably aimed at those who wanted the engraved plates of the roads but without the hefty price tag.[9]

Ogilby's geographic information was almost immediately copied by London booksellers Thomas Bassett and Richard Chiswell, who converted the maps into typographic word maps which arranged the place names in order and in their approximate direction upon an imaginary map of England and Wales.[10] Copies of these maps were inserted into Speed's *Theatre of the Empire of Great Britain* and also bound in a pocket volume called *The English Travellers Companion*.[11] As noted in chapter two, Ogilby complained to the Secretary of State about this copying but also responded in the marketplace, producing his own typographical road maps, although without the orientational accuracy, in 1676.[12] In that same year, he and Morgan also published *Mr Ogilby's Tables of his Measur'd Roads*. This publication was squarely aimed at the traveller as it contained the tables of roads and distances, as well as market days and fairs. This work, as well as the typographical road maps, were clearly designed to meet Bassett and Chiswell in the market; as

[5] JB Harley, 'Introduction' in J Ogilby, *Britannia: John Ogilby, London 1675* (Theatrum Orbis Terrarum, 1970) v, xv.

[6] C Delano-Smith and RJP Kain, *English Maps: A History* (London, The British Library, 1999) 169.

[7] Hodson (n 4) 442.

[8] C Delano-Smith, 'Milieus of Mobility: Itineraries, Route Maps and Road Maps' in JR Akerman (ed), *Cartographies of Travel and Navigation* (Chicago, University of Chicago Press, 2006) 61.

[9] Hodson (n 4) 484.

[10] ibid 506.

[11] *The English Travellers Companion* (London, Thomas Bassett and Richard Chiswell, 1676). An example of one of the sheets bound up with the 1767 edition of Speed's *Theatre of the Empire of Great Britain* can be found in Delano-Smith (n 8) fig 2.11, 42.

[12] Hodson (n 4) 497–503.

the advertisement after the title page explained, Ogilby had been compelled to publish first the two works

> to prevent the Injury design'd Him and the Kingdom, by the Publishers of certain Tables stolen out of his Book (so ignorantly and carelessly Collected & Printed, that they are fill'd with false Computations and Distances; often sending the Traveller 10 or 20 Mile out of the Way).[13]

By its fourth impression in 1689, the *Tables* was being published as *Mr Ogilby's and William Morgan's Pocket Book of Roads.*[14] It eventually ran to 24 editions, the final one appearing in 1794.[15]

By the early eighteenth century, several mapmakers and booksellers were copying Ogilby's strip map format and adapting it to create their own pocket-sized editions, with added letterpress. The most popular of these was Emanuel Bowen's *Britannia Depicta or Ogilby Improved*, first published in 1720.[16] Other such works included *Bowles' Post-Chaise Travelling Companion; or, Traveller's Directory Through England and Wales*[17] and *Kitchin's Post-Chaise Companion, Through England and Wales.*[18] It was thus apparent from the time of Ogilby that survey data of the roads was highly valued and sought after in a range of formats. It would be another 100 years until the data was comprehensively updated in England and, unlike in the time of Ogilby, unauthorised copying would then lead to litigation. Before describing the cases that arose in England, however, we turn to examine a road book dispute that occurred a few years earlier in Scotland.

[13] ibid 506.

[14] J Ogilby and W Morgan, *Mr Ogilby's and William Morgan's Pocket Book of the Roads, with their Computed and Measured Distances … the Fourth Impression. To which is added several Roads … With a Table for the ready finding any Road, City, or Market-Town, and their Distance from London. And a Sheet Map of England … By William Morgan, Cosmographer to their Majesties* (London, Printed for the Author, and Christopher Wilkinson, 1689). For details of this and subsequent editions, see HG Fordham, *John Ogilby (1600–1676), His Britannia, and the British Itineraries of the Eighteenth Century* (London, Oxford University Press, 1925) 168–74.

[15] Hodson (n 4) 506.

[16] Bowen published it with Thomas Bowles, and Bowen's share was taken over by Thomas's brother John. Carington Bowles acquired his uncle Thomas's share, presumably after his death, when John purchased Thomas's business for his son Carington (I learnt of John's purchase of Thomas's business through the personal notes of Michael Treadwell). Carington Bowles published a new edition in 1764: *Britannia Depicta, or, Ogilby Improved: Being an Actual Survey of all the Direct and Principal Cross Roads of England and Wales: Shewing all the Cities, Towns, Villages, Churches, Gentlemen's Seats, &c. Situated on, or Near Any of the Roads / Engraved by Emanuel Bowen …; To Which is Added An Accurate Historical and Topographical Description of all the Cities, Boroughs, Towns Corporate, and Other Places of Note; Compiled from the Best Authorities, by John Owen.; The Whole Illustrated with Maps of all the Counties of South-Britain, and A Summary Description of Each* (London, Carington Bowles, 1764).

[17] *Bowles' Post-Chaise Travelling Companion; or, Traveller's Directory Through England and Wales* (London, Carington Bowles, c1775).

[18] *Kitchin's Post-Chaise Companion, Through England and Wales* (London, John Bowles, Carington Bowles and Robert Sayer, 1767).

III. 'You Take the High Road': Taylor and Skinner and the Roads of Scotland

In 1775 Scottish surveyor George Taylor, in partnership with Andrew Skinner, determined to do for Scotland what Ogilby had done for England and Wales a century earlier.[19] Like Ogilby, they had difficulty raising the funds for the undertaking. Taylor had worked as an estate surveyor for Sir James Grant of Grant and wrote to him in April 1775 seeking his patronage and also his influence with the Commissioners of the Forfeited Estates. This was the body set up to administer the estates of landowners who had supported the Jacobite cause and part of their task was to distribute funds for the 'improvement' of the Scots ('civilising the inhabitants' and 'promoting amongst them the Protestant Religion, good Government, Industry and Manufactures').[20] In July 1775, Taylor and Skinner petitioned the Commission directly, appealing to this objective and noting that

> much attention has been always paid to render the high roads of Scotland regular and commodious, as a free and easy intercourse through the different parts of a country must be considered as a most interesting object of its policy.[21]

But, going on to point out that 'in many parts of Scotland the form of the highways is not itself sufficient for the accommodation of travellers',[22] they proposed to remedy this by undertaking a survey of the roads, which they had already begun. The survey would be supplemented with additional information such as noblemen and gentlemen's seats, cities, towns, villages near the roads, rivers, bridges, and ferries, and they would also advise on places where it appeared to them that bridges should be erected.[23]

The Commission approved the undertaking but did not offer financial assistance. Taylor and Skinner had already been advertising for subscribers for their volume, which was to be based upon Ogilby's *Britannia*. The *Maps of the Roads of North Britain* was published on 8 February 1776. It opened with a map of Scotland, based upon James Dorret's *Map of Scotland*, to which they added roads, and followed with 60 plates featuring strip maps in the style of Ogilby.[24] (see Figures 14 and 15). The work had cost them a total of £1,433: £306 on surveying, £487 to engrave and bind 3,000 copies, and £640 on distribution and the booksellers' discount.[25] The volume had originally been advertised at 6s in sheets and 7s 6d bound but the price had had to be raised, and copies bound in red leather were

[19] For a biography of Taylor, see IH Adams, 'George Taylor, a Surveyor o' Pairts' (January 1975) 27 *Imago Mundi* 55, 59–60. Of Skinner, almost nothing is known.
[20] ibid.
[21] ibid 60.
[22] ibid.
[23] ibid.
[24] ibid.
[25] ibid 61.

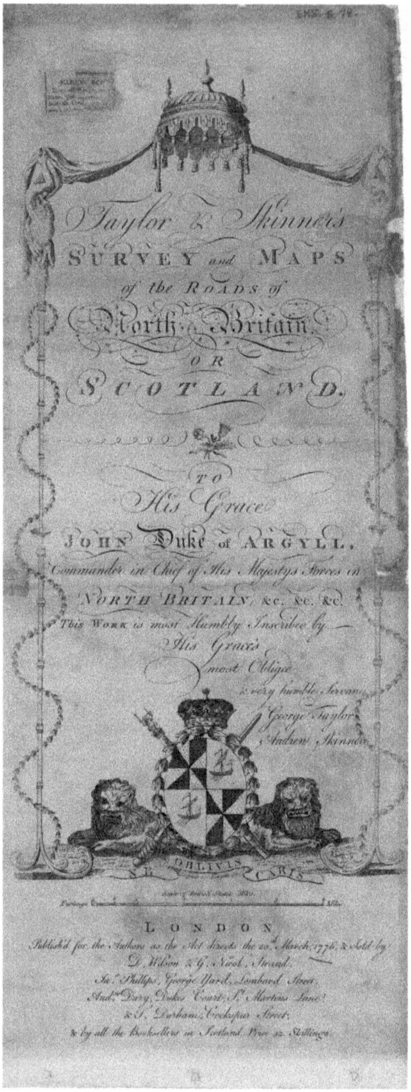

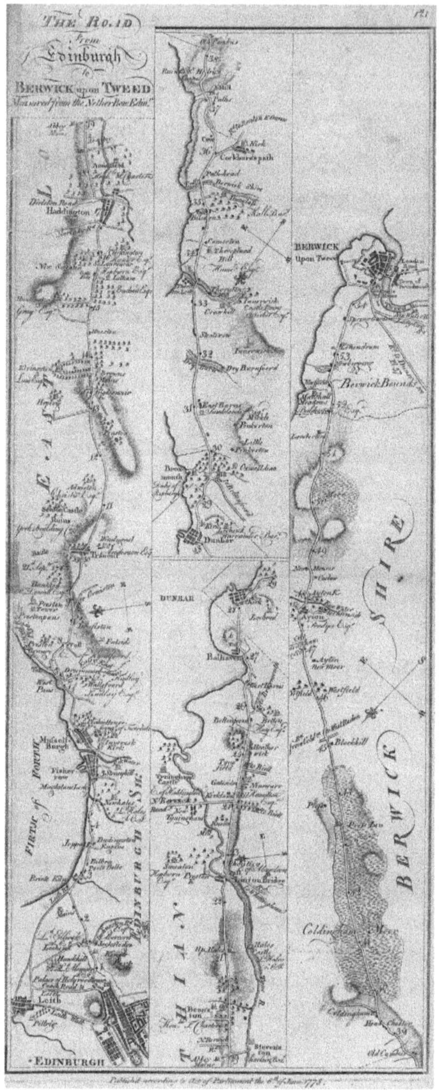

Figures 14 and 15 Taylor and Skinner's *Survey and maps of the Roads of North Britain or Scotland*, published in 1776, showed over 3000 miles of roads in Scotland, and was modelled on Ogilby's *Britannia* (1675)

Reproduced with the permission of the National Library of Scotland.

delivered to subscribers at 10s 6d and on sale for 12s.[26] They immediately sold 1,000 copies and the Commission awarded them 100 guineas, leaving them £300 out of pocket.[27] The book included an abstract or index of roads with measured

[26] *Caledonian Mercury*, 1 April 1775, 3; *Edinburgh Advertiser*, 17 May 1776, 7.
[27] Adams (n 19) 61.

distances. No doubt hoping to capture the segment of the market that could not afford the larger work, Taylor and Skinner also published this abstract separately under the title *The Traveller's Pocket Book, or an Abstract of Taylor and Skinner's Survey of the Roads of Scotland.*[28] Both publications were entered at Stationer's Hall, the first on 30 March 1776 and the second on 30 May 1776.[29]

As indicated by the sales numbers, the works were immediately popular. One correspondent wrote into the *Weekly Magazine* that he had 'often seen Ogilvie's Roads of England, which is indeed comprised in a neat pocket volume; but this new publication is far preferable to it in every respect, save that of bulk or size'.[30] He enthused that he had travelled a great deal 'but I never spent three weeks on the road with greater pleasure than in the company of this useful director'.[31] As well as helping travellers to find their way and entertaining them en route, the volume offered another advantage: as an authoritative and purportedly accurate measurement of mileage for use by coachmen and those employing them. Taylor and Skinner used this in their marketing, inserting an advertisement in the *Edinburgh Advertiser* of 27 August 1776, which concluded:

> Being informed that disputes have arisen between travellers and chaise-hirers of the stage between Perth and Cupar of Angus, they assure the public, that the distance of that stage is only twelve miles three quarters, as by their book, and not fifteen miles, as charged by the hirers.[32]

The existence of such new and useful information proved too tempting to Robert and Richard Wilson, publishers of *The Town and Country Almanac*, who included the abstract of roads from *Maps of the Roads of Northern Britain* in their 1777 edition. In December 1776, Taylor and Skinner petitioned the Court of Session for an interdict (injunction) against the Wilsons and Donald Bayne, a typefounder, claiming they had unlawfully copied 14 pages of the *Maps of Roads in Northern Britain* – comprising the list of distances between Edinburgh and various cities and towns – on the final pages of their almanac.[33] Taylor and Skinner's petition argued: 'There is not a single line in the Traveller's Pocket Book that was not acquired by the labour of travelling many miles, and measuring every footstep of the road as they travelled'. They argued that they were entitled to reap the benefit arising from the publication and the defenders, 'who have not laid out a shilling of expense', could not be permitted to ruin their sales.[34]

[28] As set out in the Summons: *Taylor and Skinner v Bayne and Wilson*, 4 April 1777, CS237/T/1/80/1 (NRS). See entry in Moir, *The Early Maps of Scotland* 30.

[29] Certificates of Entry in Stationers' Hall, CS237/T/1/80/2 and C237/T/1/80/3 (NRS).

[30] *The Weekly Magazine, or, Edinburgh Amusement*, 1 August 1776, 33.

[31] ibid.

[32] *Edinburgh Advertiser*, 27 August 1776, 5.

[33] *The Petition of George Taylor and Andrew Skinner, Surveyors* (18 December 1776), Session Papers, vol. 594, no. 23 (Advocates Library).

[34] George Taylor and Andrew Skinner, Pursuers, against Donald Bayne and Robert and Richard Wilson, 21 December 1776 in WM Morison, *The Decisions of the Court of Session, From its Institution Until the Separation of the Court into Two Decisions in the Year 1808, Digested Under Proper Heads, in the Form of a Dictionary Vol XIX–XX* (Edinburgh, printed for Archibald Constable, 1811), Appendix, 7.

The defenders responded that they did not dispute the merit of the work, but that the 'mere list of stages annexed to the survey cannot be considered such a part of the work as that the publication of them should be any encroachment upon the pursuers' property'.[35] Indeed, they argued, this would be 'the most groundless and chimerical of all the claims of literary property, that have hitherto appeared'.[36] In addition, lists of roads were always included in almanacs and, by making a survey of the roads, the pursuers could not prevent anyone from 'mentioning that such and such are the stages from one town to another'.[37] They pointed out that the Statute of Anne, under which the work had been registered, was an act for the encouragement of learning and publishing a list of roads could not be deemed an infringement of such a statute. Finally, they thought that if the pursuers' argument was accepted, it would put an end to all periodical publications of the sort as all almanacs, magazines, and reviews consisted of transcripts from other books.[38]

The Court of Session did not accept the defenders' arguments; indeed, the report claims that the court labelled the defenders as 'pessimi exempli' (the worst example or bad precedent).[39] Some of the judges observed that finding otherwise 'would put an end to the property of authors altogether' and that the defenders' had taken the substance of the book 'in an evasive way, which was hard and cruel'.[40] It granted the interdict requested.[41]

The matter was not, however, so clear to others and a debate erupted in the pages of the Edinburgh-based *Weekly Magazine*. An editorial on 19 December 1776 criticised the decision as 'a new species of literary property, and a heavy restraint on the liberty of the press'. The author alleged that Taylor and Skinner's book was 'almost in everybody's hands who has been able to purchase them, and they have been amply and deservedly rewarded by the public for their assiduity and correctness'. However, they went on, 'it would be unaccountably hard if a man, who cannot afford to throw away twelve shillings, should be debarred the information of the distance in miles and furlongs he has to ride betwixt Edinburgh and Glasgow'.[42] The following week Taylor and Skinner responded in the pages of the same publication. They rejected the allegation that the roads were

[35] ibid Appendix, 8.

[36] ibid.

[37] ibid.

[38] ibid, Appendix, 9.

[39] ibid 8309.

[40] ibid, Appendix, 9.

[41] ibid. In April 1777 a Summons was issued against Bayne and the Wilsons ordering them to appear in the Court of Session, seeking an order for the penalties under the Statute of Anne (amounting to 100 pounds, half of which would go to the Lords of Council and Sessions and half to the pursuers) as well as damages for 500 pounds: see the summons ordering defenders to appear, CS237/T/1/80 (NRS). Whether the matter went to trial is unknown, but as it was not reported on further it seems unlikely.

[42] *Weekly Magazine, or the Edinburgh Amusement*, 15 December 1776, 415.

'a new species of literary property', stating: 'They are a property that have cost us more money than most publications that have appeared in this country, and, with all publications of the same nature, are an express object of the legislature'.[43] They also disputed that they had been amply rewarded, noting that they were still 'some hundred pounds in advance, notwithstanding the public assistance that has been given us, which with gratitude we acknowledge'.[44] Their letter, however, was immediately followed by another, authored by 'A Friend to Liberty', who complained that, although he had been an original subscriber, he had been unhappy with the volume's 'incommodious form' and 'confused arrangement'. Now he thought that, while the monopoly of 'the exclusive property in books for a limited time, is perhaps necessary for the encouragement of literature', this was an attempt to extend that monopoly to 'an unusual latitude' and 'a dangerous encroachment upon the liberties of the press'.[45]

The dispute continued on through January. As editor of a broadsheet offering a digest from other magazines, reviews, and newspapers alongside its own content, Walter Ruddiman unsurprisingly supported the almanac publishers and inserted a justification of the *Weekly Magazine's* role and position (including observing the anonymity of its correspondent, despite Taylor's demands to name them publicly).[46] The debate now took on a broader shape, revisiting some of the themes that had been aired more fully in the argument, judgments, and commentary relating to common-law copyright in England, and the earlier cases of *Millar v Taylor* (1769)[47] and *Donaldson v Becket* (1774),[48] but with a specific focus on so-called 'facts' and extracts. 'A Friend to Liberty' offered a range of examples of adverse results that would flow from Taylor and Skinner's victory, including the inability of historians to cite dates copied from works by other historians, philosophers to write about the length of a meridian by consulting the works of Condamine, or Gazetteers to state accurate observations about longitude and latitude if the astronomer who made those observations had registered his book at Stationers' Hall. Likewise, they argued, it would not be possible for mapmakers to make new and accurate maps by consulting other works or for the authors of travel accounts, such as Thomas Pennant, to mention Taylor and Skinner's calculated distances in their publications.

'A Friend' rejected the argument that Taylor and Skinner's property rights arose because of the expense involved in making the survey, because it would not be possible for any subsequent user to know who had or had not been at expense in compiling their facts; 'therefore, if this doctrine were admitted he could never

[43] *Weekly Magazine, or the Edinburgh Amusement*, 26 December 1776, 31.
[44] ibid.
[45] ibid 31–32.
[46] *Weekly Magazine, or the Edinburgh Amusement*, 9 January 1777, 94–96.
[47] (1769) 4 Burr 2303.
[48] (1774) 7 Bro PC 88; 4 Burr 2408.

know in what case he might adopt a fact borrowed from another, or in what cases he might refrain.'[49] 'A Friend' also disagreed that the Almanac's publication of the information would interfere with Taylor and Skinner's sales: '[F]or if a man find satisfaction from these detached parts of the work, he naturally wishes to be possessed of the whole, from which he hopes to receive a still higher degree of satisfaction.'[50] Finally, they argued, if the law be correct,

> there is not, perhaps, one book nor news-paper printed among a million, in which the law has not been infringed – so that the printer or publisher is at the mercy of them, who, by claiming the privilege that the law allows them, shall be able to crush them at pleasure, or to fill their pockets with hush money.[51]

The following month the *Weekly Magazine* published a response by 'GM'. This correspondent drew on some of the terms of the arguments that had been employed in the literary property debates, which had culminated several years earlier in the House of Lords decision in *Donaldson v Becket*.[52] 'GM' stated that the question to be asked was 'whether the works of the mind can become property?' Answered in the affirmative, they went on to explain that:

> The property of the labour of the mind, exhibited in the author's original copy of a book, is not restricted to that copy itself, merely as a composition of paper and ink, but extends to the author's ideas therein expressed.

Furthermore, 'GM' rejected the analogies of 'A Friend' in relation to extracts on quotation, saying they would only apply to cases where 'the author has no intention to enrich himself at the expense of his neighbour'.[53]

In the discourse that arose in and surrounding the case, a key point of contention was how the property right could arise in such a list of facts. One side argued that the right arose from the labour and expense involved in collecting that data, the labour in question being both physical and mental, a claim which the other side rejected in relation to the textual description. That side did, however, recognise a distinction between the information presented visually in map form, which Bayne and Wilson were prepared to accept as protectable, and the information presented as a list. Ruddiman, writing editorially, was critical of the commercial strategy employed by Taylor and Skinner, pointing to one advertisement in which they had said that the *Pocket-Book* would be available only to subscribers for the *Survey*, contradicting a second public statement in which they claimed that the object of the *Pocket-Book* was 'to supply the public with it at a price that may suit

[49] *Weekly Magazine, or the Edinburgh Amusement*, 30 January 1777, 167.
[50] ibid 168.
[51] ibid.
[52] For a detailed discussion of the debates around the nature of copyright as property and the role of mental labour, see B Sherman and L Bently, *The Making of Modern Intellectual Property Law* (Cambridge, Cambridge University Press, 1999) ch 1.
[53] *Weekly Magazine, or the Edinburgh Amusement*, 27 February 1777, 298–99.

every individual'.[54] Ruddiman considered this a 'striking contradiction'.[55] To him it seemed Taylor and Skinner were trying to usurp the role of the almanac and other miscellanies by capturing a market those publications had historically served. He also considered it illegitimate to do so by packaging up the same information in different formats. He considered that the difference between the two works was 'a distinction without a difference … [the *Pocket-Book*] has all the essentials of the great work (as they call it): the one contains in print what the other does on copper-plates'.[56]

But the pursuers, too, struggled to explain why the copying of the list of distances infringed their property in the book of maps. As noted above, they had registered both works at Stationers' Hall in accordance with the provisions of the Statute of Anne but also in argument insisted that the copperplates were protected by the Engravings Act. The point for them was that both works 'have been the results of a very laborious and very expensive survey; they are separate and distinct works, and without having actually made the survey, no person could possibly have been the author of either'.[57] For them, the key was the labour involved in both which gave rise to the property rights. They argued,

> if the statute of Queen Anne applies with peculiar energy to any case, it applies so to this; for the labour and trouble that it has cost the petitioners, in collecting materials for the publication, is beyond any idea that can be formed from its size; and as they have been at a very great expence, as well as much trouble, of which they are yet to be indemnified, it is reasonable they should have the protection of the law for their indemnification.[58]

For Taylor and Skinner, the labour and expense went largely into creating and compiling the *information*, not its material form. Thus, labour dictated that the information be protected in whatever form they chose to put it on the market.

IV. The Legal Travails of *Paterson's Roads*

While Taylor and Skinner were attempting to do for Scotland what Ogilby had done for England a century before, south of the border Ogilby's work was seen as ripe for revision. In 1771 Daniel Paterson entered into an agreement with the bookseller Thomas Carnan to print and publish a travel itinerary, which would become the most enduringly popular road book of the late eighteenth century, popularly known as *Paterson's Roads*.[59] However, the author and his publisher

[54] *Weekly Magazine, or the Edinburgh Amusement*, 9 January 1777, 95.
[55] ibid.
[56] ibid.
[57] *The Petition of George Taylor and Andrew Skinner* 5.
[58] ibid 7.
[59] D Paterson, *A New and Accurate Description of all the Direct and Principal Cross Roads in Great Britain* (London, T Carnan, 1771) (*Paterson's Roads*, 1771).

soon found themselves entangled in the labyrinthine processes of the eighteenth-century Court of Chancery in an action for breach of copyright.

Of the man Daniel Paterson himself, little is known beyond the bare facts of his life and death available on his tombstone and what can be gathered through his publications.[60] His first foray into the publishing world was a single engraved sheet, which gave a table of distances between the principal cities and towns of England, accompanied by a skeleton map.[61] His next venture was the road book for which he would become known. Then commissioned as an ensign in the 30th Regiment of Foot, Paterson described himself in the book as 'Assistant to the Quarter Master General of His Majesty's Forces' and dedicated the book to Lieutenant-Colonel George Morrison, then Quartermaster General.[62]

The book he produced for Carnan as a *New and Accurate Description of all the Direct and Principal Cross-Roads in Great Britain*, or *Paterson's Roads*, was essentially, as its title indicated, a list of the direct roads and principal cross-roads of Great Britain, with their various distances calculated from a fixed point (eg, London Bridge or Westminster Bridge).[63] In addition to listing the roads of England, Wales, and Scotland, it contained details of the circuits of the Judges and an index to the country seats of the aristocracy and landed gentry, as well as short descriptions of some of the great houses and their owners near the particular route described. Over subsequent editions a single map of the country was added, the roads of Scotland were omitted and moved to a separate publication, and a list of all the fairs in England and Wales was added.

Despite the claims made in its title, however, *Paterson's Roads* was not particularly new (nor is it likely to have been particularly accurate, at least by today's standards). Paterson carried out no new surveys and made no new maps; instead, he gathered and collated information from a variety of sources, many of which were no doubt associated with his employment, and used them to update the road distances measured and surveyed by Ogilby.[64] Paterson himself explained that his original motivation had been

> a desire of excelling in his profession and of executing the duties of his staff employment with that degree of accuracy and precision necessary for conducting the movements of an army, in such regularity and good order as is absolutely requisite for the good of the service.[65]

[60] See HG Fordham, '"Paterson's Roads": Daniel Paterson, His Maps and Itineraries, 1738–1825' (1925) s4-V(4) *The Library* 333.

[61] ibid 333; D Paterson, *A Scale of Distances of the Principal Cities and Towns in England: by Daniel Paterson* (London, 1766).

[62] Paterson (n 59).

[63] ibid.

[64] He also appears to have received assistance from the Post Office in 1790 and 1791, according to Letter from Francis Freeling, Post Office Secretary to the Postmaster General, 1801, POST 10/286 (PM).

[65] D Paterson, *Paterson's British Itinerary, Being a New and Accurate Delineation and Description of the Direct and Principal Cross Roads of Great Britain* (London, Carington Bowles, 1785) (*Paterson's British Itinerary*) iii.

Considering that 'a thorough knowledge of the Roads, Towns, and even Villages of Note in the Kingdom, must be allowed the first essential towards the wished-for accompaniment',[66] he began compiling information first for his own use and was then persuaded by friends to present it to the public. He wrote that, having done so,

> The success attending that first Essay (notwithstanding its many imperfections) and the reception it has been honoured with from a generous public, has encouraged the Author to persevere in his favourite pursuit, sparing neither pains nor expence in procuring such materials as would enable him to improve upon the subject.[67]

His book was certainly successful. In the 10 years after its first publication in 1771, *Paterson's Roads* ran to four further editions; each time, Carnan paid Paterson for making additions and corrections. However, it seems that after 1781 they had a parting of the ways. The sixth edition, published in 1783, was prepared for Carnan by a hack writer named Richard Johnson,[68] while Paterson found a new publisher: London print and mapseller Carington Bowles. It is possible that money lay at the root of the dispute. Carnan had originally paid Paterson the sum of £50 and undertook to provide him with 300 copies of the book for the first edition. For corrections and updates, Carnan paid Paterson £11 16s 3d, £15 6s 6d, and £10 10s for the second, third, and fourth editions respectively.[69] In 1783, however, he paid Johnson half what he had paid Paterson; namely, £5 5s for corrections resulting in the fifth edition. Bowles, meanwhile, paid Paterson the considerably larger sum of £263, 13s 3d and 50 copies for the right to publish a book that he called *Paterson's British Itinerary.*[70]

Carington Bowles, whom we met in chapter four, ran a substantial wholesale and retail print business and was already involved in publishing some of *Paterson's Roads*' main competitors, notably Emanuel Bowen's *Britannia Depicta*, *Bowles' Post-Chaise Companion*, and *Kitchin's Post-Chaise Companion.*[71] Bringing Paterson and his reputation into this publication list was likely to have been a good business strategy. But Bowles had grander plans for this publication. Both *Britannia Depicta* and *Kitchin's Post-Chaise Companion* included strip maps of the kind popularised by Ogilby and copied by Taylor and Skinner. In producing *Paterson's British Itinerary*, Bowles added 179 strip maps to accompany the letterpress, making it a much larger work in two volumes.

Carnan was not one to turn a blind eye to such a potential threat. He was known as being 'litigious, cantankerous, a born rebel and fighter against "the establishment",

[66] ibid.
[67] ibid.
[68] *The Records of the Stationers' Company* (Cambridge, Chadwyck-Healey, 1986), Series 1, Box O (Richard Johnson, father and son 1734–1860). For more on Richard Johnson, see MJP Weedon, 'Richard Johnson and the Successors to John Newbery' (1949) s5-IV(1) *The Library* 25.
[69] Complaint of Thomas Carnan, 5 July 1785, C12/136/25 m1 (UKNA).
[70] Answer of Daniel Paterson, C12/135/25 m2, 15 July 1785 (UKNA).
[71] See above nn 14, 15, 16.

but brave and tenacious of purpose in a high degree'.[72] Famous in the annals of copyright and publishing history as the man who broke the longstanding monopoly held by the Stationers' Company on printing almanacs in the 1770s, he had also successfully petitioned against a bill seeking to reinstate the monopoly in 1779.[73] By the mid-1780s, therefore, he was an experienced legal player, who had tasted victory in the courts and legislature, and was fully aware of the possibilities offered by the 1710 Statute of Anne.[74] As discussed in the previous chapter, being a book, *Paterson's Roads* fell within the statute's scope. When fighting against the interests of the Stationers, Carnan had extolled the virtues of competition, arguing in the case of almanacs that 'their whole authority depends on their correctness. The way to make them correct is to permit an emulation and rivalship'.[75] Unsurprisingly, he felt differently when it was his property that was invaded and on 5 July 1785 he brought a bill of complaint in Chancery.

Carnan engaged several high profile counsel for his battle against Bowles and Paterson, including the Solicitor-General, Archibald Macdonald, and John Scott (later Lord Eldon[76]), and brought a bill of complaint in Chancery on 5 July 1785.[77] Bowles and Paterson made their answers 10 days later[78] and the following week the Solicitor-General moved for an injunction to restrain the sale of the book.[79] Like Carnan, Bowles was not unfamiliar with the courts or the law of copyright, having been involved in copyright litigation on two previous occasions.[80] In response to Carnan's suit, Bowles and Paterson also engaged a number of eminent counsel to plead their case including James Mansfield and John Stainsby, both leading Chancery counsel.[81]

The case raised two separate legal issues: first, whether the copyright Paterson had assigned to Carnan had reverted to Paterson in which case Paterson would be able to make a second assignment to Bowles; and second, whether the book sold to Bowles was an infringement of Carnan's book.[82] The first question turned on the provisions of the Statute of Anne. The Act's first section provided that the author

[72] S Roscoe, *John Newbery and His Successors, 1740–1814: A Bibliography* (Wormley, Five Owls Press, 1973).

[73] *Stationers' Company v Carnan* (1775) 2 Black W 1004. See C Blagden, 'Thomas Carnan and the Almanack Monopoly' (1961) 14 *Studies in Bibliography* 23; R Deazley, 'Commentary on *Stationers' Company v Carnan* (1775)' in L Bently and M Kretschmer (eds), *Primary Sources on Copyright (1450–1900)*, (www.copyrighthistory.org, 2008), www.copyrighthistory.org/cam/tools/request/showRecord.php?id=commentary_uk_1775.

[74] Statute of Anne.

[75] *Stationers Company v Carnan* (1775) 2 Black W 1004, 1008.

[76] John Scott, Lord Eldon, was Lord Chancellor from 1801 to 1827 and generally regarded as the greatest lawyer of his age.

[77] C12/136/25 m1.

[78] C12/136/25 mm2, 3.

[79] *Carnan v Bowles* (1785) 2 Bro CC 80, 81.

[80] As noted in ch 4, these were the cases of *Jefferys v Bowles* (1770) and *Bowles v Sayer* (1780).

[81] D Lemmings, *Professors of the Law: Barristers and English Legal Culture in the Eighteenth Century* (Oxford, Oxford University Press, 2000) 352–54.

[82] 2 Bro CC 80, 81.

of any book, or his assigns, should have the sole right and liberty of printing and reprinting for the term of 14 years.[83] The final section of the Act stated that 'after the expiration of the said term of 14 years the sole right of printing shall return to the Authors thereof if they are living for another Term of 14 years.'[84] Paterson and Bowles were relying on this section, arguing that Paterson's initial assignment to Carnan in 1771 ended in 1785 and returned to Paterson in order that he could reassign it to Bowles.

Carnan raised two possible grounds upon which he was entitled to the copyright for the second term of 14 years. The first ground was that Paterson had conveyed to Carnan his rights in the second 14-year term, as well as his rights in the first 14-year term, in the initial agreement back in 1771. The alternative ground was that the fifth edition, as amended and updated by Paterson and entered in the Stationer's Register on 3 September 1781, was a new work which Carnan had the right to publish for another 14 years (which term still had 10 years to run).

The Lord Chancellor, Lord Thurlow, apparently accepted Carnan's first argument and held that the reversionary term did indeed pass to Carnan, so that he acquired both 14-year terms in 1771. As Lionel Bently and Jane Ginsburg have observed, Lord Thurlow based his decision on the wording of the agreement and the context in which it was made.[85] First, Lord Thurlow interpreted the word 'interest' as indicating an intention to transfer the contingent right. Perhaps more importantly, however, the Lord Chancellor also looked at the context of the grant. The agreement had been entered into after the case of *Millar v Taylor*,[86] in which the King's Bench had accepted the principle of a perpetual common-law copyright which survived the passing of the Statute of Anne, but before the decision in *Donaldson v Becket*,[87] in which the House of Lords rejected that principle. Therefore, Lord Thurlow concluded, the grant 'must have been made on the idea of a perpetuity'.[88] It is worth noting that, when acting as counsel for the booksellers opposing the perpetual right at common law, Lord Thurlow had specifically referred to the contingent term as evidence against the common-law right.[89]

[83] Statute of Anne, s 1.

[84] ibid s 11.

[85] L Bently and JC Ginsburg, '"The Sole Right … Shall Return to the Authors": Anglo-American Authors' Reversion Rights from the Statute of Anne to Contemporary U.S. Copyright' (2010) 25 *Berkeley Technology Law Journal* 1475. Note that Bently and Ginsburg assign this reasoning to Master of the Rolls, Lord Kenyon, but that this is based upon a mistake as to which order is being referred to. The order they cite, C33/465, was made on 20 June 1786, and the decision as to the reversionary term was made on 23 July 1785: C33/463 f.696^{r-v}. There is a discrepancy as to dates in the reported case which dates this as 22 July 1785 (2 Bro CC 80, 81) but this could be explained if the hearing occurred over two days. The Master's Report confirms 23 July 1785 as the day on which the order was made. C38/728 (all UKNA).

[86] (1769) 4 Burr 2303.

[87] (1774) 2 Bro PC 129.

[88] 2 Bro CC 80, 83.

[89] *Tonson v Collins* (1761) 1 Black W 301, 309; *Donaldson v Becket* (1774) 2 Bro PC 129, 142–43. For a recent reassessment of the common-law right as discussed in *Millar v Taylor* and *Donaldson v Becket* see HT Gómez-Arostegui, 'Copyright at Common Law in 1774' (2014) 47 *Connecticut Law Review* 47.

However, in *Carnan v Bowles* he took a robust line, stating: 'If he [Paterson] had meant to convey his first term only, he should have said so'.[90]

Once the Lord Chancellor found that Carnan *did* continue to hold the copyright, Bowles and Paterson had to argue that they had not infringed it. The success of the defence would turn on whether the book produced by Bowles was effectively *the same* book as that published by Carnan.[91] If the former, it would infringe; if the latter, it would not. Here the differing formats of the two books became relevant. Carnan's counsel argued that the books were the same and that Bowles's was copied from Carnan's. He contended that the fact that one contained the roads as written description and the other depicted them graphically was immaterial: 'The book contains the same road; the only difference is that one is engraved on copperplates, the other is in letter-press'.[92] Bowles and Paterson responded that, on the contrary, the addition of the maps had varied the whole work and that

> this is as different from the former work as any two works of this nature can be. They must all be considerably alike, as being descriptions of the same places. *Ogleby, Kitchen, et Britannia delineata*, must all essentially be the same.[93]

Solicitor-General Macdonald countered for Carnan that merely making improvements could not make the book a new and different work to the original. It could only be a new work if surveys of different roads were included. He went further and said that the additional parts in Bowles's book were the maps and that 'there is no additional mental labour'[94] in them.

The Lord Chancellor appeared unsure as to how to decide whether copying had occurred in such a case. Faced with the issue of whether the book published by Bowles was a new work and, therefore, non-infringing, he had to confront the question of how a work that built upon existing works could itself be an original work. In addition, this raised the question whether all of the Carnan editions were new works or just the latest one. Contemplating this matter, he observed:

> In this case it is not an operation of the mind, like the Essay on Human Understanding; it lies *in medio*: every man with eyes can trace it; and the whole merit depends upon the accuracy of the observation: every description will therefore be in a great measure original. If this be so, every edition will be a new work; if it differs as much from the last edition as it does from the last precedent work: either all are original works, or none of them.[95]

[90] 2 Bro CC 80, 84. For more detail on this aspect of the case, see Bently and Ginsburg (n 85).

[91] See I Alexander, *Copyright and the Public Interest in the Nineteenth Century* (Oxford, Hart Publishing, 2010) ch 6.

[92] 2 Bro CC 80, 82.

[93] ibid.

[94] ibid 83; 47.

[95] 2 Bro CC 80, 83.

After considering the contingent interest question, he went on:

> It is an extremely difficult thing to establish identity in a map, or a mere list of distances: but there may be originality in casting an index, or pointing out a ready method of finding a place in a map. In the work Paterson sold to Carnan there seems to be some sort of this originality.[96]

He referred the case to a Master to examine 'the originality' of the books and make a report.[97]

The Master, John Eardley Wilmot,[98] made his report 10 months later on 29 May 1786. He stated that he had been attended by the plaintiff, the defendants and their solicitors, and that he had 'looked into' both books.[99] Having done so, he concluded that they were not the same book and that they differed in the following ways: the former book was 'a description only' of the roads, while the latter was also a 'delineation', containing 179 maps or charts, and therefore a great deal more information.[100] He observed that the books were by the same author, Paterson, and went on to say: '[W]ith regard to those roads which are in both Books described in Letter Press, I find there are many small differences, additions, corrections, & variations, but that the said Roads are in Substance nearly the same'.[101] Finally, he pointed out that the two books were sold at different prices, Carnan's book being sold for 2s, and Bowles's for 2 guineas.[102]

The Master of the Rolls, Sir Lloyd Kenyon, awarded Carnan an injunction on 20 June 1786 in respect of the letterpress only. He held that the Master's report had found the 'delineation' to be different in the defendant's work but that the letterpress was 'nearly the same' and that 'the mere act of embellishing could not divest the right of the owner in the text'.[103] However, Bowles and Paterson moved to dissolve the injunction in November of that year and, having heard argument, the Lord Chancellor found that the Master's report was unclear and ordered him to review it.[104]

The Master took another six months to deliver his report. This time he was even more clearly in favour of Bowles and Paterson, stating again that the defendants' book was not the same as the plaintiff's book and that it was 'so essentially different from the last as to render the former a new and original composition in the following respects'.[105] He then went on to note that he considered neither

[96] ibid 84; 47.
[97] ibid 84; C33/4636 f96r-v (UKNA).
[98] Later taking the name John Eardley Eardley-Wilmot. His father was Sir John Eardley Wilmot (1709–92), Chief Justice of the Common Pleas (1766–71).
[99] C38/728 (UKNA).
[100] ibid.
[101] ibid.
[102] ibid.
[103] C33/465 f449v (UKNA); 2 Bro CC 80, 85.
[104] *Carnan v Bowles* (1786) 1 Cox 283, 285; C33/467 f23v (UKNA).
[105] C38/736, 19 May 1787 (UKNA).

book to be new and original except as compared with each other, as there were numerous books both prior to and contemporary with those in question 'of the same kind but differing in form and execution'.[106] Secondly, he observed that the greatest part of Bowles's book was the delineation of roads on copperplates and it therefore had much more information that Carnan's book. Thirdly, he found that the letterpress in Bowles's book contained many additions and corrections and so could not be said to be the same.[107]

The Lord Chancellor accepted the report but Carnan took exceptions to it and these were argued on 19 July 1787.[108] Lord Chancellor Thurlow responded by referring the report back to the Master for a third time. This time, he said, he wished to know specifically in which respects Carnan's book could be considered an original book and

> whether the said Book published by the Defendant Carington Bowles is the same as the Book published by the Plaintiff in any and which of the respects in which he finds the latter is an original Work and it is ordered that the said Master do state the respective particulars in which the said Books are different from each Other.[109]

From the report we can detect a certain terseness towards the Master from Lord Thurlow (whose nickname in court was Tiger or Lion, for his fierceness).[110] Unfortunately, we can only speculate as to what Wilmot would have said in his third report. We know that Carnan continued to pursue the case, perhaps encouraged by the Lord Chancellor's re-referral or, possibly, simply due to his litigious and cantankerous nature.[111] However, in July 1788 Carnan died and I have been unable to locate any further records regarding this case.

The case was clearly one of some public interest, attracting several mentions in the popular press.[112] Some of the reporting was incredulous at the resources being devoted to the question:

> Yesterday, there was a second hearing on that *very important* object, the Book of Roads … There was a vast quantity of talents exercised on this object, small as it is, viz. Scott, Hargrave, Mansfield, the Solicitor General, and Madocks.[113]

Unlike in Scotland, there was no extended public debate over the propriety of protecting such works but, similarly to the Scottish case, the particular nature of

[106] ibid.
[107] ibid.
[108] C33/467 f393r, C40/5, 4 June 1787; C33/467 f.429v, C33/467 f617v-618r (UKNA).
[109] C33/467 f617v–618r (UKNA).
[110] GM Ditchfield, 'Thurlow, Edward, first Baron Thurlow (1731–1806)' in HCG Matthew, B Harrison and L Goldman (eds), *Oxford Dictionary of National Biography* (Oxford, Oxford University Press, 2004) www.oxforddnb.com.rp.nla.gov.au/view/article/27406.
[111] Records from the accounts book of Richard Johnson show he was still employed by Carnan to prepare material from the case in January and February 1788, above n 68.
[112] See eg *General Evening Post*, 24 June 1786, 4; *Morning Chronicle and London Advertiser*, 28 June 1786, 3; 24 November 1786, 2; 30 July 1787, 2; *General Advertiser*, 20 July 1787, 2.
[113] *World and Fashionable Advertiser*, 20 July 1787, 2.

the works in question raised a number of knotty problems for the court. A key similarity between the two cases was the relationship between the maps and the text. Carnan's counsel argued for a dematerialised approach and protection of the information itself. As noted above, he argued the two books were the same because they contained the same information: 'The book contains the same roads; the only difference is, that one is engraved on copper-plates, the other is in letter-press'.[114]

The defendants argued that, working within an established genre, they had differentiated their book as much as they possibly could, and this approach seemed to resonate best with the Master. The fact that both books contained the same information, based on the same sources, led him to focus on the differences between the books. Clearly they differed in many respects. Most significantly, one contained maps and the other only a written itinerary. However, in some cases the distances also differed and, perhaps most importantly, they were designed for different sectors of the market. *Patersons' Roads* contained information of use to commercial travellers, such as the fair and market days and circuit dates, with a nod towards those travelling for leisure in the brief descriptions of some of the sights en route and was sold at the price of 2s. *Paterson's Itinerary*, which was sold for two guineas (reflecting the greater cost of the copperplates), was much more squarely aimed at affluent travellers, with greater printed information on local sights, views, and great houses, as well as more such detail being included in the maps. As Paterson explained in the Preface, the weakness of previous works (including his own) was that they contained only the line of the road without 'affording the least idea of the circumjacent country or describing any of those beautiful seats and other remarkable objects which attract the Traveller's attention, and excite a curiosity he cannot get satisfied'.[115]

When the case came back to the Master of the Rolls after the Master's first report, Sir Lloyd Kenyon MR sought to apply the approach adopted in the earlier case of *Mason v Murray*[116] (a case in which he had appeared, as Attorney General, for Mason). In that case, which involved publishing some poems in which the plaintiff alleged copyright alongside some in which he did not, Lord Thurlow LC had awarded a perpetual injunction and an account of profits in respect of the additional poems. Following this approach, Kenyon MR thought 'there was no difficulty in distinguishing what belongs to Mr Carnan; nor does it make any difference that it constitutes only a small part of the publication'.[117] Concluding that the letterpress was nearly the same, Kenyon awarded the injunction in respect of that part only.

[114] 2 Bro CC 80, 82.
[115] *Paterson's British Itinerary*, iii.
[116] (1777) Dick 536. Reported in more detail in *The Morning Chronicle and London Advertiser*, 3 July 1777, 2; 26 June 1777, 2; 14 July 1777, 2; 14 July 1779, 2. The pertinent order in *Mason* is at C33/452 ff.486r–487r.
[117] 2 Bro CC 80, 85.

Lord Thurlow, however, seemed to be seeking a compromise between the two polarities offered by Carnan's counsel and the Master in Ordinary, and a more nuanced solution than that offered by the Master of the Rolls. He stated:

> As the roads of Great Britain were open to the inspection and observation of all mankind, every one was at liberty to publish the result of such observation: the subject matter of these books were therefore *in medio*: but the question will be, whether the author has exhibited any new and distinct idea in the exposition of them; and then whether the subsequent editor has in substance adopted the same .... Now here if the scheme of exhibiting this information to the public is substantially and fundamentally the same in the second work as in the first, and the former is merely reprinted with such differences as not to amount fundamentally to a different project of exhibition, the law ought to interfere and protect the exhibition.[118]

It is notable that this formulation moves away from the emphasis on labour that we saw in Taylor and Skinner's case against Bayne and Wilson. Indeed, Carnan made no mention of the labour and expense involved in making *Paterson's Roads*, perhaps because Paterson had not carried out his own survey. Carnan's case for property rights was based upon the series of agreements he had made with Paterson. Meanwhile, in his answer Paterson referred to the 'great labour and expense' he had been to in making the new work for Bowles, that Bowles 'was at a great Expence in Procuring Surveys and purchasing Books maps and other necessary Materials', and he emphasised the new information and material he had added, as well as adding new roads and removing discontinued or unfrequented ones.[119] Because Paterson and Bowles had invested additional labour and finance in the new edition, their case was a more complex one.

Thus, in repeatedly sending the report back to the Master, Lord Thurlow was seeking to ascertain more precisely the similarities between the two books, in order to assist him in identifying what Bowles had copied and what was '*in medio*'. This phrase can be translated as 'open to all', which looks rather like today's concept of the public domain. If the case could not turn on a simple appropriation of labour, then it was necessary to look at what else might distinguish *Paterson's British Itinerary* from *Paterson's Roads*. What Lord Thurlow then emphasised was the 'idea' or mental labour exerted on openly available material. If this mental labour were copied, then there would be an infringement but if the defendant had exerted their own mental labour then there would not be.

The delays associated with Chancery procedure meant that the suit would not be resolved during Carnan's lifetime. However, had he lived, he would have seen the market provide his victory. A second edition of the expensive *Paterson's British Itinerary* was not published for another 11 years, while *Paterson's Roads* notched up a further four editions in that time. This was not, however, the end of its legal wrangles.

[118] 1 Cox 283, 284–5.
[119] C12/136/25 m4 (UKNA).

V. John Cary and the Post Office

Following Carnan's death his stepbrother, Francis Newbery, inherited his copyright in *Paterson's Roads*. The brothers had been in business together until they quarrelled and Francis left to concentrate on the patent medicine business. Now, with his nephew, Francis Power, Newbery arranged for the printing of several further editions.[120] However, in 1798 the road became rocky once again. The cause of the trouble was a new competitor: John Cary. Cary had set up his own London business engraving, publishing, and selling maps and prints in around 1783.[121] In 1784 he issued his first road book[122] and, by 1786, Cary's maps were recognised as being of higher quality than the usual offerings. The *Monthly Review* noted that Cary's surveys were the 'most accurate and elegant of any that have appeared since the days of Rocque.'[123]

In 1793 or 1794, Cary embarked upon the first comprehensive survey of the roads of Britain since Ogilby. He did so at the instigation of the Post Office, an institution established in the sixteenth century for the use of the King and conveying official letters and documents.[124] By the end of the eighteenth century, it was an office under the control of two Postmasters-General, receiving and transporting private letters from and to all parts of the Great Britain, Ireland, and overseas. In 1784, the first mail coach began to run between London and Bristol, provided by contractors at a cost of 3d per mile, and by the end of the year over 15 coaches were running.[125] In 1793, the Post Office was subject to a range of reforms.[126] At this time it appears that a survey of the roads was desired, likely to settle disputes over the prices charged by the mail coach contractors, which were calculated by mileage.[127] Cary was thus engaged by Thomas Hasker, the superintendent of the mail coaches, upon the order of Postmaster-General Lord Walsingham, to carry out this survey.[128] The Post Office agreed that Cary should receive payment of 9d per mile but, as this was the actual amount he had to pay his surveyors, it would only cover his costs.[129] It was therefore agreed he would also receive the

[120] Roscoe (n 72) 27.

[121] D Smith, 'The Cary Family' (1988) 43 *Map Collector* 40, 43.

[122] D Hodson, *County Atlases of the British Isles published After 1703 Volume III: Atlases Published 1764–1789 and Their Subsequent Editions* (London, British Library, 1997) 173.

[123] ibid 175.

[124] JC Hemmeon, *The History of the British Post Office* (Cambridge, MA, Harvard University, 1912) 3.

[125] ibid 34–41.

[126] ibid 44–45.

[127] Hodson (n 122) 181.

[128] *Cary v Longman* (1800) 3 Esp 273, 273; 170 ER 613, 613. See also the Affidavit of John Cary, C31/294, 18 November 1799 (UKNA). Cary's association with the Post Office probably began in relation to his production, *A New and Correct English Atlas*, published 1787–89, in the preface of which he thanks the Comptroller General of the Post Office for permission to consult important documents.

[129] Or so he claimed. Newbery later alleged that the going rate was only 6d per mile, suggesting Cary was making an adequate profit without the copyright. D Paterson, *A New and Accurate Description of All the Direct and Principal Cross Roads in England and Wales and Part of the Roads of Scotland: The Thirteenth Edition* (London: Longman & Rees, 1803) xiii.

exclusive right to publish his survey, which would allow him to make a profit through sales.[130]

Cary began to sell the results of his survey under the title of *Cary's New Itinerary* in 1798.[131] Newbery immediately accused him of having copied the 'plan and design'[132] of *Paterson's Roads*. According to his own account, Newbery decided not to bring legal proceedings but,

> instead of the slow warfare of legal restraints and prosecutions, … determined upon the bolder measure of reprisals: for two reasons, – one, that retaliation was more summary; – and the other, that the Public would probably be the gainers by the establishment of a competition.[133]

He therefore published a new edition of *Paterson's Roads*, containing additions and corrections copied from Cary's book.[134] Newbery's retaliation spurred Cary to legal action and he brought a bill in Chancery against Newbery's printers and publishers, the well-connected cartographer and engraver William Faden, Geographer to the King, and prominent booksellers Thomas Norton Longman and Owen Rees.[135]

Newbery was not Cary's only threat. One of his surveyors, Nathaniel Coltman, was also attempting to undercut Cary's publication by publishing his own book, *The British Itinerary*, which would be sold at 3s. Coltman advertised the book as written by 'Nathaniel Coltman, Surveyor, employed by the Post-Office to measure the Roads of Great Britain.'[136] Cary wrote crossly to the General Post Office, asking the Postmaster-General to declare publicly that no person other than himself had been appointed Surveyor of the Roads to the General Post Office.[137] The request occasioned some embarrassment, as the Post Office could find no evidence that Cary had ever been appointed to such a position and, consequently, did not wish to make a public declaration that he had. However, it did not wish to show a lack of appreciation to Cary (particularly in light of the fact that Cary had been styling himself under that title in the book).[138] The correspondence does not reveal a resolution and Cary may have chosen to focus his attention on the more significant threat presented by Newbery, Longman, Rees, and Faden.

Cary sought an injunction in Chancery to restrain the defendants from printing their book, which he alleged was a copy of his work, in part or in whole.[139] Cary alleged that Newbery could only offer the book so cheaply because he had

[130] *Cary v Longman* (1800) 3 Esp 273, 273; C31/294.
[131] John Cary, *Cary's New Itinerary: Or, An Accurate Delineation of the Great Roads, Both Direct and Cross, Throughout England and Wales* (London, John Cary, 1798).
[132] *Paterson's Roads 13th edn* (1803) vi.
[133] ibid viii–ix.
[134] *Paterson's Roads 12th edn* (1799).
[135] Complaint of John Cary, 14 November 1799, C12/256/9 m1 (UKNA).
[136] See eg *The Star*, 6 July 1799, 1.
[137] Letter from John Cary to Francis Freeling, 18 July 1799, POST 10/28 (PM).
[138] ibid. See notes made on the back of John Cary's letter.
[139] C12/256/9 m1.

copied it.[140] Seeking to obtain his injunction without waiting for the Defendants' answer, Cary put in an affidavit further setting out his case. A significant grievance was that Newbery's work was being offered at 4s 6d, which was cheaper than Cary's book at 7s.[141] Newbery responded with an affidavit, in which he claimed that

> the general plan or design of the said Complainant's Book is not new or original but is the same as that of the said Original book published by this Defendant and that the additions or improvements made by the said Complainant form but a very small part of the said Complainant's Work the remainder being copied in some instances almost page for page from this Defendant's said Book.[142]

On 21 November 1799, the case came before Lord Loughborough, the Lord Chancellor. Cary was represented by the Solicitor-General, Sir William Grant, while Newbery had retained the Attorney-General, Sir John Mitford. In response to the accusations of copying by Newbery, Mitford countered that Cary had copied from Paterson so closely he had even copied a road that did not exist.[143] The Lord Chancellor inspected the works himself and found them to be very different. According to the report in Vesey (Junior), Lord Loughborough complimented Cary, stating: 'He has made a very good map; with which it is very pleasant to travel',[144] but added that if he were to do 'strict justice', he would order the defendants to take everything out of their book that they took from the plaintiff and the plaintiff to take out everything he took from the defendants. According to Newbery's account, the Lord Chancellor also observed that, 'as they were useful publications, rather than reduce them as it were to skeletons, both Books should be left to take their chance with the Public'.[145] Upon Newbery's counsel observing that only Mr Cary's book would be a skeleton, the Lord Chancellor added: 'That Mr Cary might think himself well off, if Mr Newbery, the Proprietor of *Paterson*, did not file a Bill against him'.[146] He did not grant the injunction and awarded costs against Cary.[147]

The remaining defendants, Longman, Faden, and Rees put in their answer on 29 January 1800, admitting that they had sold the book, but stating they only did so as the agents of Newbery, who had the sole right to print and publish the work.[148] In the meantime, Cary commenced an action in the King's Bench. On 6 November 1800, the Court of Chancery ordered him to elect in which court he wished to proceed.[149] He elected the Courts of Law but, according to Newbery's

[140] Affidavit of John Cary, C31/294, 18 November 1799 (UKNA).
[141] ibid.
[142] ibid.
[143] *The True Briton*, 22 November 1799, 3.
[144] *Cary v Faden* (1799) 5 Ves 24, 26.
[145] *Paterson's Roads 13th edn*, ix–x.
[146] ibid.
[147] (1799) 5 Ves 24, 26.
[148] Answer of William Faden, Thomas Norton Longman and Owen Rees, 29 January 1800, C12/256/9 m2 (UKNA).
[149] C33/512 f52v, 6 November 1800 (UKNA).

account, after the day of the trial was fixed, Cary withdrew the case and approached Newbery through intermediaries with a proposal. He told Newbery that he had heard that, as the copyright term in *Paterson's Roads* was about to expire, the booksellers (meaning London booksellers in general) were about to publish their own version of it. Cary suggested that the two of them join together in a new publication as 'from the command they had over the trade, they would be able to supersede or annihilate both Paterson's Roads and Cary's Itinerary'.[150] Again according to his own account, Newbery reacted with righteous outrage:

> To a proposal, so repugnant to the Statute of the 8th of Queen Anne (which was intended to limit such monopolies) and so hostile to the Booksellers, the Proprietor of Paterson's Roads sent the following reply:– 'That neither his character nor his feelings would allow him to enter into any such compromise or coalition.'[151]

Cary therefore renewed his case in the King's Bench, now only against Newbery, Longman, and Rees.[152] Here he was represented by Thomas Erskine, along with another silk, James Mingay, and George Holroyd.[153] One of Newbery's compositors was a witness for Cary, and gave evidence that, in setting up the new edition of *Patersons' Roads*, '[t]he major part of it was Copy from Cary. *Pieces* were cut out of *Cary's book* and interwoven Manuscript put between'.[154] On further questioning he confirmed that 'there were Eight or Ten times as much Print as Manuscript'.[155] A particularly inculpatory admission by the compositor was that 'fractional parts' were inserted in order to deviate from Cary's book. When asked: 'Was this done to disguise it?' the answer was: 'I suppose so, yes'.[156]

Newbery responded, as he had before the Court of Chancery, that Cary's work was itself a piracy of *Paterson's Roads* and his counsel adduced evidence of errors in *Paterson's Roads* that Cary had copied. Similar evidence was led on behalf of Cary. Newbery further argued (at least in his publication if not before the Court) that Cary could have no such exclusive right in it. Knowing that the survey was paid for by the Post Office, 'he naturally concluded, that after it was delivered out for publication, it was the property of the public for whose use and at whose expense it had been made'.[157]

It was once again Lord Kenyon, now Chief Justice, who heard the case. As in *Carnan v Bowles*, Lord Kenyon had no difficulty in finding that copyright subsisted in Cary's book, notwithstanding that he might have copied parts of it from elsewhere. Relying again on the decision in *Mason v Murray*, he commented: 'It is not

[150] *Paterson's Roads 13th edn*, x–xi.
[151] ibid xi.
[152] J Cary, *Cary's New Itinerary: or, an accurate delineation of the Great Roads, both direct and cross, throughout England and Wales*, 2nd edn (London, J Cary, 1802) 862. Note that this report says that Erskine described Longman and Rees as being 'only nominal defs', the real defendant being Newbery.
[153] Holroyd had been the arbitrator in *Mason v Murray*, referred to above.
[154] ibid 865.
[155] ibid.
[156] ibid 866.
[157] *Paterson's Roads 13th edn*, xvi.

necessary that a plaintiff who brings an action of this sort should have the whole property in the work which he publishes'.[158] He continued:

> Lord Walsingham, by whose direction the survey was made, has given the copy-right of that part of the work arising from Mr Cary's survey to him, and as it has been used by the defendant's assignee, in his last publication of Paterson's Road Book, without his consent, I think the copy-right has been infringed.[159]

Unsurprisingly, given the overwhelming evidence of copying, the jury found in favour of Cary. However, he was awarded only 1s in nominal damages.

Not willing to let the matter rest there, Newbery's counsel brought a motion for a new trial in the King's Bench, arguing that Cary could not be considered the author of his book, as the greater part of it had already been published by Newbery.[160] However, the motion was refused by Lord Kenyon, who emphasised that, although

> the plaintiff had no title on which he could found an action to that part of his book he had taken from Mr Patterson's; but it is as clear that he had a right to his own additions and alterations, many of which were very material and valuable.[161]

Cary then returned to Chancery seeking an injunction, delivery up of infringing copies and an account and disgorgement of profits.[162] In their answers to the Chancery bill, Longman, Rees, and Newbery first argued that Cary had no right to any aid from Chancery, having earlier elected to proceed at Law.[163] However, on being ordered to put in further answers, they all confirmed that they had ceased to sell the 12th edition after the King's Bench judgment. Newbery stated that he had sustained an overall loss of £238 12s 5d, having printed 10,000 copies, of which 4,500 remained unsold.[164] Once again, in the absence of any profits to be accounted for, the case petered out[165] – or at least out of the courts, as Cary and Newbery continued the battle in the pages of their respective publications. Newbery, Longman, Rees, and Faden produced a 13th edition of *Paterson's Roads* in 1803, which included an 'Advertisement' at the front describing the legal proceedings and accusing Cary of plagiarism, and an Appendix which compared the two texts (see Figure 16).[166] Cary rebutted the allegations in his *Itinerary* and included a transcript of the King's Bench cases as proof.[167]

[158] *Cary v Longman* (1800) 3 Esp 273, 275.
[159] ibid.
[160] *Cary v Longman* (1801) 1 East 358, 360.
[161] ibid.
[162] Complaint of John Cary, 13 May 1801, C13/2/37 m1 (UKNA).
[163] Answer of Thomas Norton Longman and Owen Rees, I June 1801, C13/2/37 m2; Answer of Francis Newbery, 3 June 1801 (UKNA).
[164] C33/513 f807r, C33/516 f.172r, Further Answer of Thomas Norton Longman and Owen Rees, 22 March 1802, C13/14/46 m3, Further Answer of Francis Newbery, 22 March 1802, C13/14/46 m4 (UKNA).
[165] The final records I have located were the further answers of Newbery, Longman and Rees, ibid.
[166] *Paterson's Roads 13th edn.*
[167] *Cary's New Itinerary*, 2nd edn (1802) 862–68.

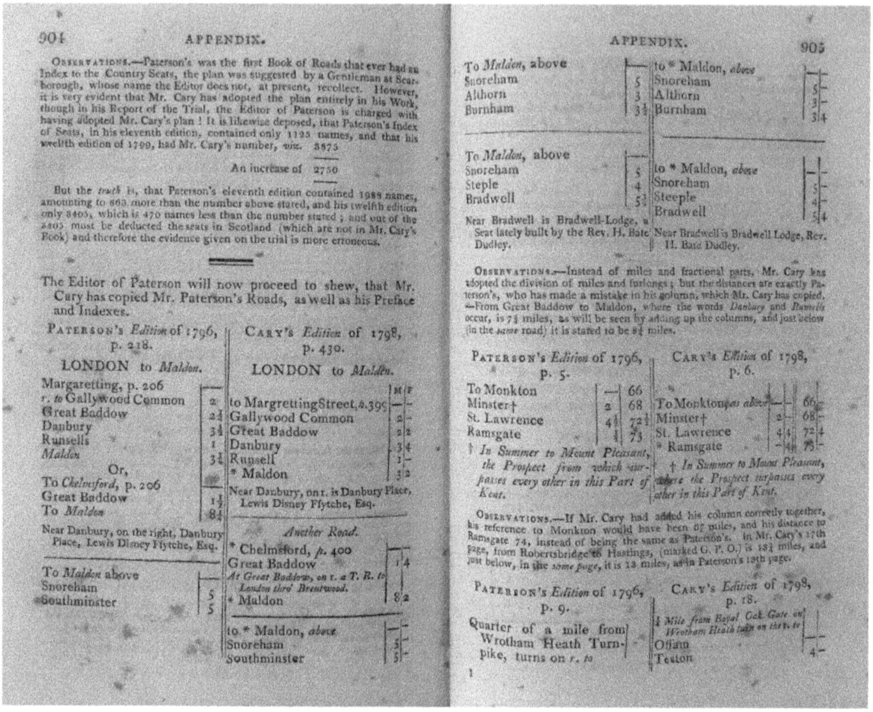
904 APPENDIX.

OBSERVATIONS.—Paterson's was the first Book of Roads that ever had an Index to the Country Seats, the plan was suggested by a Gentleman at Scarborough, whose name the Editor does not, at present, recollect. However, it is very evident that Mr. Cary has adopted the plan entirely in his Work, though in his Report of the Trial, the Editor of Paterson is charged with having adopted Mr. Cary's plan! It is likewise deposed, that Paterson's Index of Seats, in his eleventh edition, contained only 1125 names, and that his twelfth edition of 1799, had Mr. Cary's number, *viz.* 3875

An increase of 2750

But the *truth* is, that Paterson's eleventh edition contained 1988 names, amounting to 663 more than the number above stated, and his twelfth edition only 3405, which is 470 names less than the number stated; and out of the 3405 must be deducted the seats in Scotland (which are not in Mr. Cary's Book) and therefore the evidence given on the trial is more erroneous.

The Editor of Paterson will now proceed to shew, that Mr. Cary has copied Mr. Paterson's Roads, as well as his Preface and Indexes.

PATERSON'S *Edition* of 1796, p. 218. LONDON to *Maldon*.

CARY'S *Edition* of 1798, p. 430. LONDON to *Maldon*.

Margaretting, p. 206 / *r. to* Gallywood Common / Great Baddow / Danbury / Runsells / *Maldon*

to MargrettingStreet, 4.395 / Gallywood Common / Great Baddow / Danbury / Runsell / * Maldon

Or, To *Chelmsford*, p. 206 / Great Baddow / To *Maldon*

Near Danbury, on the right, Danbury Place, Lewis Disney Flytche, Esq.

Another Road. * Chelmsford, *p.* 400 / Great Baddow / *At Great Baddow, on r. a T. R. to London thro' Brentwood.* / * Maldon

To *Maldon* above / Snoreham / Southminster

to * Maldon, *above* / Snoreham / Southminster

APPENDIX. 905

To *Maldon*, above / Snoreham / Althorn / Burnham

to * Maldon, *above* / Snoreham / Althorn / Burnham

To *Maldon*, above / Snoreham / Steple / Bradwell

to * Maldon, *above* / Snoreham / Steeple / Bradwell

Near Bradwell is Bradwell-Lodge, a Seat lately built by the Rev. H. Bate Dudley.

Near Bradwell is Bradwell Lodge, Rev. H. Bate Dudley.

OBSERVATIONS.—Instead of miles and fractional parts, Mr. Cary has adopted the division of miles and furlongs; but the distances are exactly Paterson's, who has made a mistake in his column, which Mr. Cary has copied. —From Great Baddow to Maldon, where the words *Danbury* and *Runsells* occur, is 7½ miles, as will be seen by adding up the columns, and just below (in the *same* road) it is stated to be 8½ miles.

PATERSON'S *Edition* of 1796, p. 5.

CARY'S *Edition* of 1798, p. 6.

To Monkton / Minster† / St. Lawrence / Ramsgate

To Monkton, *as above* / Minster† / St. Lawrence / * Ramsgate

† *In Summer to Mount Pleasant, the Prospect from which surpasses every other in this Part of Kent.*

† *In Summer to Mount Pleasant, where the Prospect surpasses every other in this Part of Kent.*

OBSERVATIONS.—If Mr. Cary had added his column correctly together, his reference to Monkton would have been 67 miles, and his distance to Ramsgate 74, instead of being the same as Paterson's. In Mr. Cary's 17th page, from Robertsbridge to Hastings, (marked G. P. O.) is 13¼ miles, and just below, in the *same page*, it is 13 miles, as in Paterson's 19th page.

PATERSON'S *Edition* of 1796, p. 9.

CARY'S *Edition* of 1798, p. 18.

Quarter of a mile from Wrotham Heath Turnpike, turns on *r.* to

¼ *Mile from Royal Oak Gate on Wrotham Heath turn on the r. to* / Offam / Teston

Figure 16 Newbery included an Appendix in the 13th edition of *Paterson's Roads* in which he set out the alleged instances of copying by Cary in a comparative table. Daniel Paterson, *A New and Accurate Description of all the Direct and Principal Cross Roads in England and Wales*, 13th edition (London, Newbery, 1803).

Newbery, moreover, was not content with simply reasserting his own innocence. He too wished to improve the accuracy of his publication. His next action, therefore, was to write to Francis Freeling, the Secretary to the Post Office, who also happened to be his son-in-law.[168] In this letter, Newbery asked for the same assistance as that given to Cary in the form of requests being sent to the Post Office's surveyors and postmasters to supply him with local information on such things as the turnpikes, milestones, river and canal crossings, gentleman's seats, inns supplying post horses, and so on. Newbery's particular concern was with the milestones because, as he explained to Freeling: 'I mean to pursue our old Plan of marking the Distances by the Mile Stones; which I find, from various correspondents, is much more agreeable to the Traveller and I shall therefore discard all Mr Cary's Admeasurements'.[169] Freeling referred the request to the

[168] Letter from Francis Newbery to Francis Freeling, 12 May 1801, POST 10/286 (PM).
[169] ibid. Note that Cary's measurements had used the General Post Office as their starting point.

Postmasters-General, who were happy for him to supply such information to Newbery.[170]

However, matters were less straightforward when Newbery requested a copy of Cary's actual survey. Although Newbery emphasised again that he only wished to use the survey to ascertain the positions of the milestones, which Cary had not used in his measurements of roads, the inquiry directed attention to the potential use of the information contained in the survey, rather than the format in which the survey was expressed or had been published. On this difficult matter Freeling sought legal advice from a barrister, John Leach (who had been Newbery's counsel in 1799), and the Attorney-General, Edward Law.[171] Leach advised that:

> Mr Carey having by his agreement with the Post Office expressly reserved the copyright in the Survey, it appears to me that the Post Office [*illeg*] only entitled to the use of it for their particular information and that they cannot authorize Mr Newbery to avail himself of it in any manner in his intended publication.[172]

The Attorney-General came to the same conclusion but with a greater emphasis on protecting Cary against competition. He considered that Freeling could not supply to Newbery the survey to be used 'in any manner which may deprive [Cary] of the Benefit of the exclusive publication of his admeasurement and survey, according to the terms of his bargain with the Post Office'.[173] He proposed that, since Cary had made no use of the milestones in his book, he might be considered to have abandoned that information to the public. However, he thought that if

> Carey has indicated or is supposed to entertain any purpose of giving this information to the Public in any new edition of his Work, or if even the immediate publication by any one else of a book of Roads with the addition and improvement in question would materially affect the Sale of Mr Carey's Work as at present published, I think it would be in some degree a violation of good faith on the part of the Post Office to communicate this Survey to any body else in such manner as that the materials furnished by Carey himself should be converted to his present or future prejudice.[174]

The result appears to be that Newbery was not furnished with a copy of Cary's survey but given the same assistance in the form of enquiries and information. In the preface to the 13th edition, Newbery thanked Freeling and the Post Office for their assistance.[175]

The dispute between Cary and Newbery reveals that, even when the competing publications were in the same format, it was still difficult to disentangle proprietary claims over geographic information. This was particularly so when the

[170] Letter from Francis Freeling to Postmasters-General and notes made on the back of the letter, 14 May 1801, POST 10/286 (PM).

[171] Later Lord Ellenborough.

[172] Notes made on document dated 27 June 1801, POST 10/286 (PM).

[173] ibid.

[174] ibid.

[175] *Paterson's Roads 12th edn*, xvii.

publications were competing in the same market. An added complication was the intervention of the state, in the form of the Post Office, whose use of public funds to generate the data added force to the argument that the publications should be open to the use of anyone. The court resolved the conflict by focussing on the evidence of direct copying. Meanwhile, the Post Office and their legal advisors sought to navigate the uncertain boundary by limiting Cary's claim to the information he planned to commercialise.

VI. Road Book to Guidebook

Although his action against Newbery was not entirely a success, Cary was not finished defending his work against copiers. In June 1802, Cary brought an action in the King's Bench against bookseller George Kearsley for infringing copyright in the *Itinerary*.[176] The allegedly infringing work, *Kearsley's Traveller's Entertaining Guide through Great Britain* (see Figure 17), was not a direct competitor to *Cary's New Itinerary* (see Figure 18). While it included the tables of roads and distances, it placed greater emphasis on the ancillary information about the areas the putative traveller would be moving through. As Kearsley explained in his Preface, despite many 'Tours' having been published describing the roads of Great Britain, '[t]here yet, however, may be found wanting a Compendium of Topography; an Itinerary, comprehending as well what is amusing and instructive, as what is necessary and useful'.[177]

Edward Law, who had advised the Post Office on Cary's survey the previous year, was now Chief Justice Lord Ellenborough. The debate before him once again focused on whether a person who both copied a work and made additions could be guilty of piracy. Cary was represented again by Erskine, who was accompanied once more by Holroyd, as well as by William Garrow, the same team that had represented William Heather against John Hamilton Moore.[178] Erskine presented Lord Ellenborough with an example involving the Chief Justice's friend William Paley: 'Suppose a man took Paley's Philosophy, and copied a whole essay with observations and notes, or additions at the end of it, would that be piracy?'[179] The Chief Justice responded:

> That would depend on the facts of, whether the publication of that essay was to convey to the public the notes and observations fairly, or only to colour the publication of the original essay, and make that a pretext for pirating it; if the latter, it could not be sustained.[180]

[176] *Cary v Kearsley* (1802) 4 Esp 168.
[177] G Kearsley, *Kearsley's Traveller's Entertaining Guide through Great Britain: or, A description of the Great and Principal Cross-Roads* (1801).
[178] See ch 4.
[179] *Cary v Kearsley* (1802) 4 Esp 168, 170.
[180] ibid 170.

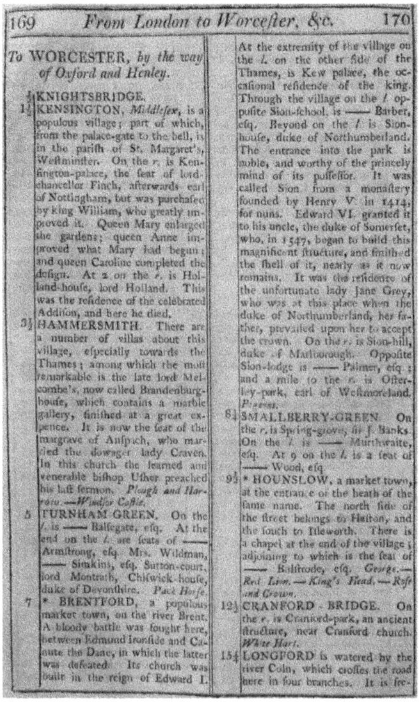

169 From London to Worcester, &c. 170

To WORCESTER, by the way of Oxford and Henley.

½ KNIGHTSBRIDGE.

1¼ KENSINGTON, Middlesex, is a populous village; part of which, from the palace-gate to the bell, is in the parish of St. Margaret's, Westminster. On the r. is Kensington-palace, the seat of lord-chancellor Finch, afterwards earl of Nottingham, but was purchased by king William, who greatly improved it. Queen Mary enlarged the gardens; queen Anne improved what Mary had begun; and queen Caroline completed the design. At 2 on the r. is Holland-house, lord Holland. This was the residence of the celebrated Addison, and here he died.

3½ HAMMERSMITH. There are a number of villas about this village, especially towards the Thames; among which the most remarkable is the late lord Melcombe's, now called Brandenburg-house, which contains a marble gallery, finished at a great expence. It is now the seat of the margrave of Anspach, who married the dowager lady Craven. In this church the learned and venerable bishop Usher preached his last sermon. Plough and Harrow.—Windsor Castle.

5 TURNHAM GREEN. On the l. is —— Ralfegate, esq. At the end on the l. are seats of —— Armstrong, esq. Mrs. Wildman, —— Simkins, esq. Sutton-court, lord Montrath, Chiswick-house, duke of Devonshire. Pack Horse.

7 * BRENTFORD, a populous market town, on the river Brent. A bloody battle was fought here, between Edmund Ironside and Canute the Dane, in which the latter was defeated. Its church was built in the reign of Edward I. At the extremity of the village on the l. on the other side of the Thames, is Kew palace, the occasional residence of the king. Through the village on the l. opposite Sion-school, is —— Barber, esq. Beyond on the l. is Sion-house, duke of Northumberland. The entrance into the park is noble, and worthy of the princely mind of its possessor. It was called Sion from a monastery founded by Henry V. in 1414, for nuns. Edward VI. granted it to his uncle, the duke of Somerset, who, in 1547, began to build this magnificent structure, and finished the shell of it, nearly as it now remains. It was the residence of the unfortunate lady Jane Grey, who was at this place when the duke of Northumberland, her father, prevailed upon her to accept the crown. On the r. is Sion-hill, duke of Marlborough. Opposite Sion-lodge is —— Palmer, esq.; and a mile to the r. is Osterley-park, earl of Westmoreland. Pigeons.

8¾ SMALLBERRY-GREEN. On the r. is Spring-grove, sir J. Banks. On the l. is —— Murthwaite, esq. At 9 on the l. is a seat of —— Wood, esq.

9¾ * HOUNSLOW, a market town, at the entrance of the heath of the same name. The north side of the street belongs to Heston, and the south to Isleworth. There is a chapel at the end of the village; adjoining to which is the seat of —— Bulstrode, esq. George.—Red Lion.—King's Head.—Rose and Crown.

12¼ CRANFORD - BRIDGE. On the r. is Cranford-park, an ancient structure, near Cranford church. White Hart.

15¼ LONGFORD is watered by the river Coln, which crosses the road here in four branches. It is fre-

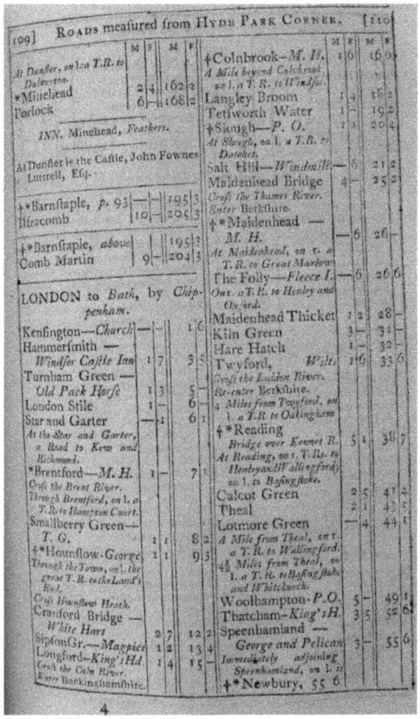

199] ROADS measured from HYDE PARK CORNER. [110

At Dunster, on l. a T.R. to Dulverton.
*Minehead | 2 | 4 | 162 | 2
Porlock | 6 | — | 168 | 2
INN. Minehead, Feathers.
At Dunster is the Castle, John Fownes Luttrell, Esq.
+*Barnstaple, p. 93 | — | — | 195 | 3
Ilfracomb | 10 | — | 205 | 3
+*Barnstaple, above | | | 195 | 3
Comb Martin | 9 | — | 204 | 3

LONDON to Bath, by Chippenham.
Kensington—Church | — | — | 1 | 6
Hammersmith — Windsor Castle Inn | 1 | 7 | 3 | 5
Turnham Green — Old Pack Horse | 1 | 3 | 5 | —
London Stile | 1 | — | 6 | —
Star and Garter | — | 1 | 6 | 1
At the Star and Garter, a Road to Kew and Richmond.
*Brentford—M. H. | 1 | — | 7 | 1
Cross the Brent River. Through Brentford, on l. a T.R. to Hampton Court.
Smallberry Green—T. G. | 1 | 1 | 8 | 2
+*Hounslow-George | 1 | 1 | 9 | 3
Through the Town, on l. the great T.R. to the Land's End.
Cross Hounslow Heath.
Cranford Bridge — White Hart | 2 | 7 | 12 | 2
SiptonGr.—Magpies | 1 | 2 | 13 | 4
Longford—King's Hd. | 1 | 4 | 15 | —
Cross the Coln River. Enter Buckinghamshire.
+Colnbrook—M. H. | 1 | 6 | 16 | 6
A Mile beyond Colnbrook on l. a T.R. to Windsor.
Langley Broom | 1 | 4 | 18 | 2
Tetsworth Water | 1 | — | 19 | 2
+Slough—P. O. | 1 | 2 | 20 | 4
At Slough, on l. a T.R. to Datchet.
Salt Hill—Windmill | — | 6 | 21 | 2
Maidenhead Bridge | 4 | — | 25 | 2
Cross the Thames River. Enter Berkshire.
+*Maidenhead — M. H. | — | 6 | 26 | —
At Maidenhead, on r. a T.R. to Great Marlow.
The Folly—Fleece I. | — | 6 | 26 | 6
On r. a T.R. to Henley and Oxford.
Maidenhead Thicket | 1 | 2 | 28 | —
Kiln Green | 3 | — | 31 | —
Hare Hatch | 1 | — | 32 | —
Twyford, Wilts | 1 | 6 | 33 | 6
Cross the Loddon River. Re-enter Berkshire.
4 Miles from Twyford, on l. a T.R. to Oakingham.
+*Reading | 5 | 1 | 38 | 7
Bridge over Kennet R.
At Reading, on r. T.Rs. to Henley and Wallingford; on l. to Basingstoke.
Calcot Green | 2 | 5 | 41 | 4
Theal | 2 | 1 | 43 | 5
Lotmore Green | — | 4 | 44 | 1
A Mile from Theal, on r. a T.R. to Wallingford.
4½ Miles from Theal, on l. a T.R. to Basingstoke and Whitchurch.
Woolhampton-P.O. | 5 | — | 49 | 1
Thatcham-King's H. | 3 | 5 | 52 | 6
Speenhamland — George and Pelican | 3 | — | 55 | 6
Immediately adjoining Speenhamland, on l. a
+*Newbury, 55 6

4

Figures 17 and 18 Comparing *Cary's New Itinerary* (1802) with a similar route from *Kearsley's Entertaining Traveller* (1801) shows that the distances may have been copied, with some variation, but a considerable amount of new material was added.

On this occasion, the approach that Erskine had used so successfully for Heather was now used against him. Although Cary pointed to the nine years he had spent making the survey, and the existence of mistakes and errors were sufficient to establish that Kearsley had copied from the *Itinerary*, Lord Ellenborough did not think that this would automatically lead to a finding of infringement, stating: 'That part of a work of one author is found in another, is not of itself piracy, or sufficient to support an action'.[181] Adopting an approach that firmly prioritised the public interest in accurate geographical information over Cary's claimed property rights, Lord Ellenborough continued:

> [A] man may fairly adopt part of the work of another, he may so make use of another's labours for the promotion of science and the benefit of the public, but having done so, the question will be, Was the matter so taken used fairly with that view, and without what I may term *animus furandi* [intention of stealing]?[182]

In this case, he considered that names of places and distances would necessarily be identical in both books if correct but that in the defendant's book there was

[181] ibid.
[182] ibid.

additional information and corrections. Therefore, he added, 'while I shall think myself bound to secure every man in the enjoyment of his copy-right, one must not put manacles upon science'.[183] He stated he would address these observations to the jury and leave it to them to decide whether what was copied 'was fairly done with a view of compiling a useful book, for the benefit of the public, – or taken colourable, merely with a view to steal the copy-right of the plaintiff'.[184] Upon hearing that this was how the Chief Justice planned to frame the issue, Erskine, Garrow, and Holroyd consented to be nonsuited.[185]

VII. Conclusion

In the eighteenth century, roads were the main conduits for the flow of information in Britain. They transported the post, which included newspapers, chapbooks, pamphlets, and books. They also, of course, carried people and were the main conduits for commerce. Over the course of the century, the quality of roads improved and their use increased as officials such as circuit judges, merchants, and other commercial travellers were joined on the road by travellers for leisure. Although roads were tools for the exercise of state power as well as essential to the economy, the state took little interest in producing and disseminating information about them between the days of Ogilby and Cary.[186] This meant that the surveying and mapping of the roads became commercial publishing ventures and even Cary and Ogilby were expected to exercise initiative and entrepreneurial methods to make their endeavours economically viable. Copyright law offered another tool for indirect state involvement, incentivising the undertaking by offering private property rights in the product. However, the courts implementing the laws recognised that information about the roads also needed to circulate in the market. Too much control would, in the words of Lord Ellenborough 'put manacles on science'. The cases discussed in this chapter reveal that mapmakers, booksellers, lawyers, judges, and members of the public were aware of the stakes involved in allowing property rights to be granted to essential infrastructure information despite their differences over where the boundaries should be drawn. However, it was not just lofty concerns in relation to social and scientific progress that concerned them. This language was also used to ensure that, as social and economic conditions

[183] ibid.

[184] ibid 171.

[185] A judgment of nonsuit is given where it appears that there is insufficient evidence to establish a cause of action and terminates the action; a plaintiff remains free to refile on the same cause of action.

[186] The situation can be contrasted to that in France where the state took a much more active role in mapping the roads. See CM Petto, 'To Know the Distance: Wayfinding and Roadmaps of Early Modern England and France' (2016) 51 *Cartographica* 240.

changed and opened up new markets for the leisure traveller, copyright did not become an impediment to enterprising new market entrants. Cary's arrangement with the Post Office raised new concerns about public access to geographical knowledge generated using public funds; these concerns would come to be amplified in relation to the much more ambitious mapmaking projects of the state to which we now turn.

6

Public Surveys, National Maps: The Rise of the Ordnance Survey

I. Introduction

Today the Ordnance Survey is an institution embedded in British life; its maps are beloved by ramblers, hikers, and cyclists, and its collection of geospatial databases, applications, platforms, and products service the public sector and commercial enterprises. A government agency led by military personnel until 1974, then an executive agency until 2015, when it became a wholly government-owned limited company, the Ordnance Survey's 'public task' requires it to 'create, maintain and improve the National Geographic Database (NGD)' and to 'provide access to the NGD with the public sectors'.[1] Nevertheless, it guards its maps and geospatial data zealously, offering access in a range of circumscribed ways and subject to an array of differently priced licences.[2] It has also brought litigation on several occasions over the last 20 years against those using its data without the correct authorisation and payment.[3]

But it was not always thus. This chapter traces the rise of the Ordnance Survey from its origins at the end of the eighteenth century through to the start of the twentieth, examining its approach to the collection, use, circulation, and control of the geographic data it gathered and the maps produced using that data. It reveals that during this period the Ordnance Survey and the various government departments to which it reported maintained a complex and frequently ambiguous relationship with copyright law. The Ordnance Survey wished to participate in the private market for maps (as chattel property) but was ill-equipped to do so. Moreover, its internal, state-directed purposes meant it was operating under different incentives to those of the private trade. While it sought to circulate its maps and data widely so that they could be useful for a range of state purposes, at the same time it needed to maintain some level of control over that circulation.

[1] Ordnance Survey, 'Our Public Task', www.ordnancesurvey.co.uk/governance/public-task/.

[2] Ordnance Survey, 'Licensing and Agreements', www.ordnancesurvey.co.uk/business-government/licensing-agreements.

[3] *Her Majesty's Stationery Office and Another v The Automobile Association* [2001] ECC 34; *The Controller of Her Majesty's Stationery Office, Ordnance Survey v Green Amps* [2007] EWHC 2755 (Ch); *77M Limited v Ordnance Survey Limited* [2019] EWHC 3007 (Ch).

It recognised that the maps it produced had both use and exchange value as chattels but that the chief use value lay in the data and information they contained. The exchange value of this data was difficult to capture and there were real questions as to the desirability of so doing. Value in both data and maps could only be maintained as long as it remained authoritative but the locus of this authority shifted over time. Copyright law, in this context, was not a mechanism to advance the claims of authorship, nor to structure markets for intangible rights, and so we do not see the tussle over claims of accuracy and copying arising through legal disputes as we did in chapters four and five. Instead, and because the Ordnance Survey was already claiming to have reached the pinnacle of scientific and mathematical accuracy, copyright became a mechanism to maintain control of the maps as physical commodities and to guard their reputation as repositories of the most authoritative geographic information.

The rise of the Ordnance Survey reflects the intensification of state involvement in geographic data collection and mapmaking. It is hardly a coincidence that territorial sovereignty reached its apotheosis in the same period. Scholars from a range of disciplines have commented on the links between the rise of a geographical nation-state and the use of survey and map technologies to render territories legible and easier to administer, as well to create cultural and social cohesion.[4] Sitting alongside other nineteenth-century projects of data collection such as the census, the work of the Ordnance Survey can be characterised as the same project of population management and use of statistics to regulate conduct that Foucault discusses in terms of governmentality.[5] The Ordnance Survey can likewise be seen as part of what James Scott refers to as a 'state map of legibility', a tool by which the modern nation-state extended its control and part of the aspirational administrative ordering of nature and society that he calls 'high modernism'.[6] William Rankin likewise sees the production of maps by state authorities as crucial to constituting the link between territory and sovereignty.[7] Where Foucault, Scott, and Rankin see this in terms of power and control, Higgs's exploration of the

[4] See eg B Anderson, *Imagined Communities: Reflections on the Origin and Spread of Nationalism* (London, Verso, 1983); C Arturo Leslie, 'Territoriality, Map-mindedness, and The Politics of Place' (2016) 45 *Theory and Society* 169; M Biggs, 'Putting the State on the Map: Cartography, Territory, and European State Formation' (1999) 41 *Comparative Studies in Society and History* 374; S Daniels, 'Mapping National Identities: The Culture of Cartography, With Particular Reference to The Ordnance Survey' in G Cubitt (ed), *Imagining Nations* (Manchester University Press, 1999) 112; J Black, *The Power of Knowledge: How Information and Technology Made the Modern World* (New Haven, Yale University Press, 2014).

[5] M Foucault, *Security, Territory, Population: Lectures at the College de Frances, 1977–78* (London, Palgrave Macmillan, 2007); M Foucault, *The Birth of Biopolitics: Lectures at the College de Frances, 1978–79* (London, Palgrave Macmillan, 2008); S Dorsett, 'Mapping Territories' in S McVeigh (ed), *Jurisprudence of Jurisdiction* (Abingdon, Routledge, 2007).

[6] JC Scott, *Seeing Like a State: How Certain Schemes to Improve the Human Condition Have Failed* (New Haven, Yale University Press, 1998) 88.

[7] W Rankin, *After the Map: Cartography, Navigation, and the Transformation of Territory in the Twentieth Century* (Chicago, University of Chicago Press, 2016) 1–7.

rise of the 'information state' takes a more positive, even empowering, view of the state's collection and use of information.[8] Whether characterised as benign or malign, increasingly centralised eighteenth- and nineteenth-century projects of data collection and use made possible the idea of a secular modern state.

This chapter's central concern is not with tracing or theorising the relationship between the Ordnance Survey and the modern state or forms of governance at a macro-level; rather, it seeks to look more closely at the actual mechanics and interactions by which Ordnance Survey maps and data were circulated, and the legal conditions against which that occurred. This detailed analysis has the potential to flesh out more high-level claims about links between maps, territory, and nation states. Before turning to this detail, some additional context in relation to the nineteenth-century state is required. While the changing nature of the state during the nineteenth century has been the focus of much theoretical, historical, and sociological study, three broad phases have been discerned. At the start of the century, state expenditure and activity were military in focus. The end of the Napoleonic Wars in 1815 was followed by the rise of the laissez-faire economy. Yet, while this period of largely unconstrained capitalism saw a reduction of state intervention in the military and economy and a contraction in government expenditure, it also witnessed a significant rise in nationally focused legislation aimed at social regulation. It is important, however, not to misread this as leading to a centralised and disciplinary form of government in Britain, as implementation remained largely left to local authorities.[9] As the nineteenth century gave way to the twentieth, the decentralised model of the classic liberal economy and polity was starting to give way to the rise of corporate action, concentration of capital, and growing state intervention and centralisation.[10]

These three periods of change in relation to the role of the state and its institutions map roughly onto three periods in the Ordnance Survey's changing relationship with copyright law. The first period, up to 1816, saw the establishment of the Survey and early decisions being made as to how its data would be collected and used. The maps' authority lay in their scientific credentials, which required them to be publicised and disseminated, and early Ordnance Survey Directors saw their role as participating in the 'republic of science'. Consonant with the ideals surrounding the 'second scientific revolution', their attitude was largely one of encouraging access and use, and links with the private map trade were critical in achieving this. However, the Ordnance Survey was not yet sure if this was a real market or one that it wished to participate in, given the maps' main purpose was military.

[8] E Higgs, *The Information State in England: The Central Collection of Information on Citizens Since 1500* (London, Palgrave Macmillan, 2004), although curiously he makes no mention of the Ordnance Survey or maps more generally. For a critique of Higgs's approach, see V Gattrell and S Hindle, 'Colloquium, *The Information State in England*' (2005) 18 *Journal of Historical Sociology* 125.

[9] Higgs (n 8) ch 4.

[10] See Higgs (n 8) ch 5; E Hobsbawm, *The Age of Empire: 1875–1914* (London, Abacus, 1994) 34; AV Dicey, *Lectures on the Relation of Law and Public Opinion* (London, Macmillan, 1917) 150–204.

The second period, from 1816 to 1870, saw the expansion of the Survey and its increasing use for a range of civilian and state-based purposes but also growing conflict over the objectives to be achieved and the costs of so doing. This concern was in turn reflected in worries over how to improve public access to the maps while ensuring their production remained commercially viable. Achieving this required increased participation in the market and growing pressure to treat the maps as commodities, but tension between realising their use value (through broad circulation) and exchange value (through controlling it) created challenges. Two key factors driving Ordnance Survey policy in relation to its circulation of data and attitude towards copyright law were the questions of *scale* and *sales*. Both were the subject of much internal wrangling, as well as debate in Parliament and in the general community, because they were core not only to identifying an appropriate role for the Ordnance Survey within the emergent modern state referred to above but also to consolidating a particular view of maps themselves – Edney's 'cartographic ideal'. The question of map sales implicated the relationship between the state and private markets, and the extent to which state interference with the latter would be tolerated in a laissez-faire economy. The growing intensity of the focus on map scale, expressed as a numerical ratio, provides yet further evidence for Edney's claims that during the nineteenth century map scale came to be seen as the defining characteristic of 'every map'.[11] Scale became integral to establishing the authority of the map as a scientifically determined and mathematically accurate representation of the earth. But it also became fundamental to distinguishing between official/unofficial and authorised/unauthorised through its adoption as the main proxy or criterion to determine legitimate and illegitimate copying and selling of maps.

The third period, the remaining 30 years to 1900, is the period during which the Ordnance Survey became an 'institution'; as Oliver explains, it transitioned from 'solving a short-term problem to being a permanent source of regularly maintained data'.[12] In the final decades of the century, there was a growing interest in controlling and commodifying the publication of all sorts of government-produced material but the case of Ordnance Survey maps demonstrated most sharply the complementary and competing nature of public and private interests in state-generated information. Copyright was invoked in attempts to segment the market for government-produced data, maintain its reputation for accuracy, and enforce authoritative attribution, rather than as a tool to assert ownership over an intangible asset or to protect authorship.

[11] MH Edney, *Cartography: The Ideal and its History* (Chicago, University of Chicago Press, 2019) 166.

[12] R Oliver, *The Ordnance Survey in the Nineteenth Century: Maps, Money and the Growth of Government* (London, The Charles Close Society, 2014) 502.

II. The Ordnance Survey Emerges: The Period to 1816

> Accurate surveys of a country are universally admitted to be works of great public utility, as affording the surest foundation for almost every kind of internal improvement in time of peace, and the best means of forming judicious plans of defence against the invasions of the enemy in time of war; in which last circumstance their importance usually becomes the most apparent.[13]

The origins of the Ordnance Survey lie in an interplay between military objectives and manpower, and the Enlightenment ambitions and values of men such as William Roy, Joseph Banks, and King George III.[14] The Ordnance Survey took its name from the Board of Ordnance, a civil department with a military organisation and staff.[15] The Board first began to direct surveying activities after 1717, when the Royal Engineers and the Drawing Room in the Tower of London were established. Surveys and maps created by these bodies were for military purposes and created in a military style, sometimes to further fortification proposals.[16] This became a more ambitious undertaking following the difficulties experienced by British troops in locating Scottish rebels in the impenetrable Highland terrain following the 1746 Battle of Culloden.[17] The Military Survey of Scotland was undertaken under the leadership of a civilian, Lanarkshire-born William Roy, and, while its main purposes were clearly military and colonial, there is some sense that other objectives may have been simmering under the surface. The work extended from the militarily significant Highland regions into lowland Scotland, perhaps for administrative reasons or perhaps because of the important symbolism projected by the image of a unified Scotland.[18]

The whole of the mainland had been mapped by the time the outbreak of the Seven Years War in 1756 turned attention elsewhere and the Scots no longer presented a pressing threat. While there is little evidence the Military Survey was ever directly employed or made publicly available, it laid the foundation for future large-scale mapping projects.[19] In 1783, when French astronomer Jacques Cassini de Thury proposed settling the long-standing dispute over the relative positions

[13] W Roy, 'An Account of the Measurement of the Base on Hounslow Heath in the Year 1784; and Also of the Trigonometrical Operations Carried On in the Years 1787, and 1788, For the Purpose of Determining the Distance Between the Meridians of Greenwich and Paris' (1785) 77 *Philosophical Transactions* 385.

[14] R Hewitt, *Map of a Nation: A Biography of the Ordnance Survey* (London, Granta, 2010) 112–13.

[15] Oliver (n 12) 51.

[16] ibid 51–53.

[17] Hewitt (n 14) xiii–xxvii, 9–27.

[18] CWJ Withers, 'The Social Nature of Map Making in the Scottish Enlightenment c.1682–c.1832' (2002) 54 *Imago Mundi* 46, 60; R Hewitt, 'A Family Affair: The Dundas Family of Arniston and the Military Survey of Scotland (1747–1755)' (2012) 64 *Imago Mundi* 60.

[19] Hewitt (n 14) 41. The only people who seem to have used the survey and maps were Roy himself, who was allowed to borrow them, and Arrowsmith, who consulted them in 1805 when preparing a map of Scotland for the Commissioners of Highland Roads and Bridges: Oliver (n 12) 53–55.

of the British and French observatories by connecting them by triangulation, Roy was appointed to take charge of the project. It was carried out under the auspices of the Royal Society, which purchased a theodolite from Jesse Ramsden, the leading scientific instrument maker of the day, and the Board of Ordnance provided manpower, in the form of soldiers, to carry out the survey and oversee it. The base was measured on Hounslow Heath, being close to London, fairly open and, most importantly, flat.[20] Both Joseph Banks and King George III took a considerable personal interest, with the King, who was keen to be seen as a patron of science, even visiting to inspect the work.[21]

The Paris-Greenwich triangulation saw the first links being made between the interests of science and the military. The French Revolution spelled the end of the shared triangulation project and Roy died in 1790, but in 1791 triangulation was resumed at the instigation of Charles Lennox, Duke of Richmond and Master General of Ordnance. Richmond purchased the Ramsden theodolite from the Royal Society and appointed William Mudge and Edward Williams, both of the Royal Regiment of Artillery, as directors of the Ordnance Survey. He also appointed Isaac Dalby, a civilian teacher of mathematics, as its assistant.[22] Richmond's precise motives in promoting the triangulating survey are not known. He had a long-standing interest in fortifications and defence but he also seems to have wished to continue the scientific project underlying the scheme. A related, but perhaps more personal, motivation was later said to be to assist William Gardner, Chief Draughtsman of the Ordnance, to complete a more accurate map of the county of Sussex, which was intended for publication under the Duke's patronage.[23]

Richmond's involvement in the Sussex survey demonstrates the interplay between public and private interests in the origins of a national institution.[24] The primacy of scientific motivations can be seen in the history of publication of results. Roy published two detailed reports of the London-Dover survey in the *Philosophical Transactions* in 1788 and Mudge, Williams, and Dalby continued the practice by publishing their own accounts in the same forum.[25] When war broke out with France in 1793, a more military impetus was given to the trigonometrical calculations, which were used for military surveys and hydrographic surveys of the coast.

Despite the threat of invasion, there was initially no attempt to keep the majority of the survey data secret. Although some key exceptions were made

[20] Oliver (n 12) 62.

[21] S Widmalm, 'Accuracy, Rhetoric and Technology: The Paris-Greenwich Triangulation, 1784–88' in T Frängsmyr, JL Heilbron, and RE Rider, *The Quantifying Spirit in the 18th Century* (Berkeley, University of California Press, 1990) 179, 185–86.

[22] Oliver (n 12) 63.

[23] Oliver (n 12) 63; W Mudge and I Dalby, *An Account of the Operations Carried on for Accomplishing a Trigonometrical survey of England and Wales; From the Commencement in the Year 1784, to The End of the Year 1796* (London, Faden, 1799–1811) xi–xii.

[24] Oliver (n 12) 63.

[25] Widmalm (n 21) 187.

(such as in relation to the 1799 survey of the coasts of Hampshire and the Isle of Wight, plans from which were lodged in the Tower and not available for public inspection[26]), in most respects Mudge and Williams welcomed and even encouraged use of the new, accurate data they were producing. In 1795 they wrote in the *Philosophical Transactions*:

> As it is probable that some individual will avail himself of the particulars given in this performance, by forming more correct maps of the counties over which the triangles have been carried, and who consequently may wish to visit certain of the stations, it is proper to observe, that small stakes are placed over the stones sunk in the ground, having their tops projecting a little above it.[27]

At this stage, the Ordnance Survey was solely producing trigonometric and topographic data, which it left to others to integrate it into maps alongside other source material from existing maps. Joseph Lindley and William Crosley's 1793 map of Surrey both copied John Rocque's map of Surrey and made use of William Roy's measurements.[28] Likewise, the 1803 edition of *Paterson's Roads* also incorporated material from 'the very ingenious Major Mudge', and Mudge assured its publisher Newbery that 'he may depend upon every information that the further progress of this great undertaking can supply'.[29] The relationship also went in both directions. In 1795 Faden used Ordnance Survey material in his map of Sussex; he also offered to supply a copy of his incomplete map of Norfolk to the Ordnance Survey on condition they did not publish it, since it had already cost him £2,000.[30]

In this same year, a significant change occurred: the Trigonometrical Survey began to collaborate with the Tower of London draughtsmen (known as the Interior Survey) to turn its measurements into maps.[31] From this point we can begin to discern more clearly a second technological transformation taking place in relation to mapmaking – one that involved the organisation of labour. While private mapmakers such as Faden and Cary had already begun to take active roles as organisers, hiring subcontractors to make surveys and producing the finished map product in London, the involvement of the state through the Board of Ordnance took this organisation to the next level. Over the course of the eighteenth century, the Board of Ordnance had built up a 'scientific corps' – officers trained in military engineering and mathematics.[32] Initially the draughtsmen and surveyors, whose

[26] Mudge and Dalby (n 23) xii.

[27] E Williams, W Mudge and I Dalby, 'An Account of the Trigonometrical Survey Carried on in the Years 1791, 1792, 1793, and 1794, by Order of His Grace the Duke of Richmond, Late Master General of the Ordnance. By Lieut. Col. Edward Williams, and Capt. William Mudge, of the Royal Artillery; And Mr. Isaac Dalby. Communicated by the Duke of Richmond, F. R. S.' (1795) 85 *Philosophical Transactions of the Royal Society of London* 414, 474.

[28] JB Harley, 'English County Map-Making in the Early Years of the Ordnance Survey: The Map of Surrey by Joseph Lindley and William Crosley' (1966) 132 *The Geographical Journal* 372.

[29] Advertisement, *Paterson's Roads 13th edn*, xviii.

[30] WA Seymour, *A History of the Ordnance Survey* (Folkestone, Wm Dawson & Sons Ltd, 1980), 68 citing WO47/2366 335 (UKNA).

[31] Hewitt (n 14) 149.

[32] Seymour (n 30) 3.

offices were locating in the Drawing Room at the Tower of London, were civilians but this changed in 1800 when a new Corps of military surveyors and draughtsmen was established, and which survived until 1817.[33] While the arrangement may not have always assured control, consistency, or quality, its significance lay in its organisational capacity – for the first time, the process from survey to map was carried out by a body of men working for the same employer and for the same purpose.

In 1795, when the decision to make maps was first taken, the intention developed for these maps to be sold to the public. There is no direct evidence of the reasoning behind this decision, although it is now seen as the most innovative aspect of the Ordnance's national topographic mapping.[34] Hewitt suggests that Mudge's determination to make both maps and trigonometrical measurements available to the public may have been in part designed to avoid accusations of espionage or suspicions on the part of the populace that the surveys were a precursor to raised taxes or further enclosures of public land.[35] Harley has suggested the decision was instigated by Faden, who had been allowed to publish the map of Kent in return for letting the Ordnance see his map of Norfolk before publication.[36] However, it is also clear that the Survey leadership was keen to bring both maps and data into the public sphere, where they could participate in scientific discourse of the day. In 1799 Mudge and Dalby explained:

> It has been very justly expected by the Public, that from the present undertaking, they should derive the advantage of an improvement in the geography of their country, and possess some general Map, published on the same principle with the *Carte de France*, a performance highly celebrated.[37]

This reasoning was again emphasised in 1816–17, when a case prepared by legal counsel related to copyright (discussed further below) explained that: 'Colonel Mudge, considering that the survey would be a loss to the public unless published for their use, the Master General and Board, on his recommendation permitted Mr Faden … to publish the work'.[38]

However, entering the commercial map market was not a simple matter; the Tower draughtsmen were neither engravers nor mapsellers. The Survey therefore turned to William Faden for assistance.[39] Having been provided with the Ordnance surveys, Faden and his assistants reduced the six-inch surveys to one inch upon

[33] ibid 48.
[34] Oliver (n 12) 68.
[35] Hewitt (n 14) 155.
[36] Seymour (n 30) 68.
[37] Mudge and Dalby (n 23) xiii.
[38] W Garrow and S Shepherd, Case, 8 January 1817, WO 44/299 (UKNA).
[39] Faden had taken over Thomas Jefferys' business in 1783 and was appointed as Geographer to the King in that same year: L Worms and A Baynton-Williams, *British Map Engravers: A Dictionary of Engravers, Lithographers and Their Principal Employers to 1850* (London, Rare Book Society, 2011) 224.

Mudge's instruction.[40] This was the scale first adopted by John Ogilby and since established as standard for the commercial county maps through the efforts of the Society of Arts and its county map premiums.[41] Faden arranged for the engraving and printing of the map, with Mudge verifying the place names on proof copies.[42] On 1 January 1801, Faden published the Ordnance Survey's first map, *An Entirely New & Accurate Survey of the County of Kent, with Part of the County of Essex.*

Authority for each stage of production can be traced through the cartouche, which proclaimed the map to be 'An entirely new & accurate Survey', that has been 'Done by the Surveying Draftsmen of his Majesty's Honourable Board of Ordnance, on the basis of the Trigonometrical Survey carried on by their Orders under the direction of Captn. W. Mudge of the Royal Artillery. F.R.S.' It stated the map was published by W Faden, giving the place as Charing Cross and the date. A second cartouche contained a dedication to Charles, Marquis Cornwallis, the Master-General of the Ordnance 'and the rest [of] the Principal Officers of His Majesty's Ordnance', from Mudge. The map's slip-case proclaimed it to be sold by W Faden, 'Geographer to the King'.

Two other county maps, of the significant military areas of Essex (1805) and Devon (1809), followed. These appear to be designed as independent county maps but Mudge's intention was eventually to publish maps covering the whole of Britain.[43] After the publication of this first map, however, Mudge sought to bring more of the production processes 'in-house'. Two engravers who had worked on the Kent map were employed to work permanently in the Tower and Faden was given oversight and appointed 'Agent for the sale of Ordnance Maps'.[44] From this point, Faden's name no longer appears on the maps as publisher. The map of the Isle of Wight, published on 1 June 1810, is the first to have abandoned the highly decorative cartouche, placing its title inside a framed border, which for the first time, identifies itself as the 'Ordnance Survey of the Isle of Wight and Part of Hampshire'. Mudge is named as the publisher in the bottom left corner and the engravers are named on the bottom right.

It is notable that the publication details appear designed to comply with the provisions of the Engravings Acts (explained in chapter three). However, whether this marked an emerging intention to assert exclusive rights in the maps or was simply a case of following a by now increasingly accepted convention for demonstrating the map's authorising entity is not clear. Before any clarity could be reached, the scientific character of the maps suddenly gave way to the military and in September 1811 the maps were withdrawn from sale. The Peninsular War

[40] Hewitt (n 14) 160.

[41] JB Harley, 'The Society of the Arts and the Surveys of English Counties 1759–1809' Part (i) (1963) 112 *Journal of the Society of the Arts* 45.

[42] ibid 161.

[43] Oliver (n 12) 71.

[44] Hewitt (n 14) 175.

had been underway for four years and the new Master-General of the Board of Ordnance, Henry Phipps, first Earl of Musgrave, appears to have decided that the Ordnance Survey maps presented a security threat.[45] Seymour suggests that inter-departmental rivalry between the Quartermaster General's Department and the Ordnance Survey may also have been a factor.[46] Although engraving continued, the maps were not made publicly available again until 1816.[47]

This first period in the Ordnance Survey's existence thus saw an initial interweaving of motives military, personal, and scientific. The key individuals who drove it forward, Roy, Richmond, and Mudge, placed its significance firmly within the purview of late Enlightenment scientific advances in navigation, scientific instrument-making, and geodesy, as well as broader scientific discourses centred around the Royal Society. Mudge's efforts in particular sparked considerable public interest in the Ordnance Survey; newspapers reported its progress and writers and poets (most famously Wordsworth) inserted Mudge himself into their texts.[48] The decision to put the maps on sale to the public can be seen in the context of fostering public participation in scientific discussion and sharing of knowledge in line with Enlightenment ideals. Mudge was pleased to share both trigonometric survey data and credit for the map itself with the private map traders in these early years. At the same time, he saw map sales as way of defraying the cost of the engraving and, in time, recovering some of the costs of the survey itself.[49] That these objectives might be to some extent in tension with each other was not immediately apparent but would soon become so.

III. Surveys, Scales, and Sales: From 1816 to 1870

Over the course of the next 70 years, the Ordnance Survey extended its survey and map coverage to the whole of Ireland (now part of the UK following the Act of Union 1800[50]), then England and Scotland. However, this was far from being a straightforward process. With the war over, civilian and private needs could be given greater consideration, leading to a growing list of competing demands on the Ordnance Survey's resources. As early as 1816, the gentlemen of Lincolnshire were pressing for a survey of their county to be made, which could be used for

[45] Seymour (n 30) 71.
[46] ibid.
[47] Hewitt (n 14) 215.
[48] R Hewitt, '"That Experienced Surveyor, Colonel Mudge": Romantic Representations of the Ordnance Survey Map-Maker, 1791–1830' in S Bushell, JS Carlson, and D Walford Davies (eds), *Romantic Cartographies: Mapping, Literature, Culture, 1789–1832* (Cambridge, Cambridge University Press, 2020) 50. See also ch 8, below.
[49] Commissioners of Military Inquiry, Parliamentary Papers (1812) Vol 4, Paper 5, 168.
[50] 39 & 40 Geo III c67.

agricultural improvement as well as foxhunting.[51] Captain Thomas Colby, Mudge's deputy, was in favour of taking up the offer, writing:

> [T]o what more proper object can the survey be directed, in a time of peace, than to aid the general improvement of the country: and how can that be done more effectually than in giving maps of those counties where the most beneficial changes are taking place?[52]

This approach demonstrated the existence of demand for the Survey and other counties soon began petitioning for similar arrangements.[53] However, the Lincolnshire map foreshadowed the challenges the Ordnance Survey would experience in trying to meet these expectations. Despite Colby's enthusiasm, the Board of Ordnance was not willing to contribute additional funding, so the Survey resorted to the traditional approach taken by commercial mapmakers – the raising of funds through subscriptions – and the map was not completed until 1825.[54]

The call on the Ordnance Survey to meet a private demand (and its inability to meet it promptly) spoke to a growing tension in the relationship between the Survey and commercial mapmakers during the period between 1811 and 1816 when sales were prohibited. The prohibition disappointed Mudge in his ambition to use sales to cover engraving costs. Moreover, it by no means prevented the data that the Ordnance Survey produced from circulating in public because the private mapsellers were under no such restriction. In 1813 John Cary published a map of Devonshire, which he proudly proclaimed as 'Reduced from a Survey made by the Board of Ordnance Under the Direction of Col. Mudge'.[55] Mudge was also aware of privately published reduced copies of the Essex maps and that London mapmaker Aaron Arrowsmith had incorporated most of the Devonshire map into his own map of England. Following the lifting of the prohibition on sales in 1816, Mudge wrote to the Board complaining of this growing practice.[56] He noted that, in addition to the above, the Ordnance Survey's map of Cornwall had been reduced to the scale of half an inch to the mile within a fortnight of being published and was about to be put into the hands of an engraver. Mudge lamented that

> an Idea has gone abroad among the mapsellers of London that as a portion of the Public at whose expence the Ordnance Survey is carried on, they have a right to reduce from

[51] Oliver (n 12) 78, Seymour (n 30) 76.

[52] Quoted in Oliver (n 12) 79.

[53] Seymour (n 30) 77, Oliver (n 12) 79.

[54] Lewis to Colby, 24 October 1820, Letterbook 152; Brownlow to Faden, 22 March 1818, Letterbook 154–5; Colby to Lewis, 26 October 1820, Letterbook 155–6; Mudge to Chapman, 7 February 1818, Letterbook 156 OS3/260 (UKNA); Also Seymour (n 30) 76.

[55] See W Ravenhill, 'The South West in the Eighteenth-Century Re-mapping of England' in K Barker and RJP Kain (eds), *Maps and History in South-West England* (Exeter, University of Exeter Press, 1991) 1, 22. *A Topographical Map Of Devonshire, Including Parts of the Adjacent Counties* (London, Cary, 1813). A copy can be found here: digitalarchive.mcmaster.ca/islandora/object/macrepo%3A79498.

[56] Mudge to Board of Ordnance, 28 Sept 1816, WO 44/299 (UKNA).

> and publish Copies of the Ordnance Survey on Scales suited to their own convenience; a circumstance, whether they have that right or not, that seems likely in a greater or less degree to affect the sale of the original work.[57]

Mudge's complaint about 'Scales suited to their own convenience' highlights the problem. Already the choice as to the most appropriate scale had undergone revision. The earliest surveys had been made at the scale of six inches to the mile, which was seen as suitable for military purposes. However, surveying at the six-inch scale took a long time, and Mudge was concerned at the cost involved at carrying out such large-scale surveys, which then had to be reduced by the engraver. To speed things up, the survey of Kent was completed at the three-inch scale. For the second map, of Essex, Mudge directed the Interior Survey to reduce further the scale to two inches to the mile, prioritising 'what is of real use to the Public' over the minute detail needed for military purposes, as well as making a considerable saving of expenditure and time.[58] When maps were published from the surveys, the scale was reduced still further; in creating the map of Kent, Faden reduced the six-inch Interior Surveys to the scale of one inch to the mile.[59] As noted above, there were several reasons for this. One was that the scale of one inch to the mile had become seen as standard for a commercially produced map, due to that being the scale required to be eligible for a Society of Arts premium.[60] County maps at this scale were also small enough to be carried around and used 'in the field'.

The private mapmakers, however, sought to reach markets other than the military and were clearly keen to produce still smaller maps – perhaps for display on walls or in other commodity forms – but equipped with the most up to date geographical information. Concerned that these maps would interfere with the market for Ordnance Survey maps, now that the latter were again permitted to be sold, Mudge requested advice on whether there was any legal impediment to mapmakers doing this and, if not, whether the Board would take other steps to prevent it.[61] The matter was referred to the Board's solicitors, who identified the Engravings Acts as the relevant laws. They pointed out to the Board that 'the Term "Proprietor or Proprietors" is used to denote the description of persons to whom, to whom only, the sole right of publishing their own works is given'. They considered that the question of whether this was Mudge was 'the question which the Mapsellers mean to agitate'.[62] The wording here is of interest, suggesting some communications over the matter with the private trade may have already occurred.

The solicitors identified two potential problems: first, whether Mudge could be considered the proprietor of the maps and, second, if he was, whether he had

[57] ibid.
[58] Hewitt (n 14) 173–74.
[59] Oliver (n 12) 66–67.
[60] See Harley (n 41).
[61] Mudge to RH Crew, 28 September 1816, WO 44/299 (UKNA).
[62] Smith & Sons to Board of Ordnance, 14 October 1816, WO 44/299 (UKNA).

complied with the formalities specified in the Engravings Acts by engraving on the plates the date of publication and the name of the proprietor. If these conditions were not met, the solicitors said that the maps would be 'thrown upon the public' and the mapsellers at liberty to copy and reduce them.[63]

It was clear that Mudge's approach for the Kent map of distributing authority among the various bodies responsible for different aspects of production did not necessarily address the key question of copyright law; namely, who was the owner of the right? Mudge himself explained that in putting his own name on the maps, along with the date and place of publication, he had followed the example of Captain Hurd in relation to the Admiralty Charts, and that he understood 'the act of the official man to be the act of the government who, by that deed were represented as proprietors'.[64] Mudge had heard that the mapsellers had obtained legal advice to the effect that both Ordnance Maps and Admiralty Charts were 'the property of the public at large and equally liable with impunity to be used for the purposes of Individual advantage'.[65] However, he went on to complain that even if the maps were covered by the Engravings Acts, there was still a problem in that the Acts gave an insufficient period of protection and that it was obvious to him that the right to the Board should be 'in fee or an extensive term'. He finished by suggesting an Act of Parliament was required to protect the Ordnance Maps from piracy.[66]

The Board's solicitors were not convinced that placing the name of Mudge as agent to the government on the map was sufficient to meet the criteria of the Acts and thought it expedient to get the opinions of the Attorney-General, William Garrow, and Solicitor-General, Samuel Shepherd, on the matter.[67] In stating the case, the solicitors noted that, while Cary and other mapsellers were prepared to abandon their plans to produce reduced individual county maps, they considered themselves entitled to incorporate the information from the Ordnance Survey maps into a general map of England.[68] Garrow and Shepherd took a bullish view of the matter, stating confidently that should the mapsellers use any of the Ordnance Survey's maps to produce a general map of England this would amount to piracy and give rise to a legal liability. They did not consider it an impediment that Mudge's name was placed on the maps, stating that he was the 'Inventor' of the maps under the Acts and might be considered to be the proprietor, although holding ownership on trust for the Board of Ordnance.[69] In support of this latter point, they cited the case *Cary v Kearsley* (in which Garrow had appeared for Cary)

[63] ibid.
[64] Mudge to RH Crew, 23 October 1816, WO44/299 (UKNA).
[65] ibid.
[66] ibid (note that the version/draft of the letter on file with the Hydrographic Office LP1857/G/267 (UKHO) only refers to the right being 'in fee').
[67] Smith & Son to Board of Ordnance, 4 October 1816, WO 44/299 (UKNA).
[68] Case, W Garrow and S Shepherd, 8 January 1817, WO 44/299 (UKNA).
[69] ibid.

as establishing that a publisher had a right of action against a pirate even if that publisher were employed by others and might be responsible to them.[70] They also recommended seeking an injunction as the best course of action.[71]

The Board was initially keen to institute proceedings against Arrowsmith or one of the other mapmakers. It was now Mudge, however, who sounded a note of caution, pointing out such an approach might damage relations with the commercial mapmakers and that the outcome might be 'to force the Trade into a combination amongst themselves to injure the sale of the Ordnance-Maps at the Tower, or at other authorised places'.[72] The Board ultimately determined to proceed more cautiously by inserting a notice in *The London Gazette* (the government's official newspaper) and other newspapers that warned private mapmakers and sellers against copying, reducing, or incorporating all or any of the Ordnance Maps without prior authority in writing of the Master-General.[73] The cautious approach reflected the symbiotic relationship between the private trade and the Ordnance Survey – the former needed data while the latter needed access to distribution networks, an advertising strategy, and the trade knowledge developed over previous centuries. But it also reflected an uncertainty at the heart of mapselling strategy about the extent to which it was not just possible but also desirable for the Ordnance Survey to participate in that market.

From 1816 there were two ways that the public could buy Ordnance maps: directly from the Tower or through Faden as agent for the Ordnance Survey. Faden could sell at a trade price and at a selling price, while those who bought maps from the Tower received the trade price. Mudge remained an advocate of the importance of selling maps to the general public and was keen to increase their circulation, In December 1817 he urged the Board that the maps' sale 'depends entirely on their Publicity'.[74] Colby, his successor, took the same view.[75] He observed that sales always improved when the maps were advertised and cautioned that 'many persons have been deterred from becoming subscribers from a suspicion that the work might at some future period be suspended and that the money they paid would be uselessly sacrificed in the purchase of an incomplete map'.[76] The Ordnance Survey was far from being the trusted institution it would later become and would-be subscribers to ambitious mapping (not to mention literary) projects were accustomed to disappointment when finances failed because the projectors had overstretched themselves. Colby addressed this by drawing up an advertisement to be placed in the newspapers with the aim of restoring the public's confidence and publicising

[70] See ch 4.

[71] Case, W Garrow and S Shepherd, 8 January 1817, WO 44/299 (UKNA).

[72] Smith & Son to Board of Ordnance, 27 January 1817, WO 44/299 (UKNA).

[73] ibid.

[74] Crew to Mudge, 24 December 1817 Letterbook 15, OS3/260 (UKNA).

[75] Colby to Crew, 26 May 1820, Letterbook 47; Colby to Crew, 8 June 1820, Letterbook 56, OS3/260 (UKNA).

[76] Colby to Crew 27 July 1820, Letterbook 86–87 OS3/260 (UKNA).

what was available to date.[77] In addition to placing advertisements in newspapers, Colby also directed copies to be sent to contacts in county towns, as 'their celebrity is materially increased by their being seen by Gentlemen in the Country'.[78]

Having made it his object to identify and remove the causes of poor sales of the Ordnance maps, Colby observed an additional problem to that of poor publicity – the opposition of the London mapsellers. This opposition, he believed, arose from the Ordnance maps 'being so accurate and so beautifully engraved that the taste and expectations of the public are not so easily satisfied with … [the mapsellers'] imperfect productions'.[79] A second factor was that the allowance granted to those selling the Ordnance maps was much lower than the ordinary trade discount, making the profit margin too small to make it worth the mapsellers' while to promote them. Furthermore, the fact that the public could buy maps from the Tower at the trade price was considered by the private mapmakers and mapsellers to be a violation of the general principles upon which the trade operated.[80] Colby suggested that the system could be made more efficient if Faden were granted an agency of 10 per cent on all maps, being the lowest rate of profit at which he could supply the trade.[81] This proposal was approved by the Board on 30 August 1820.[82]

The difficulty of reconciling the Board's desire to maintain a level of control over the sale of its maps with prevailing views – held by the trade and in line with laissez-faire economics – about the extent to which the state could interfere in the market meant that the relationship between the Ordnance Survey and the mapsellers remained fraught. The system of selling maps through both Faden and the Tower continued to be unsatisfactory, particularly as Faden continued to sell his own maps alongside those of the Ordnance and the 10 per cent discount proved insufficient to induce him to push their sales.[83] When Faden retired in 1823, a more formal Ordnance Agency was established and London mapmaker James Gardner was appointed to the position of agent. He agreed to use his best efforts to promote Ordnance maps and not to sell any others that would compete with them.[84] Later, in 1835, the Dublin booksellers Hodges and Smith were appointed agents for the sale of the Ordnance Survey Maps of Ireland.[85]

It was clear that notices placed in the *Gazette* and other newspapers in 1817 were not having the desired effect and that the London mapsellers were not just failing to promote Ordnance maps but also selling their own maps reproduced from Ordnance Maps. Investigating the situation in 1820, Colby found that both

[77] ibid.
[78] Circular letter from Dawson, 30 June 1820, Letterbook 64, OS3/260 (UKNA).
[79] Colby to Crew, 9 August 1820, Letterbook 97, OS3/260 (UKNA).
[80] Richard Mudge to Parry 15 January 1829, MLP 62 Folder 1 ii (UKHO).
[81] Colby to Crew, 9 August 1820, Letterbook 97 UKNA OS3/260 (UKNA).
[82] Crew to Colby, 30 August 1820, Letterbook,112 UKNA OS3/260 (UKNA).
[83] Richard Mudge to Parry 15 January 1829 MLP 62 Folder 1 ii (UKHO).
[84] Richard Mudge to Parry 15 January 1829; MLP 62 Folder 1 iii, Copy of agreement with James Gardner, 21 January 1829 MLP 62 Folder 1 ii (UKHO).
[85] McCulloch to Trevelyan, 13 November 1845, WO44/702 (UKNA).

Cary and Faden had made use of Ordnance Survey data in their own maps of Devonshire and Cornwall. However, whether or not they had had permission to do so was unclear.[86] Colby was hesitant to embark upon legal proceedings, pointing out that it would not be possible to obtain an injunction in time to prevent the majority of copies being sold and that, considering the 'extreme delicacy' of the matter, he thought it wise to 'defer coming into Court until every precaution can be taken to secure a successful issue'.[87] In October 1820, the Board's solicitor, James Elder, advised that no action for damages would lie against Cary in the particular case but that an injunction might be possible, so they should keep him apprised of any future piracies.[88] Reluctance to take legal action continued over the next two decades. In July 1840, the Ordnance Survey's solicitor noted there were complaints over James Wyld's publication of a map of Ireland referred to as 'compiled from the Survey of the Board of Ordnance', and that Lewis & Co were using the expression 'reduced from the Ordnance Survey'. However, he observed, there was

> a prevailing belief in the trade that they have a right to Maps constructed at the Public expence in the same way as is done with the Reports on Charities etc and that whatever the Law of the case might be, a Jury would in case of action, bring in a verdict of Not Guilty.[89]

From 1840 a much greater control on finances began to be exercised, as the Treasury, under Assistant Secretary Charles Edward Trevelyan, began to focus much more closely on efficiency and minimising public expenditure wherever possible. Scientific ideals were increasingly giving way to financial pressure and in 1841 the Survey also became physically more isolated from the scientific community when, following a fire in the Tower of London, its headquarters was moved to a barracks in Southampton.[90] But the twin problems of getting maps into the hands of the public remained pricing and distribution. In 1845 Trevelyan wrote to the Board that it was

[86] Colby to Crew, 9 August 1820, Letterbook 97, OS3/260; Colby to Crew, 4 September 1820, Letterbook 114 OS3/260 (UKNA).

[87] Colby to Crew, 4 September 1820, Letterbook 114–15, OS3/260 (UKNA).

[88] Smith to Colby, 9 October 1820, Letterbook 142, OS3/260. Note that Smith followed up this letter on 7 September 1821, but Colby responded that Cary had not published anything further since 9 October 1820. Smith to Colby, 7 September 1821, Colby to Smith, 11 September 1821, 379, OS3/260 (UKNA).

[89] Board of Ordnance Minutes, 20 July 1840, 8,891–8, 892 (20 July 1840) WO 47/1867. James Wyld had been apprenticed to William Faden and acquired his business and stock in 1823. He was also given the title Faden had held: Geographer to the King and to the Duke of York. Wyld was not averse to more underhand measures of competition. Also the member of parliament for Bodmin, Wyld used his parliamentary power to put through a vote in the House of Commons withholding Exchequer funding for the Metropolitan Commission of Sewers' survey of London. The MCS, now under the control of social reformer Edwin Chadwick, was seeking a high quality and large-scale survey upon which to base its sanitary planning. The Ordnance was not willing to fund the survey from its own coffers but, in stopping additional funding from the Exchequer, Wyld omitted to inform the House that he had started his own large-scale map of London: Oliver (n 12) 189.

[90] Oliver (n 12) 156.

> an object of so much importance to secure the most extensive sale possible of the Ordnance Maps, both to meet in some degree the heavy expenditure arising from the Survey, and to promote the objects of public utility for which the Survey was instituted.[91]

Trevelyan's eliding of expense and public interest draws attention to the increasing, and not always complementary, demands being placed on the Ordnance Survey by the middle of the century for both government and private purposes. In 1824 a new state priority had emerged to eclipse the earlier military ones: a survey of Ireland, which would allow the British government to introduce a taxation system based on land valuation and thereby exert greater administrative control over the territory.[92] By the time the bulk of its staff returned to England from Ireland following the survey two decades later, the Ordnance Survey had become caught up in the sweeping political and social reforms of the mid-century. Reform of the House of Commons in 1830s created a need for maps to assist in defining borough boundaries.[93] The wave of social reforms that followed also had mapping implications. In the mid-1830s, the Poor Law Commission sought the assistance of the Ordnance Survey to make the large-scale town surveys and maps it needed to implement its sanitation reforms. The Tithe Commission established under the Tithe Commutation Act 1836 also required large scale maps that could accurately display parish and estate boundaries so that the tithes could be calculated. Then in 1845, the Inclosure Act[94] created the Inclosure Commission, which also required large scale maps, with the Tithe Commission Acts being insufficiently accurate for the purpose of dividing and allotting common land. The rise of railway construction represented another drain on resources as it created an enormous demand for maps to plan and construct rail routes. The problem here was not that the private companies required the services of the Ordnance Survey but, rather, that they enticed its staff to leave through offering higher rates of pay.[95] Further, in 1847 the Metropolitan Sanitary Commission requested a map of London on the scale of five feet to a mile to assist its work in improving the city's drainage.[96]

These projects were not only diversions from the Ordnance Survey's main task of completing the surveys and maps of England and Wales but also demonstrated the challenges of producing maps for different purposes and raised questions about the role or roles that the Ordnance Survey was expected to play. In 1855 the Board of Ordnance was abolished due to dissatisfaction with its activities during the Crimean War and responsibility for the Survey passed to the War Office. Real responsibility for the Survey continued to lie with Treasury and it was the Lords

[91] Trevelyan to Secretary of the Ordnance, 16 October 1845, WO 44/702 (UKNA).

[92] See J Harwood Andrews, *A Paper Landscape: The Ordnance Survey in Nineteenth-Century Ireland* (Oxford, Clarendon Press, 1975). Also, A Sills, *Against the Map: The Politics of Geography in Eighteenth-Century Britain* (Charlottesville, University of Virginia Press, 2021).

[93] Oliver (n 12) 107–10.

[94] 8 & 9 Vict c 118.

[95] Seymour (n 30) 112–13, Hewitt (n 14) 294–95.

[96] Hewitt (n 14) 298.

of the Treasury who were called to defend the Survey in the House of Commons as it increasingly came under attack over frustration at its slow progress, spiralling costs, and disagreements over the maps' proper purposes.[97]

It was not just Members of Parliament who were unhappy with the Ordnance Survey during this period but also members of the public more generally. On 17 September 1862, *The Times* published a letter from 'A Surveyor' complaining about the out of date maps he had recently purchased and lamenting that 'the very numerous defects are a disgrace to a national undertaking of such interest and utility'.[98] On 22 September, Colonel Henry James (Director of the Ordnance Survey from 1854–1875) responded in *The Times*, writing that 'no one is more conscious than I am of the fact that the old Ordnance maps do require a very extensive revision to bring them up to what they ought to be' and asserted that, nevertheless, 'half a loaf is better than no bread'.[99] But a long editorial article published the same day disagreed. The author claimed that the situation could be easily remedied if the matter had been left to private mapmakers, but that:

> Private enterprise will not venture on a field which Parliament has seized. For aught the speculators know, a Parliamentary grant next year may ruin the entire enterprise. Parliament stops the way. There are no maps of England because there is an Ordnance Map always ready to tumble on the heads of the sellers and purchasers of private maps.[100]

Writing to the *Times* the following day, Edward Stanford (who had supplied the maps to 'A Surveyor') agreed 'most fully' with the claim that the fault lay with the 'obstruction presented by the Government to the exercise of private enterprise in the production of maps'. He declared himself willing to publish maps on the large scales of one, two, or three miles to an inch, as private mapmakers had previously done, if the government would encourage, or at least not oppose, him. He alleged that the Survey's attempts to compete with the trade diverted 'the attention of officials from their proper functions – the completion and revision of their surveys', which resulted in no gain, but rather a loss, to the public.[101] The educator and cultural and literary critic Matthew Arnold also weighed into the controversy, complaining that the quality of the Survey's copperplates was poor, leading the government to neglect its responsibility: 'For a Government's first and indispensable duty in the way of map-making is … to provide a *good* map of its country, not to provide a *cheap* one … [T]he first consideration is excellence'.[102]

With this objection, Arnold put his finger on the problem: what was the state's role in mapmaking and did commercialising maps undermine it? But it also

[97] Oliver (n 12) 246.
[98] *Times*, 17 September 1862, 6.
[99] *Times*, 22 September 1862, 7.
[100] ibid 6.
[101] *Times*, 23 September 1862, 10.
[102] M Arnold, 'Ordnance Maps' in *The Complete Prose Works of Matthew Arnold*, II, 255.

begged the question: what was a *good* map? Here we return to the matter of Edney's 'cartographic ideal' and the issue of scale.[103] One of the key questions facing the Ordnance Survey was the choice of the scale at which the survey should occur. During the 1850s, this question came to a head and the period has become known as the 'Battle of the Scales'.[104] The one-inch maps comprising the First Series, while useful for military and more general purposes, were now recognised as being inadequate for more specific projects such as laying out roads and railways, geological surveys, and statistical work.[105]

In 1840 the decision had been taken to begin surveying and mapping England and Scotland at the six-inch scale, as being more useful for such purposes, but by the 1850s this scale was also under pressure for failing to offer sufficient detail to meet new demands on the maps. Railway construction and other civil engineering projects, public works such as drainage and sewage, estate surveying, geology, and land registration all tended towards adoption of larger scale maps, while Members of Parliament, drawn from the landed gentry, would have been more familiar with uses of maps for travel and field sports, which were better facilitated by the one-inch map.[106] The Treasury, however, was more influenced by economic arguments. These were connected to the arguments based on the utility of the survey: the belief that it should be at the scale which was 'most generally useful'.[107] Ultimately, financial considerations determined the adoption of the 1:2500 (roughly 25 inches to the mile) scale. Although it would initially cost more than the six-inch, it would serve more purposes, and eliminate the need for local surveys, thus offering better value for money. The 1:2500 could also be readily reduced to six-inch maps either by users themselves or by the Ordnance Survey, which, by engraving and selling six-inch reductions, could obtain still more value from the initial map.[108]

The philosophy underlying the Battle of the Scales, at least on the part of Treasury and Trevelyan, was that the Ordnance Survey would provide a basic survey and any supplementary mapping derived from it could be supplied by the private trade.[109] This meant that scale became crucial to delineating between permissible and impermissible uses of Ordnance Survey data. In the 1850s, it seems that several mapmakers applied for permission to reproduce Ordnance Survey maps. Permission was given, without payment, in cases where the proposed map was on a sufficiently different scale that it was thought it would not interfere with sale of the Ordnance Survey map, the map was published for a special purpose (such

[103] Edney (n 11) 166.
[104] Oliver (n 12) ch 5. Oliver notes the phrase consciously echoed the railway 'Battle of the Gauges' that had taken place a decade earlier.
[105] ibid 267.
[106] ibid 266.
[107] ibid 267.
[108] ibid 267–69.
[109] ibid 311.

as for insertion in a guidebook), or for district maps that involved reproducing portions of more than one Ordnance Survey sheet.[110]

An indication that attitudes were beginning to shift in relation to use of the Survey data came in 1855, when a dispute arose with Scottish mapsellers W & AK Johnston. The firm was one of the Ordnance agents in Scotland but in October 1855 they published a map under the title: *To the Nobility, Gentry and Clergy of the County of Wigtown this Map Reduced at their Request from the Ordnance Survey of Scotland is Respectfully Dedicated by the Publishers*. The War Office's solicitor wrote, apparently threatening proceedings and suggesting its behaviour was even more reprehensible as it was an Ordnance Survey agent.[111] The map produced by W & AK Johnston was at a different scale to that of the Ordnance Survey and had, in fact, featured in argument during the Battle of the Scales. Keith Johnston, the firm's co-founder, had appeared before the Select Committee investigating the Ordnance Survey in Scotland in 1851. Johnston, like other Scots appearing before the Select Committee, claimed that the lack of a 'convenient map' of Scotland was giving rise to great dissatisfaction to 'almost all classes of people in Scotland'.[112] By 'convenient', Johnston meant 'not so very large as to be inaccessible, nor too expensive to be purchased by the majority of people who wish to consult it'.[113] This was a one-inch map. Johnston urged that the survey itself continue at the six-inch scale, explaining that a six-inch survey would be more accurate but that the maps published from such a survey should be at the one-inch scale. As he elaborated,

> in every case the surveyor or other person mapping a country find it advantageous to make his sketch or drawing very much larger than is necessary for publication, because you can reduce with great accuracy, but cannot enlarge without error.[114]

He had no objection to a six-inch map also being published, as long as it did not delay the publication of the more useful one-inch map.[115]

The example Johnston gave the Committee was that of the Ordnance map of Wigtonshire in south-west Scotland. He informed the Committee that the only map of Scotland produced so far was that of Wigtonshire, but that very few copies of it had been sold in Scotland. The reason for this was that the map comprised 38 large sheets. There was then some disagreement over whether, when all laid out on the ground, these sheets would cover the same surface as the New Club in Edinburgh (200 feet by 60 feet) or the lesser space of 18 feet by 16 feet.[116] Indeed,

[110] History of Copyright of Ordnance Survey Publications (c1931), 1 OS1/233 (UKNA).
[111] ibid; 'Copyright – Messrs Bartholomew' OS1/755 (UKNA).
[112] Report from the Select Committee on Ordnance Survey (Scotland); Together with the Proceedings of the Committee, Minutes of Evidence, Appendix and Index, 10 July 1851, 76.
[113] ibid.
[114] ibid 80.
[115] ibid 78.
[116] ibid 85.

one exchange prefigured the map satires of Lewis Carroll[117] and Jorge Borges[118] of many years later:

> Supposing it were laid upon the ground, it would cover the surface which you have just stated; and if a meeting of county gentlemen had to consider upon a line of road from one point to another, they would have to cast their eyes over that enormous space? – They must walk over it.
>
> And it would be impossible to form any idea either of the features of the country or of the line which the road ought to take? – Quite impossible.[119]

The map's size made it a prime candidate for reduction but the Ordnance Survey was in fact preparing to publish its own one-inch survey of Wigtonshire, which appeared the following year.[120] Upon receipt of the solicitor's communication, the Johnstons returned a wounded letter to the Secretary of State for War, Lord Panmure, who had ministerial responsibility for the Survey. They wrote that

> it is entirely new to us, as we feel assured it will be to the general public, to be informed that the Ordnance Survey of this country, –unlike that of any other in Europe, is not for the use of the people in any way they may have occasion to employ it.[121]

The Johnstons went on to protest that, when their firm had been approached by the leading men of Wigtonshire to provide a map they could use, they never conceived they were doing anything that was against the law and added, 'if it really be the case that Surveyors, Engineers, Architects, Publishers or others are not at liberty to freely use that Survey your Lordship cannot too soon make that resolution known to the Country'.[122]

The Johnstons were also offended by the accusation that they were 'more reprehensible' because of being Ordnance Survey agents, reminding Panmure that the Survey uniformly used their company's county maps as a basis when commencing new county surveys. They also pointed out that they were the current proprietors of the only survey of Scotland in existence, worth £20,000, and that one day the Ordnance Survey would extinguish that property; thus, 'we of all others ought to be excused, in the exercise of our calling, and in ignorance of any law to the contrary, for attempting to keep the field we have so long occupied'. The Johnstons finished their letter by contrasting the position of the Ordnance Survey with that of the Hydrographic Office, stating that they had repeatedly been thanked by those interested in shipping when they have corrected the coastlines in their publications

[117] L Carroll, *The Hunting of the Snark: An Agony in Eight Fits* (London, Macmillan, 1876).
[118] JL Borges, 'On Rigor in Science' (trans M and H Boyer) in JL Borges, *Dreamtigers* (Austin, University of Texas Press, 90).
[119] Report from the Select Committee on Ordnance Survey (Scotland) 84.
[120] Oliver (n 12) 526.
[121] W & AK Johnston to Lord Panmure, 1 December 1855 ACC.5811/29 (NRS).
[122] ibid.

from Admiralty charts, which are sent to them regularly for that purpose.[123] In the end, no prosecution was pursued and W & AK Johnston continued as Ordnance Survey agent, on condition the firm would not make any more reduced maps from the Survey.[124]

The dispute with W & AK Johnston underlined the slippery boundaries between public and private interests in the Ordnance Survey maps and the data they contained. As leading Scottish mapmakers, the Johnston agency conferred an associated prestige upon the Ordnance Survey, in a vulnerable position in Scotland due to the tardiness of its surveying activities there. The Ordnance Survey also relied on W & AK Johnston's maps to accelerate its own efforts. The firm emphasised to the Ordnance Survey that it should honour its public purpose and make its data widely available. The problem was that, while W & AK Johnston needed the Ordnance Survey's superior data, having acquired it, the firm was able to produce a superior – in the sense of more commercially desirable – map.

There seemed to be no way of resolving the tension between the Ordnance Survey's desire to circulate its maps as widely as possible and yet maintain a level of control over sales. Over the years the Ordnance Survey and Treasury introduced and argued over a range of different ways to address the issues. Prices were reduced for some maps and increased for others, the sales agents changed and grew in number. A particular bone of contention was the discount offered to the agents. Those with insight into the map and bookselling trade were aware that the agents' discount needed to be large enough that they could also pass on a slightly lower discount to their own agents and other booksellers, thus ensuring all those in the distribution chain could draw in sufficient profit from the sale price. However, John McCulloch, Comptroller of Her Majesty's Stationery Office, was dismissive of Colby's statement in 1845 that the sale of Ordnance maps was dependent upon the size of the allowance to the seller, believing that, while this might be true in the case of books, it did not apply to maps which people bought not 'for amusement, but for purposes of solid utility; and they will not, speaking generally, be stimulated to buy them by the rhetoric of any book or mapseller, or hindered from doing so by his silence'.[125] No matter the measure adopted, sales figures remained modest. In 1861 Treasury ordered that the discounts given to the agents should be increased from 25 per cent to $33^{1/3}$ per cent, but sales of the one-inch maps continued to run at a loss.[126] In January 1866, a new system of agency and pricing, which it was hoped would bring in more money to cover the costs of publication, was adopted by the Secretary of State for War but led to a further drop in sales.[127] When changing the prices and methods of distribution failed to increase sales, suspicion fell back on the role of the private map trade and attention turned again to copying.

[123] ibid.
[124] History of Copyright of Ordnance Survey Publications (c1931) 2, OS1/233 (UKNA).
[125] McCulloch to Trevelyan, 13 November 1845, WO44/702 (UKNA).
[126] Oliver (n 12) 313–14.
[127] Seymour (n 30) 161.

IV. 'The most perfect maps in the world': 1870 to 1901

On 1 January 1870, the final one-inch sheet of the First Series Ordnance map of England and Wales was published. It was now 86 years since the baseline had been first measured at Hounslow Heath but there was still no map of the entire country at a uniform scale.[128] In that same year, control of the Survey moved from the War Office to the Department of Works, marking a recognition that the Survey's military purposes had been largely subsumed by the civil. It also marked a period of growing Parliamentary scrutiny of the Survey's operations. The final three decades of the century witnessed significant changes in map production and map circulation, and attitudes towards the Survey's maps and geographical data became increasingly proprietorial.

One reason for the growing interest of the House of Commons was the passing of Lord Cairns' Land Transfer Act in 1875,[129] which sought to improve the system of land registration and made provision for a public map to be kept in the Land Registry to which private maps could refer. The 1:2500 Ordnance map was specified to be the public map, where it existed. A Select Committee appointed to investigate reform of the procedures for land conveyancing reported in 1879 that the 1:2500 cadastral survey 'as regards scale and accuracy … leaves little or nothing to be desired'[130] and recommended the immediate completion of that survey. Alongside the interest in land registration and transfer, there were other demands for special mapping by government departments. Meanwhile, some members of Parliament urged that the survey be completed and one-inch maps of every county issued for more general reasons of public convenience, noting the usefulness of maps for legal and scientific purposes.[131] In June 1880, a motion was passed in the Commons that the Survey be completed immediately, which led to a significant increase in funding and subsequent expansion in terms of manpower of the Survey.[132] The 1:2500 survey of southern Britain was completed in 1886–87 and, after that, the British counties mapped at the six-inch scale before 1855 were remapped at the 1:2500 scale.

Throughout these developments and changes, the Survey remained subject to conflicting pressures. The Treasury was always anxious to reduce costs, while Members of Parliament wanted faster results.[133] At the same time, the mingling of civilian and military staff and, in particular, the treatment of the former, also gave rise to dissatisfaction within the Survey's organisation itself.[134] Gradually, the number of civil surveyors and draftsmen increased, but these Civil Assistants complained that they were always kept in subordinate positions and treated

[128] ibid 160.
[129] 38 & 39 Vict c87.
[130] Oliver (n 12) 323.
[131] Oliver (n 12) 315, 320–25.
[132] ibid 325.
[133] ibid 326, ch 7.
[134] ibid 343.

differently to other civil servants in relation to pay and superannuation. Ongoing discontent led to the appointment of a Departmental Committee in 1891, which uncovered a wide array of grievances, from pay rates and pay equity to travel allowances and promotion.[135]

While the cost of manpower was an ongoing source of tension, another way that costs could be saved was through technological innovation. One important change introduced by Major-General Anthony Cooke, who became Director in 1878, was to cease copperplate engraving of the six-inch map, instead creating it through photo-reduction of the 1:2500. The process, known as photozincography, which involved transferring a photographic negative to a zinc printing plate, was apparently discovered more or less simultaneously in 1859 by John Osborne of Melbourne, Australia, and by then-Ordnance Survey Director, Henry James, in Southampton.[136] Initially more useful for copying manuscripts than maps, in 1881–82 Cooke changed the way that the 1:2500 was drawn so that it could be directly reduced to six inches. While the style of the finished product was not so admired as that produced by engraving, it represented a saving in both time and cost.[137] Some innovations occurred also in relation to copperplate engraving, in particular in relation to hill printing and the development of steam printing in 1886.[138]

In light of the ever-constant financial pressures on the Survey, maximising sales continued to be a matter of importance. As noted in the previous section, the new arrangements of 1866 led to a reduction in sales and, in yet another attempt to address the problem, Treasury suggested setting up a map depot in London in 1872.[139] However, the depot was forced to close in 1874, when the site was needed for construction of Charing Cross Road. Meanwhile, the existing agencies were discontinued and responsibility for all map sales was handed over to the Stationery Office, which entered into an agreement with well-known publisher and mapseller Edward Stanford to act as sole agent for England.[140] He received a $33^{1/3}$ per cent commission on sales and allowed a 25 per cent discount to retail dealers. In May 1886, the sole agency was put up for tender and Stanford's offer of £600 per annum to renew the agency for 10 years was accepted (see Figure 19). In Scotland and Ireland, the maps were included in the contracts granted to the agents who sold all other government publications – Messrs Menzies & Co in Edinburgh and Messrs Hodges, Finnis & Co in Dublin.[141]

[135] ibid 348–56.
[136] Oliver (n 12) 308–309.
[137] ibid 334–35.
[138] A process was developed in 1889 which allowed the hills to be engraved on a separate plate and then overprinted on an ordinary outline plate in black or brown ink. ibid 337–39.
[139] Report of the Departmental Committee appointed by the Board of Agriculture to consider the arraignments to be made for the Sale of Ordnance Survey Maps C-8147 (London, Her Majesty's Stationery Office, 1896) (1896 Committee on Sale of Ordnance Survey Maps) Report, 6.
[140] Oliver (n 12) 362.
[141] 1896 Committee on Sale of Ordnance Survey Maps, Report, 6.

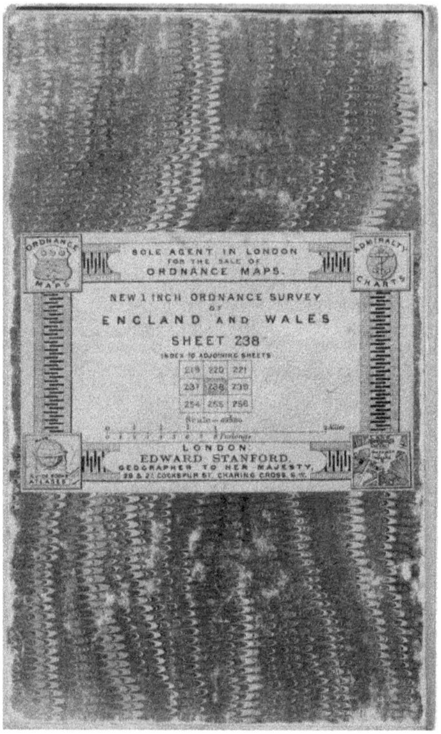

Figure 19 Cover and trade card for Edward Stanford, the Ordnance Survey's agent in London since 1853 and sole agent in London from 1887

The transfer of responsibility for printing and publishing maps to the Stationery Office meant that the question of copyright in maps was now to be considered alongside the question in relation to other government publications. The Stationery Office had been established in 1786, initially to supply the Treasury with paper, pens, ink, wax, and other items of stationery, and later expanding to carry out all business associated with printing, binding, publishing, and supply of stationery to the entire public service.[142] Over the years, an ever-increasing number of government departments sought to use its services and by 1890 it was responsible for the printing and publishing of all Parliamentary Papers, *The London Gazette*, and all Acts of Parliament.[143] But the Stationery Office too came under financial pressure to control its mounting expenditure so when commercial publishers began to reprint and sell its material this was soon perceived as a threat to its ability to recover expenditure through sales.[144]

In 1883 the Director of the Ordnance Survey, Major-General Cooke, requested legal advice from counsel, Alfred E Gathorne Hardy, on whether it was a copyright infringement to reproduce portions of a survey plan in making maps suitable for attachment to estate sale documents. Hardy responded that in all of those situations, the reproduction of an Ordnance plan would be a copyright infringement and that it would make no difference whether it was for sale or distributed for free.[145] However, he added that there was nothing to prevent those in whom copyright was vested from sanctioning the reproduction of Ordnance plans 'as they may deem them innocuous

[142] H Barty-King, *Her Majesty's Stationery Office: The Story of the First 200 Years 1786–1986* (London, Her Majesty's Stationery Service, 1986) 1–29.

[143] ibid 40.

[144] ibid 40–141.

[145] In coming to this conclusion, Gathorne Hardy relied on Vice-Chancellor Wood's statements in *Kelly v Morris* (1865–66) LR 1 Eq 697, discussed in more detail in the Conclusion of ch 8, below.

or desirable.'[146] Having received this advice, Cooke wrote to the Treasury Secretary, advising the government to consider waiving 'some of the privileges of its copyright in order to extend the utility of the maps'; in particular, in relation to one of their most important purposes, the transfer of land. He added that this would probably not lead to any diminution in the sale of the maps because it was so expensive to copy them. The government approved this course of action.[147]

However, the Stationery Office was increasingly becoming aware of the interest shown by commercial publishers in printing statutes, historical manuscripts, and the *Trade Marks Journal*.[148] Concerned, the Treasury again sought a legal opinion. Counsel responded that copyright did exist in such publications but, in order for it to be enforced, the author of a government publication would need to agree to assign the copyright to the person who had employed him or to agree to hold it as a trustee for that person – the person in question representing the government.[149] Following this advice, Treasury inserted a notice in *The London Gazette*, stating:

> Printers and publishers are reminded that anyone reprinting without due authority matter which has appeared in Government publications renders himself liable to the same penalties as those which he might, under like circumstances, have incurred had the copyright been in private hands.[150]

While the notice may have reflected government concerns about maintaining the authoritative status of official materials, it was seen in some quarters as more unwelcome state interference. The *Law Journal* issued a statement, picked up by other publications, arguing that the notice misunderstood copyright as belonging to the publisher rather than the author. It considered that

> the copyright of mere compilations made by the clerical staff of a Government office probably is vested in her Majesty, but the copyright in much more tempting productions, like the reports of commissioners and of consuls, does not become her Majesty's, simply because the Stationery-office issues them.[151]

It thought the Crown must at least show official documents were paid for with a view to their publication in order to claim copyright in them.[152]

To address some of these concerns, the Treasury issued a Minute on Crown Copyright in August 1887. The Minute set out seven classes of Government

[146] Advice of AE Gathorne Hardy (copy), 31 January 1883, History of Copyright in OS Publications, Appendix 1 OS1/233 (UKNA).

[147] History of Copyright in OS Publications, 2, OS 1/233 (UKNA).

[148] Minute (undated), STAT 12/36/1; 'Copyright – Government Publications – "Trade Marks Journal", 18 September 1886, OS1/6/3 (UKNA).

[149] History of Copyright in OS Publications, 3 OS 1/233, Richard Webster and Edward Clarke advice (copy), Copyright Government Publications, 30 August 1886, OS1/6/3; Copyright Government Publications, Case, 18 September 1886, OS 1/6/3 (UKNA).

[150] History of Copyright in OS Publications, 3 OS 1/233 (UKNA).

[151] *Morning Post*, 26 November 1886, 3.

[152] ibid.

publication, ranging from Select Committee Reports to Acts of Parliaments. Class 7 was 'Charts and Ordnance maps'. In relation to the first five categories, the Minute stated there should be no restrictions on publication, as it was desirable these works should be made known to the public as widely as possible. However, in relation to Class 6 ('Literary and quasi-literary works') and Class 7, the Minute noted that it was desirable to enforce copyright in them 'in the interests of the taxpayer, and of literature and science'. If not, then private publishers would be able to produce cheap copies of such publications and reap the profit 'at the expense of the taxpayer'. Moreover, as the production of such works was a burden to the taxpayer in the first place, 'the greater the burden, the fewer works can the Government, with justice to the taxpayer, undertake'.[153] Again, it was urged that public notice be given of the government's intention to enforce its copyright and that such notice also be directed to the publishing trade.[154] Following the Minute, in January 1888, the Director of the Ordnance Survey directed that all Ordnance maps should bear a notification stating that all rights of reproduction were reserved.[155] In 1889 it was decided that Letters Patent would be passed appointing the Comptroller of the Stationery Office to the position of Queen's Printer and holder of copyright in all government publications.[156]

Despite this explicit intention on the part of the Treasury and Stationery Office to enforce copyright in all government publications, there remained considerable reluctance to do so. In 1887 yet another dispute arose when W & AK Johnston published *Johnston's reduced Ordnance Survey maps of Scotland, coloured*. No action was taken but, in correspondence over the matter, Pigott was clear about the Stationery Office's two main concerns, observing there were two factors that would justify taking legal action: the interest of the public purse, and the duty of protecting the public from 'adulteration'. In relation to the former, he considered there were other ways of recovering the cost of printing and distributing maps, and that it was not advisable to interfere with the private trade on this basis. Thus, the government should only interfere to prevent 'actual fraud'; that is, selling a map as a genuine Ordnance map.[157] Ordnance Survey Director Wilson commented that Johnston's maps would have 'a most injurious effect' upon sales of the Ordnance Survey maps but favoured a market-based solution, suggesting that the best way of stopping such 'piracies' would be to 'make the Ordnance Maps easily and cheaply accessible to all classes. At present the Ordnance Maps are either half hidden out of sight or replaced by copies or reductions inferior to them in accuracy and finish'.[158]

The prevailing view of both the Stationery Office and the Ordnance Survey was that Ordnance Survey material could be used by the private trade as material

[153] History of Copyright in OS Publications, 3-4 OS 1/233 (UKNA).
[154] ibid 4.
[155] ibid.
[156] Copyright in Government Publications, 9 November 1889, STAT 12/36/1 (UKNA).
[157] History of Copyright in OS Publications, 4-5, OS 1/233 (UKNA).
[158] Wilson to Treasury Secretary, 19 September 1887, OS1/6/2 (UKNA).

for maps, even if they should be discouraged from copying the maps themselves. Moreover, the Ordnance Survey should not attempt to compete with the private mapmakers by publishing 'special maps of districts' or maps 'on cheap paper'.[159] There was indeed a real doubt in Pigott's mind as to whether copyright in government publications could even be successfully enforced. He took the view that if the government ever did have to fight a copyright case, 'it should be in a case in which permission has been refused for some obvious public purpose'.[160]

In the late 1880s, with the 1:2500 survey of the Southern part of the country complete, Treasury began to tighten the purse strings. Staff numbers dropped and in 1890 oversight of the Ordnance Survey was transferred from the Office of Works to the Board of Agriculture. The likely explanation for this is that most of the mapping was of rural areas but the association was to last for another 70 years.[161] 1890 was also the year in which the Survey's production and distribution of maps began to come under yet more intense public scrutiny. This was ignited by Mancunian civil engineer Henry Tipping Crook. In an address to the geographical section of the British Association in Leeds, Crook attacked the Survey for the poor sales of its maps, which he put down chiefly to their failure to meet popular requirements and, to a lesser extent, the difficulties in accessing them, their high prices, and poor presentation.[162]

Booksellers and surveyors also continued to complain about the difficulty of obtaining both information about the maps and the maps themselves.[163] In a Memorandum on the Sale of Ordnance Survey Maps of June 1891, Charles Wilson (Director since 1886) noted that as soon as Stanford took over the sole agency in England, the sales immediately fell.[164] Wilson was strongly of the view that the system was deficient, writing: 'It should not be forgotten that the country has a very valuable property in these maps, and at present derives very little profit from it in money, or from its general use by the public.'[165] He also linked the rise of copying to the sole agency, writing: 'One result in the want of facility for sale, is the great increase in the publication by private forms of maps reduced from, or based on the Ordnance Survey, which largely take the place of the Government maps'.[166] However, he went on to note that even Stanford had produced a six-inch map of London that directly competed with the Ordnance one.[167]

Meanwhile, Henry Tipping Crook's attacks continued to be echoed and amplified by complaints both within and outside Parliament about the progress of the

[159] History of Copyright in OS Publications, 5 OS 1/233 (UKNA).
[160] History of Copyright in OS Publications 6, OS 1/233 (UKNA).
[161] Oliver (n 12) 342.
[162] Seymour (n 30) 186.
[163] Charles W Wilson, Memorandum on Sale of Ordnance Survey Maps, Appendix VII to 1896 Committee on Sale of Ordnance Survey Maps Report, 78.
[164] ibid.
[165] ibid.
[166] ibid 79.
[167] ibid.

Ordnance Survey in keeping maps up to date, as well as its choices about what to depict on them.[168] In 1892 these complaints drove the House of Commons to appoint a Departmental Committee to inquire into the Ordnance Survey. Under the chairmanship of Sir John Dorington MP, this Committee was directed to consider the steps to be taken to expedite the completion of the new one-inch map of the British Isles and whether the maps satisfied the reasonable requirements of the public in terms of style, execution, form, information conveyed, and price.[169] Although not directed to consider the publication and sales of Ordnance Survey maps, the issue arose in several contexts, as did the question of copying of maps. The Committee received numerous suggestions about improvements that could be made to Ordnance Survey maps. Questions about what should appear on maps, how it should appear, and whether they should be coloured were all relevant to the larger question of the extent to which the Ordnance Survey should be meeting popular demand and the many different markets for maps that existed and were emerging. As Crook had wryly observed, many of the objections involved 'ignoring the principle upon which the Ordnance Survey has always been conducted. It does not construct maps for popular use'.[170]

Imbricated with the question of what the Ordnance Survey should be putting on its maps was the matter of whether private mapmakers should be allowed to use Ordnance Survey maps and data to meet demand not being met by the Survey, with prominent Scottish mapmakers John George Bartholomew and George Johnston of W & AK Johnston appearing before it. Bartholomew opined that the Survey should produce 'mother maps', with smaller maps left to private publishers. He suggested that the private sellers should be able to get transfers from the Survey's engraved plates upon payment of a fee or royalty on sales. Bartholomew also considered that photographic, or photolithographic, reproductions should be prohibited. Here, he drew a distinction between W & AK Johnston's map, produced in this manner, and Bartholomew's, also copied from the Ordnance Survey but produced using newly engraved plates (see Figures 20 and 21). As Bartholomew explained:

> We prepare a new map, merely using the information published in the Ordnance maps; that is the difference. This [Johnston's map] is an actual reproduction. It is very much the same as in the copyright of a book. One may use the information published in a book, but one may not actually reproduce it word for word. In the same way we use the information published by the Ordnance Department to make our map, but we do not produce it in facsimile.[171]

[168] Oliver (n 12) 363–68.
[169] Report of the Departmental Committee appointed by the Board of Agriculture to inquire into the present condition of the Ordnance Survey C-6895 (London, Her Majesty's Stationery Office, 1893) (Dorington Committee 1893), Terms of Reference, 26 April 1892. See also eg 'Travel and Geography in 1891', *Times* 7 January 1892, 3; H Crook, 'Parliament and the Ordnance Survey' *Times* 15 April 1892, 4; *Times*, 1 June 1892, 18.
[170] H Crook, 'Parliament and the Ordnance Survey' *Times* 15 April 1892, 4.
[171] 1893 Dorington Committee Report, 69.

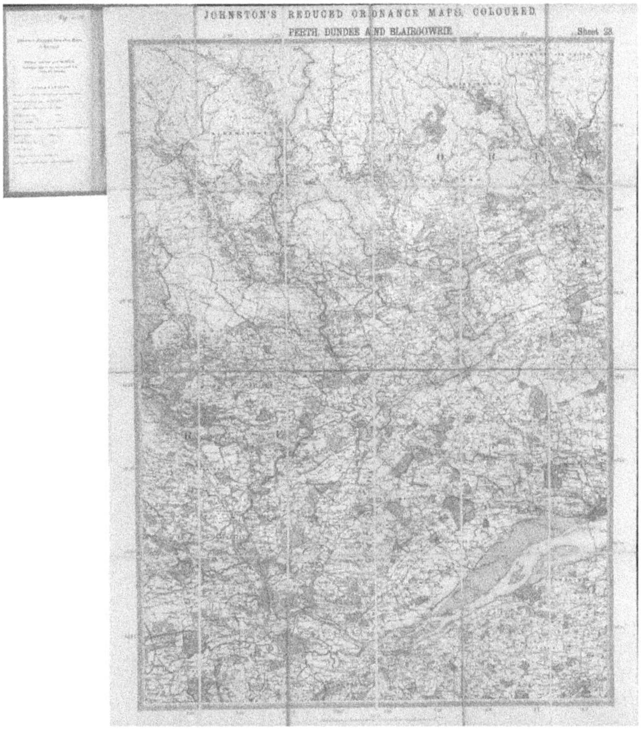

Figure 20 Johnston's maps of Scotland were direct lithographic reproductions from the Ordnance Survey's one-inch to the mile maps, reduced to roughly three-quarters of the scale and coloured with an overprint. W & AK Johnston, *Sheet 28 – Perth, Dundee and Blairgowrie* (Edinburgh, W & AK Johnston, 1896)

Reproduced with the permission of the National Library of Scotland (Maps.s.120).

For Bartholomew, the Ordnance Survey should participate only in the market for maps as commodity goods. The analogy to copyright in books relied on the distinction between idea and expression and placed the geographical data in the former category. While literary copyright could be exploited into different formats by this period, this was certainly not what Bartholomew had in mind. Other mapmakers took a similar approach. George Johnston suggested to the Committee that a better result for the public would be if the Ordnance Survey would remove the 'copyright reserved' notice from its maps and allow private publishers to make small-scale maps.[172] However, other witnesses believed the Ordnance Survey should be more proactive in exploiting its data in different ways, complaining that the new one-inch map did not serve the interests of pedestrian, cycling, or driving tourists.[173]

[172] ibid 96.

[173] ibid 113 (Evidence of George Chambers, barrister), 182–83 (Evidence of Prof J H Merivale, mining engineer).

Figure 21 The maps produced by John Bartholomew & Co were also copied from the Ordnance Survey but they used newly engraved plates to make his maps. John Bartholomew, *New reduced Ordnance Survey map of Perthshire* (Edinburgh, John Bartholomew & Co, 1891?) Reproduced with the permission of the National Library of Scotland (EMS.b.2.31).

In making its recommendations, the Committee sought to clarify the markets that the Ordnance Survey should be serving. It recommended that an edition of the one-inch map be produced that would both meet the demands of the War Office and be useful for the tourist districts, with the general outline and writing printed in black, the water in blue, the hills in brown, and the contours and altitude in some other colour. Although this would be a military map, they recommended it also be sold to the public. Trying to straddle two markets with a single map involved compromise, with the Committee observing: 'As this map would not be used for scientific purposes the slight inaccuracies resulting from defective registration in double printing would not be of importance'.[174] Having made this decision, the Committee recommended that the Ordnance Survey should print no other maps than this new, coloured one-inch version and the existing maps; that is, the engraved outline one-inch map, the one-inch map with hills, the four-mile map, and the 10-mile map. Any other maps on either the one-inch or smaller scales for special purposes should be left to the private trade.[175]

[174] ibid xxix–xxx.
[175] ibid xxx.

Further to this, the Committee recommended that reproductions of Ordnance Survey maps, either by obtaining transfers from the plates of the one-inch or smaller scales, or otherwise, should be allowed if the following conditions were met:

1. The map should not be a 'mere reproduction' but have 'some *bonâ fide* difference either in form or matter'. These differences could include shape, scale or being printed in different colours 'to bring out some special information'.
2. Any firm wishing to produce such a map should apply to the Board of Agriculture, stating the exact objects of the map, and the application would be transmitted to the Controller of the Stationery Office, who owns the copyright, and the Director-General of the Ordnance Survey should also be consulted.
3. The privilege of copying an Ordnance map should be paid for either as a lump sum or as a royalty on copies of the map sold, but that the sum should be 'rather an acknowledgment than a substantial payment'.[176]

The Committee considered that this approach would make Ordnance publications 'more useful and acceptable to the public' and that there would be no loss to the public as there was currently no charge made for such maps.[177]

The Committee made no recommendation in relation to the sales of maps, on the basis that another Departmental Committee had looked into it and Stanford was about to appoint a large number of additional agents.[178] Yet, by 1896 there were still concerns that the maps were not adequately well known among the public nor sufficiently well distributed to both public and professional users. In anticipation of the expiry of Stanford's contract, a new Departmental Committee was appointed by the Board of Agriculture to look specifically into the sale of Ordnance Survey maps. This Committee was chaired by Tory MP William Hayes Fisher and evidence was taken from London and provincial retailers of maps, as well as surveyors and other professional users. The first witness called was the current Director-General of the Ordnance Survey, Colonel J Farquharson. The tenor of the inquiry was set up by Fisher, who asked Farquharson:

> I suppose you will agree with the paragraph in the report of the Committee of 1892 which states that large sums have been expended in producing the Ordnance maps, that they are the most perfect maps in the world, that they are of the greatest value in facilitating transactions and works connected with land which lead to public improvements; that it is therefore desirable that they maps should be made known as widely as possible, not only to landlords and professional men but also to the public generally, and that persons of all classes should have within easy reach the means of obtaining information about them.[179]

Farquharson fully agreed with the sentiment and that the system under which Stanford was sole agent was not conducive to achieving that objective. He believed

[176] ibid.
[177] ibid.
[178] ibid xxxvi.
[179] 1896 Committee on Sale of Ordnance Survey Maps, Evidence, 2.

that, because most of the maps covered local areas, the public ought to have local facilities for acquiring them.[180]

The single agent system remained unpopular with the rest of the map trade. London map publisher George Bacon, who had acquired Wyld's business in 1894, told the Committee that, under the current system, other mapsellers had very little inducement to push the sale of the Ordnance Survey maps, due to the lesser discount they received of 25 per cent. Further, he considered them at a disadvantage as compared to Stanford, as they received notice of new maps later than he did. Bacon argued: 'There is thus no serious competition at present, for the system seems virtually to amount to a monopoly'.[181] Several of the witnesses also expressed dissatisfaction with their inability to return maps to Stanford. Some of the provincial sellers and one purchaser (the estate agent for the Duke of Northumberland) told of instances in which they had mistakenly ordered the wrong map and were unable to exchange it.[182] Stanley Philip, of London and Liverpool mapselling firm Philip and Son, explicitly compared the situation unfavourably with that of the Hydrographic Office, noting that Potter not only sent out monthly lists of corrected charts but accepted back obsolete maps.[183] Philip thought that if Ordnance Survey maps could also be returned they would likely double their stock, as they would no longer have to exercise such caution in relation to the maps they took from Stanford.[184]

At the same time, there was still pressure on the Ordnance Survey to meet different consumer demands. Many witnesses referred to the popularity of cycling and walking maps, and the need for maps at different scales, as well as the relative merits of coloured and uncoloured maps, contoured maps, maps with hills, maps for use in schools, and so on.[185] Julian Rogers, secretary of The Surveyors' Institution, commented that he had

> always been rather surprised that the Department has allowed the immense sale of maps for cycling purposes to pass out of its hands. There are hundreds of thousands of cyclists in the country, and the Ordnance sheets are pirated for their use.[186]

Having heard 13 witnesses over eight days, the Committee concluded the current system did not result in the largest possible distribution and recommended its discontinuance. It recommended that the Ordnance Survey Department should again take over control of sales of maps. In addition, it recommended that the proceeds of map sales should be appropriated by the Survey Vote rather than the

[180] ibid.
[181] 1896 Committee on Sale of Ordnance Survey Maps, Evidence, 45.
[182] ibid 17.
[183] ibid 54.
[184] ibid.
[185] 1896 Committee on Sale of Ordnance Survey Maps, Evidence, 51–52 (Hugh Oakley Arnold-Foster MP).
[186] ibid 29.

Stationery Office Vote (in other words, profits would now go back to the Ordnance Survey instead of the Stationery Office). The Committee also found it was absolutely necessary for a complete and full stock of maps to be maintained in London and that maintaining a government depot for the purpose was undesirable and expensive. It therefore recommended that a single agent be appointed for sale of all maps in London and that tenders be invited for the appointment. In addition, agents should be appointed for Edinburgh, Dublin, and each of the larger provincial towns, who should also keep a credit stock of the one-inch and six-inch maps in local demand. All the agents would receive a 25 per cent discount on published prices. In addition, any book or mapseller should be allowed to order maps directly from Southampton or Dublin, with the same discount of 25 per cent. However, those mapsellers would have to pay for the maps in advance and defray the cost of packing and postage.[187] Yet another initiative proposed was that an index of maps and specimen sheets for public inspection would be kept in at least 1,000 post offices throughout the United Kingdom and to also allow postmasters to order the maps for customers as well.[188] Finally, the Committee made a number of recommendations in relation to improving the advertising of the maps.[189] The recommendations were accepted by the Board and the new system commenced on 1 January 1897.[190]

Although the new system did increase net receipts, dissatisfaction continued. In April 1900, the Survey Vote occasioned considerable discussion in the House of Commons over the operation of the Survey ranging from debates over staff pensions to the accuracy of place-names and the interruptions caused to the surveyors by deerstalking season. The problems of advertising and selling the maps to the public was also discussed at length. One exchange between two MPs encapsulates the tension in views among even members of parliament. Thomas Gibson Bowles (member for King's Lynn and publisher of *The Lady* and *Vanity Fair*) argued:

> The Ordnance Surveys cost many millions … Did the Department take no steps to protect themselves in the enjoyment of their own copyright of this valuable work? … He hoped the right hon. Gentleman would be able to tell them that he intended, if possible, to take some measures whereby the Government would be secured in their copyright, and whereby if anybody used the maps they would not do it without adequate and proper payment to the Department.[191]

Yorkshire MP Commander Bethell, formerly of the Royal Navy, however, responded that

> he would not commend his right hon. friend to encourage the Department to alter the system of map-making so as to cater to the popular taste too much; nor did he see any

[187] 1896 Committee on Sale of Ordnance Survey Maps, Report 8.
[188] ibid 9.
[189] ibid 109.
[190] Oliver (n 12) 423–24.
[191] *House of Commons Parliamentary Debates*, 26 April 1900, vol 82, col 86–7.

> objection to the ordinary map-seller taking the use of the Ordnance Survey maps. What they wanted was accuracy in maps, and that was what the Ordnance Survey gave. He did not think it mattered whether the Government lost a certain amount of money by that or not.[192]

Where Bowles drew on his experience of print publishing to urge a move towards exploiting the maps as intangible property and licensing their use in different formats, Bethell may have been influenced by his naval experience to prioritise maintaining the maps' accuracy and reputation.[193] In the last years of the century, it was the latter that came to dominate attention, as the Ordnance Survey began to realise the effects of the permissive use not just of its data but also its name. The use by private mapmakers of the words 'Ordnance Survey' or 'Ordnance' in the titles or descriptions of their maps had been raised before the Dorington Committee by Edward Stanford, who argued that private mapsellers ought not be able to use the word 'Ordnance Survey' on their maps at all, even if using in the phrase 'reduced from the Ordnance', on the basis it referred to an official publication.[194] A persistent offender in this regards was the Edinburgh-based firm of John Bartholomew and Son. The firm made extensive use of Ordnance Survey maps and information in its half-inch maps of Scotland, as well as in its more limited range of one-inch and street maps. Frequently, these maps would be sold under a title which included either or both of the words 'Ordnance' and 'Survey', often 'Reduced Ordnance Survey'. The use of the words 'Ordnance Survey' to describe maps as using the Ordnance Survey's data was increasingly coming to annoy the Survey, as well as its official agents.

In 1897 it was discovered that Messrs Bartholomew were publishing a map entitled *New Reduced Ordnance Survey of England and Wales, Scale 2 mile to an inch* and a handful of other maps described in similar terms. The Board wrote to object on the basis this misleadingly suggested they were produced *by* the Survey and suggesting the alternate title of 'Maps from the Ordnance Survey', as had been used in the past. In September the firm agreed to drop the title and revert to the earlier title.[195] Farquharson was unhappy with the entire endeavour, suspecting Bartholomew of trying to steal a march on the Ordnance Survey's imminent publication of coloured maps, but he conceded that the maps themselves fitted within the Dorington Committee's rules, and that they 'had allowed so much latitude as to the titles' for so long that they could hardly start objecting now'.[196] Somewhat gallingly, the single largest customer for Bartholomew's half-inch maps was the War Office.[197]

[192] ibid.
[193] See ch 7.
[194] 1893 Dorington Committee, Evidence, 90.
[195] Letter from John Bartholomew to Secretary, Board of Agriculture, 1 September 1897, OS 1/6/3 (UKNA).
[196] Farquharson to Secretary, Board of Agriculture, 5 August 1897, OS 1/6/3 (UKNA).
[197] In 1900, the War Office ordered almost £200 worth of maps. Oliver (n 12) 431.

In 1900 Bartholomew was caught out again, this time advertising maps under the title *Reduced Ordnance Survey*. When the Ordnance Survey suggested this was in breach of their earlier undertaking Bartholomew denied he was in breach of the agreement because he was not using the word 'New'.[198] Legal advice was sought from the Law Branch, whose officers were confident that 'a reproduction or copy of an Ordnance Survey map, although on a different scale and with additions or variations in respect of colour and other particulars, constitutes an infringement of copyright'.[199] However, they also pointed out that the utilisation of Ordnance Survey maps for the production of maps by private publishers

> is regarded as permitted and even desirable, and has in fact been for many years permitted, provided that the latter maps are not mere reproductions, but are different from Ordnance Survey maps in form or matter, as in scale or in colouring or otherwise, so as to convey some special information or to meet requirements which are not satisfied by the Ordnance Survey maps themselves.[200]

In relation to the use by Bartholomew of the title *Bartholomew's Reduced Ordnance Survey*, the lawyers considered that the use of any words 'calculated to induce the belief that the maps are Ordnance Survey maps, *i.e.*, are produced by the Ordnance Survey, would no doubt be actionable and could be restricted by injunction'. However, they thought it doubtful any Court would find this to be the case in relation to those particular words were calculated to mislead, particularly given that they had for so long been used on many maps obviously not produced by the Ordnance Survey.[201]

The Bartholomew incident prompted the Board of Agriculture to seek to offer further guidance on the use of Ordnance Survey maps.[202] Because 'a certain amount of laxity' had been allowed to grow up, the Board determined that an advertisement ought to be placed in *The London Gazette*, giving notice of the government's intention and so as to enable mapmakers 'to make arrangements to regularise their position,'[203] and conditions should be drafted upon which use of Ordnance maps would be allowed. In relation to the use of the word 'Ordnance', the Board considered it potentially misleading and that it should be stopped in the interests of the Exchequer, the public, and of 'the more scrupulous mapsellers'.[204] With respect to the use of Ordnance Survey maps, the Board asserted it had no wish to exercise the rights of the Crown in a 'dog-in-the-manger' spirit and permission should be given to those who wished to use the material for maps 'likely to be of real convenience

[198] Copy of Report by Captain Williams, RE, 19 November 1900, OS 1/6/3 (UKNA).
[199] Copyright of Ordnance Survey Maps, Précis of Correspondence from January 1883 to March 1910, 19, OS1/6/2 (UKNA).
[200] ibid 20.
[201] ibid 19.
[202] 'Proposed Notice in "London Gazette" re Copyright of OS Maps, 26 July 1901, OS1/6/3 (UKNA).
[203] ibid.
[204] ibid.

and general utility to the public', where no Ordnance Survey maps of the kind had been or was about to be published. In such a case, permission should be granted if the map would materially differ from the Ordnance Survey map in size or shape, in matter or in scale, and if it served a purpose for which the Ordnance Survey maps could not be utilised. Permission should also be granted to a second category of maps – those where the map proposed seemed unlikely to 'materially injure' or compete with the sale of an Ordnance Survey map. This might include a map for insertion in a book or pamphlet or for use in connection with the sale of land. In relation to payment, the Board thought this a question for a future determination but its opinion was that, in general, the payment should be 'in the nature of an acknowledgment rather than a substantial payment'.[205]

The Controller of HM Stationery, Pigott, was not entirely approving of this intention to enforce copyright 'rather more rigidly than I have hitherto thought expedient' but acknowledged the matter was of some importance, as there was a pending case in which the applicant showed signs of intending to dispute the Board of Agriculture's decision.[206] Pigott himself thought the Board was taking 'rather too narrow a view and that the Ordnance Survey maps should be open to the tax-paying public to make use of without too much restriction', though he did object to 'cheap map makers' deceiving the public into thinking they were buying original Ordnance Survey maps. He disapproved of the Board and the Ordnance Survey going further and objecting to competing publications solely to 'make their balance sheet better'.[207]

The former Director of the Ordnance Survey, Colonel Sir John Farquharson, took a similar approach. In a speech to the Royal Geographical Society shortly after his retirement he had observed:

> The publication branch of the survey at Southampton is becoming over-weighted with the work already allotted to it, while efficient firms of map publishers like Messrs Bartholomew and Stanford are well able to supply the public with maps on other scales based on those of the Ordnance Survey. It seems to me to be in accordance with public policy that they should be encouraged to continue the production of all such maps, if not even, in case of necessity to assist the Survey in the publication of its own maps. Inferior productions on the other hand, which are, unfortunately numerous, should be discouraged as much as possible.[208]

Notwithstanding the views of Pigott and Farquharson, in August 1901 a notice was published in the London, Edinburgh, and Dublin *Gazettes* warning printers and publishers against making use of Ordnance Survey maps in ways that would infringe copyright and against using any words on the map which would lead the

[205] ibid.

[206] Pigott to Treasury Secretary (copy), 7 May 1901, OS1/6/3 (UKNA).

[207] Pigott to Desart (copy) 31 December 1900, OS11/6/3 (UKNA).

[208] J Farquharson, 'Twelve Years' Work of the Ordnance Survey, 1887 to 1899' (1900) 15 *The Geographical Journal* 565, 593. Cited in Oliver (n 12) 430.

public to think there was a connection with the Ordnance Survey Department. The notice instructed anyone wishing to use Ordnance Survey information in the production of a map to apply to the Controller of His Majesty's Stationery Office for permission.[209] The permission process was fairly onerous, involving a form to be completed containing extensive details of the planned publication. Permission, if granted, was subject to the conditions that the Ordnance Survey was duly acknowledged in the words 'Reproduced from the Ordnance Survey Map with the sanction of the Controller of H.M. Stationery Office', that any transfers supplied were used only for the specified purposes, that any royalty required was paid, and that a copy of the reproduction was sent to the Director General of the Ordnance Survey in Southampton.[210]

V. Conclusion

From its birth in the misty (and mystifying) Scottish Highlands, the Ordnance Survey evolved over the following century and a half from a military operation into a civil institution that had surveyed and mapped the entire kingdom. While not free from controversy or criticism, it had also become the most respected and authoritative source of geographical data for Britons of all social classes. During the nineteenth century, maps became embedded as a tool of state bureaucracy, as well as fully imbricated in the capitalist economy, through their roles in land registration, tax administration, railway construction, middle class tourism, and the cycling craze. Maps themselves thus became increasingly valuable commodities, as did the data they contained.

The institutionalisation of geographic knowledge produced by the Ordnance Survey entailed not secrecy but dissemination.[211] It also required that standards of accuracy be maintained and trusted; even complaints about coverage and lack of currency spoke to rising public expectations. This chapter has explored how the Ordnance Survey and the state ministries that successively oversaw its operations struggled to identify the extent to which, as a state actor, it should participate in the commercial market for geographic information, by and large preferring to treat its maps as tangible commodities, and to focus on their exchange and use values in that limited sense. There was little appetite for developing the possibilities offered by copyright in terms of a market for intangible property and, even if there had been, it would have been an impossible market to police, as successive albeit brief explorations of the affordances of copyright law revealed.

[209] Copyright of Ordnance Survey Maps, Précis of Correspondence from January, 1883, to March, 1910, 4, 22 OS1/6/2 (UKNA).

[210] See Assistant Controller, HMSO to Alfred Hinde, 19 May 1908, T1/11459/21575/10 (UKNA).

[211] Biggs (n 4) 384.

The consistent and overriding concern of the Ordnance Survey throughout the century was to build and maintain its reputation as the most authoritative source of geographical data in the kingdom, if not the world. The assertion of authority can be read upon the maps themselves, an examination of which also reveals how, over time, the locus of this authority changed. In the early decades authority was conferred by the qualifications of those making the map and it was done through the publication line – an artefact of the copyright regime. In 1828 a typical publication line read, on the bottom left-hand side of the sheet: 'Published at the Tower of London 24th November 1828 by Lieut.ᵗ Colonel of the Royal Engineers', and on the bottom right-hand side: 'Engraved at the Ordnance Map Office in the Tower under the direction of Lieut.ᵗ Colonel Colby by Benj.ᵐ Baker & Assistants _ The Writing by Eben.ʳ Bourne'.[212] On other maps additional information might be included, such as the name of the engraver who contributed the hills.

By the end of the century, the Ordnance Survey itself had come to be the authoritative source of the information. Thus, a 1:2500 map of Cambridge in 1888, by contrast, simply stated on the bottom left-hand side 'surveyed in 1886' and in the bottom centre: 'Zincographed and Published at the Ordnance Survey Office, Southampton 1888', and underneath: 'All rights of reproduction reserved'. The Revised New Series of one-inch maps, published from the 1870s, was more expansive. A typical publication line would be found on the bottom right of the sheet, stating: 'Engraved at the Ordnance Survey Office, Southampton. Surveyed in 1859–60 and Published by Col. Sir Henry James, F.R.S., M.R.I.A., R.E. Director-General, 1864 Revised in 1894, and Published by Col. J. Farquharson, C.B.R.E. Director-General, 1897'. In the centre was again placed the notice 'All rights of reproduction reserved'.[213] There we can see an emphasis on currency, through the inclusion of the date of survey and the qualifications and status of the Directors-General under whose instruction it was produced, as well as a more explicit assertion of copyright.

By the end of the century, copyright's key importance to the Survey lay in its ability to be used to control the reputation and authority of the Ordnance Survey's data and maps. It contributed to the Ordnance Survey's attempts to control the market for maps as physical commodities using the technology of scale. The fusion of the two technologies of law and mathematics operated to embed the popular understanding of maps as offering a representation of territory that directly corresponded to its features with mathematical accuracy. The use of an agreed-upon scale for all 'official' and authoritative maps is a highly significant development of modern statecraft. These maps were in turn used by a range of government departments, most significantly for the emergent practice of land registration, allowing land itself to be reduced to an abstraction, elevating its exchange value over its use

[212] Old Series Ordnance Survey Map, Sheet 44 [Cheltenham]. Surveyed 1811 to 1817 and revised before publication.

[213] One-inch Revised New Series, Sheet 2, Berwick-Upon-Tweed, 1897.

value, and facilitating the regulation of the real property market. As Alain Pottage has explained, registration 'extracted land from the network of relations and understandings which formed the "local knowledge" of different communities, relocated it on an abstract geometric map, and deciphered it according to a highly conventionalised topographic code'.[214] By the end of the nineteenth century, the Ordnance Survey had cemented its reputation as the most authoritative source of geographic information about the UK and, in doing so, had helped to cement the cartographic ideal. Copyright law was a tool it had deployed indirectly in this process but often with some ambivalence. In the next century, it would come to be used more instrumentally.

[214] A Pottage, 'The Measure of Land' (1994) 57 *Modern Law Review* 361, 363.

7

Shipwrecks and Copyrights: Hydrographic Information and the UK Hydrographic Office

I. Introduction

The second of the major state-run bodies engaged in mapmaking in the nineteenth century was the Hydrographic Office. This chapter traces the emergence, development, and activities of this body, in many ways the maritime counterpart of the Ordnance Survey. It covers the period from when it was established in 1795 until the end of the nineteenth century, a time during which Britain's domination of the oceans was unparalleled and unchallenged. Following decisive naval victories in the Napoleonic Wars, the peacetime Navy continued to be critical to Britain's foreign policy, imperial ambitions, colonial control, and global trade. Jeremy Black has written that:

> The charting of the oceans was a key theme of the nineteenth century, one that brought together the search for information, its accumulation, depiction and use. This process was linked to power: Britain's global commitments and opportunities, naval and commercial, made it both easiest and most necessary for it to acquire and use the information.[1]

Viewed like this, we can see a Whiggish, inevitable, unfolding of events, whereby the British state recognised the importance of accurate sea-charts to achieve its imperial and trade objectives, and then encouraged the development of technologies to improve navigation – first through the longitude prizes and then by setting up the Hydrographic Office.

However, examined more closely, the story is both more complex and more interesting, in particular as it relates to the control and circulation of the maritime information acquired. This chapter uncovers some of the same themes and tensions observed in the previous chapter between publicly gathered data and privately made maps; private profit and public benefit; and control and access. The Hydrographic Office of the nineteenth century was, like the Ordnance Survey, very

[1] J Black, *The Power of Knowledge: How Information and Technology Made the Modern World* (New Haven, Yale University Press, 2014) 237.

much a part of the administrative state, exemplifying the new, and growing, concern with gathering, recording, organising, and publishing information.[2] Like the Ordnance Survey, the Hydrographic Office was highly dependent upon the private map trade, in its early years for the acquisition of charts and later on for supply and distribution to the public. Also, like the Ordnance Survey, the Hydrographic Office was increasingly subject to pressure from Parliament and other executive branches to recoup the enormous costs of surveys and map production. Keeping the seas both peaceful and clear of pirates did not come cheap and the amount and deployment of money voted by Parliament for the Navy each year was frequently contentious.

Given that the economic and political strength of Britain depended so heavily on her Navy, it might be expected that she would jealously guard the navigational data that the Navy both generated and relied upon. In fact, the opposite is largely true. Setting aside a couple of occasions upon which maps and information were kept secret,[3] the Hydrographic Office's chief objective was to disseminate its charts as widely as possible. The imperatives were similar to those we saw at work in chapters four, five, and six, attended with perhaps even greater emphasis on the adverse effects of doing otherwise. As George Henry Richards (Hydrographer 1863–74) noted in 1868, mistakes in maritime charts 'might be attended with results of a most fatal character'.[4]

In examining the role played by copyright, the dynamics were similar in many ways to those affecting the Ordnance Survey. Once again, there was uncertainty over the commodity nature of the chart. The state clearly had an interest in producing charts for its own strategic, naval, and economic purposes and they therefore had significant use value for the state. They also had exchange value in the market. However, while the state was on the one hand keen to recoup some of its investment in the labour it had underwritten to produce the charts, on the other hand it had serious reservations about whether it could or should do so in a free market. This is because it needed to maintain control over the charts as both physical goods and the locus of intangible rights. The charts themselves were in constant circulation and in a constant state of flux. As Barford explains:

> Ships returning to the dockyards would return their charts, so that they might be issued with the latest navigational information. Before being sent from the Hydrographic Office, the charts would be checked and mounted onto linen, so that they might better

[2] See eg A Fyfe, 'The Information Revolution' in D McKitterick (ed), *The Cambridge History of the Book in Britain, Volume VI: 1830–1914* (Cambridge, Cambridge University Press, 2009) 567; M Barford, 'Naval Hydrography, Charismatic Bureaucracy, and the British Military State, 1825–1855' (PhD Thesis, University of Cambridge, 2016).

[3] One such exception was the conflict over the d'Entrecasteaux maps in the late eighteenth century, see below. A second such exception is the rare occurrence of a private publisher being refused access to a chart occurred in 1870 when Edward Stanford sought six copies of the chart of Portsmouth Harbour for the purposes of ongoing litigation but was refused on the basis that the chart was 'considered confidential and has never been for sale'. Minute Book (MB) 15 Jan 1869 to May 1870, 531 (UKHO).

[4] MB14, 17 December 1868, 506 (UKHO).

> withstand use as navigational aids. If correction was needed, additions would be made either by hand in red ink, or by pasting a printed correction over the relevant section on an existing chart. As new charts were published, or updated versions printed, they too would be added to the boxes sent out, and old charts returned to the office would be checked for information and for disrepair before either being corrected and reissued or condemned as waste.[5]

Losing control over chart circulation had the potential to cause serious harm – in terms of loss of life but also, with longer term effect, to the reputation of the Admiralty. In examining the relationship between copyright law and the circulation of hydrographic charts and data, this chapter offers yet another perspective on the different types of roles that copyright has performed. In this context, copyright could not be deployed as a means of raising revenue through exploitation of intangible rights. Rather, copyright was significant because it allowed property rights to be asserted over intangible aspects of the charts, thus assisting in controlling their entry into and circulation within the market as physical objects, as well as creating and upholding the Admiralty's reputation for accuracy and authority in the information they contained. In this way, the charts could be made more useful for the naval and economic objectives of the state. Maintaining their use value was thus more important than controlling their exchange value.

This chapter divides the narrative into three chronological stages. The first period, from 1795 to 1808, describes the establishment of the Hydrographic Office and its approach towards copyright through its interactions with the private chartmakers it relied upon to carry out its initial objectives. During the second period, 1808 to 1850, the Hydrographic Office became a printer, publisher, and seller of charts, and a chief focus was to find the best way of getting the most up to date charts into the hands of those who needed them. The final period, 1850 to 1900, saw growing emphasis on the need for better charts to reduce the loss of life at sea, whether in the Navy or the merchant marine, accompanied by increased pressure from the Treasury to become more economically efficient. In each period, the Hydrographic Office, Admiralty, and Treasury found different ways to work through the tangle of interests at play. Copyright law was one tool used to broker public and private interests in useful maritime data in a market that could not be completely free if the authority of the charts, and thereby their utility, were to be maintained.

II. The Establishment of the Hydrographic Office: Information and Honour, 1795–1808

By the start of the nineteenth century, Britain unquestionably ruled the waves. Over the previous 100 years, the navy had been transformed from a somewhat

[5] Barford (n 2) 24.

haphazard outfit, operating defensively and locally, and deeply controversial in political terms, into a professional, disciplined, and aggressive military force deployed to wage war, exert imperial ambitions, and create and protect trade across the globe.[6] One effect of the rise of a professional and disciplined navy with an increasingly central role in imperial society was that hydrographic chartmaking was, for the first time, established as an official naval activity. If it seems surprising that the British navy could exert such power without an official provider of sea-charts, it is because the cartographic ideal holds such sway over us that we cannot imagine travel without maps. Yet, before the middle of the eighteenth century, navigation was carried out using written sailing directions known as rutters, and later using volumes known as 'waggoners', which were rutters accompanied by charts. Until the eighteenth century, these charts were fairly crude, leading Fisher to suggest that many navigators used them simply as visual aids to reading the sailing directions.[7]

However, in not assuming responsibility for surveying and chartmaking until 1795, the British state trailed behind its main rivals; the French had established their Hydrographic Office in 1720 and the Dutch in 1784.[8] As we saw in chapter four, by the middle of the eighteenth century, the private trade had stepped in to serve the growing market for charts, which were increasingly useful due to advances in marine survey and navigational technologies. In particular, the use of chronometers and lunar tables allowed ships to find and record longitude at sea. While some surveying was sponsored by the state, most famously the voyages of Captain James Cook, the Admiralty was only indirectly involved in publishing the resultant charts.[9]

This began to change when, on 12 August 1795, the Hydrographic Office was established by an Admiralty Order in Council. The Order explained:

> The great inconvenience which has constantly been felt by the Officers of Your Majesty's Fleet, especially when ordered abroad, from the want of sufficient information respecting the navigation of those parts of the world to which their services may be directed, and with which they are sometimes totally unacquainted, has led us to consider of the means most advisable to be adopted for furnishing such information, and for preventing, as much as possible the difficulties and dangers to which Your Majesty's Fleet must constantly be exposed from any defect on this head.[10]

[6] See S Kinkel, *Disciplining the Empire: Politics, Governance, and the Rise of the British Navy* (Cambridge, MA, Harvard University Press, 2018).

[7] S Fisher, 'The Organisation of Hydrographic Information for English Navigators – Five Hundred Years of Sailing Directions and Charts' (2001) 54 *Journal of Navigation* 158–59.

[8] A Day, *The Admiralty Hydrographic Service 1795–1919* (London, Her Majesty's Stationery Service, 1967) 12.

[9] See I Alexander 'Copyright, Nature, and Travel Narratives: Publishing Cook's Voyages' in J Bellido and B Sherman (eds), *Intellectual Property and Nature* (Cambridge, Cambridge University Press, forthcoming 2023).

[10] Day (n 8) 334.

At the time of the Order in Council, Britain had been at war with France for two years. There had been a significant amount of naval expansion and exploration in the Pacific, particularly under Captains Cook and Vancouver. Trading routes to the East lay around the Cape of Good Hope and required numerous island and coastal ports of call, some of which were held by the British but others by rivals France, Spain, and Portugal. The East India Company, originally granted its trade charter by Elizabeth I in 1600, was expanding from India through Penang and into China, although the Crown was assuming some responsibility for this trade from 1784.[11]

Notwithstanding the sheer scale of Britain's naval operations, it is clear that the Admiralty did not envisage this would be a particularly difficult or expensive task. It rather sanguinely noted that:

> On a cursory examination of the plans and charts which have from time to time been deposited in the office, we find a considerable mass of information, which, if judiciously arranged and digested, would be found to be of the greatest utility to Your Majesty's Service.[12]

The Admiralty considered the total annual cost would not exceed £470 but allowed up to £650.[13]

The first Hydrographer to be appointed was Alexander Dalrymple. Hydrographer to the East India Company since 1779, Dalrymple was able to hold both roles at once, employing an assistant, first Aaron Arrowsmith and then John Walker, as well as a draughtsman.[14] As set out in the Order in Council, Dalrymple's chief task was to sort, classify, and arrange the existing materials held by the Admiralty, then assess them and compile information for use by Her Majesty's ships. These materials had been acquired in an ad hoc manner. A few surveys were commissioned directly by the Admiralty, while others compiled by serving naval officers were supported by the Admiralty subscribing to them or purchasing multiple copies. The latter was the Admiralty's preferred method for obtaining materials as it did not require the Admiralty putting up publication money in advance and risking a poor return.[15]

The work of organising these charts, plans, and associated materials was complete by 1800 and Dalrymple had produced a list of charts 'fit to be engraved'.[16]

[11] ibid 11–12.

[12] ibid 334.

[13] ibid 335.

[14] ibid 13–19; AS Cook, 'Alexander Dalrymple (1737–1808), Hydrographer to the East India Company and to the Admiralty as Publisher: A Catalogue of Books and Charts, Volume I' (PhD Dissertation, University of St Andrews, 1993) 22–23. Arrowsmith had worked as a surveyor for John Cary before setting up his own map and chartselling establishment. Walker had worked privately for Dalrymple as an engraver since 1783. E Baigent, 'Arrowsmith, Aaron, the Elder (1750–1823), Cartographer and Map Publisher', *Oxford Dictionary of National Biography*, 23 September 2004, www-oxforddnb-com.rp.nla.gov.au/view/10.1093/ref:odnb/9780198614128.001.0001/odnb-9780198614128-e-698.

[15] A Webb, 'The Expansion of British Naval Hydrographic Administration, 1808–1829' (PhD Thesis, University of Exeter, 2010) 97–98.

[16] Cook (n 14) 164.

It seems that he envisioned the private map trade would carry out this engraving but, on 22 March 1800, he requested that the Office be supplied with a rolling press. This was provided later that year and additional staff were employed for draughting, engraving, and press operation. However, it was still not the case that all engraving was done in-house. The work deemed non-confidential (charts obtained from foreign sources) was sent to private chart and mapmakers. The charts produced were provided to ships; there was no provision for selling them.[17]

A constant source of frustration for Dalrymple was his inability to order new surveys of areas that were urgently required, in particular the coasts of Britain. Forced to follow naval interest rather than lead it, he also chafed at his lack of control over the results.[18] The ongoing involvement of the private chart trade also hampered his ambition to acquire complete coverage of waters of naval and strategic importance. It remained the practice for many naval officers to approach the private chart trade to publish their surveys without even informing the Admiralty of their existence or sending a copy. In a letter to William Wellesley Pole, Secretary to the Admiralty, on 10 October 1807, Dalrymple sought to identify all extant charts, including those produced privately, but observed there was a question 'whether any use can be made of them in the Hydrographical Office without infringing on Private Property'.[19]

The letter was responding to a request for the Lords of Admiralty that he make a selection of 'the best and most necessary Charts and Plans of Ports'.[20] However, as Dalrymple explained, it was impossible for him to decide on the merits of different publications for several reasons. One was the fact that it was rare for charts to be accompanied by memoirs, explaining the authority upon which it was constructed. He thought it would 'certainly be of very great Publick Utility if the Data, on which all Original Charts are constructed, were delivered into the proper Office and a Certificate of Originality expressed thereon'.[21] Dalrymple went on to link the difficulties of obtaining accurate and authoritative charts with concerns over copyright:

> As General Charts must be constructed, at least in part, from Particular Ones; proper Persons should determine what proportion of the Property belongs, in right to the Original Publisher of the Particular Charts, of which the General Chart is composed; and the Publisher of such General Chart, should be required to make a special Declaration of the Materials used in constructing such General Chart; at present Property in Charts is very insecure, and pirated Publications are made, to the Loss of the Original Proprietor; and often to the serious disadvantage of the Publick, by obtruding erroneous Charts upon Them.[22]

[17] ibid.
[18] ibid 167–68.
[19] 'Dalrymple to Pole, 10 October 1807, ADM1/3522 (UKNA).
[20] ibid.
[21] ibid.
[22] ibid.

In these early days of the Hydrographic Office's operations, copyright was thus perceived as a hindrance to the Admiralty's objective of obtaining accurate charts for its own use because of the control it allowed the private trade to exert over the data those charts contained. At the same time, the difficulty in enforcing the rights in that data also allowed a market in unauthorised, inaccurate charts to flourish. They key then and for the remainder of the century was authority and accuracy.

The Admiralty's request marked the start of a change in the role and purpose of the Hydrographic Office and the beginning of the end of Dalrymple's career. Continuing to insist it was not possible for him to assess which charts were accurate or not, Dalrymple suggested that the Board establish a separate committee of naval officers who would know from their own experience which charts and surveys were best.[23] A committee was quickly set up, consisting of three serving naval officers: Thomas Hurd, Sir Home Popham, and Edward Henry Columbine. By 29 February 1808, the Committee was able to report that it had carried out its first task. They had:

> minutely examined every principal position in the General chart of the Atlantic; but for determining the accuracy of the same, we have compared every authority which we have been able to procure, with a view to discover all the geographical errors (which concern navigation) existing within the limits of that extensive ocean and to correct them as far as lay in our power.[24]

The Committee went on to report that: 'Truth requires us to declare that not one of the General Charts which we have, as yet, examined in our Committee, has proved exempt from several errors' and that the great mass of charts were 'dangerously erroneous'.[25]

Relations between Dalrymple and the Committee were initially respectful but they quickly degenerated. The Chart Committee was eager to demonstrate its ability to purchase the best, publicly available maps from private mapsellers in order to provide Her Majesty's ships on demand – a function Dalrymple considered outside his purview and rather beneath him. As he wrote to John Barrow, 'I am neither a Stationer & Bookbinder, an Admiralty Messenger nor a Clerk in the Hydrographical Office'.[26] Indeed, Dalrymple's view of his own role and its relationship with the private trade and the Admiralty was to prove a particular source of conflict. The first flashpoint came when Aaron Arrowsmith wrote to Dalrymple, asking for access to some unfinished charts that the Chart Committee had told him were being held in the Hydrographic Office and that he wished to use to update charts he was currently working upon 'for the immediate advancement

[23] Darlymple to Pole, 20 November 1807, ADM1/3522 (UKNA).
[24] Hurd to Pole, First Report of the Chart Committee 29 February 1808, ADM1/3523 (UKNA).
[25] ibid.
[26] Cook (n 14) 181–83; Dalrymple to Barrow, 1 April 1808, ADM1/3522 (UKNA).

of the Hydrography of this Nation'.[27] Dalrymple was enraged, writing to Pole on 23 February 1808:

> When, at the Instance of the Admiralty by Memorial, his Majesty in Council was graciously pleased to establish the Hydrographical Office, an avowed purpose was to supply the Royal Navy with good charts.
>
> Their Lordships will please to consider that this Intention can never be carried into effect, if the Surveys and Observations sent to the Hydrographical Office are delivered to private Chart-Makers to publish, mixed with materials of doubtful or unknown authority.[28]

Dalrymple believed the solution to improving accuracy and reliability was for the Admiralty to take over publication, pointing out it was the

> bounden duty of all Officers in His Majesty's Navy to send their Observations, and Charts laid down from those Observations, to the Admiralty: If these Materials have been given, or sold to Mr Arrowsmith and not sent to the Admiralty, these Officers have committed a reprehensible breach of duty.[29]

For Dalrymple, the private trade could simply not be trusted to produce charts of acceptable accuracy.

Dalrymple argued that the Hydrographical Office was 'the proper Channel for Publication'. He went on to claim that this would also make good economic sense:

> I beg leave to observe also that it is an extravagant waste of Public Money to buy Charts from Chart Sellers, constituted from Publick Documents, when Engravings might be made at much less expence to the Publick; and the Plates then belonging to the Admiralty, any additions or corrections, which may be found wanting can be made from time to time.[30]

The response from the Admiralty came the same day: 'Refer the Hydrographer to my letter of the 19th last and direct him to give Mr Arrowsmith the information accordingly'.[31]

Dalrymple grew increasingly suspicious of Arrowsmith, complaining in a letter of 5 March 1808 that he returned to his office to find Arrowsmith in there seeking charts to be pasted on cloth – a practice Dalrymple rejected as an unnecessary expense and as distorting the scale.[32] The final showdown came when the Chart Committee sought access to charts made by French explorer Antoine Bruni d'Entrecasteaux. The charts had come into the possession of the Hydrographic Office when the British had captured a Dutch vessel that happened to be carrying Charles-François Beautemps-Beaupré's charts of d'Entrecasteaux's expedition.

[27] Arrowsmith to Dalrymple, 19 February 1808, ADM1/3523 (UKNA).
[28] Dalrymple to Pole, 23 February 1808, ADM1/3523 (UKNA).
[29] ibid.
[30] ibid.
[31] Note on letter, ibid.
[32] Dalrymple to Pole, 5 March 1808, ADM1/3523 (UKNA).

Dalrymple refused to turn over the charts to the Committee on the basis that they were 'a secret and sacred trust'.[33] The Chart Committee wrote to the Admiralty Board complaining:

> Mr Dalrymple having refused to let us have Entrecasteaux's valuable surveys of the Coasts of New Guinea, New Britain etc etc we have to request that their Lordships will be pleased to give him orders to comply with our requisition. The above charts being the principal authentic materials for those extensive, but very little known coasts, it is absolutely necessary that we should be allowed to have the use of them to guide our judgement in the selection of the charts which have been published of these seas. These charts were taken about twelve years past, on their way from Britain to Europe, a Copy of them was liberally communicated to the French government, and the originals have since that time been carefully concealed from the world in the Hydrographic Office.[34]

Dalrymple responded that he could not possibly give up the charts, based upon the honourable understanding of all nations engaged in voyages of discovery that charts created by one nation would not be published by another should they fall into their hands. He explained that he had had some copies made 'to prevent the accidental loss in the passage to France'[35] and that

> on no other pretence but security against accident could Copies have been honourably made; and on no account can they be published, till the French publish them, without a disgraceful breach of Public Faith.[36]

He went on to point out that: 'As these Charts have never been published they cannot afford any assistance in "forming a judgement of the correctness of other Charts, which have been published of these very little known Coasts"'.[37]

Dalrymple also wrote directly to Sir John Barrow, stating that 'the Charts in question cannot be made use of without a disgraceful and flagrant breach of the Public Faith, which I cannot suppose their Lordships would knowingly countenance'.[38]

Hurd and Columbine, however, continued to make representations to the Board, writing to Pole on 21 May:

> As the Coasts of New Guinea, New Britain, new Ireland, the Arsacides etc etc are very little known, and have hitherto been most erroneously placed upon the Charts, we take the liberty of suggesting to their Lordships the expediency of obtaining from Entrecasteaux's valuable surveys, such corrections as may be necessary for the more accurately placing of the principal points of those Coasts upon our general charts only; without entering into any details of the particulars, or publishing a Copy of Entrecasteaux's work. As these places lay in the direct track of our Ships between China

[33] Dalrymple to Columbine, 11 May 1808 ADM1/3523 (UKNA).
[34] Hurd and Columbine to Pole, 13 May 1808, ADM1/3523 (UKNA).
[35] Dalrymple to Pole, 14 May 1808, ADM1/3523 (UKNA).
[36] ibid.
[37] ibid.
[38] Dalrymple to Barrow, 14 May 1808, ADM1/3523 (UKNA).

> & Botany Bay, it is extremely desirable that our navigators should be furnished with better information respecting them than has yet been afforded; and as we have the means in our power, it is presumed there can be no impropriety in using it, in the very limited manner above pointed out, particularly as every facility for their complete publication has been liberally given to the French Government by the Admiralty about twelve years past, when the entire originals were sent to France. The French have declined publishing them, probably from the consideration that they had no trade or navigation at present which could benefit from the result, which on the other hand might be of great value to England.[39]

Dalrymple was ordered by the Board to give up the Charts and eventually succumbed. On 28 May, he was removed from office by decision of the Admiralty Board. The reason given to him was that new arrangements were being made for the office which would require 'great and continual exertion on the part of the Hydrographer' which Dalrymple would not be able to manage at his 'advanced period of life'.[40] Dalrymple himself ascribed his removal to the d'Entrecasteaux incident.[41] He died three weeks later.

The episode demonstrates the competing ideas in play as to the place and role of sea-charts. For Dalrymple, charts were instruments of state, documents of national importance and diplomatic significance, and the rules that governed their use were those of national comity and the international order. The information they contained could be used for national purposes but the charts themselves could not be put onto the market. In other words, they had use value for the state but to exploit their exchange value would be to overstep the conventions of state relations. In his letter of 14 May, Dalrymple noted:

> Fully convinced of this Public Duty I have abstained from making use of them myself, altho' I have a Chart partly engraved, of those parts from original documents, not published; but knowing M Entrecasteaux's Discoveries exist, I am prevented from publishing for the East India Company which I do know.[42]

By contrast, Dalrymple suggested, Arrowsmith had no such scruples. Dalrymple went on to accuse him of pirating a proof of one of Dalrymple's charts of the coast of New Guinea, which Arrowsmith acknowledged he had 'got from my Engraver's Son without [Dalrymple's] knowledge or permission'.[43]

Dalrymple had not kept the d'Entrecasteaux charts completely secret. He had shown them to Matthew Flinders when the latter had visited the Admiralty in preparation for his voyage in the *Investigator* in 1801 and provided Flinders with manuscript copies of the charts to take with him.[44] Looking at these charts,

[39] Hurd and Columbine to Pole, 21 May 1808, ADM1/3523 (UKNA).
[40] Day (n 8) 19.
[41] Cook (n 14) 184.
[42] Dalrymple to Pole, 14 May 1808, ADM1/3523.
[43] ibid.
[44] G Ingleton, *Matthew Flinders: Navigator and Chartmaker* (Guildford, UK, Genesis Publications, 1986) 100.

Dalrymple pointed out a particularly useful innovation – the idea of indicating ships' tracks on charts and showing which portions had been run in daylight and which at night, since only those geographical features that had been seen could be fixed. Flinders adopted this technique in three of his own charts that were published by Arrowsmith in 1801.[45] While Dalrymple was haggling with the Chart Committee over the Beautemps-Beaupré charts in 1807, Flinders was being held captive at Ile de France (Mauritius) and spent some of his time compiling charts from his prior surveys. The position of Flinders seemed to be preying on Dalrymple's mind. In his correspondence with the Admiralty, Dalrymple observed: 'In such voyages of Discovery the Public Faith has been mutual and even Buonaparte has given orders, in Triplicate, for Captain Flinders Release'.[46]

The opposing view, apparently espoused by Hurd and the Chart Committee, was that the information the charts contained should be made to serve the public interest in the best way possible, including being placed on the private market, where exploiting exchange value would lead to wider dissemination and, thus, greater utility. In the Chart Committee's first Report of 29 February 1808, it observed that

> the many fatal disasters resulting to our shipping of every description, from the incorrectness of charts in general, must inevitably continue to accumulate, unless means far more prompt and efficacious than any hitherto employed, shall be adopted to remedy so serious an evil.
>
> We humbly conceive that the consideration of this truly important subject is, of itself, sufficient to impress on their Lordships the necessity of establishing a system, which may enable the government to offer to the British Marine, as well commercial as military, a collection of correct charts, adapted to the general purpose of navigation, in every quarter of the globe. The great number of lives, and the vast amount of property which would be annually saved to the nation, by such a measure, would amply compensate for the expense of its execution. The sale of charts, constructed from correct data, might be made to repay, in part, this temporary expense; while among other permanent advantages, it would speedily check and ultimately stop the publication of spurious and unauthenticated charts, which could not, by any other means, be so effectually prevented.[47]

The entire situation was rendered somewhat absurd by the fact that Beautemps-Beaupré published his atlas, including the charts, in France in 1807, the same year that Dalrymple was refusing to release them.[48] Moreover, the Admiralty's treatment of Flinders indicates they did not place such high emphasis on the charts as instruments of state as did Dalrymple or even the French. Arriving back in England in October 1810, Flinders found that the publication of

[45] Ingleton (n 44) 93–94.
[46] Dalrymple to Pole, 14 May 1808, ADM1/3523 (UKNA).
[47] First Report of Chart Committee, 29 February 1808, ADM1/3523 (UKNA).
[48] Ingleton (n 44) 362.

his charts was not a high priority for the Admiralty, notwithstanding their significant advances over previous surveys. The Admiralty agreed to pay the expense of engraving the charts and other engraved plates but thought that the financial profits hoped to flow from publication would pay for the cost of paper, printing, binding, and all other expenses, including the fees for the artists.[49] The Admiralty also refused to put Flinders on full pay while he wrote up the voyage, agreeing only to give him an allowance of £200 to be deducted against publication profits (essentially a royalty advance). Both Flinders and Sir John Barrow were convinced that at least part of the French rationale for keeping him so long imprisoned was to steal a march on Flinders' discoveries. Flinders wrote in the second volume of *A Voyage to Terra Australis* that Napoleon 'had granted a considerable sum' to Peron to bring his publication of the French voyage of discoveries to market.[50] Flinders also complained that although he had met French hydrographer and explorer Nicolas Baudin and given the latter information on his own voyage, 'French names were given to all my discoveries'.[51] He thought this 'but an ill return to deprive me of the little honour attending the discovery'.[52] Barrow was blunter still: 'That the prolonged confinement was a trick to rob him of the merit of his discoveries, we think will admit of little doubt'.[53]

III. From Supplying to Selling Charts: 1808–1850

Dalrymple's replacement was his nemesis, Thomas Hurd. Under Hurd, the Hydrographic Office began to implement the Board's plan that the Office should supply charts directly to the Navy.[54] To achieve this, Hurd needed to acquire as many charts as he could find. Large quantities were purchased from the private map trade. By 29 March 1809, he had run up bills amounting to £4,574 1s 2d with Arrowsmith, and fellow chartsellers Faden, Heather, and Steel (all introduced in chapter four) and Laurie & Whittle, former assistants to Robert Sayer who had continued the business after his death.[55] He also purchased charts from serving naval officers. Sometimes Hurd would agree to buy the copyright in these charts

[49] ibid 386.

[50] M Flinders, *A Voyage to Terra Australis,* Vol 2 (London, Nichol, 1814) 470.

[51] ibid.

[52] ibid.

[53] J Barrow, 'A Voyage to Terra Australis, undertaken for the Purpose of completing the Discovery of that vast Country, and prosecuted in the Years 1801, 1802, and 1803, in his Majestys Ship Investigator, and subsequently in the Armed Vessel Porpose and Cumberland Schooner. With an Account of the Shipwreck of the Porpoise, Arrival of the Cumberland at Mauritius, and Imprisonment of the Commander during six Years and a half in that Island. By Matthew Flinders, Commander of the Investigator. In Two Volumes, wih an Atlas. London. 1814' (1814) 12 *Quarterly Review* 1, 11.

[54] In response to a suggestion from the Board, Hurd and Popham, as members of the Chart Committee, had suggested purchasing 100 copies of charts of the Atlantic and Indian seas for Her Majesty's ships: Chart Committee to Pole, 22 April 1808. Pole endorsed the plan on 10 June (marked on letter), ADM1/3523 (UKNA).

[55] Hurd to Pole, 29 March 1809, ADM1/3523, (UKNA).

and surveys, but for surveys of areas considered less important he would often merely undertake to purchase a number of copies for Admiralty use. Indeed, one of his earliest acts as Hydrographer was to ask the Admiralty Board if he could engrave and publish his own chart of the Bermuda Islands 'for the general benefit of science and navigation'.[56] The request was refused by their Lordships as 'the Survey in question was made at the Public Expense'.[57] Instead, Hurd was instructed to have the chart engraved in the Hydrographic Office and produce as many copies as would be necessary to supply Her Majesty's Ships.[58]

Another valuable cache of material came from Dalrymple, who bequeathed his manuscript charts to the Hydrographic Office.[59] The Ordnance Survey supplied copies of coastal maps and Trinity House also supplied information on such matters as the placement of buoys and beacons.[60] Charts acquired from captured enemy ships were also valuable acquisitions and, when hostilities ended, international cooperation was pursued. On 12 July 1808, Hurd wrote to Pole that it would be wise to purchase maps from Spain now that communications were open again and that any not used by the Office 'will be thankfully taken off our hands by Mr Arrowsmith'.[61]

It was apparent that many parts of the globe had yet to be charted and more specialist officers were needed to achieve this. However, it was not until the Peace of 1815 that there was any real opportunity to direct more men and ships to this task.[62] From this time, the Navy Board began to send out survey ships, although the Hydrographer had little control over who was chosen for such voyages.[63] As noted above, since his time on the Chart Committee, Hurd had believed that a crucial flipside to supplying charts to the Navy was their commercial sale to the public. He returned to the point on 12 October 1816, writing to John Barrow, Second Secretary to the Admiralty, suggesting:

> [W]ith a view of defraying a part of the expenses of the department that after a plate has been engraved and a sufficient number of charts struck off for Naval uses, that the remaining impressions be disposed of at a moderate price for the benefit of the Trading Interest.[64]

In the same letter, Hurd also suggested the establishment of a corps of specialised maritime surveyors, similar to the Engineers of the Army. This second suggestion was acted upon but Hurd claimed that the Admiralty made no response to his

[56] Hurd to Pole, 18 June 1808, ADM1/3523 (UKNA).

[57] Hurd to Pole, note on reverse, 18 June 1808, ADM1/3523 (UKNA).

[58] Hurd to Pole, note on reverse, 18 June 1808, ADM1/3523 (UKNA).

[59] Cook (n 14) 206–207; A David, 'The Emergence of the Admiralty Chart in the Nineteenth Century', (10 September 2008). Paper presented at Symposium on 'Shifting Boundaries: Cartography in the 19th and 20th Centuries', Portsmouth University, Portsmouth, United Kingdom, 10–12 September 2008, 5.

[60] Webb (n 15) 128–29.

[61] Hurd to Pole, 12 July 1808, AMD1/3523.

[62] Webb (n 15) 62–63.

[63] ibid 65ff.

[64] Day (n 8) 27; David (n 59) 8.

first suggestion.[65] In 1818 Hurd was still in favour of the plan, as his response to a letter from Thomas Jones, a chartseller in Liverpool seeking Admiralty charts for resale, makes clear. Hurd responded that he regretted being unable to supply Jones and that he was

> of opinion that it would be a good & advisable policy to adopt such a measure for the use & benefit of the Mercantile Interest of this Great Commercial Empire. I have long been in the habit of considering Shipwreck'd Merchant vessels to be a great National calamity, not only in the sacrifice of useful & valuable subjects to the state; but also a heavy and real loss to the Revenue and Finance of the Country – on which account I should feel delighted in being directed to carry such measure into effect.[66]

While the Admiralty ignored the request, the private chart trade filled the gap. However, this created problems of its own. Hurd received several complaints from chartsellers that Messrs Steel were incorrectly holding themselves out to be the chartsellers appointed to the Admiralty and had even stamped their publications with the Admiralty Seal of office.[67]

Eventually, on 16 November 1819, in response to a petition from Laurie & Whittle, the Admiralty changed its mind. A Minute was drawn up instructing the Secretary to enable 'the public to purchase Admiralty charts at reasonable prices'.[68] The Board decided that all charts printed by the Hydrographic Office would be sold 'at a fair price to any one inclined to buy as is done by the Ordnance – if not, then the chartmakers to have use of our surveys'.[69] The Minute reflected an emerging, peacetime understanding that state affairs and mercantile affairs were closely intertwined and state-produced charts had use value for a larger pool of private actors. The effect was that the Admiralty chartmakers became a bureaucracy, part of whose role was to broker public and private interests in both charts and data. Association with the Admiralty was clearly seen as advantageous for the private chartsellers, as illustrated by Messrs Steel's actions and the complaints to which it gave rise. However, the Admiralty was less enthusiastic about the connection. When it did eventually agree to selling the charts, Melville (First Lord of the Admiralty, 1812–1827, 1828–1830) drew up an additional minute expressing concern that chartsellers might incorrectly copy the Hydrographic Office's charts, issuing erroneous charts attributed to the Admiralty, which could lead to their being held liable in case of damage or disaster.[70]

Hurd continued to have faith that the problem of inaccurate and unauthorised maps could be resolved by the market, writing to his Danish counterpart, Rear Admiral Löwenörn:

> It is necessary you should keep in mind that many Charts are published in this Country over which we have no control – neither can we from the nature of our Government

[65] Letterbook (LB)1, f408, Hurd to Croker, 28 June 1821 (UKHO).
[66] LB1, f170, Hurd to Jones, 26 August 1818 (UKHO).
[67] LB1, Hurd to Croker, 14 June 1819; Hurd to Barrow, 29 January 1819 (UKHO).
[68] Cited in Webb (n 15) 327, ADM 1/3461 (UKNA).
[69] ibid 327–28.
[70] ibid 328.

> prevent either their publication or Sale, notwithstanding their known errors – these however will die a natural death when our own Surveys make their appearance.[71]

None of these views, however, suggested that any party had any interest in restricting or commercialising the information the charts contained. Copyright, as a tool for brokering interests in maritime data, was irrelevant in this context. It is interesting, therefore, that its formalities were observed upon the charts themselves. Hurd was careful to place his own name upon charts produced under his leadership and, in so doing, he was following the practice of his predecessor, Dalrymple, who had been making and publishing charts on his own account since 1769. As noted above, Dalrymple had concurrent positions with the Hydrographic Office and the East India Company, the latter covering some of his chartmaking expenses but leaving the copyright with him to exploit commercially as he chose.[72] It is not surprising the Dalrymple would continue to place his name on the charts he printed and published at the Hydrographic Office. A typical publication line would read: 'Hydrographical Office *Published according to Act of Parliament Feb 1st 1803 by A Dalrymple* Hydrographer *to the Admiralty*'. Elsewhere on the map would appear information about the name of the surveyor, their ship, and the date of the survey.[73] As Dalrymple's charts were republished over the following decades, Hurd would replace Dalrymple's name with his own and the date of republication.[74] This seems more about following what was by now accepted convention in mapmaking and ensuring it was his reputation and expertise being recognised than it was about asserting copyright. The practice was, however, followed by Colonel Mudge of the Ordnance Survey which, in 1816, was concerned about private mapsellers copying Ordnance Survey maps. As noted in chapter six, Mudge sought legal advice on copyright and in particular the question of compliance with the Engravings Acts. He explained that

> when the first maps were printed and published by the Ordnance, I had recourse to the Admiralty Charts and found that the name of Captain Hurd the Hydrographer was subscribed to each plate with the period and place of its publication; and I naturally took it for granted that if I followed his example, I should give equal security to the Ordnance maps.[75]

This correspondence, and legal advice, were sent to the Hydrographic Office. However, Hurd had a different plan to deter copying, which again relied entirely on the market for the charts as physical commodities. As he explained in his letter to the Admiralty Board of June 1821, the charts to be disposed of to the mercantile fleet and the general public would be sold 'at a price so moderate as shall leave no

[71] LB1, Hurd to Löwenörn, 30 December 1819 (UKHO).
[72] Cook (n 14) especially 113–14, 174.
[73] A Dalrymple, *Chart of King's Island in Bass's Strait and Plan of Port Phillip in Bass's Strait Discovered & partly Surveyed by Acting Lieut John Murray in the Lady Nelson January 1801* (London, Hydrographical Office, 1803).
[74] David (n 59) 5–6.
[75] LB1857/G/276 (UKHO). See also WO44/299 (UKNA).

temptation or inducement to the compilers and venders [sic] of such articles for copying & reprinting them on their own account'.[76]

Having taken this approach, the more pressing problem for Hurd was distribution, and here the private chartsellers remained integral to the Hydrographic Office's plans. They had the networks, the customer base, and the shopfronts necessary to get the charts to the public. However, they continued to operate in a world characterised by intricate relations of cooperation and competing claims of authority. Even as Hurd issued his catalogue of charts and plans for sale, he noted he was unable to finalise the title page, due to 'an extraordinary claim made by Mr Faden the King's Geographer to have his name inserted therein as the Publisher and Sole appointed Agent' for their sale.[77] Faden proposed to nominate Arrowsmith, RH Laurie,[78] and John Norie as secondary dealers. Hurd was very much against this proposal, thinking it quite improper to announce Faden as the publisher of charts that had been printed before he began to sell them, as well as considering it would represent a 'great injustice' to Arrowsmith as King's Hydrographer.[79] Moreover, he pointed out that the Office was much indebted to Arrowsmith

> on many occasions for the use of various documents necessary to the compilation of our Office compilations during & since the late War – all of which he freely & gratuitously lent whenever a requisition of that nature was made to him.[80]

Hurd proposed either that Faden and Arrowsmith both be appointed agents for the sale of charts, or that all four mentioned by Faden be appointed as equals but that Faden's name could appear at the head of the list. Initially, Faden and Arrowsmith were appointed but in December 1822 two further agents were appointed in Liverpool on the same terms as Faden.[81] By 1824 Norie had also become an agent[82] and in 1824 Messrs Kingsbury, Parbury, and Allen of Leadenhall Street, as well as RH Laurie of Fleet Street, were also appointed as agents by the Admiralty Board.[83] The terms on which agents operated were set out by William Edward Parry, who had succeeded Hurd as Hydrographer in 1825. The agents would receive the stock on sale or return, and settle their accounts every six months, at the same time specifying every single chart sold and at what price. They would receive 25 per cent of everything sold. In addition, they had to keep a standing stock of two copies of each chart, which could be returned or exchanged if soiled or damaged by fair wear.

[76] Hurd to Croker, 28 June 1821, LB1 f407 (UKHO).

[77] ibid.

[78] Richard Holmes Laurie took over the business of Laurie & Whittle following the retirement of his father Robert Laurie and death of James Whittle: S Fisher, *The Makers of the Blueback Charts: A History of Imray, Laurie, Norie & Wilson Ltd*, (St Ives, Imray, Laurie, Norie & Wilson, 2001) 64.

[79] Hurd to Croker, 28 June 1821, LB1 f408 (UKHO).

[80] ibid.

[81] Minute 5 December 1822, Hurd to Jones, 14 December 1822 LB1 f517 (UKHO).

[82] Request to agents to forward an account of Admiralty charts sold, 6 January 1824, LB2 f20 (UKHO).

[83] Parry to Messrs Kingsbury, Parbury & Allen, 17 February 1824, LB2, f29 (UKHO).

They could also request additional charts by written application. The agents would also receive new copies of any charts that had been materially corrected and return any superseded charts still on hand to the Hydrographic Office.[84] Prices were set using a calculation that included the cost of engraving, agency fees, and an estimate of the number that needed to be sold to recoup the cost of the plate and the cost of paper and printing.[85]

By this arrangement, the Admiralty sought to assert control over the market for charts as physical commodities. However, the market was not so easily tamed. Hurd's strategy of selling the charts at a relatively low price in order to deter copying had unfortunate unforeseen consequences because the agents and other chartsellers had a greater incentive to push sales of the more expensive, privately produced charts on which they would make a larger commission.[86] The next seven years saw some agents removed and others added but by 1829 it was clear that the existing system was occasioning significant, unnecessary labour for the Hydrographic Office.[87]

Problems were also arising because there was an additional market for the marine data that the charts contained and, while the Admiralty did not wish to commercialise this market, it nevertheless impacted upon their interests. On 12 January 1829, Lieutenant William Sheringham, Naval Assistant to Hydrographer Parry, prepared a report in which he set out his concern that the chief motivation to become an Admiralty agent did not arise from a trader's anticipation of profits but from their 'flagitious intention of transferring such portions of our new matter as may be introduced into their own publications'.[88] For Sheringham this led to two further problems. First and most important, it resulted in them presenting to the world 'garbled extracts' of incorrectly compiled information under the authority of the Admiralty, because of their coming from the hands of accredited agents. The second 'evil' was that the pecuniary benefit that might have flowed from this new information was transferred 'from the public purse to the pockets of the agents'. Rather than suggesting that the Admiralty try to control this market directly, Sheringham emphasised propriety over property, suggesting that the agents ought to be encouraged to treat their role as one of 'respectability' and 'responsibility'.[89]

Sheringham suggested the problems be addressed by reducing the number of accredited agents to one Chief Agent in London, who would have complete discretion in selecting the branch agencies. That agent should be bound to a bond of £1,000 not to publish hydrographic matter on his own private account nor to be

[84] ibid.
[85] Webb (n 15) 330.
[86] ibid.
[87] Miscellaneous Letters and Papers (MLP) 62 Folder 1 v (UKHO). Adrian Webb identifies this paper as being prepared by a Lieutenant Becher, c1829. Webb (n 15) 338–39.
[88] William Louis Sheringham, 'Report', 12 January 1829, MLP 62 Folder 1, iv (UKHO).
[89] ibid.

an accessory to the pirating of works under his charge. The agent would be allotted a sum of money to assist with advertising the charts and the amount that the agent should retain of the money received for such sales would rise to 35 per cent. Should his suggestions be adopted, Sheringham was confident that: 'It would have the effect of leading Seamen in general to look up to the authority of Government (most properly) for the best Hydrographical knowledge extant'.[90]

On 27 May 1829, Parry and his successor, Francis Beaufort, prepared a memo for the Admiralty. Parry and Beaufort explained to their Lordships their belief that the current system was suppressing sales:

> From the small quantity of charts sold by these agents it is not too much to infer that one of their principal objects in accepting the agency is the advantage of being furnished with the earliest Hydrographical Information which they immediately insert on their own charts, and it is obvious that the sale of their own charts is far more profitable to them, and therefore more their interest to urge, than the sale of the Admiralty charts.[91]

Further, they pointed out the existence of so many agents led to complex accounting that occupied much of Sheringham's time. They proposed appointing a sole agent, who would be bound not to be directly or indirectly concerned in the publication of any charts, and to supply him with charts 'at his own choice and risk, for sale alone and not on return'.[92] The agent would have discretion as to the appointment of sub-agents and 'to remunerate him for the capital he must employ, and the risk he must run under these restrictions' he would be allowed a 40 per cent discount on all charts delivered to him from the office.[93]

In making this suggestion, Parry had consulted with Colonel Mudge as to the arrangements the Ordnance Survey had made with its agent, Gardner of Regent Street. Mudge replied, explaining the previous arrangement with Faden had been unsatisfactory, as Faden had continued to sell his own maps alongside those of the Ordnance Survey, but the new arrangement with Gardner bound him not to sell any maps that would supersede the Ordnance maps.[94] Mudge later forwarded a copy of the agreement with Gardner for Parry's reference.[95] Parry in fact approached Robert Bate of 21 Poultry for the position. Bate was not a chart or map publisher or seller and had not been an agent. Therefore, unlike Faden, or Sheringham's preference, James Wyld, Bate had none of his own charts to sell in competition. He was, however, connected with the world of maritime navigation through his principal business as a scientific instrument maker.[96]

[90] ibid.
[91] Minute Book (MB) 1 Nov 1825–February 1832, f.257, 27 May 1829 (UKHO).
[92] ibid f258.
[93] ibid f258.
[94] Richard Mudge to Parry 15 January 1829, MLP 62 Folder 1 ii (UKHO).
[95] Richard Mudge to Parry 29 January 1829, MLP 62 Folder 1 iii (UKHO).
[96] Webb (n 15) 339.

Melville and the rest of the Board accepted Parry and Beaufort's suggestions and Bate was appointed on 25 September 1829.[97]

Bate continued as the sole agent for the next 18 years. However, the appointment of a sole agent and, thus, sole source of authority did not resolve the Admiralty's problems. In May 1843, Bate wrote that he had been 'woefully disappointed in my expectations from all my Agents'.[98] He put the poor sales of Admiralty charts down to three factors: 'the want of General Charts, the antiquity of their dates, and the paucity of their appearance to the eye'.[99] The first and third of these points disclosed the issue that the demands of the Navy, met by the Hydrographic Office's charts, were not identical to those of the merchant marine, and the two markets could not in fact be serviced by the same charts. The charts made by private publishers were known as 'bluebacks', a name derived from the blue manilla paper backing that the private chartsellers used to strengthen the unbound charts. In the eighteenth and early nineteenth centuries, the paper was grey-blue in colour and, by the middle of the nineteenth century, was royal blue. This was a cheaper way of strengthening charts than printing them on heavy paper, as the Admiralty did, or putting them on a linen backing. The name came to be applied to any privately published chart, whether or not it had a blue backing, and was used to distinguish them from the Admiralty charts.[100]

Bluebacks were the chart of choice for the mercantile marine for several reasons. In the nineteenth century, bluebacks tended to be small scale charts covering as large an area as possible. Inset plans would provide detailed coverage of ports and narrow sea passages (see Figure 22). They were often more decorative than the Admiralty charts and might also include rhumb lines, which were used by navigators who used dividers to lay a course rather than the more modern parallel rulers. Merchant shipmasters preferred a chart that contained both their departure and destination points. They would keep well out to sea so far as possible and so did not need a large-scale chart containing detail of dangerous coasts. When arriving at port they would use a local pilot. Bluebacks were thus ideal for their needs.[101] Sold at 7 or 8s, the bluebacks were more expensive than the Admiralty charts which sold for 1 or 2s but, because they were on a smaller scale, the shipmaster needed far fewer of them.[102] Ships of Her Majesty's Navy did not keep to well-known and recognised routes but were required to serve across the globe and

[97] MB1 November 1825–February 1832, f.257, 27 May 1829 (UKHO).

[98] Bate wrote this in a letter to Captain Washington (Hydrographer 1855–1862) which he forwarded to the Hydrographic Office's Naval Assistant, Alfred Miles on 26 May 1843, LP1857/B/939 (UKHO). Also quoted in Anita McConnell, *RB Bate of the Poultry 1782–1847* (London, Scientific Instrument Society, 1993) 44.

[99] ibid.

[100] Fisher (n 78) 1.

[101] ibid 11–12.

[102] ibid 12–13.

be able to approach known ports as well as uninhabited and remote coasts. They were more utilitarian and less decorative in appearance and fine engraving was important to show the necessary detail. Fisher observes that these features were not appreciated by the merchant shipmasters; one private chartseller complained to the Hydrographer that she had to trace over some coastlines in Indian ink so that they could be seen.[103]

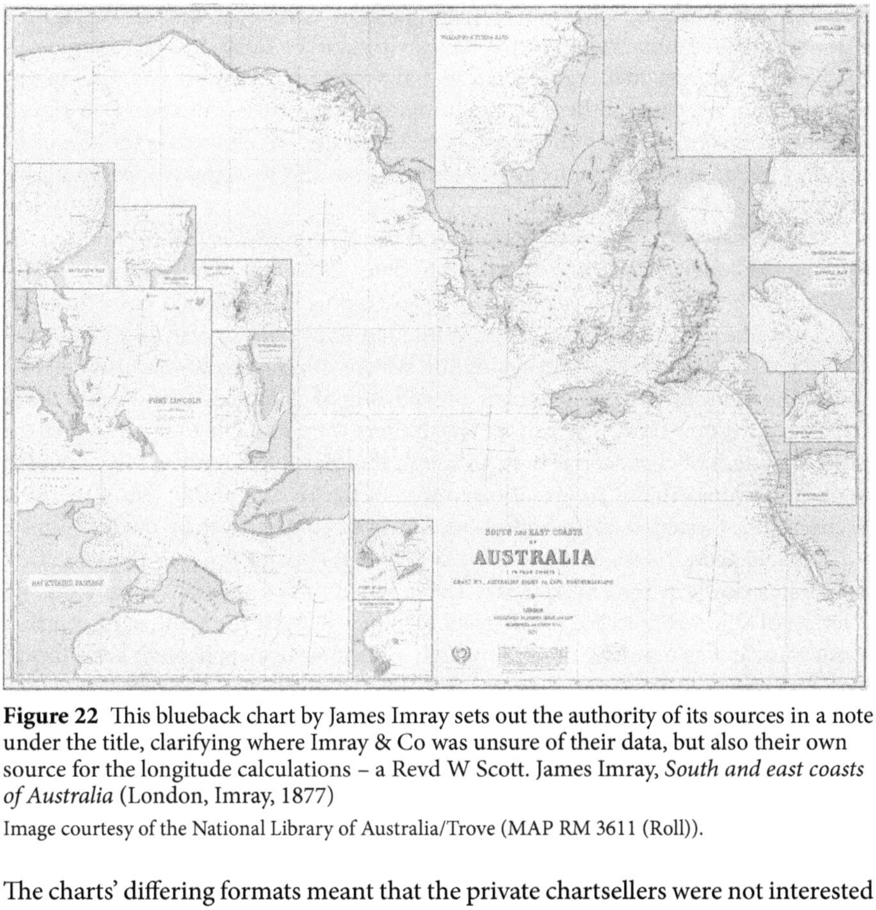

Figure 22 This blueback chart by James Imray sets out the authority of its sources in a note under the title, clarifying where Imray & Co was unsure of their data, but also their own source for the longitude calculations – a Revd W Scott. James Imray, *South and east coasts of Australia* (London, Imray, 1877)

Image courtesy of the National Library of Australia/Trove (MAP RM 3611 (Roll)).

The charts' differing formats meant that the private chartsellers were not interested in copying Admiralty charts in their entirety; what they needed was the data they contained. Sometimes this was seen as a problem, as noted above, but at other times the Hydrographic Office was happy to oblige. As Hydrographer from 1829 to 1855, Francis Beaufort was particularly concerned with improving both the Royal and Merchant Navy by collecting and disseminating useful maritime knowledge.

[103] ibid 12.

Beaufort played roles in the leading scientific societies of the day, and had long been involved in the Society for the Diffusion of Useful Knowledge and committed to its Whig-utilitarian agenda.[104] To carry out his objectives, he established the *Nautical Magazine*, which was funded by the Admiralty and contained a mix of sailing directions, nautical notices, announcements of newly published charts, voyage reports, papers on nautical topics, letters to the editor, and notices of promotion, births, deaths, and marriages.[105] The *Magazine* was not only aimed at a domestic audience but received plaudits from navigators and hydrographers in Russia, France, and Denmark. Its 'key sentiment' of 'open and communicated knowledge' was one that embraced a global scientific community.[106] Eschewing participation in a data market and encouraging its wide dissemination also played an important role in cementing the British Admiralty's reputation as the source of best and most up to date hydrographic knowledge and its claims of authority for its charts.

Nevertheless, both the private trade and the Hydrographic Office experienced ongoing challenges in keeping charts up to date. As well as publishing new information in *The Nautical Magazine*, the Hydrographic Office issued corrections in *Notices to Mariners* from 1834. It also remained important to control the circulation of charts as physical objects using the system of chart agents and sub-agents. The authorised agents could return unsold out of date charts and have them exchanged for new ones. The private chartsellers were not able to operate such an efficient system of chart correction, although the *Mercantile Marine Magazine* did begin publishing similar information to that of the Hydrographic Office in 1854. Accusations of inaccuracy on both sides, however, continued to be made.[107]

The sole agency system evidently worked well enough for it to be continued until Bate's death in December 1847. This opened up a potential vacancy for the position of Sole Agent to the Hydrographic Office. Despite the challenging market conditions, it was a prestigious role which a number of people were keen to fill. Bate was barely in the ground before Beaufort received offers to take over from Letts, Son & Steer (a printing and publishing company famous for having popularised the diary)[108] and George Taylor, husband of the scientific instrument maker and chartseller Janet Taylor.[109] In the end the firm passed to Bate's widow, who retained the Chart Agency until her retirement in 1850.[110] On 20 April 1850, Bate's former shopman John Dennett Potter took over the Agency, remaining at the same address at 21 Poultry.[111]

[104] Barford (n 2) 76–77.
[105] ibid 81–82.
[106] ibid 83–85.
[107] Fisher (n 78) 16–17.
[108] MB 6, November 1846–August 1849 f.183 (UKHO).
[109] McConnell (n 98) 45–46.
[110] ibid 53.
[111] ibid 46.

The first half of the nineteenth century was the period in which the Industrial Revolution fundamentally transformed not only Britain but the world. Britain was the world's leading political, military, and economic power; her success on spectacular display at the Great Exhibition of 1851. The Great Exhibition showcased Britain's economic might, technological advances, and consumer goods, emphasising the centrality of global trading networks and imperial markets. It also captured another truth – the success of an emergent capitalist system based on free flows not just of capital and commodities but also of information. Liberal attitudes towards free trade might seem to be reflected in the Hydrographic Office's attitude towards charts, particularly following the peace of 1815, but Britain still sought to dominate oceanic trade at a global level. This meant that the market for charts as commodities could not be completely free if the Hydrographic Office were to succeed in its core aim of improving maritime information and its claims to authority were to be encouraged and preserved. However, there was little need to interfere in or exploit a market in the data those charts contained.

IV. Commerce, Competition, Monopolies, and the Merchant Marine: 1850–1900

The period up to 1850 was the era of the sailing battlefleet. The second half of the nineteenth century was the age of steam. It also saw a rising number of military conflicts in which Britain became involved, although the involvement of the Navy was less significant than it had been during the Napoleonic Wars. However, it was commercial shipping that underpinned British economic success. Globally, Britain was the chief exporter of manufactured goods and the foremost importer of food, raw materials, and industrial commodities.[112] Britain's position at the centre of the web of global trade also placed her at the centre of global financial services. With the political economy of free trade in the ascendant, the navy was crucial in keeping sea lanes open and safe, and in opening new markets, as in the case of the Opium Wars. In such circumstances, the Admiralty was ever increasingly relied upon for accurate hydrographical information.

In 1850 the Board of Trade took over supervision of merchant shipping matters and soon began to take an interest in the sale and distribution of Admiralty charts. Three years later, the Board suggested to the Admiralty that the price of its charts be raised or that it find some other way to increase their sale but neither suggestion was adopted.[113] In 1860 the Board received a report from

[112] M Daunton, *Wealth and Welfare: An Economic and Social History of Britain 1851–1951* (Oxford, Oxford University Press, 2007) 225.

[113] Marine Department, Board of Trade, Memorandum relating to supply and correction of charts, Departmental Paper 79, August 1882, App 1.

Samuel Robert Graves, a shipowner, chairman of the Liverpool Local Marine Board and soon to be Mayor of Liverpool, complaining about the deficiencies of the current system of supplying correct charts to the merchant marine. The Board responded by writing to the Admiralty, suggesting it do more to publish charts of the frequented seas and channels in a more convenient and popular form, and backed like the private charts, that all chartsellers should receive the same discount, and that all charts should be checked, verified, and stamped by the Admiralty.[114] In other words, the Board wished the Hydrographic Office to offer a product with a broader commercial appeal while also guaranteeing its accuracy. The Hydrographic Office was not keen to take on either task. Becher, the senior naval assistant, pointed out that the Hydrographic charts were 'tolerably correct' but 'far from perfect' and that if ships were lost while using them it would be the Admiralty that was blamed.[115]

In the decade between 1858 and 1867, Admiralty chart sales fluctuated considerably. From annual sales of 57,981 in 1858, they increased to 68,270 in 1860 before dropping to a low point in 1861 of 53,000. The following year, however, they were up to 74,247 and reached a high point of 119,138 in 1864, but then sold 83,324 copies in 1865, 99,082 copies in 1866, and 83,619 copies in 1867. It seems likely the geopolitical realities played a significant role in the market. In 1869 Hydrographer Sir George Henry Richards suggested the surge in 1864 was due to the crisis of the American War, while the high point in 1866 could be attributed to the 'Danish and Prussian difficulty'.[116]

The unpredictable nature of the trade drew the attention of the Navy's Accountant General, who began to take an interest in the chartselling arrangements in 1868. When Richards requested that Potter be allowed to submit his accounts quarterly instead of monthly, the former was sent a memo drawn up by Arthur Henry Bather of the Accountant-General's office. Bather appeared to have a number of concerns with the existing arrangements and to have been influenced by the War Office's approach to the sale of the Ordnance Survey maps. He proposed increasing the number of chart agents to follow the practice of the War Office, apparently with a view to increasing sales and profits, and queried the difference in discount received by the agents compared to that of the Ordnance maps, as well as the practice of replacing old charts which was not done by the War Office. He also implied that Chart Agent Potter was asking for replacement charts whenever his stock was damaged and that he was obtaining an unearned advantage in relation to his scientific instrument business through the arrangement.[117]

Richards was not impressed by Bather's points, which he considered 'neither relevant nor logical'.[118] He replied that 'the first and greatest object has always been

[114] ibid.
[115] Fisher (n 78) 16–17.
[116] MB15, 8 February 1869, 57 (UKHO).
[117] MB14, 17 December 1868, 504–506 (UKHO).
[118] ibid 504 margin.

to circulate correct Charts as widely as possible for the benefit of navigation & the preservation of life and property – the object of making money by the Sale has been secondary'. To achieve this object, 'it is necessary that the Hydrographer should exercise a considerable control over the Chart Agent'.[119] Richards rejected any imputation that Potter received replacement charts in any case except when they were so erroneous to have been cancelled, and that he received any unfair advantage in relation to his sales of scientific instruments. As to the comparisons between the discount offered by the War Office and that of the Admiralty, he pointed out that the War Office could offer short credit and get prompt payment as their market was largely confined to the UK, whereas the Admiralty supplied charts all around the globe.[120] Finally, addressing the point that the War Office did not replace out of date charts, Richards noted:

> It seems almost puerile to reply to this argument – the absence of a hedge or a house on the Ordnance Map might be attended with inconvenience. The absence of a rock or shoal on a Navigating Chart might be attended with results of a most fatal character.[121]

In December 1868, Hugh Childers was appointed First Lord of the Admiralty in Gladstone's government and began implementing his goals of 'improved administration and economy'.[122] The following three years, until Childers's resignation in May 1871, were a turbulent period for the Admiralty from which the Hydrographic Office was not immune. As the Accountant General's office continued to look for ways to make savings, pressure to allow the charts to circulate more freely in the market arose from a second source. Samuel Robert Graves, now sitting in the House of Commons as member of Liverpool, suggested to the House that more use needed to be made of Admiralty charts by the public. He believed that the system of a single chart agent operating in London was not successful and 'it was desirable that everything should be done to induce shipowners and ship captains to use the authorized charts'.[123] Graves also wrote directly to Childers suggesting that the Agency be extended or that all firms wanting more than £5 worth of charts be able to acquire them direct form the Admiralty or on the same terms as the Chart Agent. Complaints about the system were simultaneously raised by Philip & Sons, chartsellers in Liverpool.[124]

Richards considered that the current system was satisfactory. He noted it was only other chartsellers who complained and that he had never had any complaint on the part of the public.[125] Nevertheless, he proposed two alternative

[119] ibid 504.
[120] ibid 504-6.
[121] ibid 506.
[122] W Carr and HCG Matthew, 'Childers, Hugh Culling Eardley (1827–1896), Politician'. *Oxford Dictionary of National Biography*, 23 September 2004, www-oxforddnb-com.rp.nla.gov.au/view/10.1093/ref:odnb/9780198614128.001.0001/odnb-9780198614128-e-5296.
[123] *Hansard*, Supply – Navy Estimates, 30 March 1870, vol 199, 1302.
[124] MB15, 19 April 1870, 467–68 (UKHO).
[125] ibid 468.

options: increasing the number of chart agents to six, one in each of the main ports (London, Liverpool, Bristol, Belfast, Aberdeen, and Leith); or, that the Admiralty establish a depot of its own in the Strand and sell direct to the public.[126] Richards himself preferred the second option. The former would require the Hydrographic Office to administer six sets of accounts and to supervise six agents, reducing its ability to prevent the circulation of erroneous charts.[127] This would disrupt its lines of command and control. For Richards, the monopoly complained of was not something to be remedied but in fact critical to the Hydrographic Office's mission of improving safety at sea. He wrote: 'I believe that we cannot morally divest ourselves of this responsibility for the reason that we are, and must be monopolists, for we alone can provide correct Charts'.[128] The depot option was preferable as it would make it easier to the Hydrographic Office to recall incorrect charts and he believed it would be more attractive to the public as everyone would be able to purchase charts on the same terms.[129] However, Richards warned that this option would be less popular with the private trade, as the discount offered by the government would be reduced to cover the new costs.[130]

The extent to which the Hydrographic Office should embrace sale of charts to the public as an important part of its mission remained a point of tension. Richards was cautious about selling to the public more generally. He warned that the Hydrographic Office was not in a position to supply unlimited charts; when it was tried in the past, demand was so high that it almost ruined the copper.[131] For him, supply to the Navy was its chief object, to which all other considerations must be subordinated. The use value of the charts to the Navy was what mattered to Richards, not their use value to the merchant marine nor their exchange value for the private chart and map trade.

Nevertheless, the private trade continued to agitate for greater access to the exchange market, linking it to questions of access to data. In June 1873, William Lamport (co-founder of the Lamport & Holt Shipping Line) complained to the Royal Commission on Shipping that the Hydrographic Department did not do enough to disseminate their nautical information. Richards responded that

> about five sixths of the results of grounding of merchant vessels have arisen from the use of Charts other than Admiralty Charts, and that the inferiority in accuracy of private publishers are not recognized generally by Merchant Captains or Owners of Ships.[132]

In March 1876, the new Hydrographer, Captain Frederick Evans (Hydrographer 1874–84), was again defending the Office against accusations of responsibility in

[126] MB15, 30 March 1870 442–54 (UKHO).
[127] ibid 443.
[128] ibid.
[129] ibid 444.
[130] MB15, 19 April 1870, 470 (UKHO).
[131] MB15, 30 March 1870, 443 (UKHO).
[132] MB18, 26 June 1873, 200 (UKHO).

relation to the loss of merchant ships through erroneous charts. Writing to Thomas Gray at the Board of Trade, he stated:

> I do not see how anything more can be done than is now carried out by this Department to put within the reach of all Merchant Captains and others interested in the safe navigation of ships, the latest reliable Hydrographic information.[133]

Rather than proposing a loosening of control over the chart market, Gray wondered if it should in fact be increased by making it compulsory for merchant ships to be navigated by Admiralty charts. He observed this was a question on which he hesitated to express an opinion but that such a step would require the authority of Parliament.[134]

A different way of increasing control and reducing the use of erroneous private charts was suggested by Captain Kiddle of Dublin: restricting use of the Hydrographic Office's data. Drawing, perhaps for the first time, on the language of public property, Kiddle wrote that 'Admiralty charts are the property of the nation which should be secured from Piracy as any other literary work'.[135] While Evans agreed with the first part of the sentence, he was not sure about the second. He pointed out that the private charts were seldom 'transcripts' of Admiralty charts but, rather, 'compilations presenting in a compendious form the information often scattered through a series of charts' He asked: 'Would the law of copyright apply in such cases?' and suggested that legal advice would be needed to resolve it.[136]

The problems associated with supplying Admiralty charts to the merchant marine were raised again in Parliament in 1879 by James Stewart, MP for Greenock, a borough adjacent to Port Glasgow.[137] Stewart again characterised the single agent system as a monopoly and proposed appointing more agents, in particular in Liverpool and Glasgow, to better serve the merchant ships.[138] Liverpool chartsellers Philip, Son & Nephew (formerly Philip & Son) continued to complain about the system through 1881.[139] They were joined by Greenock chartsellers A & H Carmichael & Co, who threatened to complain again to Stewart, their MP, of the many occasions upon which they had been unable to obtain the charts they needed.[140] The Hydrographer continued to reject the characterisation of the system as a monopoly, pointing out that while Potter received a discount of 40 per cent of the published price, and 13 copies for the price of 12, the sub-agents received an abatement of 35 per cent and six to nine months credit, compared to Potter who had to account to the Treasury every month.[141] Evans also continued

[133] MB20, 30 March 1876, 177 (UKHO).
[134] ibid.
[135] ibid 178.
[136] ibid 178.
[137] House of Commons *Debates*, 19 June 1879, Hansard vol 247, c181 (James Stewart MP).
[138] MB22, August 1879, 493 (UKHO).
[139] MB24, 11 May 1881, 408, insert to 408 (UKHO).
[140] MB25, 17 June 1881, 43 (UKHO).
[141] MB25, 11 August 1881 (UKHO).

to insist that the primary role of the Hydrographic Department was to 'provide for the efficient navigation of the fleet' and the supply of the merchant trade could be only a 'moral responsibility'.[142]

However, concerns about marine safety and the role of Admiralty charts continued. In August 1882, the Board of Trade produced a Departmental Paper written by Thomas Gray, Assistant Secretary to the Board. Gray noted that, despite all the Board's efforts since 1851, inquiries into wrecks 'show clearly that ships are still lost through the use of antiquated and insufficient charts, or the absences of charts'.[143] Gray conceded that the charts of private publishers were extensively used, giving three reasons. First, he explained, they were more attractive and convenient in size and arrangement, and more comprehensive than the Admiralty charts. Moreover, the master of a ship preferred to have one chart of a convenient size with a lot of information than several small charts and reference to sailing directions. Second, the bluebacks were more durable because they were mounted on linen. Third, they were more expensive. He went on to explain this apparent contradiction lay in the fact that the agents selling the charts received a greater profit from the private charts and, so, pushed their sale harder.[144]

Gray's report concluded that the evidence established it was possible for 'an intelligent man to obtain new charts which are correct in all essential details'.[145] He observed that the Admiralty charts formed the basis of the private publications but that the latter were preferred as being more compendious. He went on to note that

> it seems strange that private chartmakers should be able to dish up information admittedly procured from official sources in a more attractive and useful form than that in which it is presented by the Hydrographer to the Admiralty, but the fact is not disputed by the Admiralty.[146]

He concluded that there was no improvement that could be made on the current arrangements as to the correction of charts and no reason to disturb the arrangements for their sale. The challenge was in convincing masters and ship owners to purchase new charts rather than continuing to use their older, outdated ones.[147] If the Board of Trade were in charge of the sale and distribution of charts to merchant ships, Gray would have recommended that all Admiralty charts be backed with cloth, that their prices be increased to cover the expenses of the agencies, than an officer be appointed to correct and stamp useful charts as approved and to stamp as 'obsolete' those charts which were so incorrect as to be dangerous. As the Board did not have that charge, he instead recommended that improvements be made to the means of selling the newest charts at the ports. He also recommended the

[142] MB25, 11 July 1881 (UKHO).
[143] Marine Department, Board of Trade, Memorandum relating to supply and correction of charts, Departmental Paper 79, August 1882, MLP Folder 2 i, 3 (UKHO).
[144] ibid 4.
[145] ibid 18.
[146] ibid.
[147] ibid App 1.

creation of an agency to correct charts and that ship owners bear the responsibility for providing proper charts for ships.[148]

Evans, however, did not adopt the more extreme position that it be made compulsory for all merchant ships to use Admiralty charts and he resisted the Board of Trade's plans for the Admiralty to take on a greater role in chart correction. This, he considered, would put it under extreme strain in carrying out its official duties towards marine surveying and supplying the Navy with charts. It would, moreover, be impractical and should be done by the private chartmakers themselves, with the information provided by the Hydrographic Department.[149] Evans was also sceptical about the allegations in relation to the role of defective charts in shipwrecks, noting he had looked at the list of cases provided and thought that: 'A very large majority of the cases are reckless allegations, in which the chart is ostentatiously made to bear the blame, instead of the negligence, blundering or incompetence of the Master.'[150]

It is clear that both Admiralty and Board of Trade were still struggling to identify the best way to improve safety at sea. Although there was pressure from the private chart trade and the merchant marine to achieve this through a completely free market for charts as commodities, the Admiralty and Board recognised that, in order to maintain control over the meaning and use of charts, they needed to control the market to some extent. However, at the same time they also recognised they were ill-equipped to compete in the commercial market because the format of their charts was less attractive to the merchant trade and their use of the sole agent meant it was harder to compete on price. Nevertheless, more direct forms of control were ruled out as too expensive or onerous, and there remained no appetite to exploit commercially the maritime data the charts contained. Thus, copyright continued to be largely irrelevant.

In September 1882, Potter died. He was succeeded by his son Septimus until the latter's death in 1898, whereupon Septimus' brother Edward Octavius was appointed.[151] By this time, the tide was decisively turning away from the private chart trade. The rise of steam power in shipping changed marine navigation, as it allowed vessels to run close to coasts and cut corners, meaning that large-scale maps such as those produced by the Hydrographic Department were now in more demand. In addition, the private publishers were not able to keep their charts up to date with the growing numbers of lighthouses that, while assisting navigation when known, could present a source of danger if navigators were not aware of coastal depths.[152] Accompanied by the pressure from the Board of Trade

[148] ibid 5.

[149] Enclosures to MB 28, 20 March 1884, 256 (UKHO).

[150] Enclosures to MB28, 20 March 1884, 256 (14) (UKHO).

[151] MB26, 10 October 1882, 473–74; Enclosure to MB 28, 1 September 1884, 485; MB43, 22 February 1898, 5 May 1898 (UKHO).

[152] Memorial of Kettle trading as Laurie, MB47, 1 June 1899 (UKHO).

for shipowners to supply the latest charts, which in general meant the Admiralty charts, these factors led to a serious reduction in business for the private sellers.

By the end of the century, only three family firms remained in business. In 1899 James Imray & Son amalgamated with the firm of Norie & Wilson to become Imray & Norie.[153] Brothers David and William Kettle were now running the firm of Laurie's and, in the same year, they approached the Admiralty, offering to sell them their chart plates and other stock in trade. The current Hydrographer, Rear Admiral Sir WJL Wharton (Hydrographer 1884–1904), prepared a memo to the First Lord in which he mentioned another firm (almost certainly Imray's) had approached him with a similar offer several years earlier.[154] Wharton recommended that the Admiralty reject the offer, as the plates would be of no use to them. Rebuffed by the Admiralty, the Kettles continued in trade for another six years but eventually bowed to the inevitable and joined in the amalgamation, forming the company Imray, Laurie, Norie & Wilson Ltd in 1905.[155]

Wharton's response to the Kettles' offer encapsulates the difficulties of the relationship between the Hydrographic Office and the private trade. He noted that he rejected their offer with regret, stating: 'It has been with a great deal of sorrow that I have seen the gradual diminution of the private chart trade'.[156] This diminution presented its own problems for the Admiralty because it put additional pressure on the Admiralty chart plates, wearing them out more quickly. Wharton thought that if the firm of Imray & Norie should also go out of business it would put the Hydrographic Department in the awkward position of having to provide 'the special form of chart still used and liked by many Merchant seamen, and now provided by the Private Firms but not by us'.[157] He also rejected the suggestion that the Hydrographic Department could have protected the private trade by refusing to allow their charts to be used by the mercantile marine or by raising their prices. He considered this would have led to a public outcry at the misuse of public money spent in making the surveys only to produce charts that were difficult to acquire. It would also be contradictory to the long-established policy of 'permitting the results of the labour of the Government Department to be obtained at the lowest possible price, with a view of saving losses at sea in general'.[158] Despite their superior understanding of the merchant marine market's needs, the private trade was eventually less able to compete in the market for charts as commodities because the real use value lay in the data the charts contained. When changing shipping technologies eroded the significance of the different physical formats of the two types of chart, the private trade found its market too small to support multiple suppliers.

[153] Fisher (n 78) 106.
[154] ibid.
[155] ibid 108.
[156] MB47, 1 June 1899, 4 (UKHO).
[157] ibid 5.
[158] ibid 4.

V. Conclusion

This is a book about copyright and, so, it might seem remarkable to include a chapter where copyright is barely mentioned. But it is the non-relevance of copyright that is of significance in relation to the generation, use, publication, and circulation of both maritime charts and data, particularly in light of the contrasting position in the twenty-first century.[159] Copyright, in the sense of being an intangible property right that could be leveraged to extract exchange value for reproductions in different markets, did not develop in this case because it was not clear there was a market for the specific physical charts, as commodities, that the Hydrographic Office produced. Moreover, while there would have been a market for the data underlying them, it was not a market that the state wished to exploit. If it had, it seems unlikely that it could have successfully used copyright to do so, given the limitations on using information from maps to make better maps established in the case law discussed in chapters four and five.

What interested the Admiralty and the Hydrographic Office, and other state organs such as the Board of Trade, was ensuring that the charts produced were as accurate as possible and that the Admiralty was recognised as the authoritative source of this accuracy. Here, copyright did have a role to play through the operation of its publication conventions. As noted above, Alexander Dalrymple had begun the practice of putting his own name upon the charts, in part to establish their authority and in part to identify a copyright owner. In the middle decades of the century, the name of the Hydrographer ceased appearing on the charts, instead being replaced by words along the lines of 'Published according to Act of Parliament at the Hydrographical Office of the Admiralty', followed by the date. It was, however, accompanied by the name of the selling agent (Bates or Potter) and that of the engraver. And elsewhere upon the chart (in an area empty of features) would appear the name or names of the surveyors and dates upon which the surveys were made (see Figure 23). By the 1860s, the name of the Hydrographer, Richards, was again appearing in the publication line and the practice was continued by his successors. As was the case with the terrestrial maps, the publication line and other textual information placed upon the chart worked to identify some of those involved in 'authoring' the chart (engravers, hydrographers, surveyors), while rendering invisible others (printers, draftsmen, sailors, naval officers).

[159] See eg the disputes over marine data in the Canadian case *Nautical Data International Inc v C-Map USA* (2013) CAF 63, (2013) FCA 63 and in the Australian case of *Commonwealth v Oceantalk Australia Pty Ltd* (1998) 79 FCR 520. The Canadian case arose from similar tensions observed in this chapter; namely, the relationship between the state hydrographic authority and the private trade, and involved a dispute over the terms of an agreement for nautical data used to produce (paper) navigation charts. The court held copyright could subsist in the charts but not in the data, as copyright did not protect information. The licence in question purported to assert ownership in data giving rise to an ambiguity the court could not resolve. The Australian case raised some of the difficulties discussed in the next chapter, ch 8, namely copyright subsistence and authorship.

Furthermore, as in the case of the Ordnance Survey, it subsumed all of them within a government office, constituted as the copyright owner and providing the authoritative source of the data therein.

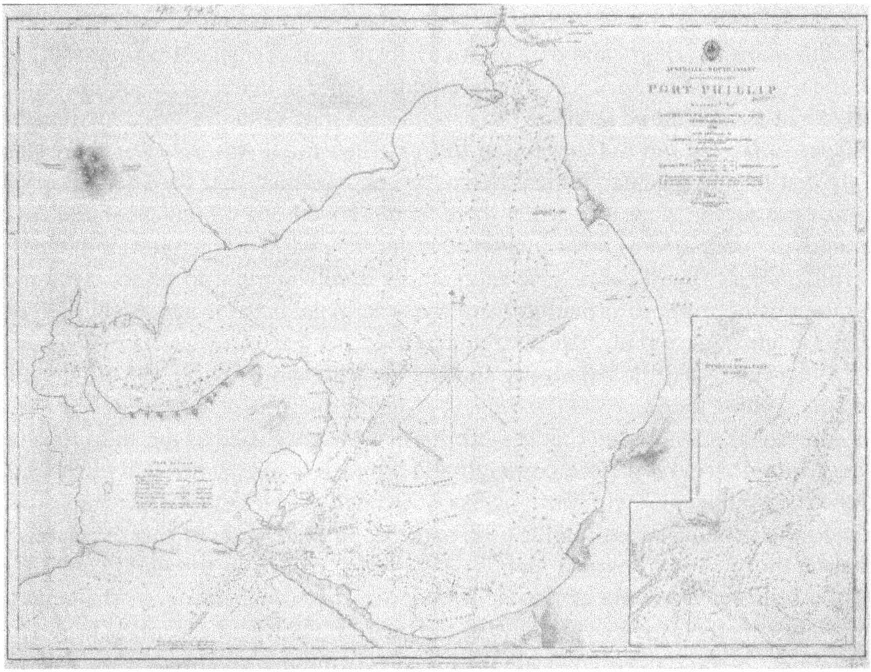

Figure 23 A UK Hydrographic Office chart of Port Phillip, Australia, lists the surveyors and their ships by date, referring also to the official agent Potter. Australia, South Coast, Port Phillip (London, UKHO, 1854)

Image courtesy of the National Library of Australia/Trove (MAP RM 1304).

In an age where Britain's national security and economic prosperity were linked so closely to her maritime strength and effectiveness, it was more important that information was accurate and widely available than secret and protected or controlled and commercialised. The state's interest was best served by more accurate charts and those accurate charts needed to be on board the ships and trusted by the officers that would use them. Both private markets and public investment were needed to achieve this but the private regulatory and market opportunities offered by copyright law were not necessary, despite the fact that the charts were costly to produce and had exchange value which could have been leveraged to recoup those costs. At the end of the day, it was the utility of the charts that mattered most and this was dependent on their accuracy and the authority of the body asserting it.

8

'A Painted Assemblage of Facts': Private Mapmaking in the Nineteenth Century

I. Introduction

The previous two chapters explored the rise of Britain's two major national mapping agencies of the modern era – the Ordnance Survey and the Hydrographic Office – and the effects they had on the creation, collection, management, and circulation of geographic data. Historians often single out the creation of these bodies as two major mapping events marking the British state's incursion into the collection and management of geographic data and, thus, completing the creation of the modern nation-state as a geographic entity. Focusing on national, state-led mapping has meant much less attention has been paid to the private mapmaking that continued throughout the century. This chapter looks at the activities of private mapmakers of the nineteenth century and their attempts to use copyright law to regulate changing market conditions, which flowed on from the changing social and economic conditions observed in previous chapters: the rise of the middle classes with rising expendable income, the rapid growth of the industrialising cities, a more mobile population taking advantage of improved roads and railways, and Britain's global trade dominance. Such changes, considered broadly, stimulated demand for consumer products that could inform Britons about the changing world around them – locally, nationally, and internationally. A cluster of copyright disputes, mostly occurring in the middle years of the century, reveal thriving markets for a range of maps and map-based products – war maps, railway maps, newspaper maps, maps printed on silk handkerchiefs, cheap maps aimed at working-class readers, and expensive atlases aimed at middle- and upper-class readers.

The state bodies discussed in previous chapters had been ambivalent participants in a market for maps and charts, aware that it offered a means of recouping some of the considerable labour required for their production but, at the same time, attentive to its potential to undermine their products' usefulness. Conversely, the private mapmakers of the nineteenth century were always on the lookout for ways to exploit their useful commodities more effectively. However, they too struggled to articulate the basis of their proprietary claims in products of such obvious public interest, now increasingly using data created using public funds. Much of the complexity for both mapmakers and lawyers arose from the understanding of maps as factual, objective representations of the earth. Flowing from the growing influence of the 'cartographic ideal', this understanding created uncertainty for the operation of several aspects of copyright law: how to prove that a product that objectively and scientifically represented parts of the earth could be a subject of copyright protection; even if it could, how to prove that any other map depicting the same parts of the earth was a copy; and who out of myriad people involved in production could be an author and an owner, and what their contribution had to be.

Sherman and Bently have persuasively argued that the nineteenth century was the period in which intellectual property law transitioned from its pre-modern form, which was reactive and subject specific and which did not sharply delineate between different types of intangible property rights arising from mental labour, into a modern, abstract, and forward-looking regime, which organised copyright, patents, designs, and trademarks into distinct categories.[1] While maps, which were marketable commodities with artistic and literary qualities, as well as claims to scientific authority and impact, straddled these different regimes, it was copyright law to which mapmakers habitually resorted to protect and expand their markets. Yet, even within copyright law, the shift towards categorising copyright subject matter by reference to its qualities, rather than its physical form, meant that maps sat uneasily within a statutory scheme dividing the literary from the artistic. At the same time, the emphasis placed upon the idea of maps as objective, scientific, and factual within the legal process and the courtroom worked to further consolidate the cartographic ideal as the essential attribute of any and all maps. This did not so much displace creative authorship as the key to copyright protection as require it to be reimagined as located in other forms of labour – artisanal, skilful, scientific, and entrepreneurial.

This chapter starts by exploring how the cartographic ideal of maps as factual representations of the earth complicated both copyright subsistence and claims of infringement, and how this was resolved by continuing to emphasise both labour and financial investment. In this way, geographical knowledge of the world was transformed into a commodity. The next section looks at the emergence of new uses and, thus, new markets for that commodity and how mapmakers sought to use copyright law to navigate entry into these markets. Exploring three cases of the 1830s, it observes that the rights began to be seen in more abstract terms, as being able to control copying beyond the initial form in which the particular commodity was placed upon the market. The fourth section examines how the emphasis on the objective qualities of correct and accurate maps in copyright law and the collaborative process of their production sat in tension with the rising influence

[1] B Sherman and L Bently, *The Making of Modern Intellectual Property Law* (Cambridge University Press, 1999).

of Romantic theories of authorship, which emphasised the role of the individual and their personal expression. It does this through a detailed examination of a dispute between two leading Scottish mapmakers: the firm of W & A K Johnston, and that of A Fullarton and Company. The fifth section explores the legislative changes of the Literary Copyright Act 1842, leading to an uneasy positioning of maps between the artistic and the informational, and its effect upon two disputes over birds'-eye view prints.

II. The Cartographic Ideal, Labour, and Copying

Nineteenth-century Britain is often characterised as witnessing the birth of the modern information state[2] and was a time when the growing interest and investment in the collection of geographic data by the state trickled down to other parts of society. While the owners of large estates had long had an interest in surveying and mapping their private lands, now other commercial enterprises began to take an interest, in particular those constructing canals and railways. The availability of more comprehensive and more accurate data spurred new interest in longstanding formats such as atlases and new technologies allowed maps to move into more accessible formats such as newspapers. The period thus saw consolidation of 'map-mindedness' throughout much a broader swathe of society.[3] This in turn led to the emergence of new market opportunities.

As noted in chapter six, even had it wished to do so, the Ordnance Survey would not have been able to meet all the needs of a society increasingly clamouring for geographic information. The commercial publishers were quick to fill the gap, pioneering the use of colour and varying scale to cater to differing consumer purposes and tastes.[4] Specialist maps for mining, tunnelling, and agriculture were produced, as were thematic maps, such as those displaying health statistics. Edney highlights this growing public demand for information as one of the key factors in the creation of the cartographic ideal during the nineteenth century.[5] Another was a continued commitment to the notion that maps were by definition 'scientific'. As we have seen, this approach had its roots in Enlightenment thinking of the eighteenth century. However, over the course of the nineteenth century, what was once considered 'natural philosophy' became reconceived as 'science', characterised by specialisation and professionalisation, which were brought together under

[2] E Higgs, *The Information State in England: The Central Collection of Information on Citizens Since 1500* (London, Palgrave Macmillan, 2004) 64–98.

[3] Camilo Arturo Leslie claims to have coined the phrase in CA Leslie, 'Territoriality, Map-mindedness, and The Politics of Place' (2016) 45 *Theory and Society* 169.

[4] D McKitterick, 'Organising Knowledge in Print' in D McKitterick (ed), *The Cambridge History of the Book in Britain, Volume IV: 1830–1914* (Cambridge, Cambridge University Press, 2009) 543.

[5] MH Edney, *Cartography: The Ideal and its History* (Chicago, University of Chicago Press, 2019) 114.

the umbrella label through a shared method and approach. Cartography, employing direct observation and mathematical measurement of the world, came to be a branch of this newly conceived science. Importantly, the characterisation of maps as rational and scientific chiefly found expression in the centrality of map scale as a numerical ratio, such that a direct mathematical relationship between map and world must always exist for a graphic representation to qualify as a map.[6]

The assumption of a direct correlation between map and world had not only been absorbed by lawyers at the start of the century but was also reinforced through its deployment in judicial reasoning. How then could such a map be owned, or copied? In one 1806 case, the Lord Chancellor, Lord Erskine, discussing the earlier decision of *Faden v Stockdale*,[7] posed the question:

> It might be asked, how is it possible to have a Copyright in a Map of the Island of St Domingo? Must not the mountains have the same position: the rivers the same course? Must not the points of land, the coast connecting them, the names given by the inhabitants, every thing constituting a map, be the same?[8]

The answer lay in the labour that the mapmaker had expended or directed to be expended. In that case, Lord Erskine explained that copyright could subsist because the plaintiff had made his map at great expense from original surveys. The next problem to be considered was: how could you tell if the map was copied? The answer offered was that if the two maps were identical, then one was likely to be a 'servile copy'. However, if the second identified errors or omissions in the first and rectified them, that was acceptable because 'every man may take what is useful from the original work; improve, add, and give to the public the whole, comprising the original work, with the additions and improvements'.[9] Three years later, Lord Eldon took a similar approach:

> Take the instance of a map, describing a particular county: and a map of the same county, afterwards published by another person: if the description is accurate in both, they must be pretty much the same: but it is clear, the latter publisher cannot on that account be justified in sparing himself the labour and expence of actual survey, and copying the map, previously published by another.[10]

The following year Lord Eldon made the same assertion in a slightly different way: '[O]ne man publishes the map of a county: another man, with the same design, if he has equal skill and opportunity, will by his own labour produce almost a *fac simile*'.[11]

The cases reveal a commitment to the notion of maps as factual, rational, and scientific representations of the earth, which could be transformed into

[6] ibid 166–227.
[7] See above ch 4.
[8] *Matthewson v Stockdale* (1806) 12 Ves 270, 274.
[9] *Matthewson v Stockdale* (1806) 12 Ves 270, 275.
[10] *Longman v Winchester* (1809) 16 Ves Jnr 269, 271.
[11] *Wilkins v Aikin* (1810) 17 Ves Jun 422, 425.

a proprietary commodity through the 'right kind' of labour. Thus, copying was permissible if it too employed the right kind of labour, demonstrated through improvements and additions. The oft-repeated word 'servile' was used to denigrate the 'wrong' kind of labour, which would lead to a successful infringement claim. The same approach can be seen in an 1830 dispute between two Cambridge surveyors, Richard Grey Baker and Alexander Watford.[12] Reported in newspapers of the day, the case involved a map of the county of Cambridge published by Baker in 1821. In 1828 Watford published a map of Cambridge and its environs, adding in new roads, toll-houses, bridges, and milestones. In the Court of the King's Bench, Lord Tenterden applied the earlier cases, instructing the jury that 'it was competent for one man in the compilation of a map to make reasonable use of the maps of his predecessors; but he had no right to make a servile copy of imitation of them'.[13] According to the slightly shorter report in the *Morning Post*, Lord Tenterden 'agreed that a person publishing a map was entitled to avail himself, in a reasonable way, of previous publications'.[14] The jury found for the defendant and Lord Tenterden apparently told them he quite agreed.[15]

III. Commodities, Markets, and Formats

Labour turned the map into a commodity that was both useful and economically valuable. However, as new needs and uses arose for maps, mapmakers saw their labour and investment being exploited by others in different markets. In order to prevent this, it became necessary to conceptualise maps in more abstract terms. Three disputes that came before the Court of Chancery in the 1830s illustrate this shift.

A. *The Havell* Cases (1832): Silk and Paper Maps

The first of these was in fact a series of suits all brought by one complainant, Robert Havell, an aquatint artist, engraver, and printseller of Oxford Street. Havell had recently published and exhibited his engraving, *An Aeronautical View of London*, of which he was selling copies at 15s coloured and 10s uncoloured (see Figure 24). He was clearly most displeased to find that a number of London traders were selling

[12] The latter operated a considerable business in Cambridge, surveying for a number of the colleges as well as private landowners. On his death in 1844 his estate was valued at £2,000. See AS Bendall, *Maps, Land and Society: A History with a Carto-Bibliography of Cambridgeshire Estate Maps c.1600–1836* (Cambridge, Cambridge University Press, 1992).

[13] ibid.

[14] 'Law Intelligence' *Morning Post*, 19 July 1830, 4.

[15] 'Court of King's Bench, July 17, Baker v. Watford', *Cambridge Chronicle and Journal*, 23 July 1830, 4.

silk handkerchiefs printed with copies of his print. On 3 April 1832, Havell sought injunctions in Chancery against several merchants, including a linen draper, a hosiers and glovers, and a partnership of haberdashers.[16] Ten days later, he sought another injunction against and John Baker and Joseph, Ely and John Tucker.[17] It appeared that this group of silk manufacturers and bandana printers had printed a large number of silk handkerchiefs, which they then supplied to a range of other merchants for retail sale. The handkerchiefs were sold in lots of seven at 4s 3½d each.[18] Two traders submitted to the injunction without responding. The haberdasher partners, Matthew Halling, John Pearce, and Edward Stone, submitted an answer, as did linen draper James Collier and hosier and glover Samuel Castle.

Figure 24 *An aeronautical view of London drawn and engraved by Robert Havell* (London, Havell, 1831). A hand-coloured acquatint on a single sheet
Image courtesy of the Yale Center for British Art, Paul Mellon Collection.

The complaints and answers are of considerable interest in this novel attempt to assert rights in a paper print against a silk handkerchief. To twenty-first-century eyes, the matter appears to engage design rights and the copyright/design overlap. But the case occurred seven years before the Copyright of Designs Act 1839 widened the scope of protectable designs to include those printed upon silk.[19] To fit the claim into the copyright law of the time required a certain level of abstraction and it is notable that Havell constructed his argument in the now traditional way of emphasising investment as well as both physical and mental labour. He explained that he, 'at a considerable expence etched and engraved a certain print from his own invention and design', that he was thus the sole proprietor of the said engraving, and that the defendant made or sold a '*fac simile*' copy knowing that

[16] *Havell v Samuel Castle* (1832) C13/988/7; *Havell v Edward Churton* (1832) C13/1001/61, C33/826/f1269v; *Havell v Charles Cliff* (1832) C13/1001/59, C33/826 f1260v-r; *Havell v Matthew Halling, John Pearce and Edward Stone* (1832) C13/986/6, C33/826 f1260r; *Havell v Collier* (1832) C13/987/21, C33/826 f1260r.

[17] *Havell v John Baker, Joseph Tucker, Ely Tucker, John Tucker* (1832) C33/826 f1260v-1261r (UKNA).

[18] Answer of Matthew Halling, John Pearce and Edward Stone (11 May 1832), C13/986/6 m2 (UKNA).

[19] See Sherman and Bently (n 1) 64.

Havell was the sole proprietor of the engraving. The result was that the sale of the print was 'considerably lessened and depreciated' to his great injury and loss. At the same time, Havell also emphasised his physical possession of the copperplates, claiming that he was

> the sole inventor and designer of the drawing from which the aforesaid Engraving is made and that the plate of the said Original Engraving is in your Orator's possession and that he has the sole and exclusive right to the title of the said Engraving.[20]

The implication seems to be that Havell expended (artisanal) labour upon the copperplates, making them a specific commodity, which carried with it the right to use them to make prints. Copies made not using these plates interfered with this right.

Samuel Castle, in his answer, simply replied he had sold only two handkerchiefs so far, one on credit for which he had yet to be paid, and removed the remainder from sale upon receiving notice from Havell's solicitor.[21] However, the other defendants pushed back against Havell's claims in slightly different ways. Halling, Pearce, and Stone argued that the methods of preparing the designs, of placing the designs onto the blocks or rollers, and of transferring the designs from the blocks or rollers onto silk were 'peculiar and original',[22] and completely different to the methods used for printing onto paper. Moreover,

> no paper prints or engravings could be produced from the blocks on which the designs used for printing silks are cut or stamped and that no silk articles could be printed from the plates on which designs intended for paper prints or engravings are etched or engraved.[23]

In other words, they claimed that Havell had no claim over the plates and the process that they used because they were so different to the plates and process he used. They likewise disputed Havell's claim of damage, arguing that the articles were so aesthetically distinct and useful for such different purposes that there could be no effect on Havell's market:

> [N]o sale however extensive or silk handkerchiefs printed or stamped with a design similar to that or any paper print or engraving would have the least effect in injuring or lessening or depreciating the sale of such paper engraving inasmuch as the fabric or texture or silk is unfitted to receive clear or fine or accurate impressions of any engraving or subject and because the purpose for which stamped or printed silk is applied and

[20] Complaint of Robert Havell C13/988/7 m1 (against Samuel Castle, 2 April 1832), C13/1001/61 (against Edward Churton, 3 April 1832), C13/1001/59 (against Charles Cliff, 3 April 1832), C13/986/6 m1 (against Matthew Halling, John Pearce, Edward Stone, 3 April 1832), C13/987/21 m1 (against James Collier, 3 April 1832) (UKNA).

[21] Answer of Samuel Castle (4 July 1832) C13/988/7 m2 (UKNA).

[22] C13/986/6 m2 (UKNA).

[23] ibid.

> for which alone it is made an article of trade and purchased is wholly apart from this preservation or use as a vehicle for the publication of engravings.[24]

Collier also disputed the basis of the claim. He stated that he did not know the handkerchief *Birds-Eye View of London* was a copy of *An Aeronautical View of London* but that if it was,

> he should never have supposed that it was any infringement of the laws of copyright as to prints and engravings both from the different material and uses of the prints which must of necessity prevent the sale of the one and in any way interfering with the sale of the other.[25]

He also stated it was common to print popular prints onto silk handkerchiefs without the licence of the owner or publisher of the original print.[26] Collier went to the further expense of retaining Sir Edward Sugden KC to contest the injunction.[27] In argument before the Lord Chancellor, Henry Brougham, Sugden pointed out he had seen handkerchiefs printed with portraits of celebrated and popular personages, including Brougham himself.[28] To this Brougham responded, to laughter, that it was 'a doubtful kind of honour, when you consider the use to which the handkerchief is applied'.[29]

The Solicitor-General, appearing for Havell, argued that the print on the handkerchief might be used the same way as the print on paper: 'A person might frame it as he would an engraving, and when he was tired with seeing it hang upon his walls, he could take it down and use it as a handkerchief'.[30] He then produced an actual handkerchief, 'framed and glazed' to make his point. Sugden responded that 'his client was never more astonished than in seeing the way in which the plaintiff had treated his handkerchief' and called it 'an absurdity'.[31] For Sugden, the purpose of placing the print on the handkerchief was aesthetic but this was subordinate to its proposed use:

> A man buying a handkerchief might say, 'If I have one, I may as well have a pretty one,'... but still he would not buy the handkerchief for the sake of the picture alone; he would buy it for a certain use.[32]

Lord Brougham stated that as this was the first occasion on which the matter had come up, and because it was important, he would take time to consider

[24] C13/986/6 m2–3 (UKNA).
[25] Answer of James Collier, C13/987/21 m2 (13 April 1832) (UKNA).
[26] ibid.
[27] *Morning Chronicle*, 18 June 1832, 4; C13/987/21 (3 April 1832) (UKNA).
[28] *Morning Chronicle*, 18 June 1832, 4.
[29] ibid. Given the well-known friction between Sugden and Brougham at this time, this exchange may have been less amicable than it appears.
[30] ibid.
[31] ibid.
[32] ibid.

his decision.[33] On 30 June 1832, he delivered his judgment, finding that there was infringement, as the Engravings Acts gave the right to print 'without reference to the nature of the materials'.[34]

The trivial, even humorous, nature of the case should not obscure the significance of Lord Brougham's finding that rights in a two-dimensional print upon paper could be used to restrain production of a three-dimensional article. What Lord Brougham identified here was the emergence of an abstract, intangible right that was separate to the medium of its production or the material format in which it was realised and, thus, a property *in itself*. This was a startlingly modern approach to the law.

B. *Cruchley v Edwards* (1833): Maps for the Masses

The next two cases did not require the court to address a work printed in quite such different formats, but they did involve maps printed for different markets. In 1833, a dispute came before the Court of Chancery, this time over the alleged unauthorised copying of a plan of London containing street and place names, published by Ludgate Street mapmaker George Frederick Cruchley.[35] Cruchley, who had been apprenticed to Aaron Arrowsmith (whom we met in previous chapters), had been making and regularly updating his maps of a rapidly transforming London since 1826.[36] In 1833 he sought an injunction against William Edwards, printer of *The Guide to Knowledge*, a weekly publication aimed at improving the working classes, which its editor, William Pinnock, sold at 1d. Pinnock had apparently determined to include a series of maps of London and Cruchley accused him of copying his map of London. Cruchley commenced his bill of complaint with the usual reference to investment and labour, noting that he had 'at a considerable expense etched designed and engraved' Cruchley's *New Plan of London* and emphasised his original contribution: '[I]n the margin whereof are engraved the names of streets and places contained in the said map with alphabetical letters thereto as references'.[37]

Edwards put in an answer, arguing that the map was not 'an original' because it was merely copied and compiled from other previously published maps.[38] This point did not trouble the Court of Chancery as much as Edwards's second argument: that Cruchley had not included a date 'as required by the Acts of Parliament'.

[33] ibid.
[34] *Legal Observer, or Journal of Jurisprudence* Vol 4 (1832) 220 (4 August 1832).
[35] Complaint of George Frederick Cruchley, 6 Feb 1833, C13/1849 m1–4 (UKNA).
[36] L Worms and A Baynton-Williams, *British Map Engravers: A Dictionary of Engravers, Lithographers and Their Principal Employers to 1850* (London, Rare Book Society, 2011) 173–74.
[37] Complaint of George Frederick Cruchley (6 Feb 1833) C13/1849 m1 (UKNA).
[38] Answer of William Edwards, C13/1849 m5 (22 April 1833) (UKNA).

The case was sent to the Court of Exchequer to resolve the matter but the injunction was continued.[39] Edwards's map would have been printed at a much lower quality to Cruchley's, served a different market, and performed a different purpose. It was a demonstrably distinct commodity and yet the court seemed prepared to accept Cruchley's rights extended to preventing its publication.

C. *Cheffins v Wyld* (1837–1838): Maps of the Railways

The third case also required the court to consider the extent to which property rights in a map prepared for one purpose and market could be used to curtail production of a map prepared for a different purpose and market. This dispute was one of many that arose out of the British railway mania of 1836–37. With the rise of the railways, surveying and mapping took on a whole new order of importance. Although railway construction was carried out by private companies, it was necessary to obtain an act of Parliament to enable the compulsory purchase of land along the proposed route (a requirement dating back to 1663 and turnpike road construction). From 1803 this process required that the sponsors of a railway bill submit a surveyed plan of the route, along with financial details about the undertaking's viability.[40] One ambitious civil engineer, Charles Frederick Cheffins, who had worked on the plans of the London and Birmingham Railway (L&BR) under the company's instruction, later saw an opportunity to exploit some of that work for his own profit.

The first surveys had been made along the route in 1832 in preparation for an act of Parliament, which was eventually passed in 1833, allowing the railway's construction under the newly incorporated L&BR to proceed. The creation of the map involved combining private and public data: company employees drew on original and unpublished surveys and measurements made or commissioned by the company; unpublished surveys made by the Board of Ordnance, with its permission; and maps that had been published by the Ordnance Survey.[41] In August 1835, the company agreed to sell the copperplates and the copyright in the map to Cheffins for the sum of £158.[42] Cheffins made some changes to the copperplates, adding the names of many towns and villages, as well as extending the map to include country to the north[43] (see Figure 25).

[39] *Morning Post*, 8 August 1833, 4. I have not found any records of the Exchequer proceedings.

[40] D Milbank Challis and A Rush, 'The Railways of Britain: An Unstudied Map Corpus' (2009) 61 *Imago Mundi* 186, 186–88.

[41] *Cheffins v Wyld* (1837) Bill of Complaint, C13/385/2 m1 (5 October 1837) (UKNA).

[42] C13/385/2 m2 (UKNA).

[43] ibid.

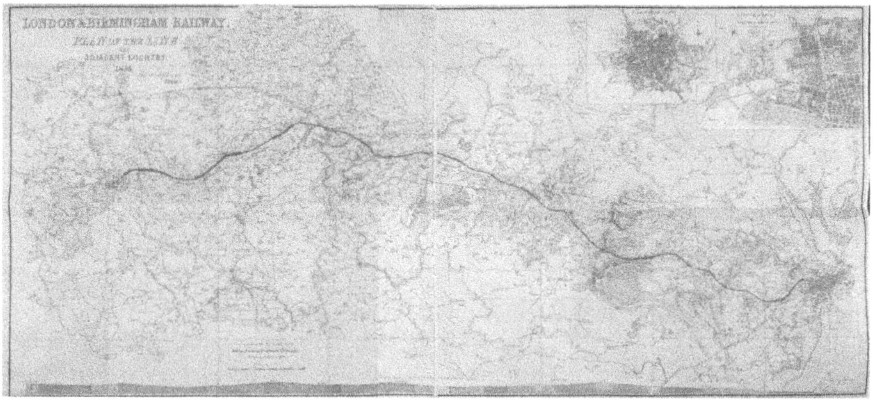

Figure 25 Robert Stephenson, *London & Birmingham Railway Plan of the Line and Adjacent Country* (London, Cheffins, 1835) Cheffins' map was a hand-coloured copperplate engraving, which included detailed insets of the Birmingham and London depôts
© The British Library Board (Maps.1223.(.2)).

Clearly perceiving there would be a market for such works outside the railway company, Cheffins arranged for this new map to be engraved, printed, and published and in January 1837 sent some copies to James Wyld to be sold or returned at the end of six months, as was the custom of the trade. The railway mania had initially proved profitable for Wyld, who had joined the mapmaking firm of his father, also James Wyld (whom we met in chapter six), in 1830.[44] He built up a business of supplying the prospectus maps and plans that the railway companies needed to deposit in order to get parliamentary approval. However, the collapse of the bubble left him with considerable debts owing, which he pursued unsuccessfully through the courts.[45] Wyld did sell some copies of Cheffins's map, priced at a guinea but, according to Cheffins, Wyld then published his own map, which was a copy of Cheffins's, entitled *Wyld's Map of the London and Birmingham Railway*, to be sold at 2s 6d (see Figure 26). On 5 October 1837 Cheffins brought a Complaint against Wyld in the Court of Chancery, accusing him of copying his map.[46] Wyld entered an answer on 9 April 1838.[47]

[44] Wyld the elder died in October 1836 leaving his son in sole charge of the firm: E Baigent, 'Wyld, James, The Younger (1812–1887), Cartographer and Geographical Publisher', *Oxford Dictionary of National Biography* (online), 23 September 2004.
[45] ibid.
[46] C13/385/2 m1 (UKNA).
[47] Answer of James Wyld (9 April 1838) C13/385/2 m5 (UKNA).

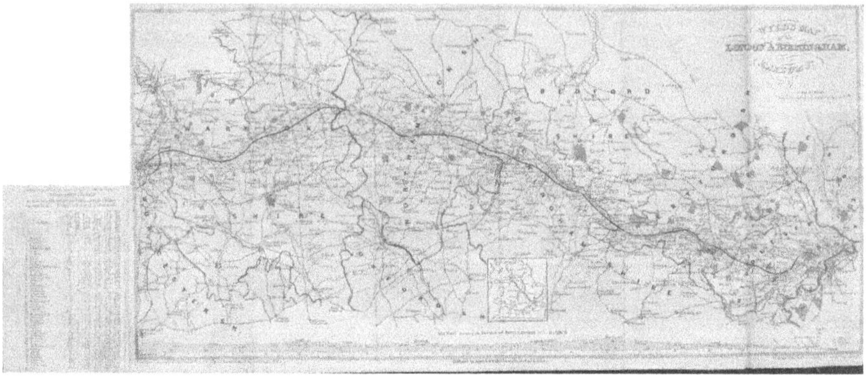

Figure 26 Wyld's Map of the London & Birmingham Railway (London, James Wyld, 1837) A hand-coloured copperplate engraved, folding map, which was a near-identical copy of Cheffins' map of the same section, even including the railway inclinations, but replacing the depot insets with one showing the entire plan for the line on a map of England

One of the key issues in the pleadings that framed the dispute was whether Cheffins's map was capable of ownership as an item of property and subject of copyright. Cheffins argued that his map was 'a wholly new and original map', despite being based on existing materials, because the materials had been 'collected and compiled with great care skill and labour and at considerable expence', and the cost of engraving borne by the L&BR.[48] Cheffins himself then 'expended a considerable sum of money and bestowed much care skill and labour' in making his own alterations and, thus, became entitled to the print and sell the map for the remainder of the copyright term.[49] He accordingly pointed to authorial collection and compilation, as well as financial investment.

In response Wyld disputed Cheffins's proprietary claims by denigrating the labour involved. Wyld asserted that the maps made by the L&BR were compiled from existing Board of Ordnance maps and that 'neither the materials thereof nor of either of them were collected or compiled with great or more than ordinary care skill or labor at a considerable or more than very moderate expence'.[50] He further denied that, in altering the map, Cheffins 'expended a considerable sum of money or bestowed much skill care or labor' in making the alterations and additions.[51] He conceded that Cheffins might be entitled to the sole right to print and publish his own alterations and additions but later Wyld added that the lengths of roads

[48] C13/385/2 m2 (UKNA).
[49] ibid.
[50] C13/385/2 m5 (UKNA).
[51] ibid.

and distances of towns in Cheffins's maps were also not 'the result of laborious or accurate compilation in as much as from existing materials such compilations may be made with little labor and this Defendant has discovered various inaccuracies' so that he would 'submit to the judgment of this Honorable Court whether the Plaintiffs said engraving is of itself wholly new or original'.[52]

Wyld also denied that the Company was competent to acquire copyright but that, if it had, it had abandoned that copyright by the gratuitous publication of its prospectus, by not objecting to the publication of other maps of the line of the Railway, and by not engraving the date of the publication or name of the publisher on the map itself. Further, he argued,

> the line and section of the Railway was dedicated to the public by the public use made thereof by depositing the same with the Clerks of the Houses of Parliament and the Clerks of the Peace of various Counties for public purposes.[53]

Finally, a proper instrument of assignment was not executed and, so, the copyright could not have been assigned to Cheffins.[54]

In addition to the difficulty of establishing ownership, proving copying was also challenging because Wyld argued he had simply used the same sources: an earlier map published by his father; Ordnance Survey maps; and railway prospectuses. In pointing out the similarities that that gave away the copying, Cheffins pointed to his inclusion of a baseline that did not, in fact, show the low-water level mark but was dictated by the need to increase the margin of the map.[55] Wyld could not, therefore, argue that the baseline was the same in both maps because it represented the actual low water mark. A further piece of 'conclusive evidence' of copying was a line drawn on Wyld's map, which represented a

> mere blunder and could not have been made but by reason of the fact of the said Engraving of your Orator having been copied on the map of the said defendant by some person who did not understand the use and meaning of the said Section on your Orator's said Engraving.[56]

For Wyld, the situation was to be treated the same way as mapsellers treated the Ordnance Survey maps, in that the data could be adapted for a different market. He explained that his map would not interfere with sales of Cheffins's, because they were

> designed for totally different purposes that of the said Complainant being an elaborate map for scientific purposes and that of this Defendant being a small pocket map

[52] C13/385/2 m6 (UKNA).
[53] ibid.
[54] ibid.
[55] C13/385/2 m4 (UKNA).
[56] ibid.

> for the use of travellers and general reference as to the line of the said Railway and its Neighbourhood.[57]

Thus, 'persons requiring a map of the description of the Plaintiffs would not purchase this Defendants as a substitute'.[58]

It appears that case settled before proceeding to a judgment, perhaps when Wyld became enmeshed in more pressing litigation over his railway-related debts. Yet the pleadings are of interest because of their framing of the questions such cases raised, some of which echoed earlier questions raised in the eighteenth century, and some of which were new. Could you claim property rights in a map based on the labour of compilation, expenditure, or by the addition of new information? If the data used was generated using public money or otherwise for public purposes, did it undermine private property rights? In relation to copying, could the complainant point to copied errors such that a failure to correspond accurately to the territory being represented could also be the telltale fingerprint of the copier? And in relation to infringement, could it be avoided if the copy improved the original or was catering to a different market? All of these questions were designed to extract information about the significance of the labour employed in mapmaking and the scope of the rights to which that labour gave rise.

IV. Owners, Makers, and the Scientific Author

A. Maps and Romantic Authors

By the fourth decade of the nineteenth century, it was clear that an objective, factual representation of the earth (or sea) could be capable of ownership through copyright law due to the application of mental labour, and investment of financial resources. Such maps could be considered 'original'. But this framing raised another question for those who characterised copyright as an authorial right: if originality in the case of maps was established by such things as labour, compilation, and the generation or addition of new data, where did that leave the matter of authorship? The emphasis on the objective qualities of correct and accurate maps in copyright law sat in some tension with the rising influence of Romantic theories of authorship on copyright's development over the course of the century. Historians have pointed to the influence of Romantic poets Wordsworth and Coleridge, as well as that of authors such as Dickens, on copyright reform through their evocation of an author as a creative genius with a natural right to their original outpourings. It has been suggested that the nineteenth century saw copyright law moving towards an understanding of its role as concerned with the protection of 'original' works

[57] C13/385/2 m6 (UKNA).
[58] ibid.

that were the product of an author's personal expression.[59] However, the Romantic model of authorship was a poor fit for maps, charts, and plans. The growing insistence on the notion that a map was simply an accurate representation or copy of the world undermined the distinction between copy and original, and the insistence on scientific method and objectivity undermined the author as creator of an original work manifesting individual, personal expression.

The extension and crystallisation of subject matters that qualified for copyright protection offered further challenges in relation to maps. Statutory reform in 1842 consolidated many aspects of the law in relation to literary works, while in 1862 new legislation protected artistic works such as paintings and drawings for the first time.[60] Yet, as will be discussed in further detail in the next section of this chapter, maps continued to sit uneasily across the two regimes because they displayed literary and artistic qualities, as well as mathematical and scientific ones. Copyright reformers also sought to increase copyright's scope in other respects, particularly increasing its duration. The rhetoric deployed to do this focused on the proprietary claims of authors in relation to their original works and drew on Romantic ideas about authorship. But the rhetoric of private property rights produced tension in relation to maps due to their claims of being both scientific and useful to the public. Furthermore, as the data they contained were increasingly generated using public funds, the conflict between private and public interests was amplified.

It perhaps not surprising that the Romantic poets were conflicted about the rise of mapping, particularly the Ordnance Survey. Wordsworth, often described as an Ordnance Survey enthusiast, evocatively wrote of its Director, Colonel Mudge:

> [On] the summit whither thou art bound,
> A geographic Labourer pitched his tent,
> With books supplied and instruments of art,
> To measure height and distance; lonely task,
> Week after week pursued!

The poem, however, concludes:

> … suddenly
> The many-coloured map before his eyes
> Became invisible: for all around

[59] M Woodmansee, 'The Genius and the Copyright: Economic and Legal Conditions of the Emergence of the "Author"' (1984) 17 *Eighteenth-Century* Studies 425; M Rose, *Authors and Owners: The Invention of Copyright* (Harvard, Harvard University Press, 1993); M Woodmansee and P Jaszi, 'The Law of Texts: Copyright in the Academy' (1995) 57 *College English* 769; K Bowrey, 'Copyright, Photography and Computer Works – The Fiction of an Original Expression' (1995) 18 *UNSW Law Journal* 278, 280–88; M Woodmansee, 'The "romantic" author' in I Alexander and HT Gómez-Arostegui, *Research Handbook on the History of Copyright Law* (Cheltenham, Edward Elgar, 2016) 53–77.

[60] Copyright Law Amendment Act 1842, 5 & 6 Vict c45, s 2 (Literary Copyright Act 1842); Fine Art Copyright Act 1862, 25 & 26 Vict c68.

> Had darkness fallen – unthreatened, unproclaimed –
> As if the golden day itself had been
> Extinguished in a moment; total gloom,
> In which he sate alone with unclosed eyes
> Upon the blinded mountain's silent top![61]

By the end of the poem, Wordsworth has come to link Mudge with Enlightenment attitudes towards classification and knowledge, of which the former is critical, and uses the poem to 'articulate scepticism about cartography's capacity adequately to represent "Nature's processes"'.[62] Mudge is a 'Labourer' and not an author.

In addition, the many different processes involved in making a map challenged the notion of an identifiable originator to perform the role of 'author'. As we have seen, the Engravings Acts focused attention on the method or act of creation (engraving, etching, working in mezzotinto etc) and rather less on the people involved. The statutes made no attempt to distinguish between the surveyors or geographers, the draughtsmen, the engravers, the printers, the colourists, or the publisher who 'procured' their labour. The potential for this lack of distinction to lead to disputes over ownership was realised in the long-running and expensive litigation between the Society for the Diffusion of Useful Knowledge (SDUK) and its publishers, Robert Baldwin and Charles Cradock, who had been publishing the Society's series of cheap maps.[63] The maps were drawn up under the superintendence of Captain Francis Beaufort (commencing in 1828, the year before he became Hydrographer to the Admiralty). Beaufort and the SDUK chose the engraver, while all arrangements for printing, colouring, and publishing were made by Baldwin and Cradock, who also bore all the costs of the arrangement.[64] Unfortunately, the agreement according to which the maps were made did not contain terms as to the copyright. Baldwin and Cradock appear to have understood that they owned the copyright, while the SDUK believed that it did. This became an issue when Baldwin and Cradock became insolvent and the SDUK wished to repossess the plates, while the publishers' creditors, now in the position of trustees, wished to continue printing and selling the maps.[65] Chancery litigation commenced

[61] W Wordsworth, *Written with a Slate Pencil, on a Stone, on the Side of the Mountain of Black Comb* (1813).

[62] R Hewitt, '"That Experienced Surveyor, Colonel Mudge": Romantic Representations of the Ordnance Survey Map-Maker, 1791–1830' in S Bushell, JS Carlson and D Walford Davies (eds), *Romantic Cartographies: Mapping, Literature, Culture, 1789–1832* (Cambridge, Cambridge University Press, 2020) 69.

[63] *The Society for the Diffusion of Useful Knowledge v Baldwin and Cradock* (1838) C13/395/7 (UKNA). For a detailed account of the mapmaking ventures of the SDUK, see MT Cain, 'The Maps of the Society for the Diffusion of Useful Knowledge: A Publishing History (1994) 41 *Imago Mundi* 151.

[64] Answer of Robert Baldwin and Charles Cradock (24 March 1838) C13/395/7 m5 (UKNA).

[65] *The Society for the Diffusion of Useful Knowledge v Baldwin and Cradock* C13/395/7; *Baldwin, Cradock, Salt, Pouncey, Smith, Hansard, Marshall v Society for the Diffusion of Useful Knowledge* (1838) C13/571/29; Answer of John Salt, Henry Pouncy, Leapidge Smith, Thomas Curson Hansard and Richard Marshall (24 December 1840) C13/430/22 (UKNA).

in 1838 and continued until 1842 when the SDUK paid the trustees £1,750 for their interest to settle the dispute out of court.[66]

B. *W & AK Johnston/The Atlas Company v Fullarton* (1853): The Scientific Author

The complexities surrounding the nature of map authorship and its relationship to copying are more fully revealed in the next dispute we will consider. This was the first case to be brought under the new provisions of the Literary Copyright Act 1842 and occurred in Scotland between two established family firms of Edinburgh mapmakers, W & AK Johnston and Archibald Fullarton and Company. In exploring this case, we are fortunate to have access not only to the original legal record but also to a printed account of proceedings, as well as to correspondence between those involved and their contemporaries, allowing an unusually full picture of nineteenth-century copyright litigation to be drawn. The legal argument reveals how questions of authorship and authority underlie assessments about copyright subsistence, the importance placed on technologies of map creation and map copying, and the emphasis on public usefulness and its tension with private protection. At the same time, the archive reveals the importance of relationships in the map trade and the human cost of conflict and litigation.[67]

The litigation involved *The National Atlas, of Historical, Commercial and Political Geography*, published by the prominent Edinburgh publishing house W & AK Johnston (mentioned earlier in chapter six). The firm had been founded by William Johnston in 1825, joined by his brother Alexander Keith Johnston in 1826, and they began publishing maps in the 1830s.[68] *The National Atlas* was their first major undertaking and Keith Johnston (as Alexander Keith was known) was chiefly responsible for preparing and engraving it.[69] The project was two years in preparation and five years in compilation, during which time 'neither time, money nor labour was spared in collecting a varied mass of geographical facts and data, and in arranging and presenting the same to the reader in the most compact, clear and useful form'.[70] The total cost, Keith Johnston estimated at the trial, was about £5,000.[71] The *National Atlas* was innovative in introducing to the British market a short section of thematic maps designed to depict and explain physical (or environmental) aspects of the natural world. For this contribution, Keith included

[66] Cain (n 63) 159.

[67] For an examination of the litigation that emphasises this aspect, see CWJ Withers, 'On Trial – Social Relations of Map Production in Mid-Nineteenth-Century Britain' (2019) 71 *Imago Mundi* 173.

[68] D Smith, 'The Business of W. and A.K. Johnston 1826–1901' (2000) 82 *IMCoS Journal* 9, 9.

[69] ibid 10.

[70] JM Duncan, *Report of the Trial at the Instance of The Atlas Company of Scotland against A. Fullarton and Company* (Edinburgh, William Blackwood and Sons, 1853) 2.

[71] ibid.

four maps of physical geography created by Heinrich Berghaus, Professor of Geography at the Bauakademie, Berlin. If these maps proved popular, Keith intended to publish further maps from Berghaus's *Physikalischer Atlas* (*Physical Atlas*).[72]

The *National Atlas* was published in 1843 and dedicated to the Royal Geographical Society. It met with approval in the scientific community and the press. Physicist Sir David Brewster wrote that the maps were 'as accurate in their geographical details as they are beautiful in their execution', while the *Literary Gazette* called it 'truly a splendid publication'.[73] Mathematician William Galbraith, who took a particular interest in surveying Scotland and was a strong advocate for extension of the national survey to cover more of that country, wrote to Keith Johnston in 1844, praising the *National Atlas* as being superior to any other he knew of. He was particularly pleased to note that:

> You appear to have availed yourself of the Ordnance Maps under the superintendency of Colonel Colby and of the Admiralty Charts published under the direction of that distinguished officer Captain Francis Beaufort Hydrographer Royal, and all these are worthy of the well known talents of their respective authors.[74]

As noted above, the *National Atlas* also contained four new maps by Berghaus, as well as an ethnographic map of Europe by Gustav Kombst, a German thematic cartographer living in Edinburgh. In the preface, Keith Johnston, referring to himself as 'Editor', acknowledged the contribution of Berghaus, the work of Humboldt, Brewster, Jameson, Whewell, and others, and further acknowledged assistance from Brewster and Jameson.[75] However, it was Keith's mapmaking reputation at stake and he who, on the strength of his contribution, was given the title of 'Geographer at Edinburgh in Ordinary to Her Majesty', while the firm was appointed 'Geographers to the Queen'.[76] According to the *Atlas*' prospectus, the work was sold in imperial folio (22 x 15 inches), half-bound Morocco,[77] for £8 8s, although cheaper issues were also produced: one on superfine thick paper for £4 14s 6d; a lithographed issue on thick paper at £3 5s; and a lithographed issue on thin paper at £2 14s 6d. All issues were in colour.[78]

Eight years later, in 1851, A Fullarton and Company issued a prospectus of a work entitled *Companion Atlas to the Gazetteer of the World, Comprehending Forty-Eight Beautifully Coloured Maps, Engraved in the First Style of Art according to the Latest and Most Authentic Information*, designed as a companion to an earlier publication Fullarton had begun issuing in parts, called *Gazetteer of the World*.

[72] See R Shirley, 'Berghaus and Johnston: Pioneers of the Thematic Atlas' (2000) 83 *IMCoS Journal* 3.

[73] Reviews included in the Prospectus for A & AK Johnston's subsequent publication, *A Physical Atlas*, to be edited by AK Johnston and Henry Berghaus. The Prospectus was entered into evidence in the litigation CS236/A/24/2 (NRS).

[74] ACC 5811/24, Galbraith to Johnston, January 1844 (NLS).

[75] *National Atlas*, 1843, Preface, I, ii.

[76] Smith (n 68) 11.

[77] 'Half-bound Morocco' means that the spine and corners are covered in Morocco, or goatskin, leather.

[78] The prospectus can be found with the papers for the legal proceedings at CS236/A/24/2 (NRS).

The company had been founded by Archibald Fullarton, a publisher, bookseller stationer, printer, and stereotyper, and had offices in Edinburgh, Glasgow, and London. Archibald died in 1836 and his son John Archibald continued the family business. Most of the maps in the Companion Atlas were engraved by George Swanston, under whose name the publication appeared. However, some were engraved by others: John Bartholomew junior, whose father, John Bartholomew senior, founded the Edinburgh mapmaking firm of that name; German mapmaker August Petermann; and John Hugh Johnsone, an artist and draughtsman.

The *Companion Atlas* was in direct competition with the *National Atlas*. It featured engraved maps of the same parts of the world and was produced in the same folio format. It was sold, however, on a subscription basis for 5s a part, allowing it to reach those for whom an initial outlay of over £8 was beyond reach. William and Keith Johnston looked at the maps of the first two numbers of the *Companion Atlas* – namely, maps of Scotland, the world in hemispheres, South America, Europe, North America, and France – and formed the view that all of them, except the map of France, had been copied from their own *National Atlas*. Fullarton refused to withdraw the maps from circulation and denied copying; so, W & AK Johnston initiated proceedings on 25 June 1852 in the Scottish Court of Session.[79] They sought £1,000 in damages and asked that the defenders be prohibited from selling and publishing the *Companion Atlas*, and either deliver up any copies or destroy them, as well as the copperplates.[80]

The case excited considerable interest among other mapmakers as well as in the press.[81] Swanston sought to draw in John Bartholomew Senior, asking him to compare the maps and 'make out it contains matter in common with other authorities'.[82] Bartholomew, however, wrote to his son, John Junior, that he was 'very reluctant to have anything to do with such a matter & I am at a loss what to say about it'.[83] On 27 July 1853, the jury was balloted.[84] The hearing then began and ran for three days.

[79] Duncan (n 70) 2–3. The manuscript report reveals that the Pursuers in the action were not only the firm of W and AK Johnston and its individual partners, William, Keith, and another brother, Thomas Brumby Johnston, but also: publishing company James Lumsden and Son and the individual partners of that firm, James Lumsden Senior and Junior; and papermakers Cowan and Company and the individual partners of that firm, Alexander Cowan, Charles Cowan, James Cowan, and John Cowan. These individuals and entities appear to have made up The Atlas Company, presumably an entity set up to bring the project to fruition and hold the copyright. The Defenders were A Fullarton and Company, and its partners, John A Fullarton and John McNab. *Atlas Company v Fullarton and Company*, Summons, 25 June 1852, CS236/A/24/2 (NRS).

[80] Summons, *The Atlas Company and others v A Fullarton and Company* (25 June 1852), CS236/A/24/1 (NRS).

[81] Reports of the trial appeared in: *Brechin Advertiser*, 2 August 1853, 2; *Dundee Courier*, 3 August 1853; *Inverness Courier*, 4 August 1853; *Elgin & Morayshire Courier*, 5 August 1853; *Aberdeen Courier*, 6 August 1853.

[82] Bartholomew Snr to Bartholomew Jnr, 24 June 1853, ACC 1022/BR/11 (NLS).

[83] ibid.

[84] Its 12 members were a plasterer, two farmers, a builder, a glass chandelier maker, a hotelkeeper, a silk mercer, a tile manufacturer, a provision merchant, a house agent, a sheep and cattle agent and a tax collector, CS236/A/24/1 (NRS).

Counsel for the Johnstons, James Crauford, opened by extolling the 'policy and justice' of the copyright statutes on copyright, and explained:

> No man could secure an exclusive right to publish a Map of Scotland, or could even prevent another man from making a fair use of his map as a guide and aid in his own labours. But the slavish or mechanical copying of a map is not a fair use of it, and against an unfair use the Law of Copyright protects the publisher.[85]

W & AK Johnston had registered the *National Atlas* at Stationer's Hall and, so, were relying on the Literary Copyright Act 1842, rather than the Engravings Acts of 1735 and 1767. This seems to have been a deliberate strategy, for the *National Atlas* was only registered on 20 May 1852, clearly in preparation for the proceedings that were about to commence.[86] A significant change introduced by the 1842 Copyright Act was that the beneficiary of protection was the 'author' rather than, as in the Engravings Acts, the inventor, designer, or engraver. It is notable, however, that Crauford emphasised that 'the Law of Copyright protects the *publisher*' and nowhere is Keith Johnston referred to as the work's 'author'. Yet, at the same time, the authorial nature of his contribution, as well as his authority as a geographer, were made central to establishing that copyright subsisted in the maps. Keith Johnston was the first witness to take the stand. He explained that the maps 'were prepared from the very best materials' and that '[t]hey were altogether original designs'.[87] He also emphasised the extent of his labour in producing the *Atlas*:

> I devoted my entire time to it for many years … I found that it was necessary for me to master several languages, especially the German, French, Italian and Spanish … I then read very extensively geographical works … I consulted every book of travels and voyages which I could get possession of in any of those languages, and also all books that bore upon the subject, whether directly geographical or not … I had a great deal of correspondence with eminent geographers … I took the benefit of all surveys that had been made at home and by foreign governments.[88]

The form of authorship Johnston described was both compilatory and deeply collaborative – he described in detail the process of making the maps themselves and who assisted him at each stage. It was also scientific in nature, with the description of his process designed to emphasise the evidence for his claims to exactitude and the robustness of his findings.

Despite over 100 years of copyright cases involving maps, two of the defender's witnesses categorically denied that copyright could even subsist in such a thing. Fullarton's first witness was Alex F Foster, the assistant editor of *Chambers' Educational Course* and the author of *Treatise on Geography*, who had worked in the Dublin Ordnance Office during the Ireland survey. He told the court that

[85] Duncan (n 70) 4.
[86] Copyright Register, COPY 3/6 p130 (UKNA).
[87] Duncan (n 70) 5.
[88] ibid 5–6.

he had '[n]ever heard of such a thing as copyright in maps, but always considered that previous maps were available within certain limits'. What those limits might be if there was no such thing as copyright remained unexplored but, under cross-examination, he explained: 'When a map is published, it becomes public property'.[89] The next witness was JH Johnsone. He too stated he had '[n]ever heard of such a thing as copyright of maps till now. I consider such a thing a practical absurdity'.[90]

Fullarton's counsel did go so far as to deny that copyright could subsist in maps but he pushed for a much narrower interpretation of 'copy' in relation to maps. His argument rested heavily on the objective nature of maps – that they were nothing more than 'a painted assemblage of facts'.[91] How to establish copying was the significant issue. The Johnstons achieved this by emphasising a particular technology of copying, a commonly used drawing aid based on parallelograms called a pantograph, and contrasting it to Keith Johnston's skilled labour. In his evidence, Johnston explained that he believed Fullarton's map of Scotland to be 'a mere mechanical copy of my map'. While the scale was reduced, he explained that this 'is very easily done by means of an instrument called a pantograph and at a trifling expense'. Moreover, Fullarton was not even copying the most up to date version of the map. Johnston stated that

> the Defenders have not in their map availed themselves of any new information since 1843. With reference to the coast lines especially, they adhere slavishly to those of my map, although subsequent information might have enabled them to correct it in many respects.[92]

His testimony elicited laughter in the courtroom, when he alluded to the notorious Scottish weather as impeding the defenders' accuracy: 'The effects of the fog are quite observable in the Defenders' map, are they not? (Laughter)'.[93]

Damning evidence was given by David Craig, an engraver who had worked for Swanston, the engraver employed by Fullarton to work on the *Companion Atlas*. Craig confirmed he had seen Swanston make the pencil drawing that copied the map of Scotland in the *National Atlas* and that he used the pantograph to do so. He added:

> There was a good deal of talk in Swanston's shop as to the drawing of the maps, and a good deal of joking about the way in which his maps were made. We had a laugh at the idea of him taking them from Johnston's Atlas.[94]

Thomas James de Bourgho, a draughtsman with the Ordnance Survey, gave evidence that the maps recovered from Swanston bore signs that the pantograph

[89] ibid 18.
[90] ibid 19.
[91] ibid 32.
[92] ibid 7.
[93] ibid.
[94] ibid 10.

had been used on them. While he admitted it to be 'a very accurate instrument in the hands of a good and careful workman' and that he had used it himself, de Bourgho was clear in his condemnation of Swanston's use of it. When asked whether someone wishing to copy a map would 'resort to the use of the pantograph', he replied: 'Unquestionably, if he merely calculated upon receiving a lucrative compensation for his trouble'.[95] Further evidence from London engraver John Dower attested to the evidence of similarity between the various maps and pantograph use. William Wood and Robert Walker, engravers employed by the Ordnance Office in Southampton, gave evidence they had been employed by Swanston and had seen him using the pantograph to copy Johnston's maps.[96]

The closing address for Messrs Johnston was given by John Inglis, the Dean of the Faculty of Advocates. He agreed with Maitland as to the rarity of such cases, using this as a point of national pride to count against the defenders:

> Literary thefts are, indeed, to the honour of Scotland and Scotsmen, rare among us; and it would have been well for the credit and respectability of the Defenders, if they had not sanctioned or adopted the piracy which has been the cause of their appearance in Court this day.[97]

Inglis reminded the jury of the labour and expense Messrs Johnston had invested in the *National Atlas* and emphasised the evidence of copying provided by the shared errors and failure to update the *Companion Atlas* with the most recent information. He was scathing as to the credibility of the defenders' witnesses, pointing out that Foster and Johnsone had 'a peculiar bias against copyright'.[98] Inglis allowed himself a witticism at their expense:

> Mr Foster, and his friend Johnsone, came here to instruct us that there was no such thing as copyright in maps; they had never heard of such a thing. But, gentlemen, 'there be land sharks and water sharks – I mean pirates;' and although these gentlemen do not commit piracies on land or water, I very much fear they do commit piracies on the representation of seas and continents.[99]

He then explained in detail the use of the pantograph, which he described as 'unfair', 'dishonest' and 'contemptible'.[100]

The closing address for the defenders was given by their counsel Robertson. Addressing the jury, he too waxed lyrical about the high stakes involved but sought to cast his clients as the heroes rather than the villains. He informed the jury that

> the eyes of the literary world were at this moment resting upon them, awaiting with anxious expectation their verdict – a verdict which was either to vindicate the cause of a free and wholesome competition in the production of literary and artistic works,

[95] ibid 12–13.
[96] ibid 14.
[97] ibid 21.
[98] ibid 27.
[99] ibid 29.
[100] ibid 26.

> or to impose a fatal check upon the advancement of science and the diffusion of useful knowledge.[101]

The central plank of his defence was that the maps of the defenders would necessarily contain many similarities to those of the pursuers because they both depicted the same, factual reality. Rhetorically, he asked:

> Ought the Defenders to have misrepresented the different outlines of these countries, that they might vary them from those of the Pursuers? Were they to impose upon the public in their 'Scotland' or 'America,' and give them as outlines of those countries, what were outlines of neither, that they might be able to lay claim to originality at the expense of truth? And granted that in the Defenders' 'Scotland' they chanced to take the outlines of that country from the Pursuers' maps, were they guilty of any fraud in so doing? Were they not in this just making of his map the same use as he has made of the maps of others?[102]

By using the geographical work of Messrs Johnston, Messrs Fullarton had 'testified their confidence in the accuracy of its information, and paid to it the highest compliment which it was in their power to do'.[103]

Seeking to undermine any claim that Fullarton might have to authorship of the maps, Inglis had also made much of the defenders' failure to put Swanston himself on the stand as a witness:

> Where is their engraver Swanston? Is he dead, or sick, or mad, or incapable of giving evidence, that he has not been examined at this trial? No! he has been in Court during the trial, but he has not been called, just because the Defenders dared not put him in the witness box.[104]

Robertson sought to counter this blow by suggesting Swanston was too modest an author to appear, stating he would not have 'humiliated' himself by putting on 'a similar display of his learning' as that made by Keith Johnston.[105]

The Lord President then instructed the jury, urging them to restrict their deliberations to the matter before them: 'You have nothing whatever to do either with the effect which your verdict may have upon the parties to the present action, or to publishers or authors generally'.[106] The jury retired for 20 minutes before returning a verdict in favour of Messrs Johnston. However, the damages they awarded were £200 – less than half of what had been estimated by the pursuers' witnesses and a fifth of what the original Summons had requested.[107]

On 30 July 1853, Bartholomew Senior wrote again to his son John, letting him know the trial had ended in a verdict for Johnston and observing 'which with the Costs will be a heavy blow to Fullarton it being generally thought that £1000

[101] ibid 30.
[102] ibid 33.
[103] ibid 32.
[104] ibid 22.
[105] ibid 34.
[106] ibid 38.
[107] ibid 44. *Atlas Company v Fullarton and Company*, Interlocutors, 29 July 1853, CS236/A/24/2 (NRS).

will scarce clear them'. Again, Bartholomew was reluctantly involved: Swanston, he said was 'pretty much in my debt' and was concerned about the effect 'if he goes to the wall'.[108] Bartholomew was sceptical as to the correctness of the decision. He thought that the differences between the two works were 'astonishing' but believed that the courtroom had fallen under the spell of the pantograph:

> The idea of the pantograph seemed to absorb everybody – & I was asked by a person beside me what sort of thing this Pantograph was – & if it did not transfer the whole work to the plate, letters and all.[109]

Bartholomew's rivalry with Johnston appears in his next, rather snide, comment:

> Johnston was somewhat cross-questioned about it, & strove to make it appear that he made very little use of it – no doubt from being such a great & original Geographer – but the fact is, that when before he had any Pantograph of his own he employed me to do that sort of work generally & in particular at the time the National Atlas was commencing.[110]

However, the focus on the pantograph allowed the pursuers to draw a distinction between Keith Johnston's use of a range of sources to create the *National Atlas*, which could be cast as authorial, despite the assistance he had received from others, and the activities of Fullarton, which could not. It also continued to prioritise the contribution of the creator's hand in giving rise to authorial rights and suspicion of copying technologies that seemed to remove this element from the process of creation.

The trial had negative impacts upon both Fullarton and Swanston. Bartholomew wrote to his son that Fullarton

> have been in a tottering condition for some time back but which the lawsuit has brought to a crisis – they are said to be offering their Creditors a compromise of 12/6 per pound to be paid in 3 years.[111]

Meanwhile, Swanston suffered when another Edinburgh publishing firm, WR Chambers, immediately upon hearing the decision in the trial,

> went & got away all their Plates and materials out of Swanston's hands so that they may get them thoroughly tested and overhauled, being in a consternation as to being brought into the same scrape as Fullarton, seeing that some of their Maps are just reductions from Fullarton's.[112]

The case demonstrated to the trade that the use of technology such as the pantograph, while scientifically valid as a means of production, could undermine the case for copyright protection where the mark of the creator's hand could not be seen in production of original or copy.

[108] Bartholomew Snr to Bartholomew Jnr, 20 July 1853, Acc.10222/BR/11 (NLS).
[109] ibid.
[110] ibid.
[111] Bartholomew Snr to Bartholomew Jnr, 5 October 1853, Acc.10222/BR/11 (NLS).
[112] ibid.

V. Literary or Artistic? Copyright and Categorisation

A. Copyright Law Reform

The litigation just discussed drew attention to the different uses to which maps could be put and, how their circulation into different markets might change depending on the information they conveyed or the way that they looked. The *Havell* cases raised the question: if a second party wished to copy a paper print – in that case one valued more for its aesthetic than informational qualities – into a useful but decorative article (in three dimensions), could that be said to be an infringement? The court was clearly of the view it could be but the need to distinguish between these attributes was reanimated following significant copyright reform that occurred 10 years later. The copyright reform campaign, supported by Wordsworth, Dickens, and other well-known figures, was driven by author, lawyer, and MP Serjeant Thomas Noon Talfourd. Increasing the copyright term was a key aim of the reformers for improving the ability of copyright law to reward authors and artists for the products of their genius and labours.[113] At the same time, Talfourd sought to bring uniformity to the law of copyright by bringing engravings, etchings, maps, and charts into the same statute as books, where they would receive the same term of protection. These works should also, he proposed, be registered at Stationer's Hall as was the case for books.[114]

By December 1837, Talfourd had been forced to drop the provisions relating to engravings and paintings from the bill, on the basis they were 'encumbrances'.[115] However, the final version of the bill, which was enacted into law on 1 July 1842, included within the definition of 'book' any 'Map, Chart, or Plan separately published'.[116] Under this statute, maps, charts, and plans would now be protected not for 28 years but for the life of their 'author' plus seven years after the author's death, or for 42 years, whichever was longer.[117] 'Author' was not defined in the Act but a further provision set out that when a person employed another person to compose any book or part of a book, the person who employed the second person would be the proprietor of the copyright.[118]

The Literary Copyright Act 1842 represented the early stages of a reshaping of copyright law which Sherman and Bently have termed the emergence of 'modern' copyright law. This was a shift away from 'primarily a backward-looking, subject-specific law which tended to respond to specific (sometimes minor) problems', into 'an abstract law which extended "to *all* works of literature and art in the

[113] See C Seville, *Literary Copyright Reform in Early Victorian England* (Cambridge, Cambridge University Press, 1999).
[114] *Parliamentary Debates*, House of Commons, vol 38 col 871 (18 May 1837).
[115] *Parliamentary Debates*, House of Commons, vol 39, col 1092 (14 December 1837).
[116] Literary Copyright Act 1842.
[117] Literary Copyright Act 1842, s 3.
[118] Literary Copyright Act 1842, s 18.

widest sense"'.[119] However, in 1842 copyright did not yet extend to all works of art; drawings and paintings remained outside its purview and the rearrangement of maps to fall within the subject matter being protected as literary copyright was not complete. The Engravings Acts were not repealed or amended, with the result that maps and charts were now protected under two different types of statute. The new Act extended its protection to maps, charts, and plans because of their literary and informational qualities, similarities they shared with books. Meanwhile, the Engravings Acts continued to apply to maps based on the artistic techniques used to produce them (engraving, etching, and so on).

Retaining the Engravings Acts necessitated further reform later in the century as technologies changed. By the middle of the century, lithography was becoming increasingly popular in map production. Cheaper and faster than copperplate engraving, lithography made it easier to keep maps up to date, as it avoided the expense and technical difficulty of updating copperplates. However, it was not mentioned as one of the printing technologies to which the Engravings Acts applied, leading to uncertainty over whether they protected lithographs. An opportunity to clarify matters came in 1852, when Parliament passed a statute enabling it to carry into effect a copyright treaty it had recently concluded with France. Most of the statute related to the treatment of translations but a final provision stated that there had been raised some doubt as to whether lithographs were protected under the Engravings Acts and that it was 'expedient to remove such Doubts'. Thus, the Act went on to provide that all of the provisions of Engravings Acts were 'intended to include Prints taken by Lithography, or any other mechanical Process by which Prints or Impressions of Drawings or Designs are capable of being multiplied indefinitely'.[120]

Lithography also offered a technological and commercial solution to the problems caused by the need to print pictures and text separately.[121] The ability to print images and text at once through this new technology was significant for copyright law. At the same time as reformers such as Serjeant Talfourd were beginning to urge an approach to copyright law that treated literary works in the same way as different types of print and even paintings, lithography offered a way for the material object to be produced as a single artefact. If text and image could be produced by the same process, then their separation into different statutes was beginning to make less logical sense from a material point of view. Yet the failure of the legislature to address this overlap reveals the ongoing uncertainty about the nature of the intangible property being created and the physical objects to which it related. Was it an intangible right over an abstract work, whose essential characteristics could manifest themselves in different formats and commodities in different markets?

[119] Sherman and Bently (n 1) 119.

[120] International Copyright Act 1852, 15 & 16 Vict c12. Remarkably, there is almost no comment or analysis of this development either in E Cooper's significant work, *Art and Modern Copyright* (Cambridge, Cambridge University Press, 2018), or A Scardamaglia's 'A Legal History of Lithography' (2017) *Griffith Law Review* 1. The background to this section is therefore a story that remains to be told.

[121] D Bryans, 'The Double Invention of Printing', (2000) 13 *Journal of Design History* 288.

Or was it an intangible right over a specific physical object in a specific market, extending only to copies of the same object in the same market?

This lack of certainty as to the answers to these questions is reflected in the litigation. In *Atlas Company v Fullarton*, counsel for W & AK Johnston chose to make use of the new Literary Copyright Act 1842 when bringing the action against Fullarton. Neither the defenders nor the judge challenged this characterisation, perhaps because the maps in question were clearly part of a book, and the book itself had been properly registered at Stationers' Hall. Another case, decided in early 1852, had addressed the question of whether prints (not maps) within books ought to be protected under the regime of the Engravings Acts.[122] In that case the Lord Chancellor had found that prints published as part of a book did not need to meet the requirements of the Engravings Acts if the book had been registered at Stationer's Hall, as the Literary Copyright Act 1842 would apply. However, he had expressly limited this to the entitlement to an injunction in equity and the plaintiffs had agreed to bring an action at law to try the right.[123] No evidence has been found that such an action was brought.

B. The Stannard Cases (1870): Bird's-Eye Views – Map or Print?

Twenty years later, however, a pair of cases highlighted the difficulty in characterising maps as a subject of copyright law under the new legislative approach – were they works of information of a literary character or visual works of an artistic character? Unlike the atlases at issue in *The Atlas Company v Fullarton*, the works in these cases were not expensive, luxury items designed to showcase the learning of their maker and the discernment of their purchaser. They were a series of lithographed birds'-eye views but, unlike Havell's print, there were relatively cheap works, produced to address a relatively fleeting popular interest in the most accessible manner possible.

The two cases in question had the same plaintiff – the lithographic printing company of WT Stannard & Son. William Thomas Stannard was the son of a London postman but became one of the city's leading lithographic printers. His son William joined him in partnership until November 1891. The firm specialised in sheet music covers and theatrical posters but, during the Crimean War (1853–56), it found a particularly valuable stream of work in birds'-eye views, particularly of battlefields. Stannard worked frequently with Alfred Concanen, a famous commercial artist, who was resident artist in the former's Poland Street shop for some time.[124] Seeking to repeat their success during the Crimean War,

[122] *Bogue v Houlston* (1852) 5 De G & Sm 267.
[123] ibid.
[124] Stannard had a colourful domestic life. His first wife suffered poor mental health and was admitted to asylums on several occasions between 1845 and 1870. He had an illegitimate child with his mistress Elizabeth in 1861. On the night of the 1871 census, he was recorded in two separate locations – his

Stannard & Son published a map entitled *Stannard & Son's Panoramic Birds-Eye View of France & Prussia and the Surrounding Countries Likely to be involved in the War, with the railways & strategic positions of each army, & the great fortresses of the Rhine provinces* (see Figure 27) on 21 July 1870, only two days after France declared war on Prussia. Sold at the price of 2s, it proved a profitable venture for the company.[125] But, on 3 August 1870, William Stannard noticed that the *Daily News* and *The Daily Telegraph* were both carrying advertisements for:

> Thos. W. Lee's Shilling Panoramic Bird's-eye View of the Seat of War, from special drawings by French and German artists, showing the Rhine, France, Prussia, Belgium and surrounding countries, rivers, roads, railways, fortresses, and strategic positions of reach army, beautifully tinted, size 28 by 22 inches, post free 12 stamps. – Lee's Lithographic Works, Grosvenor Mews, Bond Street, W. – Trade supplied.[126]

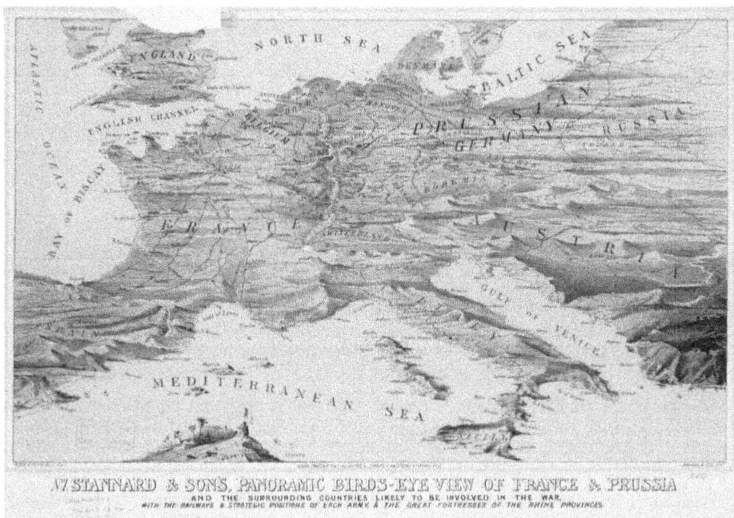

Figure 27 *Stannard & Son's Panoramic Birds-Eye View of France & Prussia and the Surrounding Countries Likely to be involved in the War, with the railways & strategic positions of each army, & the great fortresses of the Rhine provinces* (London, Stannard & Son, 21 July 1870). The lithographic print was the first in a series of prints depicting the battlefields of the Franco-Prussian war

Image from the Norman B Leventhal Map Center Collection at the Boston Public Library.

family home in St Pancras and a second home in Battersea with his mistress Selah Sands and their baby, Emily. When his wife died in 1887, he married Selah: L Worms and A Baynton-Williams, 'STANNARD, Willam Thomas', www.britishmapengravers.net/entries/s-entries/william-thomas-stannard/.

125 Amended Complaint of William Thomas Stannard and William Stannard, 9 August 1870, C16/678 S229, 2 (UKNA).

126 ibid.

To make matters worse, the advertisement appeared directly below that for Stannard's own map. The seller, Thomas Wales Lee, also specialised in theatrical prints and had worked with Stannard in the past. He too was connected with Concanen, with whom he had set up in partnership in the 1860s, along with a third partner, Henry Herapath Siebe.[127] William Stannard promptly arranged for a copy of the print to be purchased from Lee's shop and later that day called upon Lee and accused him of piracy. According to Stannard, Lee denied the piracy, alleging he had simply used the same sources as Stannard.[128] Stannard then sought legal advice and commenced proceedings. An injunction was obtained on 5 August 1870.[129] Lee asked repeatedly for extensions to put in his plea and eventually did so on 8 November 1870.[130] His plea amounted to a single point – the map in question fell within the Literary Copyright Act 1842 and, because it had not been registered at Stationers' Hall, the suit could not be maintained against him.[131] Vice-Chancellor Malins heard argument on 16 November 1870 and held the plea was insufficient.[132] The injunction therefore remained in place, although no order was made as to costs.

Lee appealed the decision, as well as the decision refusing to dissolve the injunction, and the case was heard by Lord Justices Sir William Milbourne James and Sir George Mellish.[133] Before the Chancery Appeal Court, Lee's counsel argued that, in the Literary Copyright Act 1842, 'book' was defined 'to mean and include every volume, part, or division of a volume, pamphlet, sheet of letter-press, sheet of music, map, chart or plan separately published'. Section 24 of the same act provided that no copyright owner could bring an action or suit in law or equity unless before commencing such proceeding the book had been entered in the Stationers' Company registers. Because the words 'any copyright' were general, the plaintiffs could be proprietors of a copyright in a map under the earlier Engravings Acts but still had to comply with the provision for registration before enforcing their right.[134]

Counsel for Stannard argued that, since 'the time of Queen Anne there have been two parallel series of statutes, one relating to books proper, the other to works in the nature of prints'.[135] The Literary Copyright Act 1842, they claimed, was designed to apply to maps forming part of books. They sought to address the section that referred to maps being 'published separately' by suggesting that it

[127] Worms and Baynton-Williams (n 124).
[128] Complaint, C16/678 S229, 2 (UKNA).
[129] C33/1169 2250r. On 18 August Bacon VC (standing in for Malins VC as Vacation-Judge) refused to dissolve the injunction: C33/1170 2859v (UKNA).
[130] C33/1169 2546r; C33/1169 2554v; C13/1169 2591r; C33/1169 2641v (UKNA).
[131] Answer of Thomas Wales Lee, 2 November 1870, C16/678 S229 (UKNA).
[132] C33/1170 f2884r (UKNA).
[133] *Stannard v Lee* (1871) LR 6 Ch App 346.
[134] ibid 347. He cited the authority of *Cassell v Stiff* (1856) 2 K & J 279, which addressed the provisions of the *International Copyright Act 1844*, 7 & 8 Vic c12, in relation to an illustrated periodical.
[135] *Stannard v Lee* (1871) LR 6 Ch App 346, 348.

simply meant maps that formed part of a book by being referred to in the book and accompanying a book, even though materially separate to the book. They went on to argue that the Engravings Acts remained in force and, even if they had acquired a new right under the Literary Copyright Act 1842, that did not take away the old one.[136]

Neither of the judges found this argument convincing. James LJ thought that, if the argument of Stannard's counsel were correct, it would lead to two kinds of maps or two kinds of copyright, either of which would be inconvenient. Adopting the modern approach to the law and focusing on the abstract characteristics of the work, he held that the inclusion of maps within the category of literary works was what the Legislature had intended and, moreover, correct:

> The object of the enactment is very clear. Formerly maps had been considered artistic works, now they were to be brought into their proper place as literary works. And rightly so, in my opinion, for maps are intended to give information in the same way a book does. A chart, for instance, gives similar information to sailing rules; maps give instruction as to the statistics and history of the country portrayed; they point out the amount of population, the places where battles were fought, the dates when provinces were annexed, as in maps of *India*, and give other geographical and historical details. It was quite reasonable, therefore, to take them out of the law of artistic works, and to give them greater protection by bringing them under the law of copyright of literary works.[137]

His counterpart, Mellish LJ, agreed, with the result that Lee's plea was successful and Stannard's case could not be maintained.[138]

This decision had important implications for a second case that the Stannards had commenced in September, six weeks after they commenced their suit against Lee. This case involved a different birds'-eye view from the same series as the previous one. This print was published on 1 September 1870 and was entitled *No 8 Stannard & Son's Perspective View of Paris and its Environs Shewing all the Fortifications and Redoubts Together with the Lines of Defence Recently Thrown Up and the Roads Rivers and Railways Communicating with the Interior Compiled from the Latest Official Sources by Alfred Concanen*. Also sold at 2s, this print was similarly proving popular and profitable when, on 26 September, Stannard discovered that a weekly periodical, the *Gentleman's Journal and Youth's Miscellany*, was selling a print entitled a *Bird's-eye View of Paris and its Fortifications*, along with the 51st issue of the *Journal*, at the price of 2d for both journal and print.[139]

The proprietors of the *Journal* were Edward Harrison and Edward Viles and, once again, Stannard visited them to remonstrate, with no success. Harrison denied the print was a copy, although he admitted he had made use of Stannard's

[136] ibid 348.

[137] ibid 349.

[138] A second, less detailed, report of the case can be found at (1870) 19 *Weekly Reporter* 615.

[139] Complaint of William Thomas Stannard and William Stannard, 28 September 1870, C16/678 S248 (UKNA).

plan. Stannard bought two further copies from street hawkers on 27 September for the prices of 1d and 3d respectively and was told by one of the hawkers he had already sold 52 copies that same day.[140] The following day he submitted his bill of complaint to the Court of Chancery and an injunction was granted the next day.[141]

On 19 November 1870, Harrison and Viles' counsel consented to an order awarding a perpetual injunction against them.[142] However, two factors soon made it clear to them that they had made a serious mistake. The first was in February 1871, when their solicitor informed them that in such cases the Vice-Chancellor took the view that defendants had to account to the plaintiffs for every copy sold and pay the plaintiff the profits he would have received if he had sold those copies. According to the plaintiffs, this was the point at which they decided to appeal the consent order on the basis that their counsel had consented to it without their knowledge or instruction to do so.[143] However, it seems more than probable that an equally, if not more, influential factor was their discovery of the result in Lee's appeal in March.

Harrison and Viles engaged William Fooks QC and his son, also William, the same counsel who had acted for Lee. They petitioned the Court of Chancery for a rehearing on the basis that they had never consented nor instructed their counsel to consent to the order, but also added that Stannard was not entitled to maintain the action, as he had not registered the 'bird's-eye view or plan' at Stationer's Hall and that, as this case involved exactly the same kind of 'bird's-eye view or plan' as that in *Stannard v Lee*, the same result should follow.[144] Vice-Chancellor Bacon quickly dismissed the first argument, pointing out that if parties were able to make such claims, in the absence of evidence of fraud or mistake, then the entire system of legal representation would come undone as no party would be able to rely on agreements made in court.[145] The second argument, however, warranted more consideration. Harrison and Viles had, it seems, put two issues into contention. The first was that the print had not been registered under the 1842 Copyright Act; the second was that the print had not been 'designed and invented' by Stannard & Sons (and so, presumably, could not be protected by the Engravings Acts). It is important to note the different language employed in this case, as compared to the earlier one against Lee. Where in that case the print was routinely referred to as a 'map', in this new round of litigation Stannard referred consistently to the print as a 'view or plan'. This seems to have impacted upon the outcome as we shall soon see.

Bacon VC dealt with the second point first. For this argument, evidence had been given in court for Stannard & Sons by Alfred Concanen, while a deposition was made and attested to in court for Harrison and Viles by Concanen's (and Lee's)

[140] ibid.
[141] C16/678 S248; C33/1169 2561r (UKNA).
[142] C33/1170 2802r – v (UKNA).
[143] *Stannard v Harrison* (1871) 19 WR 811, 811.
[144] ibid.
[145] ibid 812.

former partner, Henry Herapath Siebe.[146] Siebe deposed that he had watched Concanen design and draw the view or plan in question, using as reference a plan of Paris Concanen had purchased in that city. He described the process of lithographing such a works and swore that he knew Stannard & Son, as he had sold his business to them. In the case of this print, they were merely the printers, as 'they are not artists nor capable of designing or drawing'.[147]

Bacon VC was not inclined to treat the words of the Engravings Acts so literally. Focusing on the prints as commodities in a market, he thought it was clear that the 'view or plan' was

> an invention in trade – a novelty in trade; for, although a bird's-eye view of a particular place may be many hundreds of years old, yet there is a novelty in the lithographer, by his ingenuity and skill, conceiving the idea of presenting such pictures as these to the public which they will speedily and readily receive, and from which he knows he will receive a very large tradesman's profit.[148]

Having concluded the print in question was an 'invention', Bacon VC then considered whether it was the invention of Stannard, a question he resolved in the affirmative:

> That Mr Stannard cannot draw himself is a matter wholly unimportant, if he has caused other persons to draw for him. He invents the subject of the design beyond question. He prescribes the proportions and the contents of the design; he furnishes a part of the materials from which the drawing has to be made in the first instance; and afterwards collects daily from the proper sources, and even (if it be necessary to say so) from official sources, the decrees, the reports, the bulletins, and accounts, contained in the newspapers, of the different phases of the war … These he communicates to the man whom he has employed to make a drawing for him. Not having the skill in his own had to do it, he stands by and (as Mr. Concanen says) comes to him daily with materials from which this lithograph is to be compiled. Can there be anything more plain, within the words of the Act of Parliament, than that Mr Stannard did himself invent, that he did procure another person to design and draw for him, and do that which he himself could not do?[149]

It is notable that this description of the activities required to ground a claim of copyright ownership blended a range of preparatory activities, instructions, and entitlement through employment or contract. Yet it responded directly to the statutory language in place at the time, as well as the by-now long-accepted view that mapmaking could be carried out by a range of participants forming different roles, some intellectual and some manual, with the copyright holder identified as the person who brought them all together to create the final commodity, itself an item to be placed into mass production.

[146] It appears that Lee also swore an affidavit in the case that Siebe refers to in his deposition, but I have not been able to locate it.

[147] Deposition of Henry Herapath Siebe, 24 April 1871, C16/678 S248, 3 (UKNA).

[148] *Stannard v Harrison* (1871) 19 WR 811, 812.

[149] ibid 812–13.

The next question was whether the work in question was required to be registered because of falling within the scope of the Literary Copyright Act 1842. Here, Vice-Chancellor Bacon's views sharply diverged from those of the appeal judges in *Stannard v Lee*. Now the significance of the language of 'view or plan' becomes clear. Referring to the Engravings Act 1767, he noted it gave a property to those who caused or procured to be designed any prints including landscapes. He asked:

> Can anybody look at that drawing and say it is not a landscape? … It is clear to my mind that this is a work of diligence and industry and, for aught I know, of genius on the part of the plaintiffs.[150]

While disavowing any intention to call into question the judgment of the Lords Justices in *Stannard v Lee*, or declining to follow it, Bacon VC carefully picked his way through the reasoning to come up with the opposite conclusion.[151] Characterised as engravings, registration was unnecessary. He dismissed the petition and awarded costs against Harrison and Viles.[152]

The *Stannard* cases demonstrate the challenges maps posed to copyright law due to the overlapping of their aesthetic and informational qualities. However, the works in question presented a second challenge because they also fell between two genres. Were they maps or decorative prints? Following Matthew Edney, the nineteenth century was the period during which the cartographic ideal emerged but had not yet reached hegemonic status.[153] Although the images in question made use of some of the features of the cartographic ideal, such as the panoramic view from above, and named geographic features, they did not employ a numerical ratio or scale to effectuate a mathematical, proportionate correspondence between territory and map. In the twentieth century, works like birds'-eye views that did not employ scale began to be categorised in different ways, such as 'cartoral arts'.[154] While the litigants and judges in the first Stannard case recognised the images as 'maps', those in the second did not do so. The result was that the first image fell within the Literary Copyright Act 1842 and its specific category of 'maps', with the judges insisting upon the informative and factual, or 'textual', aspects of the work. The second image, meanwhile, was treated as an artistic work, thus falling into a separate regime.

In 1893 a case came before the courts requiring almost the reverse assessment. In a dispute that arose over alleged copying of cardboard sewing patterns for a sleeve for a lady's dress, the defendant alleged that the pattern did not fall within the Literary Copyright Act 1842.[155] Justice Wright in the Chancery Division, held that the pattern was not a book, but that it fell within the words 'map, chart,

[150] ibid 813.
[151] ibid.
[152] ibid 814.
[153] Edney (n 5) in particular ch 4.
[154] See, eg, M Brückner, 'Maps, Pictures, and the Cartoral Arts in America' (2015) 29 *American Art* 2.
[155] *Hollinrake v Truswell* [1893] 2 Ch 377.

or plan'. Wright J found that '"map, chart, or plan" need not necessarily be topographical' and the sleeve pattern might be regarded as 'a chart or plan of the female arm in relation to dressmaking'.[156] He held that the Copyright Act did not require *literary* merit but could apply 'to all notations by figures in a form suitable for dissemination' and found in favour of the plaintiff.[157] An appeal against this decision, however, was successful. In giving judgment, Lord Justice Davey agreed with Wright J that the words 'map, chart, or plan' need not be limited to geographical maps or navigational plans but the sleeve pattern was, nevertheless, not an appropriate subject for copyright. Davey LJ made his finding on the basis that the statute was designed to protect literary works, which 'intended to afford either information and instruction, or pleasure, in the form of literary enjoyment', and the pattern did none of these things. Rather, it was a mechanical contrivance or tool and more appropriately protected by patent law.[158]

The other two judges took the same approach but, in agreeing that what the plaintiff was seeking to protect was more appropriately protected by patent law, they drew a sharper distinction between the material and immaterial. As Lord Chancellor Farrer Herschell explained:

> The object of the Copyright Act was to prevent any one publishing a copy of the particular form of expression in which an author conveyed ideas or information to the world. These may be retained by any one, though the book, map, or chart which embodied them has passed out of his possession.[159]

By contrast, the words and figures on the sleeve chart

> are intended to be used, and can only be of use, in connection with that upon which they are inscribed. They are not merely directions for the use of the cardboard, which is in truth a measuring apparatus, but they are part of that very apparatus itself, without which it cannot be used, and except in connection with which they are absolutely useless.[160]

In this case, then, we observe the courts taking a less technical view of the words 'map, chart, or plan', such that they could be used in relation to other things that could be metaphorically mapped, charted, or planned; for example: 'types of physiognomy, or the artistic principles of proportion, or molecular proportion'[161] or 'an anatomical or physiological plan, shewing the structure and distribution of the muscles and bones of the human arm'.[162] At the same time, they were explicitly recognising that the object of copyright was to protect the intangible, abstract, elements of the work and not its physical form. If, when separated from their

[156] [1893] 2 Ch 377 (Ch D), 379.
[157] ibid 380.
[158] [1894] 3 Ch 420 (CA), 428.
[159] ibid 424.
[160] ibid.
[161] [1893] 2 Ch 377, 379.
[162] [1894] 3 Ch 420, 427.

material embodiment, the abstract elements were simply an idea about how the material embodiment works, then this would not be copyright subject matter.

VI. Conclusion

An examination of copyright litigation in the nineteenth century reveals a number of important aspects about the relationship between mapmaking, mapselling, and the law. First, we can see that copyright law reinforced the cartographic ideal at the same time as it was challenged by it. A growing commitment to the idea of the map as a scientific, factual, mathematically accurate, objective, and scaled representation of the earth forced litigants to construct a different kind of author to that found in other areas of copyright law; rather than the creative individual of literary property, this was the objective, rational authority of science. Moreover, the collaborative mode of map production necessitated a blurring between the author, who contributed mental labour, and the owner, who incurred expenditure in bringing the parties together and producing the physical commodity to be put on the market. Changing technologies of production, as mapmaking became less artisanal and the hand of the engraver gave way to the lithograph and pantograph, added to the legal uncertainty surrounding the appropriate contribution of owner and infringer.

The understanding of maps as mere factual representations, or 'assemblages of fact' now began to influence a doctrinal shift in copyright law more generally. Where we saw eighteenth-century courts taking a fairly permissive approach to map copying where the result was an improvement, by the middle of the century, a second, and more restrictive line of authority began to emerge. In the case of *Kelly v Morris*, which involved the copying of postal directories, Vice Chancellor Wood held that:

> In the case of a dictionary, map, guide-book, or directory, when there are certain common objects of information which must, if described correctly, be described in the same words, a subsequent compiler is bound to set about doing for himself that which the first compiler has done.[163]

Wood VC explicitly referred to the earlier cases, discussed in chapter four, noting that 'In case of a road-book, he must count the milestones for himself. In the case of a map of a newly-discovered island … he must go through the same process of triangulation just as if he had never seen any former map.'[164] Therefore Wood VC concluded, 'generally he is not entitled to take one word of the information previously published without independently working out the matter for himself'.[165]

[163] (1866) LR 1 Eq 697, 701.
[164] ibid 701–702.
[165] ibid 702.

This approach clearly misrepresented the argument and decisions of those earlier cases. However, the insistence on maps as being no different to other factual compilations, such as lists of names and business addresses, indicated not simply the rising influence of the cartographic ideal, but also a growing emphasis on the commercial value of data, geographical or otherwise, rather than the map in which it appeared. This valuable data was generated by labour and increasingly the courts were prepared to protect the party who had initially invested the labour over another party seeking to make use of it. At the same time, intellectual property law was itself transforming in structure. With its respective categories crystallising to distinguish between the fields of art, literature, science, and manufacturing now divided into the legal regimes of copyright, patent, and designs, maps sat uneasily across all three regimes. As mapmakers sought to capture the products of their labour in new markets, it became necessary to take a still more abstract approach to an already intangible right, loosening the ties between the original commodities to which the rights related and extending the rights to cover different commodities that drew upon the initial labour and investment but served different markets. In this way, the labour directed at the creation of the geographical knowledge and its aesthetic and informational qualities took precedence over the labour of production – engraving, printing etc.

The detailed treatment of the various disputes uncovered in this chapter offers a deeper insight into the commercial and legal conditions of the map trade. Copyright was one factor working to structure the growing and increasingly diffuse markets for commodified forms of geographical knowledge but it was not determinative and in a time of considerable flux its operation was still unpredictable. Mapmakers emerge not only as collaborators and competitors, as legal actors and economic agents, but also as people moving through the world. Their maps shift between formats, and geographical information is disseminated in new ways, circulating through different markets as aesthetic art works, items of apparel, displays of erudition, tools for the entrepreneur, and vectors of public information and current affairs.

9

The Twentieth Century: For Crown and Country

I. Introduction

By the dawn of the twentieth century, the state had emerged as the main generator and supplier of geographic and maritime data through the Ordnance Society and the Hydrographic Office. It distributed this data in the form of maps and charts, which were used for a growing array of state purposes – military/naval, economic, and social. As we saw in chapters six and seven, these two institutions sought to encourage widespread circulation and use of their data, while exercising control over the market for the maps and charts containing that data in order to maintain the authority of both product and source. As such, copyright as a source of intangible rights to be exploited in a market was not a particularly relevant concern, although its convention of asserting property rights through the publication line was drawn upon to assist in establishing and maintaining the authoritative status of those maps and charts. The private map trade, which continued to make use of copyright law to discipline competitors, operated alongside these institutions and played a crucial role in helping to disseminate the data into markets that the institutions were unwilling or unable to enter.

Yet the complex relationship between the state institutions and the market for maps and charts meant that there was always tension between the institutions and the private map trade. In the first decades of the twentieth century, the policies of the Ordnance Survey and the Hydrographic Office towards copyright law diverged still more markedly. The latter continued its policy of the previous century of copyright non-enforcement, while the former looked increasingly to copyright law as a tool to resolve the tensions with the private trade in its favour. This chapter draws attention to the hitherto-overlooked role played by the Ordnance Survey in the enactment of Crown copyright provisions in the Imperial Copyright Act 1911. Comparing the respective positions and policies of the Ordnance Survey and Hydrographic Office in relation to the control and use of their maps and data demonstrates how resolving the trade-off between these two factors (control and use) depends on the nature of the market for the information, and the information itself. The chapter looks first at the attitude of the Hydrographic Office towards chart sales and copyright law in the early decades of the twentieth century, and then at the corresponding attitudes of the Ordnance Survey. It then examines the circumstances in which the Crown copyright provisions were added to the Copyright Act 1911, and the role played by the Ordnance Survey. Finally, it looks at how the Ordnance Survey responded to the new provision, which facilitated its first copyright prosecution, but left the underlying issues unresolved.

Crown copyright offered a practical, if partial, solution to problems of accuracy, authority, and access to state-produced geographic information. However, as noted at the start of chapter six, the emergence of state mapmaking bodies in the nineteenth century drew tighter the link between the representational map and a certain ideal of the territorial state as co-extensive with sovereignty.[1] As William Rankin has argued, maps reinforced the relationship between sovereignty and territory as both ideal and practical reality because 'the control over geographic space required control over the production of geographic knowledge, which in turn required control over geographic space.'[2] By the early years of the twentieth century, the Ordnance Survey and Hydrographic Office were the undisputed leaders when it came to the production of geographic knowledge over the territory controlled by the British government, and beyond that control in the case of the Hydrographic Office. Crown copyright can thus also be seen as an assertion of sovereignty over state-generated geographic information.

II. The Hydrographic Office Sails into a New Century

As we saw in chapter seven, the Hydrographic Office entered the new century with little interest in copyright law, except to the extent it could use it to maintain its oversight of the chart trade and the authority of its reputation for accuracy. Back in 1887, the Stationery Office had forwarded the Treasury Minute to the Hydrographic Department, seeking to know to which classes of publication the Admiralty wished the reservation of rights to be applied.[3] The Hydrographer replied that he saw no objection to putting a notice reserving rights on the Hydrographic Office's publications if it was understood that there would be no enforcement of such rights, especially those preventing the extraction and publication in another form of portions of information in Admiralty books, without the concurrence of the Admiralty.[4] The Minute thus had little initial effect on the Hydrographic Department's approach to copyright.

In 1905 the Admiralty decided it needed to recoup more money from sales of charts and investigated reorganising its arrangements with Potter, the Chart

[1] W Rankin, *After the Map: Cartography, Navigation, and the Transformation of Territory in the Twentieth Century* (Chicago, University of Chicago Press, 2016) 4.

[2] ibid.

[3] Piggott to Admiralty, November 1899, Enclosures to MB 32, 145 (UKHO).

[4] ibid, 145.

Agent, and increasing the prices of its charts.[5] The Hydrographer, Arthur Mostyn Field, identified the main rival at home as the bluebacks, which he considered were still preferred by the mercantile marine. However, because this preference flowed from their being 'more suitable to the needs of those who buy them'[6] and they were already more expensive than Admiralty charts, raising the prices of Admiralty charts would not be likely to result in an increase in the sale of bluebacks. While there was the possibility of producing cheaper editions of Admiralty charts using photography, the expense involved in keeping them up to date, particularly in terms of equipment and staff, compared to the smallness of the market, meant there was little chance of being undersold by a home product. Furthermore, Mostyn Field considered:

> It would, however, be unwise in spite of the risk of competition, to endeavour to maintain a copyright in them, seeing that they are compiled from all sorts of information derived from all sorts of sources. There would be, no doubt, great difficulty in obtaining information, as the Admiralty constantly does at no cost to itself, if the charts were not made freely available to everybody to make use of. Money could be demanded for information which is now freely supplied for the public good, by Engineers, Harbour Boards, Colonial authorities, &c.&c.[7]

By this time, the largest purchasers of Admiralty charts were foreign governments. No objection had hitherto been made to copying by other nations and Mostyn Field observed: 'The charts published by all Governments are freely exchanged and each Government is free to reproduce the work of others'.[8] He did note there was potential for competition from the United States and Japan, as they made similar charts that could be used by British seamen and their reproductions were also cheaper. At present, however, neither did much surveying outside its own coasts, so they remained reliant on British charts for their information of the rest of the world. Although he conceded that the Admiralty gave more information to other countries than it received in return,

> seeing the larger interests at stake in the shape of our enormous carrying trade and our large Navy, it is of great importance to encourage, at all costs, free interchange of information in order to obtain all that is available for the production of the best and most accurate charts possible.[9]

It was possible in the future that foreign charts would become a serious competitor, especially as they were cheaper. But Mostyn Field also thought that if Admiralty charts were made cheaper there would be an outcry from the merchant marine. He further noted in relation to this free global exchange of information, 'other

[5] 'Sale of Admiralty Charts: Reorganisation of arrangements with Chart Agent and proposed increase in price', MB69, 23 December 1905 (UKHO).
[6] ibid.
[7] ibid.
[8] ibid.
[9] ibid.

countries copy our charts to sell them cheaper than we do, whilst we copy theirs and sell them dearer.'[10] The strength of the Hydrographic Office's reputation as the most authoritative and comprehensive source of hydrographic data, and the lack of any real competition, meant that it could afford to increase the prices of its charts, which is what Mostyn Field recommended. Moreover, he also recommended reducing the discount given to the Agent who, in any event, was passing it on to customers or using it to bargain with shipping companies and foreign hydrographic departments for their goods.[11]

The Admiralty thus continued to walk a fine line in its relationship with the private trade, seeking some part of its market to help underwrite its expenses but not wishing to take upon the burden of supplying it completely. The long-standing financial constraints placed on the Hydrographic Office meant that it continued to struggle to incorporate into its charts the enormous amount of information it received from sources around the globe on a daily basis. In 1908 a Department Report on the Chart Branch found that it was still struggling to keep its charts up to date and that greater numbers of skilled draughtsmen (to be called cartographers) were urgently required. The Hydrographer observed that profits from selling charts to the public had increased in recent years but that sales would drop if confidence in their correctness were impaired or other nations should start to issue equally correct charts at lower prices. Should this occur, 'the cost of supplying the Fleet would fall entirely upon Imperial funds without the cost being reduced by any return from the sale of charts from the general public'.[12] He added that 'the Safety of the Fleet, and Public confidence, can only be maintained by issuing charts containing all the information available at the date of issue'.[13]

Mostyn Field remained more concerned about the potential of the US to compete for their global market than he was about any private mapmakers. The US Hydrographic Department had already realised the advantage of possessing and printing their own charts. At present they were systematically copying and updating Admiralty charts and selling them more cheaply but it would not be long before the public realised that the American charts were more up to date and Admiralty sales would decline.[14] The Hydrographic Office nevertheless continued its policy of encouraging use of its data and in 1909 the copyright notice was removed from the Admiralty Notices to Mariners, on the basis that they should be free to be used by all.[15] In the pre-war era, the lack of any real competition in the market for its charts or data, as well as their public significance, outweighed the commercial arguments in favour of using copyright law to restrict or regulate copying.

[10] ibid.
[11] ibid.
[12] Report on Chart Branch, 7 July 1908, MB80, June 1908 to September 1908 (UKHO).
[13] ibid.
[14] ibid.
[15] Memo 'All Rights Reserved', 21 December 1911 STAT 12/36/1 (UKHO).

III. The Ordnance Survey Considers Legal Action

As discussed in chapter six, the Stationery Office and Treasury entered the new century determined to tighten up on the use of the word 'Ordnance Survey' in the titles of privately produced maps, as well as to increase the control they wielded over the use of their data. The Ordnance Survey was also giving more thought to the markets that it might try to enter or encourage further growth within, in particular for the small-scale maps bought by travellers and tourists. This was a market that could be expanded and the Ordnance Survey was keen to bring these maps to the attention of these consumers through the very successful railway stall market, dominated by WH Smith. As such, a new contract for the small-scale maps was entered into in 1906 with T Fisher Unwin, a wholesaler but not a map producer, while the contract for maps of London and large-scale mapping remained with Stanford (whose agency was discussed earlier in chapter six). Further market expansion came through the supply of the one-inch map into schools and colleges.[16]

The complex process private mapmakers were expected to use in order to obtain permission for the use of Ordnance Survey maps was generally successful, in the sense that permission was generally granted for maps which materially differed from Ordnance Survey maps, which served different purposes, or which were inserted into books or pamphlets, as well as in cases where no Ordnance Survey map was likely to be published and its public usefulness was clear.[17] The amount of royalty paid in each case depended on the particular circumstances. However, the system did not eliminate unauthorised publications and many private mapmakers continued either to dispute the Ordnance Survey's entitlements or find them confusing.

The firm of Bartholomew continued to remain a thorn in the Ordnance Survey's side. On 11 March 1902, the Controller of the Stationery Office again complained to Bartholomew in respect of their use of the title *Bartholomew's Reduced Ordnance Survey* on various of their maps. After further correspondence, Bartholomew agreed in 1902 not to use the words 'Ordnance Survey', 'Ordnance', or 'Survey' as a prefix on any of their maps.[18] However, in subsequent correspondence, Bartholomew confirmed they intended to continue using such words as 'Reduced from the Ordnance Survey' *after* the titles of their maps; the Controller informed them this would be acceptable as long as they also added the words 'Reproduced by permission from'. It does not appear that Bartholomew was ever granted permission to complete their two-mile map.[19] Further disputes arose

[16] R Oliver, *The Ordnance Survey in the Nineteenth Century: Maps, Money and the Growth of Government* (London, The Charles Close Society, 2014) 423–26.

[17] Copyright of Ordnance Survey Maps, Précis of Correspondence from January 1883 to March 1910, 4, OS1/6/2 (UKNA).

[18] ibid 5.

[19] ibid 6.

over their use of portions of the two-mile map on a postcard, which the Director General decided not to pursue, and the use of the words 'Reduced by permission from the New Revised Ordnance Survey' on maps of parts of Ireland and a map in the Glasgow Directory, for which no permission had been sought.[20] In 1908 a question arose as to whether, having been granted permission to use maps from one Ordnance Survey series, Bartholomew was entitled to use portions of maps from that series to create a map of a different area. The Controller referred the matter to Treasury but its legal advice indicated the former permission covered Bartholomew's use and no further action was taken.[21]

In 1909 there was yet another dispute over Bartholomew's attempt to license another publisher, JD Miller, to reproduce a section of a Bartholomew map of the Forres District in Scotland, itself copied from the Ordnance Survey maps. Legal advice was again sought and the Treasury's solicitor, Mr Clark, suggested Bartholomew's permission from the Ordnance Survey would not extend to authorising Miller to produce a map indirectly copied from an Ordnance map. However, he thought that, as the map was one which was hardly likely to compete with the Ordnance maps, it might suffice to send Bartholomew a letter setting out the legal position.[22] Later that same year, the Stationery Office had further occasion to write to Bartholomew over series of holiday pamphlets containing maps issued by the North Eastern Railway Company, claiming the copyright was owned by Bartholomew. In this case, Bartholomew responded that the maps in question had been published by them for 40 and 20 years respectively and that from time to time they were revised by railway engineers. He claimed that the only use made of the Ordnance Survey maps was that which he considered all publishers did; namely, checking the markings that were sometimes roughly done.[23]

From 1901 the Ordnance Survey was also embroiled in a series of minor disputes with a second publishing company, GW Bacon & Co. George Washington Bacon was an American-born map publisher who acquired the business of James Wyld in 1893.[24] Bacon was an opportunistic publisher and aggressive exploiter of opportunities at the lower end of the market, including touring, cycling, and thematic maps. His maps were generally copied from elsewhere, sometimes with permission, and sold cheaply in an array of formats with colourful covers.[25] GW Bacon had issued several maps that appeared to be reproductions of Ordnance Survey maps and for which no permission had been sought or granted. As with Bartholomew, some of the problems stemmed from the ways the maps were

[20] ibid 7.
[21] ibid 8–9.
[22] ibid 9–10.
[23] ibid 10.
[24] D Smith, 'Bacon, George Washington (1830/31–1922), map publisher' (2004) *Oxford Dictionary of National Biography*, www-oxforddnb-com.rp.nla.gov.au/view/10.1093/ref:odnb/9780198614128.001.0001/odnb-9780198614128-e-41117.
[25] D Smith, 'George Washington Bacon 1862-c.1900' (1993) 65 *Map Collector* 10.

advertised. In one case, in 1903, Bacon produced a map of the British Isles, which they stated included 'the whole of the New Ordnance Survey'. When the Controller objected on the basis that it had not been granted permission by the Ordnance Survey, Bacon responded it had thought the addition of the words 'reduced into a handsome quarto volume' had sufficiently distinguished its map but suggested altering the words to read: 'This popular edition includes maps of the whole of the United Kingdom based on the New Ordnance Survey'. Upon being informed this did not meet the Controller's objections, they offered a different form of wording: 'This Popular Edition includes the whole of the United Kingdom revised from the latest Surveys and forms an exceedingly handsome volume'. Again, this was not accepted and the company's director, George Bacon, had a meeting with the Controller. After this meeting, he wrote that he was now better able to understand their requirements

> respecting the use of the Ordnance maps for basing a new map upon or for revising existing maps … We were not aware that the notice in the *Gazette* of August 29th, 1901, had so wide a meaning as we now understand it to have.[26]

The Board of Agriculture and Fisheries was sceptical of Bacon's protestations of innocence and recommended the firm was not granted permission to use any Ordnance Survey maps until they came up with a more satisfactory explanation.[27]

In 1907 and 1908, there were reported instances of agents of Bacon holding themselves out to be Government officials when soliciting orders for new maps. In one case, Bacon & Co brought actions in the Omagh petty sessions against two farmers who had not paid for the maps they ordered and the magistrate dismissed both cases with 5s costs, as Bacon's agents appeared to have misrepresented themselves as selling Government publications. One of the maps in question had a copyright notice on it stating it belonged to Bartholomew's, but Bartholomew denied using any Ordnance material after 1904 to update the map.[28] In addition to these repeat offenders, the Controller and the Board also pursued a number of smaller firms in the period between 1897 and 1909 for various instances of copying, using information, or use of the words 'Ordnance Survey' in map titles.[29] This included a dispute with a Berlin-based mapmaker, Pharus, over a map of London.[30] In that case, it was decided there was not a strong case for legal proceedings as, while there was no doubt the Ordnance map was used in its production, the map had been 'entirely redrawn' in a different style, on a different scale, filled with colour, and omnibus routes added. It was also noted that the Ordnance Survey did not produce a map

[26] Copyright of Ordnance Survey Maps, Précis of Correspondence from January 1883 to March 1910, 4, OS1/6/2 (UKNA), 11–12.

[27] ibid 12.

[28] ibid 14–15.

[29] ibid 15–17.

[30] Elliott to Controller, 15 May 1905; Brown to Codling, 27 May 1905; Elliott to Controller, 1 July 1905, Treasury T1/11725/7153/14 (UNA).

of the area on a single sheet except on a much smaller scale.[31] The matter, as with all other disputes, was addressed simply by correspondence between the offending party (either the mapmaker or retailer/distributor) and the Controller.

The steady stream of correspondence and complaint illustrates the difficulty of enforcing the policy that the Ordnance Survey had adopted and the slipperiness of the boundaries that it had determined upon to delineate acceptable and unacceptable uses of its maps, data, and name. The approach of allowing data to be used in cases where that use would not impact upon the markets that the Ordnance Survey considered its own was supposed to bolster the position of the Ordnance Survey as the authoritative source of that data. The problem was that, even in the case where the map produced would not compete directly with any Ordnance Survey map, the producer of the map needed its customers to know that the data was obtained from the Ordnance Survey *because* of its reputation for accuracy. Allowing this information to be placed prominently on the maps was crucial to their marketability but ran the risk of diluting the Ordnance Survey's reputation when placed on maps it had not directly authorised. The approach of controlling the market for the maps as commodity goods was less and less sustainable as the Ordnance Survey's reputation had made the use value of the data they contained so important. Yet the Survey still hesitated to exploit its exchange value, granting permission liberally to make use of its maps and charging only nominal fees.

One long-running dispute, however, brought the Ordnance Survey to the brink of legal action. This was the case known as the Wolverhampton Red Book case. It involved a map of Wolverhampton, on a scale of 8.8 inches to one mile, which appeared to involve the copying by Wolverhampton bookseller Alfred Hinde of a number of Ordnance Survey sheets of Staffordshire, first surveyed in 1884–85 and revised in 1900–01.[32] The matter had first come to the attention of the Stationery Office in 1901, when it first wrote to Hinde requesting an explanation and reminding him of the notice in the *Gazette*.[33] Hinde responded, explaining that the map in question had been published in the Wolverhampton Red Book for many years and was corrected annually by the Borough Surveyor. It was printed by Edward Stanford and Hinde had assumed that Stanford had the necessary permissions from the Board: 'As Mr Stanford is the Government Agent, I naturally concluded that in dealing with him I was practically dealing with the department'.[34]

Hinde also stated he had assumed that as he had received permission once, it was not necessary to get it every year. The Stationery Office corrected this erroneous assumption by return mail – he would, in fact, need to ask for permission each year the map was published.[35] He duly applied the following year.[36]

[31] Elliott to Controller, 1 July 1905, Treasury T1/11725/7153/14 (UTNA).
[32] Elliott to Controller, HM Stationery Office, 28 November 1910, T1/11459/21575/10 (UKNA).
[33] Plowman to Hinde, 11 October 1901, T1/11459/21575/10 (UKNA).
[34] ibid.
[35] Plowman to Hinde, 29 October 1901, T1/11459/21575/10 (UKNA).
[36] Hinde to Pigott, 8 November 1902. T1/11459/21575/10 (UKNA).

However, he did not apply again for permission until May 1908, at which point the Board of Agriculture noticed the map had been published each year from 1904 to 1908 without permission.[37] Hinde claimed he no longer needed permission as he had ceased using the reproduction of the Ordnance Survey map in exchange for one specially drawn for him by Stanford.[38]

Stanford too was defiant in the face of the Controller's inquiries. He admitted that he had prepared the map for Hinde and it was '"based", like every other modern map of any part of the British Isles, on the Ordnance Survey publications'. However, he stated there was no need for permission in such cases: 'There must be some legitimate right of user by the public in the case of maps produced for the public with public money'. This was a good example of such legitimate use, he argued, because it was produced on a third of the scale of the Ordnance Survey map, was redrawn and relithographed, new streets and additions were made each year by Hinde, the wards were coloured, and the map was published 'for special and local purposes to the advantage of the public'. Surely, he asked, the copyright vested in the Controller does not extend to such a different publication? If OS maps could not be 'used as material', then no new map could be prepared by any private firm in Britain. Stanford added he would be glad to see a test case brought 'to settle how far copyright in the Ordnance Survey extends'.[39] Stanford and Hinde were both sternly rebuked, and Hinde applied and was granted permission for use of the map in the Red Book of 1909.

However, in February 1910 a new edition of the Red Book appeared with a new version of the Wolverhampton map, for which Hinde had again neither applied for nor received permission to reproduce. The Assistant Controller wrote to Hinde, asking him to explain his copyright infringement, whereupon Hinde sought legal advice.[40] His solicitors wrote to Rowland Bailey, the Controller of the Stationery Office, stating that Hinde had only previously paid the royalty of £2 12s under protest, as he contended his map was not a reproduction or reduction of the Ordnance Survey map. It contained different information, was on a different scale, and was drawn up independently by Stanford. Furthermore, he could not afford the royalty payments, as the Red Book was supplied at below-production cost because it provided 'a public convenience.'[41]

The Board of Agriculture decided it was time to see if copyright law could be used to enforce the regulations more effectively. It suggested to Bailey, the Controller, that the facts of the matter be brought before the Treasury Solicitor, AH Dennis, to consider the desirability of instituting proceedings against Hinde.[42]

[37] Hinde to Bailey, 18 May 1908; Secretary, Board of Agriculture and Fishery to Controller, HM Stationery, 13 June 1908, T1/11459/21575/10 (UKNA).

[38] Hinde to Bailey, HM Stationery, 20 June 1908, T1/11459/21575/10 (UKNA).

[39] Stanford to Bailey, 25 June 1908 T1/11459/21575/10 (UKNA).

[40] Newton to Hinde, 4 March 1910, T1/11459/21575/10 (UKNA).

[41] Thorneycroft to Bailey, 11 March 1910, T1/11459/25575/10 (UKNA).

[42] Middleton to Controller, HM Stationery, 19 July 1910. UKTNA T1/11459/21575/10 (UKNA).

Dennis advised that what Hinde had done probably amounted to copyright infringement. He added, however, that the question of copyright in government publications was 'not free from difficulty'. The Law Officers had considered the matter on several occasions and opined that copyright was initially owned by the government servants who produced them (ie, the actual authors) and then transferred either implicitly or explicitly to become vested in the Crown. Dennis added that the question of who the author of an Ordnance map was might also 'be a matter of some difficulty'; he requested a statement be drawn up showing the conditions under which the map was prepared and indicating who was the Director General or other officer under whose personal supervision the preparation of the map took place. In light of the fact no action had ever been brought for the enforcement of Crown copyright, Dennis did not think that proceedings should be threatened without obtaining the advice of the Law Officers.[43]

The Law Officers confirmed that the ordinary rules of copyright law in relation to employees would apply, such that when a public servant acting in the course of his duty for which he was paid composed a document, copyright in that document would prima facie belong to the Crown. The fact that the Crown's rights had been transferred by patent to the Controller of the Stationery Office was not relevant as the Controller was also an ordinary employer. The Law Officers thought that, if the case were taken, 'it should be a strong one, provided that the requisite details of authorship can be given'.[44] Treasury was careful to emphasise that in bringing a case it would not be seeking to prevent publication but 'only to obtain recognition on behalf of the tax-payer'.[45]

Increasingly frustrated, Elliott, Secretary to the Board of Agriculture, also wrote to Treasury to complain of continued failures to comply with the permission process and the difficulties in pursuing them. The map trade continued to chafe at the Ordnance Survey's interference, with Elliott noting that 'serious complaint is made by publishers who desire to comply with all the requirements of the Board that some of their less scrupulous competitors are allowed an unfair advantage'.[46] Given that the value of the small-scale maps sold in 1909 was £8,075, this was not an unimportant matter and Elliott suggested a Committee be appointed to make a further attempt to define the conditions under which Ordnance Survey maps could be used, and that greater efforts be made to enforce those conditions.[47] The Treasury was not in favour of appointing a Committee at this time, in case it prejudiced the position in relation to Hinde.[48] However, at this point a new development arose that seemed to offer a more promising way of enforcing copyright and the Wolverhampton Red Book case was placed on hold.

[43] Dennis to Barstow, 31 August 1910, T1/11459/15129/10 (UKNA).
[44] MFH? to Barstow, 14 October 1910, T1/11459/15129/10 (UKNA).
[45] ibid.
[46] Elliott to Secretary, Treasury, 26 September 1910, T1/11459/17533/10 (UKNA).
[47] ibid.
[48] MFH? to Barstow, 14 October 1910, T1/11459/15129/10 (UKNA).

IV. Statutory Crown Copyright

The new development was found in legislative copyright reform. In 1908 international developments required the UK government to pass new copyright legislation.[49] Publishers, authors, artists, and others, such as the makers of mechanical musical instruments, had long been campaigning for changes to the law, and they now saw their opportunity to influence the legislative process.[50] Increasingly determined to find more effective ways of asserting copyright, Elliott likewise seized upon the resulting legislation, the 1911 Copyright Bill, as providing a possible solution. On 19 April 1911, he wrote to the Treasury and the Board of Trade, noting that the extension of copyright term provided in clause 3 of the bill, which would last for the life of the author and 50 years after their death, made it necessary to consider who is 'the author' of an Ordnance Survey map or, indeed, all other Government publications produced through the cooperation of several persons employed by the Crown. The solution he proposed was to avoid the question of authorship altogether by making copyright in Ordnance Survey maps perpetual. This was justified, he believed, because the expenditure incurred in producing Ordnance Survey maps was large and it was

> reasonable that work done at the cost of the community should remain the property of the community, subject only to such concessions in favour of private individuals as it may be desirable to make, in the public interest, from time to time.[51]

A conference was hastily organised at the Board of Trade, under whose auspices the bill was proceeding through Parliament. George Askwith of the Board of Trade presided at the conference and also present were Colonel Samuel Charles Norton Grant, Director General of the Ordnance Survey; Rowland Bailey, Controller of the Stationery Office; Liddell, legal advisor to the Board of Agriculture; and representatives from the Home Office and Treasury.[52]

It was not just Ordnance maps causing problems in this area. Another matter troubling some in the government was the publication by the Fabian Society of Beatrice Webb's 'Minority Report of the Poor Law Commission', with questions asked in Parliament in 1909 about whether the Treasury was considering bringing an action for copyright infringement.[53] However, it was Ordnance Survey maps upon which most of the discussions at the conference focussed, rather to the

[49] The UK had entered into the Berne Convention for the Protection of Literary and Artistic Works in 1886. In 1908 the Convention was altered at the Berlin Revision Conference, which introduced provisions that were incompatible with UK domestic law, requiring it UK law to be amended.

[50] I Alexander, *Copyright Law and the Public Interest in the Nineteenth Century* (Oxford, Hart Publishing, 2010) 266–87.

[51] Elliott to Bailey (copy), 19 April 1911, T1/11459/7774/11 (UKNA).

[52] Note of AW Brown, Treasury, 2 May 1911, 1/11459/8839/11 (UKNA).

[53] *Parliamentary Debates* 24 February 1909, Volume 1, 717 (extract included in T1/11459/8839/11 (UKNA)).

surprise of the Treasury representative, AW Brown.[54] Askwith and Liddell were opposed to adding in any special protection for the Crown, pointing out that under the existing law they could claim Crown copyright in government publications and the term would increase to fifty years under the new Act. The Treasury had formed no view but expressed their willingness to be guided by the Conference.[55]

The Director General of the Ordnance Survey, Colonel Grant, urged the adoption of perpetual copyright for Ordnance Survey maps. For Grant, perpetual copyright would solve two problems in relation to copyright infringement. First, it would avoid the difficulty of knowing whether an alleged infringer had copied the most up to date Ordnance map or an older map in which copyright had expired and they had updated themselves. Second, it would solve the problem of linking copyright duration to the life of an author, since 'it is practically impossible to say who is the author of any particular map produced by the Survey'. Grant believed that perpetual copyright would protect the Ordnance Survey from 'unfair competition', which was particularly necessary as the Survey was expected to cover its expenses by map sales but pirated maps could undercut their market. At first he argued that if they could not get perpetual copyright they might as well have no copyright at all but he later suggested an additional period of 25 years, making a total of 75 years, might suffice.[56]

Rowland Bailey observed that some at the meeting had expressed doubt as to whether copyright should be claimed at all in government publications. He pointed out that it was important to remember that 'the State disburses very large sums in the preliminary work necessary for the issue of its Ordnance Maps', as well as the textbooks published for other departments including the War Office, Admiralty, and Board of Education. If the copyright were waived, he believed 'the advantage must be reaped by the few individuals who as publishers will reproduce the Government works' and argued that the 1887 Minute demonstrated that no 'undue' restrictions would be placed on those wishing to reproduce such publications. Bailey too pointed out the difficulties in identifying 'authors' of government publications and, thinking no doubt of the Poor Law Commission Minority Report, pointed out that often the content was provided gratuitously and the writer was not an employee. The solution he proposed was that copyright in all publications issued by any Department should vest in the Controller of the Stationery Office, and the term of copyright be fixed at 75 years from the date of publication.[57]

The pressure from the Ordnance Survey, the Board of Agriculture and Fisheries, and the Stationery Office to introduce a statutory provision for Crown copyright and longer, even perpetual, terms of protection was responding to a different logic from that of the broader push for copyright reform that was underway. Where that

[54] Note of A Brown, Treasury, 2 May 1911, T1/11459/ 8839/11 (UKNA).
[55] ibid.
[56] ibid.
[57] Bailey to Secretary, Treasury (copy), 2 May 1911, UKNA T1/11459/8839/11 (UKNA).

broader reform was a matter of international trade and the protection of domestic markets, as well as the intangible rights of authors, Crown copyright was almost a mirror image. Rather than supporting authors, it sought to remove the human author from the equation so that the state could retain authority over its publications and extend that authority into the market. Economic pressures did play a role, as the Ordnance Survey and other Departments were expected to use sales of their publications to keep down rising costs, but the rationale for preventing unauthorised publication, or piracy, was not simply because it interfered with a commercial market for these publications. Rather, these official publications provided a public service. It was not only morally abhorrent for private publishers to reap the benefit of goods paid for with public money but also their interference in the market would mean that the government would not be able to afford to keep publishing and keep its own prices low. As George Barstow, Assistant Secretary to the Treasury, wrote to Sir Thomas Heath and Sir George Murray of Treasury on 3 May 1911,

> I should have thought Crown Copyright was in precisely the opposite position to copyright vested in private persons, and that [the Board of Trade] could easily be persuaded to allow the Crown ie the State to retain copyright in perpetuity or for lengthened periods, on an assurance that it will be used only for the purposes of regulation and control, so as not to allow the produce of taxpayers' efforts to enure for private benefit.[58]

The Board of Trade remained opposed to a clause for Crown copyright, telling Treasury officials that they were 'afraid of the section of the Committee who are opposed to all copyright'.[59] Another source of contention was the large disparity in the types of government publications that the clause would cover. One Treasury official noted that for everything except Ordnance Survey maps 12 months of copyright protection, or even less, would be enough.[60] A further distraction for the Government departments was created when Josiah Wedgwood suggested the inclusion in the Bill of a clause that would encourage the Secretary of State to enter into negotiations to purchase the copyright of any literary, dramatic, or musical work 'of sufficient merit or value to the community to make its production in the cheapest form advisable'.[61] The clause was strongly opposed by Treasury and the Board of Agriculture and eventually dropped.

On 24 May 1911, Dennis, the Treasury solicitor, prepared a memorandum at Barstow's request expressing Treasury's view that it would be desirable to take advantage of the codifying bill to place Crown copyright on a more satisfactory basis. Dennis too framed Crown copyright as a question of protecting the public's interest in such publications as Ordnance maps, and manuals and pamphlets produced by other government departments. Producing such works

[58] Barstow to Heath and Murray, 3 May 1911, T1/11459/8839/11 (UKNA).
[59] ibid.
[60] File note, T1/11459/8839/11 (UKNA).
[61] File note, undated, T1/11459.

involved a 'large outlay and is justified as being a work essential for the public welfare and of a nature such as to be incapable of proper execution by private enterprise'.[62] Allowing indiscriminate copying would prejudice their sale at low prices and 'enriches the pirating publisher at the expense of the State'.[63] He argued that preventing infringement might lead to increased sales for the Ordnance maps, which would justify a further reduction in price or the undertaking of some other publicly beneficial work. Dennis stated that, although they had received legal advice that the Crown might rely on the Acts as an employer, the Law Officers had expressed doubt in a recent case relating to an Ordnance Map (presumably the Hinde case) as to whether the Crown could take advantage of the Copyright Acts as an employer. The matter had never been tested and the Ordnance Survey had been reluctant to do so in the recent case but had decided to wait for the legislation to pass. He proposed that the Bill should provide that, without prejudice to common law rights, the Crown might have a copyright in all works 'prepared and/or published by it or under its direction authority or control; for a period of 50 years after first publication'.[64] This would be subject to any express agreement by which copyright may have been reserved to the actual author.[65] In a memo dated two days earlier, Barstow of Treasury recognised this 'rather throws over the Bd of Agriculture who would like perpetual copyright for Ordnance Survey maps'.[66]

On 2 June 1911, Askwith forwarded a draft clause on Crown copyright to Treasury, the Board of Agriculture, and the Home Office.[67] The clause followed the format suggested by Dennis: granting copyright to the Crown for 50 years from the date of first publication to any work 'prepared or published by or under the direction or control of His Majesty or any Government Department, subject to any agreement with the author'.[68] Neither Dennis nor Bailey had any objection. In September Treasury forwarded the draft clause to the Board of Agriculture, noting that the legal case they had planned to pursue was standing over, pending this clause's enactment. Assistant Secretary Thomas Heath observed that it put the copyright in Ordnance Maps 'upon a definite footing, irrespective of the question of authorship, which has hitherto rendered it doubtful whether proceedings could be taken with success'.[69]

The Copyright Bill's passage through Parliament occasioned considerable discussion and almost every clause was the subject of scrutiny and debate by Members of the House of Commons as well as the Lords. Yet the provision

[62] W Dennis, Memo, 24 May 1911, T1/11459/8839/11.
[63] ibid.
[64] ibid.
[65] ibid.
[66] Barstow to Heath, 22 May 1911, T1/11459/8839/11 (UKNA).
[67] Askwith to Treasury Secretary, 2 June 1911, T1/11459/11222/11 (UKNA).
[68] ibid.
[69] Letter from Heath to Board of Agriculture, 19 September 1911, OS1/6/2 (UKNA).

establishing Crown copyright was not commented upon in either House. The Bill was eventually passed by both houses and received Royal Assent on 16 December 1911.

V. Implementing the Act: Regulations and Litigation

The Act and its new Crown copyright clause now in place, the Board of Agriculture and Fisheries turned its attention back to the case of the Wolverhampton Red Book. However, the Treasury Solicitor, Dennis, advised that the case was not important enough to proceed with and the Board should wait to see if there was a repetition of the behaviour that could be dealt with under the new act.[70] In the meantime, Bailey sought legal advice in relation to how the new clause might be applied.[71] His first question was about the role now played by the author – was it the case that if a salaried employee were the author, then the Crown would be first owner? Dennis responded that, under the new provision, 'the actual author has ceased to be material' unless there was a special relationship with them.[72] In relation to Ordnance Maps, the Controller inquired what would be the date of first publication and whether each revision of a sheet would convey copyright. He further noted that 'the term "any substantial [part]" may be important, more particularly in relation to excerpts from Ordnance Maps'. Dennis responded that the date of first publication would be the date the map is first issued to the public and that a revision would not prolong copyright unless it were substantial.[73] The Board of Agriculture confirmed in a letter that the revision of Ordnance maps was always substantial and the date of publication was always printed on every sheet.[74] If this were accepted by the private trade and successfully maintained in a court of law, it would amount to effective perpetual protection

It was decided that new Regulations should be drawn up to govern the reproduction and use of Ordnance maps, effective 1 January 1913.[75] There was considerable negotiation over the wording between the new Director General of the Ordnance Survey, Sir Charles Close, and representatives from Treasury, the Stationery Office, and the Board of Agriculture and Fisheries, which would best draw the parameters for permissible and impermissible uses. The key tension was summed up by Close when he wrote that

> we should be wise to allow private map makers certain freedom in using Ordnance maps as material for their own small-scale maps. For many years past we have put

[70] Barstow to Bryan, 13 July 1912, T1/11459/16612/11 (UKNA).
[71] Bailey to Treasury Secretary, 14 March 1912, STAT 12/36/1 (UKNA).
[72] Solicitor Comments on questions raised by Copyright Act 1911, 22 June 1912, STAT 12/36/1 C 5673 (UKNA).
[73] ibid.
[74] Bryan to Hammond, 13 July 1912, STAT 12/36/1 (UKNA).
[75] OS 23 Reproduction and Utilization of Ordnance Maps by Map-Making Firms and Others, As Regulated by the Copyright Act, 1911, OS 1/6/4 (UKNA).

> ineffectual obstacles in their way without producing any result save a sense of irritation. The general feeling amongst geographers is that there should be no restriction in the use of geographical facts, and so far as I can ascertain, this is the view taken by foreign governments.[76]

Close sought to resolve the tension by distinguishing between the data and the maps, explaining:

> The form in which the facts are presented is of course another matter and, whilst allowing a free use of the information given on the Ordnance maps, we should be careful to prevent any direct reproduction of the maps except as indicated in the draft regulations.[77]

The Regulations, known as OS 23, provided that mapmaking firms were allowed to use Ordnance Survey 'material' in maps on scales smaller than one-inch, on the condition that the maps were 'not mere reproductions, enlargements, or reductions of Ordnance maps, but are specially drawn or engraved'.[78] The second clause forbade mapmaking firms from using in the title the words 'Ordnance' or 'Ordnance Survey' or 'any expression or form of words which would convey the impression that the maps are produced by official authority or have Government recognition'.[79] This also applied to 'endorsements, envelopes, and advertisements'.

Clause 3 clarified:

> In general, no direct reproduction, copy, reduction or enlargement for publication of the whole or of any part of an ordnance map, and no reproduction, copy, reduction or enlargement for publication, with alterations or additions, of the whole or part of an ordnance map, will be allowed.[80]

However, it provided for exceptions, setting out categories in which permission would normally be granted. Small portions of maps could be used to illustrate books or pamphlets if permission were sought and a royalty paid. For scientific and technical works, permission also needed to be sought but a royalty might not be charged. Ordnance Maps could also be used in connection with sales of land and plans advertising property sales; for Parliamentary Bills and Committees; by county and district councils for illustrating transport, water, drainage, and lighting; and by public companies.[81] In most cases, permission needed to be sought but 'will usually be granted' and in most cases a royalty would also be payable. The process for obtaining permission was described in the Regulations, and a form

[76] Note from Sir CF Close, 7 June 1912 OS 1/6/4 A1491/1912 (UKNA).

[77] ibid.

[78] OS 23 Reproduction and Utilization of Ordnance Maps by Map-Making Firms and Others, As Regulated by the Copyright Act, 1911, OS 1/6/4 Box E.7109/1918 (UKNA).

[79] ibid.

[80] ibid.

[81] ibid.

was created for applicants to use.[82] It was also ordered that all works printed for the Stationery Office should bear the words 'Crown Copyright Reserved'.[83]

The system was manifestly not designed to generate profits through exploiting copyright in the maps. However, pressure was applied from other parts of the government for it to do so in light of the Stationery Office's ever-rising printing and publishing costs. In 1913 Colonel Close appeared before a Select Committee appointed to look into whether a Printing Department under the control of the Stationery Office should be established, and to consider various other matters relating to reducing the costs of printing, while increasing the dissemination, of government publications.[84] He was placed under some pressure to explain the reasons for the Ordnance Survey Department costing the State £250,000 each year. When asked to compare those costs with Germany, Close pointed out that Germany had no equivalent body and that '[w]e are the only country in the world that produces large scale cadastral maps at a nominal cost for the benefit of the public'.[85] When questioned whether dropping the price of maps to the public would increase sales, Close insisted that it would not: 'If the 2s. maps were suddenly priced at a shilling, very likely sales would not go up. There is a price which the public expects to pay for a map'.[86]

Colonel Close reported that he received requests every day seeking permission to reproduce maps and he considered that the new rules were working well.[87] However, as the royalties were only nominal, generally 1s per 100 copies, little profit accrued to the Department.[88] Moreover, commercial maps reduced from Ordnance Survey maps on a scale of less than one inch to a mile were charged no royalty. Close explained this had been discussed and it was decided that this was 'purely geographical information', and they could not stop people using geographical information.[89] He pointed to one instance in which a private firm produced a half-inch map in which all the details were taken from the Ordnance Survey. However, the Law Officers advised against bringing an action as the map was not a direct reduction but had been re-engraved. Close broadly agreed with this approach, noting it was an 'admirable map' and that 'the firm deserved some credit for doing that which was of public advantage'.[90] When Walter Rea, Liberal MP for Scarborough, asked Close 'You look upon your Department broadly as a public

[82] ibid.
[83] Dutton to Stationery Office, 1 July 1912, STAT 12/36/1 (UKNA).
[84] Report from the Select Committee on Publications and Debates' Reports, together with the Proceedings of the Committee, Minutes of Evidence and an Appendix, 23 July 1913 (London, Her Majesty's Stationery Office, 1913) (1913 Select Committee).
[85] 1913 Select Committee, 28.
[86] ibid 29.
[87] ibid 24.
[88] ibid 24–25.
[89] ibid 30.
[90] ibid 30.

service, and not as a profit-making concern?' Close's response was telling: 'Yes. It would be wrong, I think, to suppose that we could ever make cadastral maps profitably.'[91]

The Ordnance Survey thus continued to believe that it was neither possible nor appropriate for their maps to circulate freely in the market and the chief aim of the regulations was to establish a permissions regime that distinguished between permissible use of data and impermissible copying of physical maps. However, the relative simplicity of the earlier approach, which allowed private mapmakers to make maps on scales other than the one-inch, was difficult to maintain once the Ordnance Survey was making maps on a number of different scales and seeking to regulate those markets. It was impossible to delineate a clear boundary between allowing the use of Ordnance data and forbidding copying 'parts' of maps or reducing or enlarging them. The secondary aim of the Regulations was to regain control over the Ordnance 'brand' by allowing the word to be used only on official maps. The problem here was that 'Ordnance' was no longer simply the name of the institution that produced the maps but an accurate description of the source of the data to which private mapmakers needed to refer in order to establish the authority of their own maps.

Unsurprisingly then, despite the new regulations and Close's optimism, unauthorised uses of Ordnance maps by private mapmakers continued. In 1913 the Treasury took the decision to bring its first legal proceedings against an infringer. Ernest Augustus Mutch, trading as HG Rowe & Co, was issuing various maps under the series title *A New Road Map for Cyclists and Motorists*. The case was brought not as a civil action alleging infringement of copyright by reproducing the copyright works under section 2 of the Copyright Act 1911, where an injunction and/or damages would be sought as a remedy, but as a criminal prosecution before the Court of Aldermen. Mutch was alleged to be in breach of section 11 of the Act for selling and distributing infringing copies of Ordnance maps. One summons related to maps of London, Kent, and district, and the other to a map of London, Hampshire, and district (see Figure 28). Mutch was found guilty of distributing 720 copies of the first map and 120 of the second. He was ordered to pay a fine of £20 on each summons and a total of £15 in costs. He was also ordered to hand over all infringing copies and all plates for printing infringing copies, which amounted to three zinc plates, 2,072 copies of the first map, and 3,468 copies of the second.[92] There appears to be no record of why the criminal route was chosen over the civil but it is likely it was perceived to be faster and would not require putting on evidence as to whether it was Mutch who made the copies or whether he had acquired them from someone else. In addition, it underlines that the Ordnance Survey and the Stationery Office continued to think of the map market as one for

[91] ibid 30.

[92] Guy Stephenson, Assistant Director, Public Prosecutions to Treasury Secretary, 1 November 1913, T 1/11725/21870/13; Stephenson to Treasury Solicitor, 28 December 2014, T1/11725/10837/14 (UKNA).

tangible commodity goods, such that interference with it was a criminal rather than commercial matter.

Figure 28 HG Rowe's *Gazette New Road Map for Cyclists and Motorists, London, Middlesex, Surrey, Berkshire, Hampshire, and Parts of Adjacent Counties.* Map filed with other documents relating to the litigation, held at The National Archives (UK)

Image courtesy of The National Archives (UK), ref. T1/11725/10837.

The following year two more maps produced by Ernest Mutch and his brother (trading as Nolting) were referred to the Treasury Solicitor for advice about another prosecution. In referring the matter to Treasury, the Controller of the Stationery Office, Frederick Atterbury, expressed displeasure that the OS 23 Regulations were 'not more explicit' as regarded the use of Ordnance Survey Maps as material for the production of other maps.[93] These maps were not photographic copies but newly produced by hand. However, when compared it was clear that they were not just 'slavish' copies but 'bad' copies, having introduced errors.[94] Advice was sought from criminal barrister Archibald Bodkin about proceeding against the Mutch

[93] Atterbury to Treasury Solicitor, 22 May 1914, T 1/11725/10873/14 (UKNA).
[94] Letter from Sydney Olivier, 9 May 1914, T1/11725/10837/14 (UKNA).

brothers, as well as other retailers who had been selling the maps. The Mutches claimed that they had ceased selling the infringing maps and had tried to withdraw them from the retailers to whom they had supplied them. Bodkin pointed out the difficulties of proceeding against retailers of such maps, given that section 11 required them to have knowledge that the maps were infringing, and that the right thing was to proceed against the producer of the maps.[95] Although the Mutches' excuses were treated with scepticism, in the end it was decided to send warning letters rather than institute proceedings, due to the difficulty in establishing the dates when the maps in question had been published.[96]

The Berlin mapmaking company of Pharus also continued to plague the Stationery Office, with its large city maps making use of Ordnance Survey data. In 1914 legal advice was sought as to whether action could be taken in respect of a map of Leeds.[97] In this case, the map was being sold by Richard Jackson who, particularly egregiously, was also the Ordnance Survey map agent in Leeds. The map in question stated in the legend printed underneath the scale that it was based upon Ordnance Survey material and published on a scale of six inches to one mile. It was therefore in breach of the OS 23 Regulations, despite exhibiting a number of differences, such as widened roads, different symbols, and some new streets and tramlines inserted.[98] However, as Jackson claimed he had received the maps prior to the Regulations coming into effect, the matter could not be taken further and Jackson undertook to sell no further copies when his current stock was exhausted.[99]

VI. Inculcating the 'Map Habit'

Crown copyright had provided the Treasury with the confidence to launch proceedings, but it did not resolve all issues relating to circulation and access of maps. Dissatisfaction with map sales and accessibility under Fisher Unwin, as agents for the Ordnance Survey, was growing. In May 1914, a Departmental Committee (known as the Olivier Committee) made up of Sir Sydney Olivier (Secretary at the Board of Agriculture), Frederick Atterbury (Controller of the Stationery Office), and Sir Charles Close, was appointed to consider the arrangements between Fisher Unwin and the Board and the effect of his agency, and to investigate ways of improving the sales and accessibility of small-scale maps to the public.[100] It quickly

[95] Opinion re T Mutch (Trading as Nolting & Co), A E Bodkin, 16 December 1914 T1/11725/10837/14 (UKNA).
[96] Atterbury to Treasury Secretary, 9 January 1915, T 1/11725/1019/14 (UKNA).
[97] Atterbury to Treasury Secretary, 2 April 1914, T 1/11725/7153/14 (UKNA).
[98] Charles F Close, Minute, 19 Feb 1914 T1/11725/7153/14 (UKNA).
[99] Jackson to unknown, 10 August 1914, T 1/11725/17225/14 (UKNA).
[100] Report of the Departmental Committee on the Sale of Small-Scale Maps, 26 August 1914, OS1/6/5 (UKNA) (Olivier Committee 1914).

became clear that the Ordnance Survey maps continued to struggle in the face of competition from private mapmakers. The growing demand for cheap holiday, cycling, rambling, and motoring maps, which the Committee considered 'should have tended to increase the sales' of Ordnance maps, was being met by private publishers.[101] The evidence also established there was considerable demand for town maps at scales of between one and six inches to the mile. Demand for these maps was currently largely being met by Pharus, who were using the Ordnance Survey material as a base.

The truth was that private mapmakers and mapsellers simply understood the market better. Their map covers and advertising were more attractive, their discounts and sales practices were more effective, and their maps better attuned to what different sectors of the public needed. In part, this was a problem of the Ordnance Survey's own making; choosing their agent, they had specified it should be neither a producer nor a retail seller of maps. Stanford, who had lost the agency to Fisher Unwin, thought this ridiculous as the London mapsellers knew more about the business than anyone else.[102] As the witness from Messrs Cornish (the agents in Birmingham) pointed out:

> The most important thing for these maps is that they should conform to the idea of the man who wants to sell them. Of course in a place like Birmingham there is an enormous number of people who want a map with Birmingham right in the centre, and with a radius of so many miles round, and the Ordnance Survey, of course, might print them as well as anyone else, and do them better, and also they would have the stamp of the Ordnance Survey, which is a great advantage for sale.[103]

The current Ordnance map for Birmingham was out of date, did not have Birmingham in the centre, and was 'not at all a nice looking map'. The Ordnance Survey did not provide what Messrs Cornish wanted, so they asked Bartholomew to do so.[104]

Indeed, while complaints were made about the maps of Bacon, Philips, and others, the greatest challenge remained the firm of Bartholomew. Of all the other mapmakers in the market, only Bartholomew could compete with the Ordnance Survey in terms of reputation. Fisher Unwin complained that booksellers were

> so drenched with the Bartholomew map, which they talked of as the Ordnance map, that since it came into our hands it has been all our work to get over what you may call a prejudice, custom, or habit. They had the Bartholomew habit almost.[105]

Bartholomew had the advantage over Unwin in that they were able to give larger discounts and distribute their stock on a sale or return basis, a practice Unwin opposed. But a chief concern, expressed by several witnesses, was that the words

[101] ibid Report, 5.
[102] ibid Minutes of Evidence, 13.
[103] ibid Evidence, 20.
[104] ibid.
[105] ibid Evidence, 7.

'Ordnance Survey' continued to appear on Bartholomew maps.[106] Edward Stanford gave evidence that the public preferred Bartholomew maps because 'they are good, but they had a long start, and they used the word "Ordnance" in a way that I did not approve of at all'.[107]

Close and Atterbury expressed their frustration with the situation. Close noted that he had sent out a circular two years previously stating it was prohibited to use the words 'Ordnance' or 'Ordnance Survey' in any way that might give rise to the impression that the map was official. As a result, Bartholomew had stopped using the phrase 'Reduced Ordnance Survey' in favour of 'Reduced Survey'. Close commented: 'What "Reduced Survey" means I do not know', but it was clear to everyone what Bartholomew was up to.[108] Furthermore, as witnesses pointed out, the word Ordnance, or the phrase 'Reduced by permission from the Ordnance Survey' may have been removed from the cover of the maps but continued to appear elsewhere on the map itself, as well as in advertisements.[109]

Fisher Unwin had proposed that his main task since taking over the agency had been to try to wean customers from the Bartholomew habit to 'create the Ordnance habit'.[110] Indeed, inculcating the public with a 'map habit' and then ensuring that habit was served by the Ordnance Survey was explicitly endorsed on several occasions during the Committee's work. As the Birmingham agent explained:

> [I]f you are educating them up to Ordnance Survey maps you want to keep them to it all their lives. Buying maps is a habit. There are some men, of course, who go anywhere without a map and there are other men who will not go a yard without a map, and those are the people you have to go to. It is a map habit. Of course, all intelligent people do go with a map wherever they go: they cannot live without a map, in fact they like to have it at home to look at it occasionally, and in the cultivation of that map habit there is going to be a very large increase in the sale of maps in this country within the next few years; I am convinced of it.[111]

The key to this was getting maps into schools. As the agent continued: 'We know from long experience, an experience of over 100 years, that we retain our customers because they were school children … The children grow up; they still want Ordnance maps'.[112]

The final Report of the Olivier Committee was confidential and unpublished. It made a number of recommendations that it considered would improve sales and accessibility of the maps. A key consideration was, of course, price and it was one the Committee and witnesses had agonised over. The Committee had been informed that the selling price of Ordnance maps was calculated by adding

[106] ibid Evidence, 5, 7, 11, 15.
[107] ibid Evidence, 11.
[108] ibid Evidence, 6.
[109] ibid.
[110] ibid Evidence, 7.
[111] ibid Evidence, 22.
[112] ibid.

together the cost of paper and inks, preparation of the stones and plates, mounting and folding, and the labour required. To that sum was added a further 50 per cent of the cost of labour employed to cover the cost of administrative expenses.[113] The Committee considered some reduction in price was possible, noting:

> While we do not advocate that the Department should enter upon a price-cutting opportunity against private map-producers, we think it desirable that no opportunity should be missed of increasing the popularity of the maps with the public and we are of opinion that even a slight reduction in price would probably have the effect of increasing numbers sold.[114]

The trade witnesses opposed reducing the prices of maps, while those representing consumer groups, the Federation of Rambling Clubs and the Automobile Association, disagreed.[115] The Committee recommended that prices of the one-inch and half-inch maps should be reduced from 1s 6d to 1s for unmounted maps and from 2s to 1s 6d for mounted and cased maps. The Committee insisted that 'the Ordnance Survey maps are national maps, paid for by the public, and it is only right that they should be available to the public at the lowest possible prices'.[116] It also recommended changes to the sales arrangements, the first of which was to terminate the contract with Fisher Unwin, with the Ordnance Survey taking over the sale of small-scale maps out of Southampton. Agents would be appointed in all principal towns and the rates of discount should be the same, or better, as those offered by private map companies.[117] Other recommendations aimed at improving the saleability of maps included improvements to the quality of cover designs, method of folding, and attractiveness of advertising matter. The Olivier Committee also thought the Ordnance Survey should move more definitively into different markets. Noting its terms of reference directed it only to consider small-scale maps, the evidence it received indicated demand for town maps on scales between one inch and six inches and the same for tourist districts. Noting the dominance of Pharus in the town map market, it further recommended that the principal booksellers of every considerable town should be approached and offered a map of the town on a suitable scale.[118]

Alongside the recommendations relating to the appearance and format of maps, the Committee accepted the evidence as to the 'adverse effect' of the use of titles on private maps that implied that such maps were copied from or connected with the Ordnance Survey. The Committee was of the view that copyright law could

[113] ibid Report, 10. It is interesting to note that when Stanford asked Sir Charles Close how he managed to keep the cost of mounting so low, Close revealed it was through the use of women as labour, while Stanford used boys, 238–41.

[114] ibid Report, 10.

[115] ibid Evidence, Metcalf (Manager of WH Smith & Sons), 592-4; Unwin, 61, Stanford, 221–22, 245–46; Southern (Federation of Rambling Clubs), 832–37; Fryer (Automobile Association), 949–58.

[116] ibid Report, 9.

[117] ibid Report, 13–14.

[118] ibid Report, 15–16.

solve this problem, recommending that 'the powers given under the Copyright Act 1911 shall be freely exercised in all cases where the requirements of the rules governing the utilisation of the Ordnance Survey maps are not strictly complied with'.[119] The problem of course with this recommendation was that the use of the words 'Ordnance' or 'Ordnance Survey' on maps was not a copyright matter but rather a trade mark one. It might be covered by the law of passing off but, where a mapmaker made use of Ordnance data within the scope of the regulations and, if necessary, paid the relevant fee, indicating this upon the map itself would only be an accurate statement of the source of the data. Forbidding a mapmaker from making such a statement would render the data itself less attractive as its authority could not be asserted.

The Olivier Committee's terms of reference and subsequent report signalled the start of a new era for the Ordnance Survey; one in which it would more fully embrace the market possibilities of its maps and the data they contained. The Report was delivered on 26 August, three weeks after Britain had declared war on Germany. The War had an immediate effect upon the Ordnance Survey; within months it lost almost its entire military strength and most of its civilian workforce. Not only was the implementation of the Olivier Committee's recommendations postponed but War Office regulations were drawn up and circulated to major mapmakers and sellers. They stated that 'as long as the war continues, it is not considered in the public interest that any new maps or revised editions for existing maps of the United Kingdom should be issued'. Anyone wishing to produce a map had to submit it first to the Ordnance Survey for approval, ensuring it contained no information of naval or military value.[120] Policing the regulations alongside copyright infringements brought the Ordnance Survey once more into conflict with Mutch and his brother, in relation to a cycling and motorists map of Lancashire.[121] It also led to an extended conflict with Alexander Gross and his firm, Geographia Ltd. The latter would culminate in the Ordnance Survey's second copyright prosecution but that would not occur until after the war was over.[122]

VII. Conclusion

By the outbreak of World War I, the Ordnance Survey was positioning itself towards a more commercial future for its maps and data. Unlike the Hydrographic Office, which continued to emphasise the public interest in marine safety by taking a permissive approach to its charts and data, the Ordnance Survey's distinction between exploiting its maps as physical commodities in a partly regulated

[119] ibid Report, 15.
[120] Extracts contained in letter from Meeres to Burrows, 20 July 1917, OS 1/753 (UKNA).
[121] T 1/11725/1019/14 (UKNA).
[122] *Rex v Gross and Geographia Ltd*, see TS 27/614 and OS 1/753 (UKNA).

retail market, while leaving its data free from market control, was beginning to break down. Under financial pressure from the various government departments involved in map production and sales, and following its own interest in ensuring it not only offered the most up to date data but was also recognised as the authoritative source of that data, it began to seek out new consumer markets. This meant that copyright, as the basis of intangible rights that could be exploited in different formats, was becoming more relevant to its operations. But, at the same time, the nature of both maps and geographic data meant that neither could fit neatly within the law's existing scope. The collaborative process of mapmaking put pressure on copyright's authorship paradigm, while the difficulty of separating the map as a physical object from the information it contained made it difficult to draw the line between authorised and unauthorised uses. Crown copyright could solve the former issue but not the latter.

The enactment of statutory Crown copyright provisions can be better understood once placed in the context of longstanding tensions in relation to the state production and dissemination of geographic data. On one side of the equation sat the commercial need to recoup expenses and deter free-riders, as well as to control the reputation and authority of the state institutions, their maps and their data. Weighing against those considerations was the public utility of the data, the fact it was generated using public money, and the further fact that the state institutions were its only source. Crown copyright prioritised the former, leaving the latter to be managed through judicious rights management policies. These tensions were not resolved, as has been subsequently demonstrated in periodic calls for Crown copyright reform, as well as new disputes over geospatial information coming before the courts in Commonwealth countries.[123]

Finally, we can also see Crown copyright as more than a practical, if partial, solution to problems of accuracy, authority, and access, brought about in a rather opportunistic manner. For those government officials involved in effecting it, this was of course the case. Rising above the ground-level interactions, however, Crown copyright can also be seen as an assertion of sovereignty over state-generated geographic information. The explicit creation of a statutory category for government-generated materials set them apart from, and above, created by private individuals or organisations. Recognising Crown copyright as manifesting sovereignty also explains the use of criminal procedures against Mutch, which emphasised state power in a way that a civil process would not. Placing the words 'Crown Copyright Reserved' on every map and chart further underlined the

[123] *Commonwealth v Oceantalk Australia* (1998) 79 FCR 520; *Controller of HMSO v Green Amps* [2007] EWGC 2755; *Keatley Surveying v Teranet Inc 2019* SCC 43; *Copyright Agency Limited v NSW* (2008) 233 CLR 279; *77M Limited v Ordnance Survey Limited* [2019] EWHC 3007. For discussion of reform options and opportunities see EF Judge, 'Crown Copyright and Copyright Reform in Canada' in M Geist, *In the Public Interest: The Future of Canadian Copyright Law* (Toronto, Irwin Law, 2005); also Copyright Law Review Committee, *Crown Copyright* (Commonwealth of Australia, 2005), www.austlii.edu.au/au/other/clrc/18.pdf; *The Future Management of Crown Copyright* Cm 4300 (HMSO, 1999).

state's assertion of control over the use and circulation of geographic products and the data they contained. As this chapter has shown, the introduction of Crown copyright could not, and was never intended to, lead to complete control over geospatial information. While other strategies were also needed to embed a 'map habit' which looked to the state-funded bodies as its most authoritative source, Crown copyright offered not just an additional practical tool for doing so, but an importantly symbolic one.

10

Conclusion

I. An Intimate Insight: The Case of *Laurie v Newnes* (1899)

In the final year of the nineteenth century, the mapmaking firm of John Bartholomew & Son found itself embroiled in copyright litigation, not with the Ordnance Survey but with barrister and former school inspector James Stuart Laurie. This matter, first referred to in the Introduction of this book, settled almost upon the courtroom steps but its intricacies can be traced through the extraordinary Bartholomew Archive, offering a final, detailed case study in which the themes of this book converge. In addition, the archive offers an unparalleled insight into how copyright litigation not only brings to light some of the unspoken assumptions upon which traders operated but also impacted upon the personal lives of those involved in it.

The map in question, called a 'physical map', was rather unusual, in that it had passed through several different forms and technologies over the course of its creation. Once again, its format and process of creation seems to have created uncertainty as to whether it was a work to which copyright applied. Its creator, Laurie, had previously been Director General of Public Instruction in Ceylon, as well as a School Inspector. He was the author and editor of a number of educational publications, including Laurie's sixpenny manuals of instruction and *Laurie's Educational Course*.[1] To create the physical map Laurie had first made a model, either in wood or plaster, called the 'relievo', which measured around 10 feet in length. This had, in turn, been prepared from a sketch made using a pantograph to copy the large size Ordnance Survey map of England. The relievo model was then photographed using the autotype process. The cost of preparing the model and photograph was said to be £300.[2]

In or around 1886, Laurie had a number of copies printed and sent them to various people he thought might be interested, including Messrs Bartholomew. Nine years later, upon seeing Bartholomew's Physical Map of Scotland, Laurie sent them another letter asking if they would be interested in a copy of his map, should

[1] Laurie refers to his previous employment record in his affidavit, *Laurie v George Newnes Limited*, High Court of Justice, Chancery Division, 24 March 1899 (BA/NLS).

[2] Laurie to Bartholomew, 21 October 1895; Hardman Hoyle to JG Bartholomew, 20 March 1899. (BA/NLS).

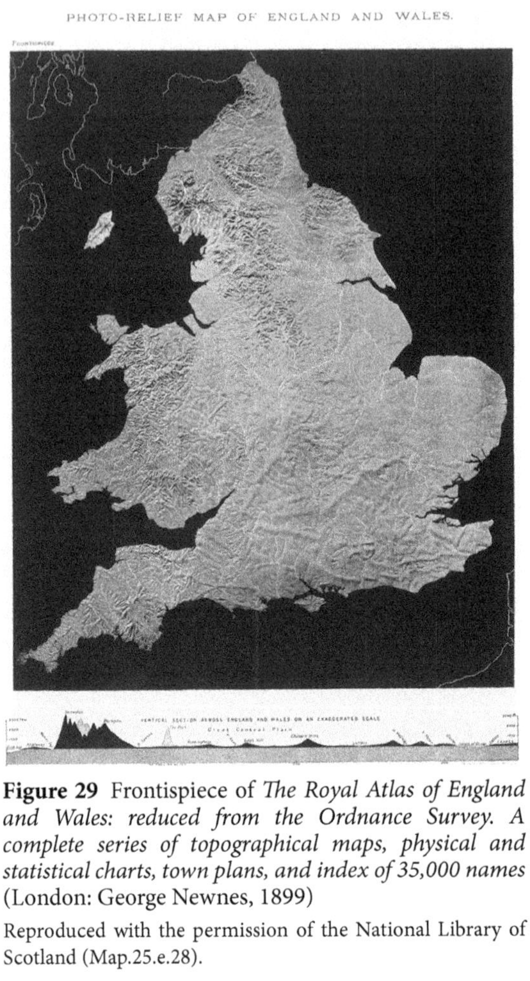

Figure 29 Frontispiece of *The Royal Atlas of England and Wales: reduced from the Ordnance Survey. A complete series of topographical maps, physical and statistical charts, town plans, and index of 35,000 names* (London: George Newnes, 1899)

Reproduced with the permission of the National Library of Scotland (Map.25.e.28).

they be producing a similar work for England.[3] Not hearing back from them, one can imagine his reaction upon seeing his work in print. On 16 February 1899, the educational publishing company established by James's brother, Thomas Laurie of 28 Paternoster Row, wrote to Messrs George Newnes, informing them that the map appearing as the frontispiece to Bartholomew's *Royal Atlas* (see Figure 29), recently published by Newnes, was a 'precise facsimile' of map made by James Laurie.[4]

Laurie had chosen to proceed against Newnes rather than Bartholomew on the basis that it was easier to bring an action in London than in Scotland.[5] The Bartholomew now involved was John George Bartholomew, grandson of the firm's founder, John Senior, whom we met in chapter eight writing to his son John Junior, in the case between Johnston and Fullarton. Although suffering from tuberculosis and almost an invalid, John George was a deeply respected geographer and cartographer with an innovative business acumen who further consolidated the leading position of the family firm.[6] In this dispute, however, we see a more vulnerable side to his usually assured business dealings. Responding to the letter from Laurie, Newnes' solicitors came back strongly, saying Bartholomew told them he had never seen the map and, if Laurie proceeded and was

[3] Laurie to Bartholomew, 21 October 1895 (BA/NLS).

[4] T Laurie to Messrs George Newnes, 16 February 1899 (BA/NLS).

[5] T Laurie to Newnes, 20 February 1899 (BA/NLS).

[6] Leslie Gardiner, *Bartholomew 150 Years* (Edinburgh, John Bartholomew & Son, 1976) 30–44 (BA/NLS).

successful in getting an injunction 'they would sue for very heavy damages'.[7] Newnes forwarded the correspondence to John George Bartholomew but received no reply, and Bartholomew's solicitor, G Hardman Hoyle, was compelled to write a testy letter accompanied by a wire, in mid-March, informing him that Laurie would be applying for an injunction the next week and could he please provide instructions.[8]

Two days later, Hoyle had seen the plaintiffs' statement of claim and was convinced they had a strong case. Their claim of copying could be established first, by Laurie's allegation that this was the only map of its kind in existence and, second, by the presence of accidental defects in Laurie's photograph (flaws either in the model itself or in the negative) that were reproduced in Bartholomew's map. The only difference between the two maps was that Bartholomew's contained rivers, which Laurie alleged had simply been inserted into the copy of his map.[9]

On 23 March, Newnes telegraphed Bartholomew that Laurie 'means practically blackmail wont [sic] consider any offer under 100 pounds and costs'.[10] An offer of £60 was made but the following day Laurie's solicitors wrote to Hoyle rejecting it and making a without prejudice counter-offer to settle for £250 plus costs.[11] They also forwarded several sworn affidavits. One simply attested to having purchased the atlas in question from Newnes, but the second was by photographer John Henry Gear, who swore that 'a careful comparison of the two maps leaves no doubt in my mind that the map published by the Defendant Company is a copy of the Map produced by the Plaintiff'.[12] To carry out his comparison, Gear described how he had photographed the defendant's map, then used an optical lantern to project the negative until it was the same size as the plaintiff's, then superimposed it over the defendant's map, so that it became 'quite apparent that the two maps were identical'.[13] A third affidavit was from Henry James Burton, technical chief at the Autotype Company Works in Ealing Dean, who had made the autotype and whose company had printed it.[14] A fourth was from James Laurie himself.[15]

As was by now usual, the affidavits sought to demonstrate that copying had occurred by pointing to defects that appeared in both works – although in this case the defects were small black spots and hairs that appeared on the photographic negative, rather than geographical errors, and 'a slight distortion caused no doubt by the several coping and projection easels not being mathematically adjusted with the plates'.[16] Gear pointed to the similarity of lighting in both maps, and Gear and

[7] Newnes to Laurie, 21 February 1899 V.

[8] G Hardman Hoyle to JG Bartholomew, 18 March 1899 (BA/NLS).

[9] ibid.

[10] Post Office Telegraph, Newington, 23 March 1899 (BA/NLS).

[11] Radford & Frankland to Hoyle, 24 March 1899. Information as to the offer can be found in the attachment to the letter from Bartholomew to Scott, 1 April 1899 (BA/NLS).

[12] Affidavit of John Davis and Affidavit of John Henry Gear, *Laurie v George Newnes Limited*, High Court of Justice, Chancery Division, filed 25 March 1899 (BA/NLS).

[13] ibid.

[14] Affidavit of Henry James Burton, filed 25 March 1899 (BA/NLS).

[15] Affidavit of James Stuart Laurie, filed 24 March 1899 (BA/NLS).

[16] Affidavit of John Henry Gear (BA/NLS).

Laurie explained that the reason that the Isle of Man appeared in the defendant's maps but not the plaintiff's was because it had been added in later (not having been mapped by the Ordnance Survey at the required scale at the time Laurie made the map).[17]

After making the initial offer, John George Bartholomew had left for a holiday in Jersey, where he was seeking to recover from exhaustion and relieve his asthma. But, as he wrote to his cousin and business partner, 'this affair has rendered rest quite impossible'. Bartholomew found the whole matter upsetting: 'It is a most sickening and worrying business and will be a lifelong warning to keep far from the tender mercies of such blackmailing sharks. I would almost fain pay the £250 and be done with it'.[18] Bartholomew's explanation for how the copying had come about can be found in the notes he made for his own affidavit. He explained that the map in question had come into his possession as an unclaimed exhibit from a Geographical Exhibition held in Edinburgh in 1866. As it had no label on it offering any claim to ownership, authorship, or publisher, it was put away. Several years later, when working upon the *Royal Atlas of England* and casting about in his mind for an appropriate frontispiece, Bartholomew remembered the relief map and, 'having come to regard it in the light of working material',[19] he used it for the preparation of the frontispiece.

Bartholomew rejected any suggestion Laurie had sent them his map and had no recollection of the letter offering to sell them the copyright but thought that, even if he had received the letter, he would not have connected it with the unclaimed map in his possession. He observed that 'the map would never have been utilized if we had thought that its publication would have interfered with any previous rights'.[20] Bartholomew considered that they had sold around 15,000 copies of the work containing the frontispiece and estimated the value of the frontispiece to be about £25. He added that the original offer of £60 was higher than he would otherwise have offered, 'owing to my anxiety to settle the matter before leaving for my holiday'. He suggested offering £25 to Laurie, along with an apology and all the plates connected with printing the frontispiece.[21]

Bartholomew's response is illuminating in what it reveals about operating assumptions as to map authorship within the trade. The map itself was created using the Ordnance Survey map as its source material. Reading between the lines, we can infer that it is likely Bartholomew had kept no record of who sent him the relief map, probably thinking it unnecessary given its derivation, and that it formed part of an extensive archive of geographic source material upon which he drew from time to time. The authorship claim of Laurie seems to have caught them off guard.

[17] Affidavit of John Henry Gear; Affidavit of James Stuart Laurie, 23 March 1899 (BA/NLS).
[18] JG Bartholomew to Scott, 25 March 1899 (BA/NLS).
[19] JG Bartholomew to Scott, 1 April 1899 (BA/NLS).
[20] ibid.
[21] ibid.

Bartholomew wondered about returning home to deal with the business but the weather in Jersey had turned 'dismal, wet-blanketty, foggy' and his asthma was not improving.[22] The weather, together with worry about the case, had spoiled his holiday.[23] By 17 April 1899, Bartholomew had been added to the action as defendant and all the defendants had undertaken not to sell any copies until the trial.[24] On 20 April 1899, Hoyle wrote to Bartholomew, now on his return from Jersey and lodging at the Royal Societies Club, telling him he had raised the matter personally with Sir George Newnes, who 'does not wish you to be in any way worried about the case but simply to let it take its course in the ordinary way for the present'.[25]

On 1 May 1899, the plaintiffs delivered their statement of claim.[26] Acting for Laurie in the matter was Thomas Edward Scrutton, a leading lawyer of his day and author of an influential treatise on copyright law. Having received the statement of claim, Hoyle sought an opinion from Arthur R Ingpen of counsel.[27] Ingpen's advice relied heavily on Scrutton's copyright treatise and one cannot help but wonder if he found it intimidating to be facing off against the acknowledged legal expert in the field. Ingpen carefully considered the copyright status of the work as a map and as a photograph. He observed that the map had been properly registered by Laurie under the Literary Copyright Act 1842, citing *Stannard v Lee*, and the photograph properly registered under the Artistic Copyright Act 1862. He further observed that, although Burton was the author of the photograph because he was the person who took it, Laurie was the proprietor of the photograph as it was taken under his direction.[28]

Ingpen did not consider the case a strong one, although he pointed out that the defendants could argue that the map had no literary value, based on an American case cited in *The Law of Copyright* by Scrutton himself.[29] However, Ingpen noted

[22] JG Bartholomew to Scott, 6 April 1899 (BA/NLS).

[23] JG Bartholomew to Scott, 12 April 1899 (BA/NLS).

[24] Hardman Hoyle to JG Bartholomew, 17 April 1899 (BA/NLS).

[25] Hardman Hoyle to JG Bartholomew, 20 April 1899 (BA/NLS).

[26] Statement of Claim, *Laurie v Newnes and another*, 1 May 1899 (BA/NLS).

[27] Arthur R Ingpen, 'Opinion', 2 June 1899 (BA/NLS).

[28] Ingpen gave it as his opinion that when a photo is executed on commission, the copyright belongs to the person who takes the photograph, unless there is an express reservation. The cases cited in support were *Nottage v Jackson* (1883) 11 QBD 627; *Melville v Mirror Co* (1895) 2 Ch 531, and *Kenrick v Lawrence* (1890) 25 QBD 106. However, as the photograph had only been registered on 15 March 1899, the plaintiff could not recover any remedy for anything done prior to that registration, following s 6 of the Artistic Copyright Act 1862 (which applied to photographs). However, Laurie was also complaining of infringement of the map itself under s 24 of the Literary Copyright Act 1842 and, under that Act, registration was only necessary to bring an action and not to recover damages for pre-registration actions. ibid.

[29] This was the case of *Perris v Hexamer* (1878) 9 Otto 674, in which the Supreme Court of the United States 'refused to allow the proprietor of the copyright in a map of New York published on a special system to prevent the publication of maps of Philadelphia on the same system'. TE Scrutton, *The Law of Copyright*, 3rd edn (London, William Clowes and Sons Ltd, 1896) 110. In fact, the case was not about whether a map had 'literary value', as Ingpen (ibid) seems to suggest, but about copying of ideas and systems. For a detailed discussion of the case, see Z Rosen, 'How Perris v Hexamer Was Lost in the Shadow of Baker v Selden' (2018) 68 *Syracuse Law Review* 231.

this would likely not be successful given the decision in *Hollinrake v Truswell*.[30] As noted in chapter eight, in that case Lord Justice Davey had held that a sleeve pattern was not a literary work, which he defined as one that 'is intended to afford either information and instruction, or pleasure, in the form of literary enjoyment'. The sleeve pattern could not be a literary work because it did not fulfil these conditions.[31] Ingpen assumed, by contrast, that the map would fulfil these criteria and thus be a literary work. The emphasis was clearly upon its factual and informational qualities rather than its artistic attributes.

Likewise, Ingpen thought an attack on the map's originality, due to it being merely a reduction of an Ordnance Survey map, was also unlikely to succeed. This assessment he also based on discussion in Scrutton's book, noting that 'a compiler from sources open to all can only claim and enforce copyright in his compilation, if it is the result in some respect or other of independent work on his part'.[32] Given Bartholomew's own extensive use of Ordnance Survey maps, arguing against independent labour conferring copyright would not have been a sensible strategy.[33] Ingpen concluded that 'it would be advisable for the Defendants to avail themselves of any opportunity which may be presented to settle the action on reasonable terms'.[34]

On 19 July, Hoyle wrote to Bartholomew, now back in Edinburgh, to tell him that the plaintiff's solicitors were prepared to settle for £150 plus taxed costs, which he estimated would be around £40.[35] Bartholomew wrote to his cousin Andrew that he thought it would be 'a great matter to get the matter settled without the publicity of a trial'.[36] Hoyle also urged settlement on the basis that 'whatever the result might be, the expense of fighting an action of this sort would be so great, it is desirable to settle if reasonable terms can be made'.[37] By the second week of August, a settlement had been agreed. Bartholomew and Newnes would pay Laurie £130 and costs (taxed at £65). Laurie would license them to continue to use the map as the frontispiece of the *Royal Atlas*. He refused to transfer copyright as part of the settlement but said he was willing to treat separately for the sale of copyright as an independent transaction.[38] The outcome was surely a relief to Bartholomew, upon whose mental and emotional health the case had taken a significant toll.

[30] *Hollinrake v Truswell* (1894) 3 Ch D 420.

[31] Davey LJ explained that 'The sleeve chart before us gives no information or instruction. It does not add to the stock of human knowledge or give, and is not designed to give, any instruction by way of description or otherwise; and it is certainly not calculated to afford literary enjoyment or pleasure'. (1894) 3 Ch D 420, 428. See the discussion of this case in ch 8.

[32] Scrutton, *The Law of Copyright* 111. Ingpen (n 27) also referred to the 1894 decision in *Leslie v Young*, which involved the copying of railway timetables, and in which Lord Herschell had affirmed that there could be copyright in a compilation: *Leslie v J Young and Sons* (1894) AC 335 (HL).

[33] See chs 6 and 9 for Bartholomew's interactions with the Ordnance Survey.

[34] Ingpen (n 27).

[35] Hardman Hoyle to JG Bartholomew, 19 July 1899 (BA/NLS).

[36] JG Bartholomew to Scott, 21 July 1894 (BA/NLS).

[37] Hardman Hoyle to JG Bartholomew, 26 July 1899 (BA/NLS).

[38] Hardman Hoyle to JG Bartholomew, 8 August 1899, 9 August 1899, 15 November 1899 (BA/NLS).

II. Re-surveying Copyright and Cartography

The story of the dispute between Bartholomew, Laurie, and Newnes that emerges from the archive makes visible the difficult, often invisible, mental and, at times, emotional, labour that went into bringing a map product to market and managing its circulation thereafter. It is the final story of many in this book that have used copyright law as a lens through which to highlight hitherto under-observed aspects of the social and cultural organisation of geographical knowledge and its circulation in print. Drawing on the legal archive, and paying attention to the use of copyright law and its antecedents by private and state mapmakers, as well as occasions on which they chose not to use it, reveals another element in what Denis Cosgrove calls 'the complex accretions of cultural engagements with the world that underpin the authoring of a map'.[39] The book also addresses the second set of questions that Cosgrove considers integral to the history of mapping; namely, those that relate to 'the insertion of the map, once produced, into various circuits of use, exchange and meaning: that is, the map as an element of material culture'.[40] However, the focus on copyright law as an element in both production and circulation of the map means that, as per Edney's urging, these two questions are not seen as relating to chronologically distinct events.[41] Even once produced and in circulation, the map is not fixed and unchanging but is transformed into different formats and adapted for different uses and markets.

This book has adopted Edney's argument that the ideal of cartography, as a complex belief system that normalised 'the map' as the product of a specific set of practices, emerged in the nineteenth century and continues to set the terms of mapping discourse to this day. The book has traced some of the features of this ideal through the late eighteenth, nineteenth, and early twentieth centuries. It has argued that copyright law and those wielding it sometimes worked to embed that ideal in social consciousness and, at the same time, the ideal impacted the development of copyright doctrine through its influence on jurists and the precedents they set.

It is also possible to discern an ideal of copyright law, which places the author at its heart and insists that the protections of copyright flow from this author's creativity and personal expression. Examining the relationship between copyright and maps from the earliest times complicates, even confounds, this ideal form. Maps cut across many of the assumptions and categories of copyright and intellectual property law. Maps are generally the product of many hands rather than a single authorial persona and many of those involved in ushering them into material form bring a mix of skilled manual and intellectual labour to the task.

[39] D Cosgrove, 'Introduction: Mapping Meaning' in D Cosgrove (ed), *Mappings* (London, Reaktion Books, 1999) 1, 9.

[40] ibid.

[41] MH Edney, *Cartography: The Ideal and its History* (Chicago, University of Chicago Press, 2019) 75.

That intellectual labour tends to be characterised as scientific and technical rather than creative and individual, such that personal, authorial forms of expression are subordinated to claims of authority and mathematical or scientific accuracy. The informational content of maps can give rise to strong claims about public rights of access that sit in tension with proprietary claims of control. Finally, maps have visual and textual elements, and their value lies in their aesthetics as well as the information they convey.

When lawyers and legal scholars think about copyright law and maps, they usually emphasise the difficulties that arise from the application of two important principles of modern copyright law. The first problem is the basic tenet that copyright does not protect facts, and the second is that copyright only protects 'original' works.[42] In Europe and the UK, 'original' is defined as 'the author's own intellectual expression',[43] while in the US more than a 'de minimis quantum of creativity' is required.[44] Because the ideal of cartography tells us that maps are objective, neutral, scientific works they appear to fall foul of the prohibition on protecting facts, and may not easily satisfy the definitions of originality, themselves drawn from the ideal of copyright. On a small number of occasions, courts in some European countries as well as the US have found that maps do not meet these threshold requirements of protection.[45] By contrast, in recent cases in Australia and Canada, courts have found little difficulty in assuming copyright subsistence in survey plans, the appearance and content of which are entirely dictated by external criteria and which retain little to no scope for individual expression.[46]

A second difficulty noted by lawyers and legal scholars lies in proving copying has occurred. There is frequent mention of 'map traps' as being necessary to provide evidence of which sources have been used and their objective similarity.[47] The assumption underlying map traps is that if a map is 'accurate' it can only take one form; two accurate maps, produced of the same place and for the same (competing) purpose, must necessarily be identical. This too is an argument with

[42] For example DS Karjala, 'Copyright in Electronic Maps' (1995) 35 *Jurimetrics Journal* 395 and cases cited in ch 1, n 40.

[43] *Infopaq International A/S v Danske Dagblades Forening* [2009] ECR I-6569.

[44] *Feist Publications v Rural Telephone Service*, 499 US 340, 111 S Ct 1282 (19th Cir. 1991).

[45] K Janssen and J Dumortier, 'The Protection of Maps and Spatial Database in Europe and the United States by Copyright and the Sui Generis Right' (2005) 24 *Journal of Computer and Information Law* 195, 201–203; DB Wolf, 'Is There Any Copyright Protection for Maps after Feist?' (1991–92) 39 *Journal of the Copyright Society of the U.S.A.* 224.

[46] *Keatley Surveying Ltd v Teranet Inc* 2019 SCC 43; *Copyright Agency Ltd v New South Wales* [2008] HCA 35. In Australia the test for originality refers to 'intellectual effort' rather than expression: *IceTV v Nine Network* [2009] HCA 14, [48]. In Canada the Supreme Court has defined originality as requiring the 'exercise of skill and judgment' involving intellectual effort: *CCH Canadian Ltd v Law Society of Upper Canada*, 2004 SCC 13, [16]. Both courts have eschewed any reference to creativity as an element of originality.

[47] See M Monmonier, 'Map Traps: The Changing Landscape of Cartographic Copyright' (2001) 6 *Mercator's World* 50.

a long history, although in earlier times it was a question of copying errors rather than deliberately inserting incorrect information.[48]

This book has sought to move the discussion about copyright and maps beyond an examination of these perceived legal mismatches, while at the same time revealing their long historical pedigrees. Widening its lens, it has engaged with critical scholarship that has identified maps as tools of empire, nation-building, and statecraft, things which could also be said of intellectual property law.[49] However, this book has been more concerned to emphasise both mapmaking and copyright as sets of social, cultural, and economic practices. Maps are both material commodities and informational commodities, travelling in circuits of use and exchange. Copyright law can set some of the terms of those circuits, easing or restricting their flow. Sometimes the circuits flow around the law or bypass it altogether. The book has traced the relationship between mapmaking and legal forms to regulate copying from early modern times to the outbreak of World War I. Through stories about mapmakers and mapping institutions it has explored interactions with changing technologies, economic conditions, and political and cultural ideologies, as well as how formal and informal laws emerged from these interactions to influence the circulation of geographical knowledge in eighteenth and nineteenth-century Britain. It has also noted the links between mapmaking and the modern state, and suggested its more granular exploration of copyright law might offer a different perspective on how these links were forged.

Finally, the book speaks to longstanding tensions around ownership of information and data, motivated on the one hand by the desire to incentivise creation, collection, and dissemination of both data and information useful to the public and on the other by the need to ensure it is accessible to all. This echoes the tension at the heart of copyright law, encapsulated for example in the WIPO (World Intellectual Property Organization) Copyright Treaty as 'the need to maintain balance between the rights of authors and the larger public interest, particularly education, research and access to information'.[50] However, it is differently inflected when it comes to maps because the concern for authorial rights is largely replaced by the economic incentives of mapmakers and the authority of the map, while the public interest in access to information is rendered more weighty by the public nature of the information involved. Not only is the data actually *in public* and thus accessible in its raw form to anyone but, since the nineteenth century, has been largely collected and produced using public funds. Crown copyright was introduced to resolve this tension but, because the state continued to rely on the market to support its investment in making and disseminating maps, it merely shifted its

[48] See also I Alexander and M Jankowska, 'Rights in Geospatial Information: A Shifting Legal Terrain' (2018) 41 *Melbourne University Law Review* 957, 967–76.

[49] See F Macmillan, *Intellectual and Cultural Property: Between Market and Community* (London, Routledge, 2020) 34.

[50] WIPO Copyright Treaty, adopted 20 December 1996, preamble.

locus to a three-way tension between members of the public, private mapmakers, and the state.

This book draws its analysis to a close in the early years of what can be seen, in hindsight, as the apotheosis of the paper, or representational, map in terms of accuracy (meaning mathematical correspondence between map and world), comprehensiveness, trustworthiness, and mass market penetration. After World War II, technologies such as GPS began to change the way maps were made and used by states, private actors, and consumers. Today, the shift from the paper map to geospatial data stored, communicated, and displayed in digital formats is largely complete. This may have engaged new forms of legal regulation, such as database protection, but the underlying tensions between control and circulation remain in place.

BIBLIOGRAPHY

Maps and Atlases

Bartholomew, J, *New reduced Ordnance Survey map of Perthshire* (Edinburgh, John Bartholomew & Co, 1891?).

Bartholomew, JG, *The Royal Atlas of England and Wales: reduced from the Ordnance Survey. A complete series of topographical maps, physical and statistical charts, town plans, and index of 35,000 names* (London, George Newnes, 1899).

Blome, R, *A Geographical Description of the Four Parts of the World taken from the Notes and Worked of the Famous Monsieur Sanson, Geographer to the French King, and Other Eminent Travellers and Authors* (London, Printed by TN for R Blome, 1670).

Blome, R, *A Discripcon of the Island of Jamaica* (London, R Blome, 1672).

Blome, R, *Britannia: or, A Geographical Description of the Kingdoms of England, Scotland, and Ireland, with the Isles and Territories thereto belonging* (London, R Blome, 1673).

Blome, R, *Speed's Maps Epitomiz'd* (London, Blome, 1681).

Blome, R, *Cosmography and geography in two parts, the first, containing the general and absolute part of geography, being a translation from that eminent and much esteemed geographer Varenius* (London, R Blome, 1682).

Bowen, E, *Britannia Depicta, or, Ogilby Improved: Being an Actual Survey of all the Direct and Principal Cross Roads of England and Wales: Shewing all the Cities, Towns, Villages, Churches, Gentlemen's Seats, &c. Situated on, or Near Any of the Roads / Engraved by Emanuel Bowen.; To Which is Added An Accurate Historical and Topographical Description of all the Cities, Boroughs, Towns Corporate, and Other Places of Note; Compiled from the Best Authorities, by John Owen.; The Whole Illustrated with Maps of all the Counties of South-Britain, and A Summary Description of Each* (London, Carington Bowles, 1764).

Bowles, C, *Bowles' Post-Chaise Travelling Companion; or, Traveller's Directory Through England and Wales* (London, Carington Bowles, c1775).

Kitchin, T, *Kitchin's Post-Chaise Companion, Through England and Wales* (London, John Bowles, Carington Bowles and Robert Sayer, 1767).

Bowles, Thomas and Bowles, John, *A New Mapp of Scotland or North Britain with Considerable Improvements According to the Newest Observations* (London: Printed and sold by Tho Bowles print and map seller next the Chapter House in St Pauls Church yard and John Bowles print and map seller at the Black Horse in Cornhill, 1731).

Camden, W, *Britannia sive Florentissimorum Regnorum, Angliae, Scotiae, Hiberniae, et Insularum Adiacentium ex intima antiquitate Chorographica descripto* (London, Per Radulphum Newbery, 1586).

Cary, J, *Cary's New Itinerary: Or, An Accurate Delineation of the Great Roads, Both Direct and Cross, Throughout England and Wales* (London, John Cary, 1798).

Cary, J, *Cary's New Itinerary: or, an accurate delineation of the Great Roads, both direct and cross, throughout England and Wales*, 2nd edn (London, John Cary, 1802).

Collins, G, *Great Britain's Coasting Pilot: The First Part being a New and Exact Survey of the Sea-coast of England from the River of Thames to the Westward with the Islands of Scilly and from thence to Carlile ... with Directions for Coming into the Channel between England and France* (London, Freeman Collins, 1693).

Dalrymple, A, *Chart of King's Island in Bass's Strait and Plan of Port Phillip in Bass's Strait Discovered & partly Surveyed by Acting Lieut John Murray in the Lady Nelson January 1801* (London, Hydrographical Office, 1803).

Gazetteer of the World, or, Dictionary of geographical knowledge (Edinburgh, A Fullarton, 1856, [1850–57]).

Gibson, Edmund (ed), *Camden's Britannia, Newly Translated into English: with large Additions and Improvements* (London, Swalle and Churchill, 1695).

Imray, J, *South and east coasts of Australia* (London, Imray, 1877).

Jeffrys, T, *The Royal Geographical Pastime, or the Complete Tour of Europe* (Thomas Jefferys, London, T Jefferys, 1768).

Jefferys, T, *The Royal Geographical Pastime Exhibiting a Complete Tour Round the World in with are delineated the North East and North West Passages into the South Sea and other modern Discoveries* (London, T Jefferys, 1770).

Jefferys, T, *The Royal Geographical Pastime Exhibiting a Complete Tour Thro' England and Wales* (London, T Jefferys, 1770).

Johnston, AK, *The National Atlas of Historical, Commercial and Political Geography* (Edinburgh, W & AK Johnston, 1843).

Havell, R, *An Aeronautical View of London, Drawn and Engraved by R Havell* (London, R Havell, 1831).

Hydrographic Office, *Australia, South Coast, Port Phillip* (London, UKHO, 1854).

Kearsley, G, *Kearsley's Traveller's Entertaining Guide through Great Britain: or, A description of the Great and Principal Cross-Roads* (London, G Kearsley, 1801).

Mayo, W, *A New & Exact Map of the Island of Barbadoes in America: According to an Actual & Accurate Survey Made in the Years 1717 to 1721 Approved by the Royal Society & Authorized by His Majesty's Royal Licence* (London, 1722).

Mudge, W, *An Entirely New & Accurate Survey of the County of Kent, with Part of the County of Essex* (London, William Faden, 1801).

Ogilby, J, *Africa Being an Accurate Description of the Regions of Ægypt, Barbary, Lybia, and Billedulgerid, the Land of Negroes, Guinee, Æthiopia and the Abyssines : With All the Adjacent Islands, Either in the Mediterranean, Atlantick, Southern or Oriental Sea, Belonging Thereunto : With the Several Denominations Fo Their Coasts, Harbors, Creeks, Rivers, Lakes, Cities, Towns, Castles, and Villages, Their Customs, Modes and Manners, Languages, Religions and Inexhaustible Treasure : With Their Governments and Policy, Variety of Trade and Barter : And Also of Their Wonderful Plants, Beasts, Birds and Serpents : Collected and Translated from Most Authentick Authors and Augmented with Later Observations : Illustrated with Notes and Adorn'd with Peculiar Maps and Proper Sculptures* (London, John Ogilby, 1670).

Ogilby, J, *America; Being the Latest and Most Accurate Description of the New World Containing the Original of the Inhabitants, and the Remarkable Voyages Thither. The Conquest of the Vast Empires of Mexico and Peru, their ancient and later wars. With their Several Plantations* (London, Printed by Tho Johnson for the Author, 1670).

Ogilby, J, *Britannia, volume the first, or, An illustration of the Kingdom of England and dominion of Wales by a geographical and historical description of the principal roads thereof, actually admeasured and delineated in a century of whole-sheet copper-sculps* (London, Printed by the author, 1675).

Ogilby, J and Morgan, Wm, *Itinerarium Angliae: Or, A Book of Roads, Werein are Contain'd The Principal Road-Ways of His Majesty's Kingdom of England and Dominion of Wales* (London, Printed by the Author at his House in White-Fryers, 1675).

Ogilby, J, *Mr Ogilby's Tables of His Measured Roads. So Digested, that any great Road or Branch may readily be found; with the General and the Particular, Computed & Measur'd Distance, and the Distinction of Market and Post-Towns* London, Printed by the Author, 1676).

Ogilby, J and Morgan, W, *Mr Ogilby's and William Morgan's Pocket Book of the Roads, with their Computed and Measured Distances … the Fourth Impression. To which is added several Roads … With a Table for the ready finding any Road, City, or Market-Town, and their Distance from London. And a Sheet Map of England … By William Morgan, Cosmographer to their Majesties* (London, Printed for the Author, and Christopher Wilkinson, 1689).

Ogilby, J, Morgan, W, and Hollar, W, *A large and accurate map of the City of London: ichnographically Describing all the Streets, Lanes, Alleys, Courtyards, Churches, Halls and Houses &c. Actually Surveyed and Delineated, By John Ogilby, Esq; His Majesties Cosmographer* (London, J Ogilby, 1677).
Ordnance Survey, Old Series Ordnance Survey Map, Sheet 44 [Cheltenham]. Surveyed 1811 to 1817 and revised before publication.
Ordnance Survey, One-inch Revised New Series, Sheet 2, Berwick-Upon-Tweed, 1897.
Paterson, D, *A Scale of Distances of the Principal Cities and Towns in England: by Daniel Paterson* (London, 1766).
Paterson, D, *A New and Accurate Description of all the Direct and Principal Cross Roads in Great Britain* (London, T Carnan, 1771).
Paterson, D, *A New and Accurate Description of all the Direct and Principal Cross Roads in England and Wales, 12th Edition* (London, Longman & Co, 1799).
Paterson, D, *A New and Accurate Description of all the direct and principal Cross Roads in England and Wales: the thirteenth edition*, 13th edn (London, Longman & Rees, 1803).
Paterson, D, *Paterson's British Itinerary, Being a New and Accurate Delineation and Description of the Direct and Principal Cross Roads of Great Britain* (London, Carington Bowles, 1785).
Petty, Wm, *Hiberniae Delineatio quoad hactenus licuit, Perfectissima Studio Guilielmi Petter Eqtis Aurati* (London, 1685).
Quesnel, F, *Map of Paris* (Paris, 1609).
Saxton, C, *An atlas of England and Wales, containing 35 coloured maps, drawn by Christopher Saxton and engraved by A Ryther R Hogenberg, C Hogius, N Reynolds, L Terwoord and F Scatter* (London, 1574–79).
Speed, J, *The Theatre of the Empire of Great Britaine Presenting an Exact Geography of the Kingdomes of England, Scotland, Ireland and the Iles Adjoining: With the Shires, Hundreds, Cities and Shire-Townes, Within the Kingdome of England, Divided and Described by Iohn Speed* (London, 1611).
Stannard & Son, *Stannard & Son's Panoramic Bird's-eye View of France and Prussia and the Surrounding Countries Likely to be Involved in the War with the Railways and Strategic Positions of each Army and the Great Fortress of the Rhine Provinces* (London, Stannard & Son, 1870).
Stephenson, R, *London & Birmingham Railway. Plan of the Line* (London, Ch F Cheffins, 1835).
Swanston, GH, *Companion Atlas to the Gazetteer of the World* (Edinburgh, A Fullarton, [1852–60]).
Taylor, G and Skinner, A, *Taylor & Skinner's Survey and Maps of the Roads of North Britain or Scotland* (London, printed for the Authors, 1776).
Tempesta, A, *Recens pro ut hodie iacet almae Urbis Romae com omnibus viis aedificiisque prospectus accuratissime delineates* (Rome, 1593).
The English Travellers Companion (London, Thomas Bassett and Richard Chiswell, 1676).
W & AK Johnston, *To the Nobility, Gentry and Clergy of the County of Wigtown this Map Reduced at their Request from the Ordnance Survey of Scotland is Respectfully Dedicated by the Publishers* (Edinburgh, W & AK Johnston, 1855).
W & AK Johnston, *Sheet 28 – Perth, Dundee and Blairgowrie* (Edinburgh, W & AK Johnston, 1896).
Wyld, J, *Wyld's Map of the London & Birmingham Railway* (London, James Wyld, 183).

Other Printed Materials

The Petition of George Taylor and Andrew Skinner, Surveyors (18 December 1776), Session Papers, vol 594, no 23. Advocates Library.
Trial of John Hamilton Moore for Pirating a Chart: Sittings after Term, March 1798, before Lord Kenyon and a Special Jury of Merchants (London, Plummer, 1798).
Adams, IH, 'George Taylor, a Surveyor o' Pairts' (January 1975) 27 *Imago Mundi* 55.
Akerman, JR (ed), *Cartographies of Travel and Navigation* (Chicago, University of Chicago Press, 2006).
Alexander, I, *Copyright Law and the Public Interest in the Nineteenth Century* (Oxford, Hart Publishing, 2010).

Alexander, I, '"Manacles Upon Science":Re-evaluating Copyright in Informational Works in Light of 18th Century Case Law' (2014) 38 *Melbourne University Law Review* 317.

Alexander, I, 'The Legal Journey of Paterson's Roads' (2015) 67 *Imago Mundi* 12.

Alexander, I, 'Sayer v. Moore (1785)' in Jose Bellido (ed), *Landmark Cases in Intellectual Property Law* (Oxford, Hart Publishing, 2017) 59–86.

Alexander, I, 'Copyright, Nature, and Travel Narratives: Publishing Cook's Voyages' in J Bellido and B Sherman (eds), *Intellectual Property and Nature* (Cambridge, Cambridge University Press, forthcoming 2023).

Alexander, I and Gómez-Arostegui, HT, *Research Handbook on the History of Copyright Law* (Cheltenham, Edward Elgar, 2016).

Alexander, I and Jankowska, M, 'Rights in Geospatial Information: A Shifting Legal Terrain' (2018) 41 *Melbourne University Law Review* 957.

Alexander, I and Martinez, CS, 'A Game Map: Object of Copyright and Form of Authority in Eighteenth-Century Britain' (2020) 72 *Imago Mundi* 163.

Alexander, I and Martinez, CS, 'The First Copyright Case under the 1735 Engravings Act: The Germination of Visual Copyright?' in W Slauter and S Delamire (eds), *Circulation and Control: Artistic Culture and Intellectual Property in the Nineteenth Century* (Cambridge, Open Book Publishers, 2021) 39–76.

Anderson, B, *Imagined Communities: Reflections on the Origin and Spread of Nationalism* (London, Verso, 1983).

Anderson, C, 'Constructing the Military Landscape: The Board of Ordnance Maps and Plans of Scotland, 1689–1815' (PhD Thesis, University of Edinburgh, 2010).

Andrews, JH, *A Paper Landscape: The Ordnance Survey in Nineteenth-Century Ireland* (Oxford, Clarendon Press, 1975).

Andrews, JH, 'Meaning, Knowledge, and Power in the Map Philosophy of J.B. Harley' in JB Harley (ed), *The New Nature of Maps: Essays in the History of Cartography* (Baltimore, The Johns Hopkins University Press, 2001) 1–32.

Arber, E (ed), *A Transcript of the Registers of the Company of Stationers 1554–1640AD*, Vol 3 (London, 1875–77).

Armstrong, E, *Before Copyright: The French Book-Privilege System 1498–1526* (Cambridge, Cambridge University Press, 1990).

Baigent, E, 'Arrowsmith, Aaron, the Elder (1750–1823), Cartographer and Map Publisher', *Oxford Dictionary of National Biography*, 23 September 2004. doi-org.rp.nla.gov.au/10.1093/ref:odnb/9780198614128.001.0001/odnb-9780198614128-e-698.

Baigent, E, 'Wyld, James, The Younger (1812–1887), Cartographer and Geographical Publisher', *Oxford Dictionary of National Biography*, 23 September 2004. doi.org/10.1093/ref:odnb/30131.

Barber, P, 'England II, Monarchs, Ministers and Maps, 1550–1625' in D Buisseret (ed), *Monarchs, Ministers and Maps: The Emergence of Cartography as a Tool of Government in Early Modern Europe* (Chicago, University of Chicago Press, 1987) 57–98.

Barford, M, 'Naval Hydrography, Charismatic Bureaucracy, and the British Military State, 1825–1855' (PhD Thesis, University of Cambridge, 2016).

Barker, T and Gerhold, D, *The rise and rise of road transport, 1700–1990* (Cambridge, Cambridge University Press, 1993).

Barnard, J, McKenzie, DF and Bell, M (eds), *The Cambridge History of the Book in Britain. Volume IV: 1557–1695* (Cambridge, Cambridge University Press, 2002).

Barrow, J, 'A Voyage to *Terra Australis*, undertaken for the Purpose of completing the Discovery of that vast Country, and prosecuted in the Years 1801, 1802, and 1803, in his Majestys Ship Investigator, and subsequently in the Armed Vessel Porpoise and Cumberland Schooner. With an Account of the Shipwreck of the Porpoise, Arrival of the Cumberland at Mauritius, and Imprisonment of the Commander during six Years and a half in that Island. By Matthew Flinders, Commander of the Investigator. In Two Volumes, with an Atlas. London. 1814' (1814) 12 *Quarterly Review* 1.

Baynton-Williams, A, 'Richard Blome', mapforum.com/2022/07/13/biography-richard-blome/.

Baynton-Williams, A, 'John Speed', mapforum.com/2022/01/14/biography-john-speed/.
Bendall, AS, *Maps, Land and Society: A History with a Carto-Bibliography of Cambridgeshire Estate Maps c.1600–1836* (Cambridge, Cambridge University Press, 1992).
Bently, L and Ginsburg, JC, '"The Sole Right ... Shall Return to the Authors": Anglo-American Authors' Reversion Rights from the Statute of Anne to Contemporary U.S. Copyright' (2010) 25 *Berkeley Technology Law Journal* 1475.
Benton, L, *A Search for Sovereignty: Law and Geography in European Empires 1400–1900* (Cambridge, Cambridge University Press, 2009).
Bhandar, B, *Colonial Lives of Property: Law, Land and Racial Regimes of Ownership* (Durham, NC, Duke University Press, 2018).
Biagioli, M, Jaszi, P and Woodmansee, M (eds), *Making and Unmaking Intellectual Property: Creative Production in Legal and Cultural Perspective* (Chicago, Chicago University Press, 2011).
Biggs, M, 'Putting the State on the Map: Cartography, Territory, and European State Formation' (1999) 41 *Comparative Studies in Society and History* 374.
Black, J, *The Power of Knowledge: How Information and Technology Made the Modern World* (New Haven, Yale University Press, 2014).
Black, J, *Mapping Shakespeare: An Exploration of Shakespeare's World Through Maps* (London, Bloomsbury, 2018).
Blagden, C, *The Stationers' Company: A History 1403–1959* (London, Allen & Unwin, 1960).
Blagden, C, 'Thomas Carnan and the Almanack Monopoly' (1961) 14 *Studies in Bibliography* 23.
Bloch, M, *The Historians' Craft* (New York, Knopf, 1953).
Borges, JL, 'On Rigor in Science' in JL Borges, *Dreamtigers*, M and H Boyer (tr) (Austin, University of Texas Press, 1964) 90.
Bottomley, S, *The British Patent System during the Industrial Revolution 1700–1852: From Privilege to Property* (Cambridge, Cambridge University Press, 2014).
Bower, DI, 'Further Light on Ogilby and Morgan's Map of London (1676)' (2013) 65 *Imago Mundi* 280–87.
Bowrey, K, 'Copyright, Photography and Computer Works – The Fiction of an Original Expression' (1995) 18 *UNSW Law Journal* 278.
Bowrey, K, *Copyright, Creativity, Big Media and Cultural Value: Incorporating the Author* (London, Routledge, 2021).
Branch, J, 'Mapping the Sovereign State: Technology, Authority, and Systemic Change' (2001) 65 *International Organization* 1.
Branch, J, *The Cartographic State: Maps, Territory, and the Origins of Sovereignty* (Cambridge, Cambridge University Press, 2013).
Brewer, J, *The Sinews of Power: War, Money, and the English State, 1688–1783* (Harvard University Press, 1990).
Brückner, M, 'Maps, Pictures, and the Cartoral Arts in America' (2015) 29 *American Art* 2.
Brückner, M, *The Social Life of Maps in America, 1750–1860* (Chapel Hill, University of North Carolina Press, 2017).
Bryans, D, 'The Double Invention of Printing', (2000) 13 *Journal of Design History* 287.
Buisseret, D (ed), *Monarchs, Ministers and Maps: The Emergence of Cartography as a Tool of Government in Early Modern Europe* (Chicago, University of Chicago Press, 1987) 1–4.
Cain, MT, 'The Maps of the Society for the Diffusion of Useful Knowledge: A Publishing History (1994) 41 *Imago Mundi* 151.
Carlyle, EI, and Howse, Rev D, 'Wales, William (bap. 1734, d. 1798), in *Oxford Dictionary of National Biography*, 23 September 2004, doi-org.rp.nla.gov.au/10.1093/ref:odnb//9780198614128.001.0001/odnb-9780198614128-e-28457.
Carr, W and Matthew, HCG, 'Childers, Hugh Culling Eardley (1827–1896), Politician'. *Oxford Dictionary of National Biography*, 23 September 2004, doi-org.rp.nla.gov.au/10.1093/ref:odnb//9780198614128.001.0001/odnb-9780198614128-e-5296.
Carroll, L, *The Hunting of the Snark: An Agony in Eight Fits* (London, Macmillan, 1876).

Challis, DM and Rush, A, 'The Railways of Britain: An Unstudied Map Corpus' (2009) 61 *Imago Mundi* 186.

Clapp, SLC, 'The Subscription Enterprises of John Ogilby and Richard Blome' (May 1933) 30 *Modern* 371.

Clarke, GNG, 'Taking Possession: The Cartouche as Cultural Text in Eighteenth-Century American Maps' (April 1988) 4 *Word & Image* 455.

Clayton, T, 'Engraving and Printing' in MH Edney and M Sponberg Pedley (eds), *The History of Cartography. Vol 4. Cartography in the European Enlightenment* (Chicago, University of Chicago Press, 2020) 1248–59.

Cohen, JE, *Configuring the Networked Self: Law, Code and the Play of Everyday Practice* (New Haven, Yale University Press, 2012).

Cook, AS, 'Alexander Dalrymple (1737–1808), Hydrographer to the East India Company and to the Admiralty as Publisher: A Catalogue of Books and Charts, Volume I' (PhD Dissertation, University of St Andrews, 1993).

Cook, AS, 'Surveying the Seas: Establishing Sea Route to the East Indies' in JR Akerman (ed), *Cartographies of Travel and Navigation* (Chicago, University of Chicago Press, 2006) 69–96.

Cook, J, Wharton, Captain WJL (ed), *Captain Cook's Journal During his Voyage Round the World made in H M Bark Endeavour 1768–71* (London, Elliott Stock, 1893).

Cook, KS, 'Reproduction of Maps by Printing' in M Monmonier (ed), *The History of Cartography, Vol 6. Cartography in the Twentieth Century* (Chicago, University of Chicago Press, 2015) 1308–11.

Copinger, WA, *The Law of Copyright in Works of Literature and Art* (London, Stevens and Haynes, 1870).

Cooper, E, *Art and Modern Copyright* (Cambridge, Cambridge University Press, 2018).

Cormack, LB, *Charting an Empire: Geography at the English Universities, 1580–1620* (Chicago, University of Chicago Press, 1997).

Cosgrove, D (ed), *Mappings* (London, Reaktion Books, 1999).

Crane, N, *Mercator: The Man Who Mapped the Planet* (London, Phoenix, 2003).

Cubitt, G (ed), *Imagining Nations* (Manchester University Press, 1999).

Curtis, GT, *A Treatise on the Law of Copyright* (London & Boston, Maxwell & Son and Little & Brown, 1847).

Daniels, S, 'Mapping National Identities: The Culture of Cartography, With Particular Reference to The Ordnance Survey' in G Cubitt (ed), *Imagining Nations* (Manchester University Pres, 1999) 112–31.

Darnton, R, '"What Is the History of Books?" Revisited' (2007) 4 *Modern Intellectual History* 4.

Daunton, M, *Wealth and Welfare: An Economic and Social History of Britain 1851–1951* (Oxford, Oxford University Press, 2007).

David, A, 'The Emergence of the Admiralty Chart in the Nineteenth Century' (10 September 2008). Paper presented at Symposium on 'Shifting Boundaries: Cartography in the 19th and 20th Centuries', Portsmouth University, Portsmouth, United Kingdom, 10–12 September 2008.

Day, A, *The Admiralty Hydrographic Service 1795–1919* (London, Her Majesty's Stationery Service, 1967).

Deazley, R, 'Commentary on *Tonson v Collins* (1762)' in L Bently and M Kretschmer (eds), *Primary Sources on Copyright (1450–1900).*

Deazley, R, 'Commentary on the Engravers' Act (1735)' in L Bently and M Kretschmer (eds), *Primary Sources on Copyright (1450–1900).*

Deazley, R, 'Commentary on *Stationers' Company v Carnan* (1775)' in L Bently and M Kretschmer (eds), *Primary Sources on Copyright (1450–1900).*

Deazley, R, 'The Myth of Copyright at Common Law' (2003) 62 *Cambridge Law Journal* 106.

Deazley, R, *On the Origin of the Right to Copy: Charting the Movement of Copyright Law in Eighteenth Century Britain (1675–1775)* (Portland, OR, Hart, 2004).

Deazley, R, Kretschmer, M and Bently, L (eds), *Privilege and Property: Essays on the History of Copyright* (Cambridge, Open Book Publishers, 2010).

Delano-Smith, C, 'Milieus of Mobility: Itineraries, Route Maps and Road Maps' in JR Akerman (ed), *Cartographies of Travel and Navigation* (Chicago, University of Chicago Press, 2006) 16–68.

Delano-Smith, C, 'Matthew Paris Itinerary Map (c.1250)' in *The Times History of the World in Maps* (London, Harper Collins, 2014) 36–39.
Delano-Smith, C and Kain, RJP, *English Maps: A History* (London, The British Library, 1999).
Delano-Smith, C, Kain, RJP and Parker, K, 'Maps and Mapping, History Of' in Audrey Kobayashi (ed), *International Encyclopedia of Human Geography*, 2nd edn, Vol 8 (Amsterdam, Elsevier, 2020) 353–65.
Dorsett, S, 'Mapping Territories' in S McVeigh (ed), *Jurisprudence of Jurisdiction* (Abingdon Routledge, 2007) 137–58.
Dicey, AV, *Lectures on the Relation of Law and Public Opinion* (London, Macmillan, 1917).
Ditchfield, GM, 'Thurlow, Edward, first Baron Thurlow (1731–1806)', *Oxford Dictionary of National Biography*, 23 September 2004, doi.org/10.1093/ref:odnb/27406.
Drahos, P and Braithwaite, J, *Information Feudalism: Who Owns the Knowledge Economy?* (London, New Press, 2002).
Duncan, JM, *Report of the Trial at the Instance of The Atlas Company of Scotland against A. Fullarton and Company* (Edinburgh, William Blackwood and Sons, 1853).
Edney, MH, 'Mathematical Cosmography and the Social Ideology of British Cartography, 1780–1820' (1994) 46 *Imago Mundi* 101.
Edney, MH, *Mapping an Empire: The Geographical Construction of British India, 1765–1843* (Chicago, Chicago University Press, 1997).
Edney, MH, 'Reconsidering Enlightenment Geography: and Map-Making: Reconnaissance, Mapping, Archive' in DN Livingstone and CWJ Withers (eds), *Geography and Enlightenment* (Chicago, University of Chicago Press, 1999) 165–98.
Edney, MH, 'Academic Cartography, Internal Map History, and the Critical Study of Mapping Processes' (2014) 66 *Imago Mundi* 83.
Edney, MH, *Cartography: The Ideal and its History* (Chicago, University of Chicago Press, 2019).
Ereira, A, *The Nine Lives of John Ogilby: Britain's Master Map Maker and His Secrets* (London, Duckworth Overlook, 2016).
Evans, IM and Lawrence, H, *Christopher Saxton: Elizabethan Map-Maker* (West Yorkshire, Wakefield Historical Publications & The Holland Press Ltd, 1979).
Eyre, GEB (ed), *A Transcript of the Registers of the Worshipful Company of Stationers 1640–1708 AD*, Vol 2 (London, Privately Printed, 1913).
Fauchart, E and von Hippel, EA, 'Norms-Based Intellectual Property Systems: The Case of French Chefs' (2008) 19 *Organisation Science* 187.
Feather, J, 'The Book Trade in Politics: The Making of the Copyright Act of 1710' (1980) 8 *Publishing History* 19.
Feather, J, *Publishing, Piracy, and Politics: An Historical Study of Copyright in Britain* (New York, Mansell, 1994).
Feather, J, 'Controlling the Press in Restoration England' (2013) 74 *Publishing History* 7.
Fernández-Armesto, F, 'Maps and Exploration in the Sixteenth and Early Seventeenth Centuries' in D Woodward (ed), *History of Cartography: Volume 3, Cartography in the European Renaissance Part I*, (Chicago University Press, 1998) 738–59.
Fisher, S, *The Makers of the Blueback Charts: A History of Imray, Laurie, Norie & Wilson Ltd*, (St Ives, Imray, Laurie, Norie & Wilson, 2001).
Fisher, S, 'The Organisation of Hydrographic Information for English Navigators – Five Hundred Years of Sailing Directions and Charts' (2001) 54 *Journal of Navigation* 157.
Fitzmaurice, A, *Humanism and America: An Intellectual History of English Colonisation, 1500–1625* (Cambridge, Cambridge University Press, 2003).
Foliard, D, *Dislocating the Orient: British Maps and the Making of the Middle East, 1854–1921* (Chicago, University of Chicago Press, 2017).
Fordham, HG, *John Ogilby (1600–1676), His Britannia, and the British Itineraries of the Eighteenth Century* (London, Oxford University Press, 1925).
Fordham, HG, '"Paterson's Roads": Daniel Paterson, His Maps and Itineraries, 1738–1825' (1925) s4-V(4) *The Library* 333.

Foucault, M, *Security, Territory, Population: Lectures at the College de Frances, 1977–78* (London, Palgrave Macmillan, 2007).

Foucault, M, *The Birth of Biopolitics: Lectures at the College de Frances, 1978-79* (London, Palgrave Macmillan, 2008).

Frängsmyr, T, Heilbron, JL and Rider, RE (eds), *The Quantifying Spirit in the 18th Century* (Berkeley, University of California Press, 1990).

Fyfe, A, 'The Information Revolution' in DMcKitterick (ed), *The Cambridge History of the Book in Britain, Volume VI: 1830–1914* (Cambridge, Cambridge University Press, 2009) 567–94.

Gardiner, L, *Bartholomew 150 Years* (Edinburgh, John Bartholomew & Son, 1976).

Gattrell, V and Hindle, S, 'Colloquium, *The Information State in England*' (2005) 18 *Journal of Historical Sociology* 125.

Gay, P, *The Enlightenment: An Interpretation, Volume 2: The Science of Freedom* (London: Wildwood House, 1970).

Geggus, D, 'British Opinion and the Emergence of Haiti, 1791–1805' in J Walvin (ed), *Slavery and British Society 1776–1846* (London, Macmillan Education UK, 1982) 123–49.

Geist, M, *In the Public Interest: The Future of Canadian Copyright Law* (Toronto, Irwin Law, 2005).

Ginsburg, JC, 'Proto-Property in Literary and Artistic Works: Sixteenth-Century Papal Printing Privileges' in I Alexander and HT Gómez-Arostegui (eds), *Research Handbook on the History of Copyright Law* (Cheltenham, Edward Elgar, 2016) 237–67.

Ginsburg, JC, 'The 1593 Antonio Tempesta Map of Rome' in Claudy op den Kamp and Dan Hunter (eds), *A History of Intellectual Property in 50 Objects* (Cambridge, Cambridge University Press, 2019) 40–47.

Gómez-Arostegui, HT, 'What History Teaches Us about Copyright Injunctions and the Inadequate-Remedy-at-Law Requirement' (2008) 81 *Southern California Law Review* 1197.

Gómez-Arostegui, HT, 'The Untold Story of the First Copyright Suit Under the Statute of Anne' (2010) 25 *Berkeley Technology Law Journal* 1247.

Gómez-Arostegui, HT, 'Copyright at Common Law in 1774' (2014) 47 *Connecticut Law Review* 1.

Gómez-Arostegui, HT, 'Equitable Infringement Remedies before 1800' in I Alexander and HT Gómez-Arostegui (eds), *Research Handbook on the History of Copyright Law* (Cheltenham, Edward Elgar, 2016) 195–234.

Great Britain, House of Commons, Select Committee on Ordnance Survey (Scotland), 'Report from the Select Committee on Ordnance Survey (Scotland); Together with the Proceedings of the Committee, Minutes of Evidence, Appendix and Index' (London, HM Stationery Office, 1851).

Great Britain, House of Commons, Departmental Committee, 'Report of the Departmental Committee appointed by the Board of Agriculture to inquire into the present condition of the Ordnance Survey [C–6895]' (London, Her Majesty's Stationery Office, 1893).

Great Britain, House of Commons, Departmental Committee, 'Committee on sale of ordnance survey maps. Report of the departmental committee appointed by the Board of Agriculture to consider the arrangements to be made for the sale of ordnance survey maps; with copy of the minute appointing the committee [C.8147]' (London, Her Majesty's Stationery Office, 1896).

Great Britain, House of Commons, Select Committee on Publications, 'Report from the Select Committee on Publications and Debates' Reports, together with the Proceedings of the Committee, Minutes of Evidence and an Appendix, 23 July 1913' (London, Her Majesty's Stationery Office, 1913).

Greg, WW, *A Companion to Arber, Being a Calendar of Documents in Edward Arber's Transcript of the Registers of the Company of Stationers of London 1554–1640* (Oxford, Clarendon Press, 1967).

Gwynn, J, *An Essay on Design including Proposals for erecting a Public Academy* (London, Ino. Brindley, 1749).

Gwynn, J, *London and Westminster Improved* (London, Printed for the Author, 1765).

Griffiths, A, *The Print Before Photography: An Introduction to European Printmaking 1550–1820* (London, The British Museum Press, 2016).

Hale, J, 'Warfare and Cartography, ca.1450 to ca.1640' in D Woodward (ed), *History of Cartography: Volume 3, Cartography in the European Renaissance Part I* (Chicago University Press, 1998) 661–79.

Hargraves, M, *'Candidates for Fame': The Society of Artists of Great Britain 1760–1791* (New Haven, Yale University Press, 2005).

Harley, JB, 'The Society of the Arts and the Surveys of English Counties 1759–1809' Part (i) (1963) 112 *Journal of the Society of the Arts* 43.

Harley, JB, 'The Society of the Arts and the Surveys of English Counties 1759–1809', Part (ii) (1964) 112 *Journal of the Society of the Arts* 119.

Harley, JB, 'The Society of the Arts and the Surveys of English Counties 1759–1809', Part (iii) (1964) 112 *Journal of the Society of the Arts* 269.

Harley, JB, 'The Society of the Arts and the Surveys of English Counties 1759–1809', Part (iv) (1964) 112 *Journal of the Society of the Arts* 538.

Harley, JB, 'The Bankruptcy of Thomas Jefferys: An Episode in the Economic History of Eighteenth Century Map-Making' (1966) 20 *Imago Mundi* 27.

Harley, JB, 'English County Map-Making in the Early Years of the Ordnance Survey: The Map of Surrey by Joseph Lindley and William Crosley' (1966) 132 *The Geographical Journal* 372.

Harley, JB, 'Silences and Secrecy: The Hidden Agenda of Cartography in Early Modern Europe' (1988) 40 *Imago Mundi* 57.

Harley, JB, *The New Nature of Maps: Essays in the History of Cartography* in P Laxton (ed), (Baltimore, The Johns Hopkins University Press, 2001).

Harley, JB, 'Texts and Contexts in the Interpretation of Early Maps' in JB Harley (ed), *The New Nature of Maps: Essays in the History of Cartography* (Baltimore, The Johns Hopkins University Press, 2001) 33–50.

Harley, JB and Woodward, D (eds), *The History of Cartography, Volume 1: Cartography in Prehistoric, Ancient and Medieval Europe and the Mediterranean* (Chicago, University of Chicago Press, 1987).

Harris, J, 'Reading the First Atlases: Ortelius, De Jode and TCD volume M.aa.9' (2004) 49 *The Long Room* 28.

Harvey, PDA, *Maps in Tudor England* (Chicago, Chicago University Press, 1993).

Helgerson, R, *Forms of Nationhood: The Elizabethan Writing of England* (Chicago, University of Chicago Press, 1992).

Hewitt, R, *Map of a Nation: A Biography of the Ordnance Survey* (London, Granta Books, 2011).

Hewitt, R, 'A Family Affair: The Dundas Family of Arniston and the Military Survey of Scotland (1747–1755)' (2012) 64 *Imago Mundi* 60.

Hewitt, R, '"That Experienced Surveyor, Colonel Mudge": Romantic Representations of the Ordnance Survey Map-Maker, 1791–1830' in S Bushell, JS Carlson and D Walford Davies (eds), *Romantic Cartographies: Mapping, Literature, Culture, 1789–1832* (Cambridge, Cambridge University Press, 2020) 50–77.

Higgs, E, *The Information State in England: The Central Collection of Information on Citizens Since 1500* (London, Palgrave Macmillan, 2004).

Hobsbawm, E, *The Age of Empire: 1875–1914* (London, Abacus, 1994).

Hobsbawm, E, *Nations and Nationalism since 1780: Programme, Myth, Reality* (Cambridge, Cambridge University Press, 1990).

Hodson, D, *County Atlases of the British Isles published After 1703 Volume III: Atlases Published 1764–1789 and Their Subsequent Editions* (London, British Library, 1997).

Hodson, D, 'The Early Printed Road Books and Itineraries of England and Wales' (PhD Thesis, University of Exeter, 2000).

Hodson, D, 'The Making of John Ogilby's *Britannia*' (unpublished paper), cited in C Delano-Smith, 'Milieus of Mobility: Itineraries, Route Maps and Road Maps' in JR Akerman (ed), *Cartographies of Travel and Navigation* (Chicago, University of Chicago Press, 2006) 16–68.

Hodson, Y, 'Maps, Charts and Atlases in Britain, 1690–1830' in MF Suarez and ML Turner (eds), *The Cambridge History of the Book in Britain: Volume V, 1695–1830* (Cambridge, Cambridge University Press, 2009) 762–78.

Hughes, J, 'Copyright and Incomplete Historiographies: Of Piracy, Propertization, and Thomas Jefferson' (2005–6) 79 *Southern California Law Review* 993.

Hughes, J, 'A Short History of "Intellectual Property"' (2012) 33 *Cardozo Law Review* 1293.
Hunt, A, 'Book Trade Patents, 1603–1640' in A Hunt, G Mandelbrote and A Shell (eds), *The Book Trade and Its Customers 1450–1900* (Winchester, St Paul's Bibliographies, 1997) 27–54.
Iljadica, M, *Copyright Beyond Law: Regulating Creativity in the Graffiti Subculture* (Portland, OR, Hart, 2016).
Ingleton, G, *Matthew Flinders: Navigator and Chartmaker* (Guildford, Genesis Publications, 1986).
Jackson, WA, *Records of the Court of the Stationers' Company, 1602 to 1640* (London, Bibliographical Society, 1957).
Jacob, C, *The Sovereign Map: Theoretical Approaches in Cartography Throughout History*, Edward H Dahl (ed), Tom Conley (trans) (Chicago, University of Chicago Press, 2006).
Janssen, Kand Dumortier, J, 'The Protection of Maps and Spatial Database in Europe and the United States by Copyright and the Sui Generis Right' (June 2005) 24 *Journal of Computer and Information Law* 195.
Johns, A, *The Nature of the Book: Print and Knowledge in the Making* (Chicago, University of Chicago Press, 1998).
Johnson, P, 'The Board of Longitude 1714–1828' (1989) 99 *Journal of the British Astronomical Association* 63.
Jones, M, 'Engraved Works Recorded in the Stationers Registers, 1562–1656: A Listing and Commentary' (2002) 64 *The Volume of the Walpole Society* 1.
Judge, EF, 'Crown Copyright and Copyright Reform in Canada' in M Geist, *In the Public Interest: The Future of Canadian Copyright Law* (Toronto, Irwin Law, 2005) 550–94.
Kagan, RL and Schmidt, B, 'Maps and the Early Modern State: Official Cartography,' in D Woodward (ed), *History of Cartography: Volume 3, Cartography in the European Renaissance Part I* (Chicago, Chicago University Press, 1998) 661–79.
Kain, RJP, 'Maps and Rural Land Management in Early Modern Europe' in D Woodward (ed), *History of Cartography: Volume 3, Cartography in the European Renaissance Part I* (Chicago, Chicago University Press, 1998) 705–18.
Kain, RJP and Baigent, E, *The Cadastral Map in the Service of the State: A History of Property Mapping* (Chicago, Chicago University Press, 1992).
Karjala, DS, 'Copyright in Electronic Maps' (1995) 35 *Jurimetrics Journal* 395.
Kinkel, S, *Disciplining the Empire: Politics, Governance, and the Rise of the British Navy* (Cambridge, MA, Harvard University Press, 2018).
Kirschbaum, L, *Shakespeare and the Stationers* (Columbus, Ohio State University Press, 1955).
Kitchin, R, *The Data Revolution: Big Data, Open Data, Data Infrastructures & Their Consequences* (London, SAGE, 2014).
Klein, B, *Maps and the Writing of Space in Early Modern England and Ireland* (Basingstoke, Palgrave Macmillan, 2001).
Klepper, H, 'Originality in Cartography: The Standard for Copyright Protection Ninth Circuit Survey: Patent & Copyright Law: II' (1980) 10 *Golden Gate University Law Review* 469.
Kostylo, J, 'From Gunpowder to Print: The Common Origins of Copyright and Patent' in R Deazley, M Kretschmer and L Bently (eds), *Privilege and Property: Essays on the History of Copyright* (Cambridge, Open Book Publishers, 2010) 21–50.
Latour, B, *Science in Action: How to Follow Scientists and Engineers through Society* (Cambridge, MA, Harvard University Press, 1987).
Lefebvre, H, *The Production of Space*, D Nicholson-Smith (tr) (Oxford, Blackwell, 1991).
Lemmings, D, *Professors of the Law: Barristers and English Legal Culture in the Eighteenth Century* (Oxford, Oxford University Press, 2000).
Leslie, CA, 'Territoriality, Map-mindedness, and The Politics of Place' (2016) 45 *Theory and Society* 169.
Linebaugh, P and Rediker, M, *The Many-Headed Hydra: Sailors, Slaves, Commoners, and the Hidden History of the Revolutionary Atlantic* (Boston, Beacon Press, 2000).
Livingstone, DN and Withers, CWJ (eds), *Geography and Enlightenment* (Chicago, University of Chicago Press, 1999).

Livingstone, DN, *Putting Science in its Place: Geographies of Scientific Knowledge* (Chicago, University of Chicago Press, 2003).

Long, JH, 'London Underground Map' in M Monmonier (ed), *The History of Cartography, Vol 6. Cartography in the Twentieth Century* (Chicago, University of Chicago Press, 2015) 788–92.

Lowndes, JJ, *An Historical Sketch of the Law of Copyright*, 2nd edn (London, Saunders & Benning, 1842).

Lytle, GF and Orgel, S (eds), *Patronage in the Renaissance* (Princeton, Princeton University Press, 1981).

Martinez, CS, 'Hogarth [née Thornhill], Jane (d. 1789), Printseller and Businesswoman' *Oxford Dictionary of National Biography*, 9 July 2020, doi-org.rp.nla.gov.au/10.1093/odnb/9780198614128.013.310187.

Martinez, CS, 'Jane Hogarth: A Printseller's Imprint on Copyright Law' in CS Martinez and CS Roman (eds), *Female Printmakers, Printsellers and Print Publishers in the Eighteenth Century: The Imprint of Women ca. 1700–1830* (Cambridge, Cambridge University Press, forthcoming).

Maugham, RA, *A Treatise on the Laws of Literary Property* (London, Longman, 1828).

McConnell, A, *RB Bate of the Poultry 1782–1847* (London, Scientific Instrument Society, 1993).

McKendrick, N, Brewer, J and Plumb, JH, *The Birth of a Consumer Society: The Commercialization of Eighteenth-Century England* (London, Hutchinson & Co, 1983).

McKitterick, D (ed), *The Cambridge History of the Book in Britain, Volume VI: 1830–1914* (Cambridge, Cambridge University Press, 2009).

McKitterick, D, 'Organising Knowledge in Print' in D McKitterick (ed), *The Cambridge History of the Book in Britain, Volume IV: 1830–1914* (Cambridge, Cambridge University Press, 2009).

Macmillan, F, *Intellectual and Cultural Property: Between Market and Community* (London, Routledge, 2020).

Mann, AJ, 'Mapping North Sea print networks during the gestation of the first atlas of Scotland: Commercial, Legal and Political Landscapes' (2005) 121 *Scottish Geographical Journal* 243.

Meese, J, *Authors, Users, and Pirates: Copyright Law and Subjectivity* (Cambridge, MA, MIT Press, 2018).

Moore, JH, *The Practical Navigator, and Seaman's New Daily Assistant*, 6th edn (London, JH Moore, 1781).

Moore, JH, *The Practical Navigator and Seaman's New Daily Assistant*, 9th edn (London, B Law and Son, GGJ and J Robinson, JH Moore, 1791).

Morison, WM, *The Decisions of the Court of Session, From its Institution Until the Separation of the Court into Two Decisions in the Year 1808, Digested Under Proper Heads, in the Form of a Dictionary Vol XIX–XX* (Edinburgh, Printed for Archibald Constable, 1811).

Moir, DG, *The Early Maps of Scotland to 1850* (Edinburgh, Royal Scottish Geographical Society, 1973).

Mokyr, J, *The Enlightenment Economy: An Economic History of Britain 1700–1850* (New Haven, Yale University Press, 2009).

Monmonier, M, 'MapTraps: The Changing Landscape of Cartographic Copyright' (2001) 6 *Mercator's World* 50.

Monmonier, M (ed), *The History of Cartography, Vol 6. Cartography in the Twentieth Century* (Chicago, University of Chicago Press, 2015).

Monmonier, M and Cameron, JH, 'Paper' in M Monmonier (ed), *The History of Cartography, Vol 6. Cartography in the Twentieth Century* (Chicago, University of Chicago Press, 2015) 1048.

Morgan, V, 'The Cartographic Image of 'The Country' in Early Modern England' (1979) 129 *Transactions of the Royal Historical Society* 129.

Mudge, W and Dalby, I, *An Account of the Operations Carried on for Accomplishing a Trigonometrical survey of England and Wales; From the Commencement in the Year 1784, to The End of the Year 1796* (London, Faden, 1799–1811).

Murray, LJ, Piper, ST and Robertson, K, *Putting Intellectual Property in Its Place: Rights Discourses, Creative Labor, and the Everyday* (New York, Oxford University Press, 2014).

Nichol, DW, 'On the Use of "Copy" and "Copyright": A Scriblerian Coinage?' (1990) 12 *The Library, 6th Series* 110.

Ogilby, J and Harley, JB, *Britannia: John Ogilby, London 1675. With an Introduction by Dr. J.B. Harley* (Amsterdam, Theatrum Orbis Terrarum, 1970).

Oldham, JC, 'The Origins of the Special Jury (1983) 50 *The University of Chicago Law Review* 137.
Oldham, JC, *The Mansfield Manuscripts and the Growth of English Law in the Eighteenth Century*, Vol 1 (Chapel Hill, University of North Carolina Press, 1992).
Oldham, JC, *English Common Law in the Age of Mansfield* (Chapel Hill, University of North Carolina Press, 2004).
Oldham, JC, *Trial by Jury: the 7th Amendment and Anglo-American Special Juries* (New York, New York University Press, 2006).
Oliar, D and Sprigman, CJ, 'There's No Free Laugh (Anymore): The Emergence of Intellectual Property Law and the Transformation of Stand-Up Comedy' (2008) 94 *Virginia Law Review* 1787.
Oliver, R, *The Ordnance Survey in the Nineteenth Century: Maps, Money and the Growth of Government* (London, The Charles Close Society, 2014).
Östling, J, Heidenblad, DL, Sandmo, E, Nilsson Hammar, A and Nordberg, K (eds), *Circulation of Knowledge: Explorations in the History of Knowledge* (Lund, Nordic Academic Press, 2018).
Pawson, E, *Transport and Economy: The Turnpike Roads of Eighteenth-Century Britain* (London, Academic Press, 1977).
Pedley, MS (ed), *The Map Trade in the Late Eighteenth Century: Letters to the London Map Sellers Jefferys & Faden* (Oxford, Voltaire Foundation, 2000).
Pedley, MS, *The Commerce of Cartography: Making and Marketing Maps in Eighteenth-Century France and England* (Chicago, University of Chicago Press, 2005).
Perzanowski, A, 'Tattoos and IP Norms' (2013) 98 *Minnesota Law Review* 511.
Petto, CM, 'To Know the Distance: Wayfinding and Roadmaps of Early Modern England and France', (Winter 2016) 51 *Cartographica* 240.
Piggott, S, 'William Camden and the Britannia' in RC Richardson (ed), *The Changing Face of English Local History* (Oxford, Routledge, 2018) 12–29.
Plumb, JH, 'The Commercialization of Leisure in Eighteenth-Century England' in N McKendrick, J Brewer and JH Plumb (eds), *The Birth of a Consumer Society: The Commercialization of Eighteenth-Century England* (London, Hutchinson & Co, 1983) 265–285.
Pocock, JGA, *The Machiavellian Moment: Florentine Political Thought and the Atlantic Republican Tradition* (Princeton, Princeton University Press, 1975).
Porter, R, *Enlightenment: Britain and the Creation of the Modern World* (Harmondsworth, Penguin Books, 2000).
Poser, NS, *Lord Mansfield: Justice in the Age of Reason* (Montreal, McGill-Queen's University Press, 2013).
Pottage, A, 'The Measure of Land' (1994) 57 *Modern Law Review* 361.
Rankin, W, *After the Map: Cartography, Navigation, and the Transformation of Territory in the Twentieth Century* (Chicago, University of Chicago Press, 2016).
Ravenhill, W, 'The South West in the Eighteenth-Century Re-mapping of England' in Katherine Barker and Roger J P Kain (eds), *Maps and History in South-West England* (Exeter, University of Exeter Press, 1991) 1–22.
Renn, J, 'From the History of Science to the History of Knowledge – and Back' (2015) 57 *Centaurus* 37.
Richardson, RC, 'William Camden and the Re-discovery of England' (2004) 78 *Transactions of the Leicestershire Archaeological and Historical Society* 108.
Ristow, WW, 'Lithography and Maps 1796–1850' in D Woodward (ed), *Five Centuries of Map Printing* (Chicago, University of Chicago Press, 1975) 77–112.
Robinson, AH, 'Mapmaking and Map Printing: The Evolution of a Working Relationship' in D Woodward (ed), *Five Centuries of Map Printing* (Chicago, University of Chicago Press, 1975) 1–23.
Rogers, S, 'The Use of Royal Licences for Printing in England, 1695–1760: A Bibliography' (2000) 1 *The Library* 133.
Roscoe, S, *John Newbery and His Successors, 1740–1814: A Bibliography* (Wormley, Five Owls Press, 1973).
Rose, M, 'The Author as Proprietor: *Donaldson v. Becket* and the Genealogy of Modern Authorship' (1988) 23 *Representations* 51.

Rose, M, *Authors and Owners: The Invention of Copyright* (Cambridge, MA, Harvard University Press, 1993).

Rosen, Z, 'How Perris v Hexamer Was Lost in the Shadow of Baker v Selden' (2018) 68 *Syracuse Law Review* 231.

Roy, W, 'An Account of the Measurement of the Base on Hounslow Heath in the Year 1784; and Also of the Trigonometrical Operations Carried On in the Years 1787, and 1788, For the Purpose of Determining the Distance Between the Meridians of Greenwich and Paris' (1785) 77 *Philosophical Transactions* 385.

Rudolph, J, *Common Law and Enlightenment in England, 1689–1750* (Woodbridge, The Boydell Press, 2013).

Ryan, S, *The Cartographic Eye: How Explorers Saw Australia* (Cambridge, Cambridge University Press, 1996).

Saunders, D, *Authorship and Copyright* (London, Routledge, 1992).

Scardamaglia, A, 'A Legal History of Lithography' (2017) 26 *Griffith Law Review* 1.

Scott, JC, *Seeing Like a State: How Certain Schemes to Improve the Human Condition Have Failed* (New Haven, Yale University Press, 1998).

Scott, K, *Becoming Property: Art, Theory and Law in Early Modern France* (New Haven, Yale University Press, 2018).

Scott, K, 'Maps, Views and Ornament: Visualising Property in Art and Law. The Case of Pre-Modern France' in R Deazley, M Kretschmer and L Bently (eds), *Privilege and Property: Essays on the History of Copyright* (Cambridge, Open Book Publishers, 2010) 255–88.

Scrutton, TE, *The Law of Copyright*, 3rd edn (London, William Clowes and Sons Ltd, 1896).

Secord, JA, 'Knowledge in Transit' (2004) 4 *Isis* 95.

Seville, C, *Literary Copyright Reform in Early Victorian England* (Cambridge, Cambridge University Press, 1999).

Shapiro, B, *Political Communication and Political Culture in England, 1558–1688* (Stanford, Stanford University Press, 2012).

Shefrin, J, '"Make it a Pleasure and Not a Task": Educational Games for Children in Georgian England' (1999) 60 *The Princeton University Library Chronicle* 251.

Sher, RB, *The Enlightenment and the Book: Scottish Authors and Their Publishers in Eighteenth Century Britain, Ireland, and America* (Chicago, University of Chicago Press, 2007).

Sheridan, RB, 'Edwards, Bryan (1743–1800), Planter and Politician', *Oxford Dictionary of National Biography*, 23 September 2004, doi-org.rp.nla.gov.au/10.1093/ref:odnb//9780198614128.001.0001/odnb-9780198614128-e-8531.

Sherman, B and Bently, L, *The Making of Modern Intellectual Property Law* (Cambridge University Press, 1999).

Shirley, R, 'Berghaus and Johnston: Pioneers of the Thematic Atlas' (2000) 83 *Journal of the International Map Collectors' Society* 31.

Sills, A, *Against the Map: The Politics of Geography in Eighteenth-Century Britain* (Charlottesville, University of Virginia Press, 2021).

Skelton, RA, 'Copyright and Piracy in Eighteenth-Century Chart Publication' (1960) 46 *The Mariner's Mirror* 207.

Skelton, RA, *County Atlases of the British Isles 1579–1850: A Bibliography Part 2 (1612–1646)* (London, Map Collectors' Circle, 1964).

Skelton, RA, *County Atlases of the British Isles 1579–1850: A Bibliography, Part 4 (1671–1703)* (London, Map Collectors' Circle, 1968).

Slauter, W, *Who Owns the News? A History of Copyright* (Stanford, Stanford University Press, 2019).

Smith, D, 'The Cary Family' (1988) 43 *Map Collector* 40.

Smith, D, 'George Washington Bacon 1862-c.1900' (1993) 65 *Map Collector* 10.

Smith, D, 'The Business of W. and A. K. Johnston 1826–1901' (2000) 82 *IMCoS Map Journal* 9.

Smith, D, 'Bacon, George Washington (1830/31–1922), Map Publisher', *Oxford Dictionary of National Biography*, 23 September 2004, www-oxforddnb-com.rp.nla.gov.au/view/10.1093/ref:odnb/9780198614128.001.0001/odnb-9780198614128-e-41117.

Stokes, D, 'Another Look at the Dicey-Marshall Publications, 1736–1806' (2014) 15 *The Library* 111.
Sullivan, GA, 'The Atlas as Literary Genre: Reading the Inutility of John Ogilby's Britannia', Thirteenth Kenneth Nebenzahl Jr Lectures in the History of Cartography, Newberry Library, Chicago, 1999.
Taylor, EGR, 'Robert Hooke and the Cartographical Projects of the Late Seventeenth Century (1666–1696)' (1937) 90 *The Geographical Journal* 529.
Taylor, EGR, '"The English Atlas" of Moses Pitt, 1680–83' (1940) 95 *The Geographical Journal* 292.
Thrower, NJ (ed), *The Compleat Plattmaker: Essays on Chart, Map and Globemaking in England in the Seventeenth and Eighteenth Centuries* (University of California Press, 1978).
Tidd, W, *The Law of Costs in Civil Actions* (London, Wheldon and Butterworth, 1793).
Turnbull, D, *Maps Are Territories; Science Is an Atlas: A Portfolio of Exhibits* (Geelong, Deakin University, 1989).
Tyacke, S, 'Map-Sellers and the London Map Trade c1650–1710' in H Wallis and S Tyacke (eds), *My Head Is a Map: Essays and Memoirs in Honour of R.V. Tooley* (London, Francis Edwards and Carta Press, 1973) 63–80.
Tyacke, S, 'Chartmaking in England and its Context, 1500–1660' in D Woodward (ed), *History of Cartography: Volume 3, Cartography in the European Renaissance Part 2* (Chicago, University of Chicago Press, 2009) 1722–53.
Verner, C, 'Copperplate Printing' in David Woodward (ed), *Five Centuries of Map Printing* (Chicago, University of Chicago Press, 1975) 51–75.
Verner, C, 'John Seller and the Chart Trade in Seventeenth-Century England' in NJ Thrower (ed), *The Compleat Plattmaker: Essays on Chart, Map and Globemaking in England in the Seventeenth and Eighteenth Centuries* (University of California Press, 1978) 127–158.
Vertue, G, *Note books*, Vol III, 22 Walpole Society (1933–4) (Oxford, Walpole Society, 1934).
Wallis, H and Tyacke, S (eds), *My Head Is a Map: Essays and Memoirs in Honour of R.V. Tooley* (London, Francis Edwards and Carta Press, 1973).
Wallis, HM, 'Geography is Better than Divinitie. Maps, Globes and Geography in the Days of Samuel Pepys' in NJ Thrower (ed), *The Compleat Plattmaker: Essays on Chart, Map and Globemaking in England in the Seventeenth and Eighteenth Centuries* (University of California Press, 1978) 1–43.
Waters, DW, 'The English Pilot: English Sailing Directions and Charts and the Rise of English Shipping, 16th to 18th Centuries' (1989) 42 *Journal of Navigation* 317.
Webb, A, 'The Expansion of British Naval Hydrographic Administration, 1808–1829' (PhD Thesis, University of Exeter, 2010).
Weedon, MJP, 'Richard Johnson and the Successors to John Newbery' (1949) s5-IV(1) *The Library* 25.
Whicher, JF, 'Originality, Cartography, and Copyright' (1963) 38 *New York University Law Review* 280.
Widmalm, S, 'Accuracy, Rhetoric and Technology: The Paris-Greenwich Triangulation, 1784–88' in T Frängsmyr, JL Heilbron and RE Rider, *The Quantifying Spirit in the 18th Century* (Berkeley, University of California Press, 1990) 179–206.
Williams, E, Mudge, W and Dalby, I, 'An Account of the Trigonometrical Survey Carried on in the Years 1791, 1792, 1793, and 1794, by Order of His Grace the Duke of Richmond, Late Master General of the Ordnance. By Lieut. Col. Edward Williams, and Capt. William Mudge, of the Royal Artillery; And Mr. Isaac Dalby. Communicated by the Duke of Richmond, F. R. S.' (1795) 85 *Philosophical Transactions of the Royal Society of London* 414.
Winchester, S, *The Map That Changed the World: The Tale of William Smith and the Birth of a Science* (London, Penguin, 2002).
Withers, CWJ, 'The Social Nature of Map Making in the Scottish Enlightenment c.1682–c.1832' (2002) 54 *Imago Mundi* 46.
Withers, CWJ, *Placing the Enlightenment: Thinking Geographically in the Age of Reason* (Chicago, University of Chicago Press, 2007).
Withers, CWJ, 'On Trial – Social Relations of Map Production in Mid-Nineteenth-Century Britain' (2019) 71 *Imago Mundi* 173.
Witt, MM, *A Bibliography of the Works Written and Published by David Steel and His Successors, with Notes on the Lives of David Steel and His Heirs* (London, Anthony & Setitia Simmonds, 1991).

Wolf, DB, 'Is There Any Copyright Protection for Maps after Feist?' (1991–92) 39 *Journal of the Copyright Society of the U.S.A.* 224.
Wood, D, *Rethinking the Power of Maps* (New York, The Guilford Press, 2010).
Woodmansee, M, 'The Genius and the Copyright: Economic and Legal Conditions of the Emergence of the "Author"' (1984) 17 *Eighteenth-Century* Studies 425
Woodmansee, M and Jaszi, P (eds), *The Construction of Authorship: Textual Appropriation in Law and Literature* (Durham, NC, Duke University Press, 1994).
Woodmansee, M and Jaszi, P, 'The Law of Texts: Copyright in the Academy' (1995) 57 *College English* 769.
Woodmansee, M, 'The "romantic" author' in I Alexander and HT Gómez-Arostegui (eds), *Research Handbook on the History of Copyright Law* 53–77.
Woodward, D (ed), *Five Centuries of Map Printing* (Chicago, University of Chicago Press, 1975).
Woodward, D (ed), *History of Cartography: Volume 3, Cartography in the European Renaissance* (Chicago University Press, 1998).
Wordsworth, W, *Written with a Slate Pencil, on a Stone, on the Side of the Mountain of Black Comb* (1813).
Worms, L, 'Maps and Atlases' in J Barnard, DF McKenzie and M Bell (eds), *The Cambridge History of the Book in Britain. Volume IV: 1557–1695* (Cambridge, Cambridge University Press, 2002) 228–45.
Worms, L, 'The Maturing of British Commercial Cartography: William Faden (1749–1836) and the Map Trade' (2004) 41 *The Cartographic Journal* 5.
Worms, L, 'The London Map Trade to 1640' in D Woodward (ed), *History of Cartography: Volume 3, Cartography in the European Renaissance Part II* (Chicago, Chicago University Press, 2007) 1693–1721.
Worms, L and Baynton-Williams, A, *British Map Engravers: A Dictionary of Engravers, Lithographers and Their Principal Employers to 1850* (London, Rare Book Society, 2011).
Worms, L and Baynton-Williams, A, 'STANNARD, Willam Thomas', *British Map Engravers – A Supplement*, www.britishmapengravers.net/entries/s-entries/william-thomas-stannard/.
Yeo, R, *Encyclopaedic Visions: Scientific Dictionaries and Enlightenment Culture* (Cambridge, Cambridge University Press, 2001).

INDEX

www.ingramcontent.com/pod-product-compliance
Ingram Content Group UK Ltd.
Pitfield, Milton Keynes, MK11 3LW, UK
UKHW020240290926
15470UKWH00002B/644

9 781509 958337